The Transatlantic World of Higher Education

EUROPEAN STUDIES IN AMERICAN HISTORY
Editor: Michael Wala, Ruhr-University Bochum

THE TRANSATLANTIC WORLD OF HIGHER EDUCATION

Americans at German Universities, 1776–1914

Anja Werner

berghahn
NEW YORK · OXFORD
www.berghahnbooks.com

First published in 2013 by

Berghahn Books

©2013 Anja Werner

Cover illustration: main building of the University of Leipzig
in 1890; Courtesy of the Leipzig University Archives

Library of Congress Cataloging-in-Publication Data

Werner, Anja.
   The transatlantic world of higher education : Americans at German universities,
1776–1914 / Anja Werner.
      p. cm. — (European studies in American history ; v. 4)
   Includes bibliographical references.
   ISBN 978-0-85745-782-0 (hardback : alk. paper) — ISBN 978-0-85745-783-7
(institutional ebook)
   1. American students—Germany—History. 2. American students—Germany—
Social life and customs. 3. Americans—Education (Higher)—Germany—History.
4. Universities and colleges—Germany—History. 5. Education, Higher—United
States—German influences. I. Title.
   LA729.A3W47 2012
   378.1'980943—dc23

                                                                2012032417

British Library Cataloguing in Publication Data

A catalogue record for this book is available from the British Library

Printed in the United States on acid-free paper

ISBN 978-0-85745-782-0 (hardback)
ISBN 978-0-85745-783-7 (institutional ebook)

To

Fletcher M. Burton
Consul General (September 2002–August 2005)
US Consulate General Leipzig

CONTENTS

TABLES

FIGURES

ACKNOWLEDGMENTS

MY SPECIAL THANKS go to the former US Consul General in Leipzig, Fletcher M. Burton, for his supportive networking. To express my sincere gratitude, I dedicate this monograph to him.

I am very grateful to Berghahn Books and specifically to Ann Przyzycki DeVita who, together with Michael Wala of the Ruhr-Universität Bochum in Germany, saw me through the publishing process. This manuscript was originally researched thanks to a three-year fellowship from the Studienstiftung des deutschen Volkes (2002 to 2005). My contact person, Roland Hain, very kindly supported me throughout the years. This book furthermore greatly benefited from a year of Postdoctoral Research at Vanderbilt University in 2006/2007 sponsored by the German Academic Exchange Service (DAAD).

I sincerely thank my three former dissertation advisors Hartmut Keil, Jurgen Herbst, and Siegfried Hoyer as well as John and Nancy Boles, Gordon Gee, and Michael Schoenfeld. Moreover, I am very grateful to Eberhard Brüning, Roger Geiger, Lester F. Goodchild, John R. Thelin, Helmut Walser Smith, and Gregory R. Zieren. My special thanks go to Elizabeth Bonkowsky and the staff and diplomats of Leipzig's US Consulate General, past and present.

I am greatly indebted to numerous archivists and librarians: the staff of the Halle University Archives; the Leipzig University Library Albertina; Jens Blecher and Petra Hesse (Leipzig University Archives); Brian A. Sullivan and the staffs of Harvard University Libraries and Archives; Tad Bennicoff and AnnaLee Pauls (Princeton); Judith Ann Schiff (Yale); Kathleen Smith and Teresa Gray (Vanderbilt, Special Collections); James Toplon (Vanderbilt, ILL); Andrew J. Harrison, Margaret Burri, and James Stimpert (Johns Hopkins); Nancy Dean (Cornell); Jennifer Ulrich (Columbia, NY); Daniel Rooney and Randall Fortson (NARA); Jim Gerencser (Dickinson); Karl Hansel (Wilhelm-Ostwald-Gesellschaft Großbothen); J. M. Duffin (University of Pennsylvania); Eric Pumroy (Bryn Mawr); Patricia Albright (Mount Holyoke); Wolfgang Knobloch (Berlin Brandenburgische Akademie der Wissenschaften); Ken Grossi (Oberlin); Peter A. Nelson (Amherst); Mark Alznauer (University of Chicago); Steve Masar (University of Wisconsin-Madison); Diana Preller and Reinhard Müller (Bibliothek Hör- und Sprachgeschädigtenwesen Samuel-Heinicke-Schule, Leipzig). I would also like to express my gratitude to the staffs of the MIT Museum and the MIT Archives, the Bentley Historical Library of the University of Michigan at Ann Arbor, and the American Philosophical Society in Philadelphia.

Finally, my friends and family supported me in numerous ways in researching and writing this book. My deep-felt thanks go to my brother Frank and his wife Kathleen Becker, Joel Dark, Constanze Kutschker and Jan Lorenzen, Archana Narasanna, Beate Renker, Susanne Schindler, Sabine Schlunk and John R. Jones, Caroline Schott, Ewa Słojka, and Charlotte Szilagyi. Moreover, I am very grateful to my American host parents Olga and Gary Jacobsen as well as to my aunt Edith Göpfert (formerly of the Carl Ludwig Institute of Physiology at the University of Leipzig) and my uncle Alfred Göpfert (formerly of the University of Halle). Last but not least, I am especially grateful to my parents, Annette and Klaus Becker, to my husband and fellow-historian Oliver Werner, and to our daughter Frieda.

Berlin, December 2012

Note on Sources and Quotations

The names of US students and registration information I gleaned from the nineteenth-century register (*Matrikel*) and the hearers lists (*Hörerlisten*) that are preserved at the Leipzig University Archives (LUA) and the Halle University Archives. The names and registration dates of regular students may be double-checked in the Leipzig student directories (*Personalverzeichnisse*) that were printed each term; they are now available online at http://ubimg .ub.uni-leipzig.de/. Students who enrolled late in a semester were not listed in the student directories.

The US student lists at Halle and Leipzig that I collected will be made available online at http://www.berghahnbooks.com/title.php?rowtag=Wern erTransatlantic. They contain registration information and additional biographical information besides references (if available). As online resources, these lists may conveniently be updated, corrected, and revised. This monograph, in turn, comprises three appendices. **Appendix I** contains several tables based on statistical analyses of available US student lists. **Appendix II** offers an overview of Leipzig professors who were of particular interest to US students. **Appendix III** lists PhD dissertations by US students who were affiliated with Leipzig before 1914.

I generally left quotations from archival and published sources as authentic as possible. Spelling idiosyncrasies of the individual authors were retained, as well as peculiar punctuation and capital letters in places where nowadays small letters would be used. I retained alternative spellings of "Leipzig" such as "Leipsic," "Leipzic," and "Leipsig." There is no such ambiguity about Halle-Wittenberg, except that it is usually abbreviated as "Halle," a practice that I adopted for the most part. I inserted the complete word in square brackets instead of abbreviations or an English translation of an interspersed German word or phrase. To ensure the reading flow, I typically translated longer German quotations into English but provide the original German in an accompanying note.

INTRODUCTION

ON 16 OCTOBER 1890, a young graduate of Princeton University by the name of Winthrop Moore Daniels registered at the University of Leipzig to take up history. That same fall, he joined Leipzig's new American Students Club, a society whose main purpose was to set up academic networks—so its statutes pointed out explicitly. Possibly during one of the club meetings, Daniels made the acquaintance of Charles Newton Zueblin, a twenty-three-year-old graduate of Northwestern University and Yale who was a Leipzig-veteran already, having enrolled at the university's theological department in October 1889. Zueblin is listed alongside Daniels as one of the club's official members.[1]

While little is known about how the two Americans had met, their acquaintance resonated well into the future: "for the sake of old Leipzig days and future unacademic insurgency," Zueblin approached Daniels more than twenty years later on 29 December 1911, "Would it be possible ... to persuade you ... to write an article for the *Twentieth Century Magazine* on Woodrow Wilson?"[2] Daniels was then a professor of political economy at Princeton, over which institution Wilson, of course, had presided before embarking on his political career that would eventually see him the twenty-eighth president of the United States of America. Zueblin, in turn, had been on the sociology faculty of the University of Chicago before committing himself to *Twentieth Century Magazine* as editor. His appeal struck the right chord at the right time. Already on 4 January 1912, Daniels answered, "enclosing short article 1500 words ±. with request not to attach my name as author."[3] Zueblin replied in late January, now addressing "my dear Daniels" rather than resorting to the more formal "Mr."[4]

The episode suggests that networking was a lasting benefit to be derived from nineteenth-century US student migration to Europe, an idea that also insinuates that there was more to the German university experience back

Notes for this section begin on page 14.

then than, for instance, merely adopting seminary and laboratory methods into US academia. Indeed, American students in Europe were looking for much more. They were looking for an educational ideal that—if successfully introduced in the United States—would achieve nothing less but to shift the educational center of the Western world from Europe to North America.[5]

A crucial part of reaching that goal was what I would call academic networking among Americans in Europe and the United States as well as between Americans and Europeans. The creation of American colonies in the form of American clubs, American churches, and other more or less formal forms of association in European cultural centers helped Americans to attain this goal as it provided platforms for networking activities. Moreover, US students abroad closely observed German (university) culture, whereby they were rather critical and selective in their perception with regard to its different aspects. Finally, once they returned home, they brought along methods, concepts, connections, degrees, and materials.

In this monograph, I examine US student migration to nineteenth-century German-speaking universities[6] more exhaustively than has been done to date. I understand student migration as a multifaceted phenomenon that connects different regions on both sides of the Atlantic Ocean for a prolonged period of time not simply in the educational realm but in direct communication with various aspects of society, such as gender-related aspects, economic well-being, and military conflicts. Up to now, studies on US student migration abroad examined individual aspects, time periods, and persons. But for the most part, they shied away from putting the different elements together to create a more comprehensive picture. Then again, historiography on US higher education tended to discuss a German element in isolated subchapters or even paragraphs.[7] As a result—while excellent research on transformations of the US educational scene and on American student cultures is available as well as studies of aspects of US student migration to Europe—we still lacked a comprehensive account of *American student life abroad* especially at a time of intense US student migration to German universities on the one hand and considerable activism to reform US higher education on the other.

I will consequently discuss US student migration to German universities throughout the long nineteenth century as a part of US reform-mindedness that fueled American university transformations with visions, concepts, and materials and that experienced a heyday between the 1860s and World War I. As, however, student migration was not exclusive to that period, I will extend my timeframe to cover the period 1776 to 1914, when US student migration to German universities first started, continued to rise in popularity, and eventually broke off.

My goal is twofold. First, I will establish patterns in student migration in the course of the period in question, and, second, focus on American colonies abroad and specifically their academic networking activities. In other words, I will provide statistical analyses of US student numbers over time and then add biographical research to reconstruct US student life at German universities. In my statistics, I compare data on US students at four German universities—I reexamine published older materials such as the US student lists of the University of Göttingen (Georg-August-Universität) and the University of Heidelberg–Ruperto Carola[8] and incorporate my own research on US students at Martin Luther University of Halle-Wittenberg and the University of Leipzig (thereafter simply Göttingen, Heidelberg, Halle, and Leipzig). My biographical research, in turn, focuses mainly on the US student body at Leipzig.

The two combined approaches allow me to draw conclusions about the different benefits to be derived from the nineteenth-century German experience as a starting point to reevaluate the significance of such an experience for the evolution of US higher education. Put differently, my monograph examines American students abroad, a chapter in historiography that was neglected but that is vital in understanding the activities of German-trained Americans in their later careers. The impact of US alumni of German universities on American academia, in turn, should be studied in a separate volume, as it would exceed the scope of this one.[9]

I consider academic networking the central concept on the basis of which both developments in numbers and also the activities of American colonies may be explained. I define academic networking broadly: it covers any activities that more or less directly helped advance (academic) careers. While one might argue that "networking" as such is a contemporary concept, I nonetheless decided on using the term for a lack of a better one and to avoid possible misunderstandings that might occur when using expressions such as "association" with multiple meanings. Employing the notion of the act of associating with someone, my idea of academic networking includes assisting one another in settling down abroad, exchanging information about US higher education, finding out about academic job prospects in the United States, making friends with would-be colleagues at US universities, traveling together to other European universities, procuring equipment for US institutions of higher learning, and preparing future professional collaborations. Americans who met at Leipzig would stay in touch and thus stayed informed about career moves of their Leipzig acquaintances. They would recommend their Leipzig friends to US institutions of higher learning and thereby shape—while abroad—the outlook of today's top US institutions of higher learning.

Part of achieving greatness lies in observing what is happening elsewhere, for which reason it is not surprising that reform movements in US
higher education accelerated as the number of US students abroad increased.
Of course, US students also established academic networks at home. But a
foreign setting added a transnational twist to the tale. Americans in Europe—and, more specifically at the then internationally renowned German
universities—experienced foreign approaches to student- and everyday life
that differed from the American way. They would discuss differences in national character as well as advantages and disadvantages of German approaches to life and education in contrast to America. They would be able
to see their homeland from a distance and thus develop a keen eye for its
potential to reform itself.

On the whole, contact with a German university did not Germanize the
American scholars but clarified their visions of what US academia was lacking to make it internationally appealing. In Europe, US students were looking for America rather than trying to understand the former in depth. They
were, of course, affected by their surroundings to varying degrees—a few
became, indeed, Germanophile, but a notable number became more patriot-
ically American. Between these two extremes, different degrees of adopting
and rejecting German (academic) culture may be traced. For the most part,
the transatlantic journey became a journey to discover one's roots—not so
much a European heritage but the meaning of the New World. The poet
William Carlos Williams was a case in point. During his stay at Leipzig as
a student of medicine in the 1909/10 fall term, he was working on a play
about Christopher Columbus, discovering America while in Germany by
tracing a US identity in the encounter with a European Other.[10]

US observations of German university culture thus were not necessarily
a reflection of the state of affairs in Germany and certainly did not match
objective German reality.[11] In 1922, Walter Lippmann, a protégé of Leipzig-
trained muckraker Lincoln Steffens,[12] mused about the encounter with foreign cultures that for "the most part we do not first see, and then define, we
define first and then see. In the great blooming, buzzing confusion of the
outer world we tend to perceive that which we have picked out in the form
stereotyped for us by our culture."[13] As Benedict Anderson observed in the
early 1980s, part of the process of defining ourselves depends on defining
ourselves as members of an imagined community,[14] which necessitates the
existence of a different Other. For US students abroad, that Other was European and, more specifically, German higher education with its international
appeal.

The search for *ideal* US education abroad would imply that there might
be *generic* US and German educational models. I would argue instead that
there is a national educational mainstream on which a people agrees. This

mainstream shifts priorities over time. If travelers rediscover "new" ideals abroad, these ideals could also be traceable as lingering "older" educational concepts back home. The "new" ideals might then simply be more clearly visible in a foreign setting, and, with larger numbers of travelers supporting them, can subsequently become a new mainstream.

Moreover, if we zoom in on one nation, its educational mainstream may no longer be noticeable quite so clearly. For example, there is German education generally, but it is not necessarily synonymous with Saxon education, Leipzig education, and, zooming in ever closer, the educational ideals of, say, three thousand students at Leipzig alone in one year during the 1870s. One consequently gets a fuller picture the more different voices one hears in addition to examining general national trends. Differentiated regional analyses would be a way to provide a more multifaceted picture of student migration and its role within the evolution of an educational national mainstream.

In addition to the shifting emphasis on different educational concepts, the American student body abroad was not static, either. It changed over time and with it its educational ideals, which reflected transformations in German higher education. In his statistical examination of US students at Göttingen, Konrad Jarausch concluded that the "German university that American students encountered ... changed considerably during the course of the nineteenth century."[15] Similarly, writing with hindsight in 1946, the Leipzig-trained Harvard zoologist George Howard Parker wondered whether universities might not undergo fluctuations.[16]

The same holds true for everyday life, an essential part of the German experience. Students of the late nineteenth century were much more mobile, and Americans in Europe much more numerous than those of the early nineteenth century. The pace of life had quickened notably. For example, when future Yale president Theodore Dwight Woolsey ventured from Paris to Leipzig in the fall of 1827, it took him ten days by carriage.[17] Similarly, in May 1836, the South Carolinian lawyer and politician Hugh Swinton Legaré expected to travel from Leipzig to Dresden, the Saxon capital, in ten hours.[18] By 1877, however, Calvin Thomas made it in less than four hours.[19] In August 1878, he took a train to go to Dresden for an afternoon. He started back in the evening.[20] In 1891, Parker marveled, "think with good travelling you could go from Cambridge [Massachusetts] to Leipzig easily in two weeks."[21]

* * *

With US student numbers in Europe ever-growing by the mid-nineteenth century, Americans began referring, somewhat humorously, to American colonies in popular cultural centers such as Paris and Berlin. In American colonies, "colonization" happened in subtle ways, not by exploiting natural resources and subjugating peoples, but—in the case of US students—by observing how internationally attractive cutting-edge research was produced. Leipzig's American colony may serve as a general example with regard to overall structures such as churches and platforms for academic and social gatherings. The term *American colony* might have been coined in Göttingen, where one of the earliest and to date best-known such colony had formed. In his 1910 list of American students at the University of Göttingen, Daniel Bussey Shumway explicitly refers to the "colony book" that was kept to chronicle American life in town.[22]

The American colony is not identical with the US student body at a local university but embraced different Americans in town (which does not mean that all Americans in town wanted to be part of the American colony). When possible—such as at Berlin and Leipzig with its oldest US consulate in the German states dating back to the 1820s[23]—local US diplomats got involved besides businessmen, artists, and travelers. Some US families established residence abroad and became centers of American colony life. The larger American colony would form an American Church, sometimes in collaboration with other native English speakers, as was the case in Leipzig after the turn of the twentieth century when US student numbers there began to decline.

Different American colonies also communicated with one another. For instance, while abroad, US students would often study at least at two or even more European universities. They would also be in touch with friends, acquaintances, and family members elsewhere in Europe. Having arrived in Leipzig, where no US student had enrolled in over a decade, Yale graduate Samuel William Johnson noted in July 1853, "Call from Hiller who brings report from the American colony at Göttingen."[24] Five days later, Johnson's travel companion Mason Cogswell Weld asked his younger brother Lewis, then at Yale, to "keep me supplied with New Haven news for my friends at Göttingen look to me for the same."[25] A Yale-Leipzig-Göttingen network was thus established in which the German universities served as extensions of Yale.

In discussing American colonies, I will focus on the perspective of US students, though the lines are not always clearly drawn as some Americans who were advanced in age also audited classes or registered at the university without having an academic career in mind. An examination of, for example, the entire American colony at Leipzig would require a systematic search of diplomatic communications from the local US consulate as well as a search of business connections between Leipzig and America, which could probably also be traced through the diplomatic exchanges as well as by researching the regular fairs, a main feature that distinguished Leipzig from other German university towns. Another main feature to distinguish Leipzig was the fact that besides the university, there was a conservatory. Disregarding some overlapping between the student bodies of the two, I will focus on the university. To include the consulate, fairs, and the conservatory on a systematic level would once again have exceeded the scope of this monograph. I therefore discuss the university but highlight connecting points with the larger American colony in town.[26]

*   *   *

My choice of the universities of Leipzig and Halle and their US student bodies will have to be explained.[27] Above all, they are both old and renowned German universities. In the eighteenth century, Leipzig, Halle, and Wittenberg were three universities in the enlightened Kingdom of Saxony. For most of the nineteenth century, however, Leipzig remained Saxon, whereas Halle-Wittenberg became Prussian. The University of Leipzig was founded in 1409 and is after Heidelberg the second-oldest German university in continuous existence. It never had a proper name, excepting the brief Cold War period when it was christened Karl Marx University. Martin Luther University of Halle-Wittenberg was founded as two separate institutions in 1694 and 1502, respectively. They were united at Halle in 1817 following a restructuring of the German countries in the wake of the Napoleonic Wars. At different moments in the nineteenth century, both Leipzig and Halle were at least as appealing to US visitors as the celebrated University of Göttingen. But hardly any research was done on either university from a US perspective—there certainly were no comprehensive case studies.

The situation of existing materials is telling not so much regarding the nineteenth century, but, to some degree, regarding the priorities of twentieth-century historiography. By the time of the Cold War, when publications appeared concerning nineteenth-century US students at Göttingen and Heidelberg, both institutions were located in what was then West Germany under US cultural influences. Leipzig and Halle, in turn, were now part of the Eastern Bloc and thus had disappeared "behind" the Iron Curtain. Although the latter two institutions had been major attractions for US students in the previous century with Leipzig surpassing other German universities in international appeal in the late 1800s, this fact virtually disappeared from historiography due to the seemingly unrelated deadlock in international politics between World War II and the fall of the Berlin Wall. Of course, under Soviet influence, Leipzig did not make its large nineteenth-century US student body a major research priority, either.[28] But even after the 1990 German reunification, Leipzig continued to be an aside.[29]

An influence such as student migration that was strongly felt in the past will have to be examined for its impact *then*. To come closer to the past, different perspectives are needed rather than stressing exclusively what appears to be of greatest interest at the moment of writing history. The references to George Ticknor's 1816 visit to Leipzig provide an example. When a selection of Ticknor's writings was published in 1876, it mentioned that he had devoted nearly an entire volume of his nine travel journals to Leipzig, Dresden, and Berlin. But only a single letter with reference to Leipzig written in 1816 and addressed to Edward T. Channing was reprinted. It started off with the observation that "Leipzig is a very remarkable place [...with] a University, one of the largest, most respectable, and ancient in the world."[30] This suggests that Ticknor was impressed with what he had seen at Leipzig. By contrast, Orie William Long's 1935 study referred exclusively to Ticknor's (then) unpublished travel journals.[31] It conveyed a very different picture.[32] To be true, Ticknor was disillusioned with Leipzig in 1816. But when his selected writings were published in 1876, the Saxon university had become the most highly frequented German institution of higher learning. Ticknor, who had been styled *the* educational pioneer abroad, could hardly be cited as speaking derisively of Leipzig, which in the meantime had moved to the top.[33]

Thousands of US students studied all over the German countries throughout the nineteenth century. I contribute to refining these estimated numbers by having counted and analyzed the actual US presence in the university registers at Halle and Leipzig, revealing that some 319 students registered at Halle and 1,530 at Leipzig—not counting the uncertain number of auditors. In addition to that, I selected about one third of the US students at Leipzig and traced them at university archives across the United States, where I found abundant sources on their future careers and also personal documents about their Leipzig venture. I focused on mainly top-twenty US institutions today, institutions that, incidentally, also sent the largest numbers of students to German universities—often on traveling fellowships as if to extend the US campus to include one (or several) in Europe. My statistical insights are derived from the available US student lists at Göttingen and Heidelberg as well as my own archival research in the university registers of of Halle and Leipzig: the matriculation records and the printed *Personalverzeichnisse* (student directories).

While I also refer to individual students and incidents from the late eighteenth and first half of the nineteenth centuries, the bulk of this monograph deals with the years from 1866 to 1914—the period of highest frequency of US students at Leipzig and other German universities. I opted for an American starting point and a European ending (that is, American independence on the one hand and the outbreak of World War I in Europe on the other), which points to the complexity of the phenomenon of student migration as a transatlantic exchange. The time frame 1776 to 1914 includes the earliest North American whom I traced in the Leipzig register, John Foulke of

Philadelphia, who enrolled on 4 October 1781 to study medicine. Foulke was an acquaintance of Benjamin Franklin, who had visited Göttingen in 1866.[34] At Halle, students from North America were traced already in the late 1760s. Foulke's trip to Leipzig is an example of a shift in US student migration that followed the Declaration of Independence; that is, a shift away from Great Britain as a preferred destination and towards France and eventually the German countries. One of the last US students in Leipzig, William Carlos Williams in 1909, illustrates yet another shift in the development—declining interest, for Williams simply followed a trend of going to Europe for higher education; he felt rather rotten about it.[35] Everyone did it by then, and many now returned doubting that much had been gained academically. I chose 1914 rather than 1917 as a closing point, for the outbreak of World War I in Europe resulted in an immediate drop of student numbers at German universities.

I differentiate my database with a regional analysis of US student migration abroad, which has not yet been undertaken for the German countries on a larger scale; neither has it been examined for the United States as a point of departure.[36] By *regional differentiation* I mean a discussion of US student migration to a German university specifically in light of the fact that location in a certain German principality or kingdom did have an impact on the standing of its university. After all, before 1870/71, a unified Germany did not exist. In historiography on US student migration, this fact is glossed over. An overemphasis on Prussian education insinuates that the terms "Prussia" and "Germany" may be used synonymously rather than pointing to regional German diversity. It is misleading to state that for the traveler who meant to witness an educational revolution the "favorite destination in the 1830s was *Germany*."[37] Göttingen did not become Prussian until 1866. Studies about Göttingen prior to that date describe the situation in Hanover rather than Prussia.[38] In fact, as regarded German dialects, US travelers did observe regional differences between northern and southern German states. Leipzig is located in Saxony rather than in Prussia and therefore requires an inquiry into Saxon educational developments.

Likewise, on the US side the idea persists that Harvard and, later in the century, Johns Hopkins University were the gateways to European learning. This idea needs to be differentiated. It seems more likely that educational reform movements hit different regions of the United States at different moments in the course of the long nineteenth century, which is reflected in the fact that different US regions sent their students to Europe at different moments in time. Considering that the appeal of German universities changed from decade to decade, different regions may be linked educationally on both sides of the Atlantic depending on which specific time-frame a historian chooses to examine. As a result of this, it cannot be concluded that New England was necessarily the starting point of US student migration abroad—instead, the South deserves credit with its eighteenth-century youth venturing to British universities (see chapter 1).

In addition to regional diversity, I stress the increasing diversity of the student body. In the course of the twentieth century, scholarship on US student migration to the German countries widened in scope but has until now refrained from approaching the student population of a German university in the *late* nineteenth century on the whole using an extensive biographical approach. By contrast, the focus has been on specific groups of the US student body abroad. US women in Germany between 1868 and 1914 were examined extensively.[39] As it stands in existing literature, the experiences of US men in German lecture halls *before* 1870 are to counterweigh the experiences of US women *after* 1870, which insinuates that male US student culture in Germany remained static throughout the nineteenth century in spite of industrial, political, and social revolutions. To illustrate the point, as regards women, a more recent publication is Sandra Singer's 2003 *Adventures Abroad*.[40] The title is a telling allusion to older studies on US men at German-speaking universities, such as Carl Diehl's "Innocents Abroad" from 1976[41] or Long's aforementioned 1935 *Literary Pioneers,* both of which concentrate on a period when US women had not yet joined student migration to Europe. Singer's title suggests that a woman could not afford to be an innocent pioneer in Germany. She had to demonstrate willpower to attain admission into the masculine universe even as an auditor.

Both male and female students were part of US academic networks. Some Leipzig-trained US men started their academic careers at women's or coeducational institutions, thus influencing—and being influenced by—female students and colleagues, some of whom would themselves go (or had already gone) to Leipzig for further study. In a few cases, US men married their classmates and students, as did Calvin Thomas, who later remembered (using his personalized spelling): "Yes, he would giv Miss Allen private lessons—for fifty cents an hour. And even so he did. At the time of it he felt much compunction over the taking of that revenue, for he knew that she needed it at least as much as he did. But it all came out right in the end. For the last thirty-five years she and I hav been illustrating wedlock at its best ... and she has got fair interest on her old investment."[42] Other wives and future wives entered Leipzig as auditors and collaborated with their husbands in the professional sphere. In two cases, US women met their future husband in a German lecture hall and described it in autobiographical novels.[43]

The US student bodies at German-speaking universities became even more diverse than that. Ethnicity, sexual orientation, and disability also played a role now besides gender diversity. Minorities and "other bodies" of interest to this monograph include an African American, a homosexual, and hearing-impaired as well as blind Americans. Their numbers were exceedingly small, but a few examples could be traced, illustrating that US student bodies particularly in the second half of the nineteenth century were diversifying. While a group experience may be traced of US students generally looking abroad for means to effect reforms at home, the different groups also may be discussed for their individual needs and objectives. Of course, categories also overlapped—such as in the case of African-American men or a hearing-impaired white woman (chapter 3).

*   *   *

Before delving into the subject matter, I would like to point out that I am an American studies scholar. My intention was to write a chapter in US history above all, tracing how the encounter with a foreign culture shaped aspects of American culture in the course of the nineteenth century. What I cannot provide in this monograph is a thorough history of Leipzig or the University of Leipzig. Instead, I am presenting US impressions of it. I point out when these impressions are not necessarily objective facts. My references to Leipzig and Saxon history consequently are limited to counterbalancing opinions of individual Leipzig Americans.

Moreover, as even primary sources on US student migration to Leipzig and Halle alone are abundant, I simply cannot present and discuss biographies of nearly two thousand persons here for various reasons. First of all, there were simply too many. Second, some students cannot be traced as they simply did not leave many traces at US universities. Sometimes information was illegible or inconclusive and thus made it impossible to ascertain a person's identity. Third, without obtaining additional information on a matriculated student, it was not always possible to identify specific research interests. That is why my statistics are close approximations, and my biographical research provides information especially of such students who were particularly ambitious to embark on academic careers, for they were more likely to be on record at different leading American institutions of higher education and to be named in relevant secondary sources.

Last but not least, I made the conscious choice not to present my findings in a chronological manner but rather to stress specific themes such as statistical and biographical approaches as well as aspects of student-professor relationships, academic networking, and free time associations. It was my prerogative to point out gaps in existing historiography on the history of US higher education and on student migration, and to provide data and interpretations to help fill these gaps. Chronology did not seem helpful as, for example, Leipzig attracted US students in notable numbers only in the late nineteenth century and thus in a rather late phase of US student migration to German universities. Earlier phases up to the 1870s were researched in other contexts—it was therefore imperative to focus on the later period, and Leipzig allowed me to do just that. Of course, the early migration helps us understand the larger phenomenon, which is why I included it in my thematic analyses when appropriate.

*   *   *

I structured my monograph into eight chapters. In the chapter 1 I establish five phases in US student migration abroad that may be linked to developments in American educational reform. These five phases are framed by military conflicts and episodes of social unrest on both sides of the Atlantic. Against this background, I subsequently reevaluate the phenomenon of US student migration to Europe by discussing existing scholarship and by focusing on the idea of education as a dynamic phenomenon, whereby the idea of dynamics applies to progress in time, regional diversity within as well as in exchange among nations, and the subject interests of students and faculty. All three aspects continuously evolved in the course of the nineteenth century, interweaving the three storylines in the process.

In chapter 2 I analyze the changing US student bodies at Göttingen, Halle, Heidelberg, and Leipzig from the late eighteenth century through the early twentieth century. While similar general tendencies may be observed at all four institutions, individual patterns for each differ sometimes rather dramatically. Moreover, the arrival patterns of US student numbers do not necessarily match patterns of an institutions' total student numbers. In addition to the general developments, I scrutinize various aspects of the US student bodies at Leipzig and Halle, including their regional origins, socioeconomic backgrounds, religion, and ages upon first enrollment—all of which was information that had to be presented upon registration. One of the more intriguing results from this analysis is that regional backgrounds changed over time, illustrating that US student migration—and thus also reform movements—hit different US regions at different moments in the course of the nineteenth century.

I move on in chapter 3 to introducing a second framework for my research—that is, rather than writing a monograph about white, able-bodied men exclusively, I integrate history by trying to intertwine perspectives from the point of view of gender, ethnicity, physical ability, and sexual orientation. I characterize the different groups by examining their chances of being admitted to a German university. Besides juxtaposing white men and women, I include a brief discussion of African-American students, disabled students, and homosexual students. Such examples add intriguing dimensions (even though they are few in number). For instance, African-American students tended to experience German universities as a mind-bogglingly positive experience, for a different racial climate in Germany allowed them to feel equal to their white fellow-students, an experience that for the most part left them determined to return home to take up the fight for equality relying confidently on their intellectual abilities.

In chapter 4 I examine Leipzig for reasons that might explain the specific US student patterns there. In doing so, I focus on reform attempts in the state of Saxony (rather than Prussia). US students were not necessarily aware of reform attempts; they simply saw the outcome, and either proceeded to enroll or moved on to another university—depending on which decade we examine. Reform movements are closely intertwined with the economic well-being of a region, which, in turn, is dependent on the state of peace and war. Moreover, even in the most prosperous times, it takes a shrewd minister of education for a typically state-run German university actually to prosper as well. It also helps if the head of state (that is, the duke or king) is interested in education, which was the case on the eve of Leipzig's heyday.

Chapters 5 through 7 explore the world of academic networking taking Leipzig as an example (though not exclusively). Chapter 5 continues to explain Leipzig student patterns by focusing on teacher-disciple relations, both the relationships of US students and Leipzig professors as well as the ones of Leipzig alumni and their own peers and students after their return to the United States. Patterns are discernible, which I describe in more detail. These patterns apply to different disciplines regardless of subject matter.

In chapter 6, I turn away from the strictly academic by examining life at Leipzig's American (student) colony as derived from letters, journals, and memoirs. US students gathered in the homes of long-term Leipzig residents from the United States to find entertainment, to have deep discussion, to ease over homesickness, to catch up on American student days, and to make valuable connections. As more and more students arrived, an American Church and an American Students Club were founded to provide official platforms for such gatherings. Such organizational structures could also be found in other cultural and educational centers in Europe. Leipzig Americans were furthermore in touch with US diplomats, some of whom were former university presidents, while others were students at Leipzig themselves.

Whereas chapter 6 presents the different organizational structures of Americans in Leipzig, chapter 7 focuses specifically on US students' perceptions of German university life to illustrate that they carefully observed and studied German culture in order to find out what would be worthwhile to be imported to America. To obtain their goal, they read guidebooks in preparation of their German venture, studied the language, and attended German club meetings. Even leisure activities were geared toward academic networking and discussions about the future of US education and how to improve it. There were, of course, jolly free-time activities, but both chapter 6 and chapter 7 illustrate that a considerable number of US students made all matters count toward getting the most out of their German experience *academically.*

Finally, chapter 8 examines how US students prepared to return to their native land. What did they take home? Increasingly, they brought higher degrees home. But merely credentialing themselves by being affiliated with a certain German authority also helped them obtain academic positions— sometimes while still in Germany. Once they had landed a job, they bus- ied themselves buying books and apparatuses to be taken home for future teaching and, above all, research. Promising career possibilities also awaited US women at home. The fact that gender restrictions could be circumvented much more easily in the United States helped to build up its educational system by making it comparatively easy for women to embark on academic careers, thus allowing for new intellectual potential to be integrated. By contrast, in Germany, women had a hard enough time to be admitted as students; their teaching would long be restricted to girls' schools (there were no women's colleges).

Just about any subject can be inspiring—if you allow yourself to be inspired. Scholarship and science today are compartmentalized to a degree that makes communication quite challenging even within a discipline. The topic of student migration provides us with an example of how different branches of history could cooperate. For, German educational culture in the nineteenth century communicated in various unexplored ways with the United States of America. In filling a gap in scholarship, this monograph discusses the history of higher education, and, even more specifically, the history of US student migration to Germany in broader contexts such as military, gender, and cultural history.

Notes

1. American Students Club, W.S. 1890/91 + S.S. 1891, Rep. II/XVI/II, Nr. 3 Bd. 11 + 12, microfilm 474/94, 0175 [7] + 0253, LUA. *Regarding the statutes,* ibid., Nr. 16, microfilm 488/94, 0185 [2].
2. C. N. Zueblin to W. M. Daniels, 29 December 1911. Winthrop Moore Daniels Papers, CO734, Box 1, Folder 1, PUL Firestone.
3. Note, W. M. Daniels, 4 January 1912. W.M. Daniels Papers, CO734, Box 1, Folder 1, PUL Firestone.
4. C. N. Zueblin to W. M. Daniels, 31 January 1912, ibid.
5. Simon Flexner and James T. Flexner, *William Henry Welch and the Heroic Age of American Medicine* (Baltimore/London: Johns Hopkins University Press, 1993 [1941]), 5. Wilhelm

Ostwald, *Lebenslinien. Eine Selbstbiographie*, vol. 3 (Berlin: Klasing & Co., 1926–27), 56–57.

6. The term "German-speaking universities" includes those that are not part of Germany today, such as the ones in Vienna, Zurich, Strasburg, and Breslau (Wrocław). My focus is, however, on German and not on German-speaking universities.

7. Foreign influences on US education were discussed in twentieth-century scholarship until about the 1960s–1970s; possibly because many German-trained Americans and their disciples were still professionally active. More recent publications did not necessarily present new archival materials. Today, interest is renewed in the context of transatlantic history. I discuss existing scholarship mainly in chapters 1 and 2; see also note 6. Examples: W. H. Cowley, "European Influences upon American Higher Education," *Educational Record* 20 (April 1939): 165–90; Thomas H. LeDuc, "German Influences at Amherst," *Amherst Graduate Quarterly* (May 1940): 205–10; Jurgen Herbst, *The German Historical School in American Scholarship* (Ithaca, NY: Cornell University Press, 1965); Winfried Herget, "Overcoming the 'Mortifying Distance': American Impressions of German Universities in the Nineteenth and Early Twentieth Centuries," in *Transatlantische Partnerschaft. Kulturelle Aspekte der deutsch-amerikanischen Beziehungen*, ed. Dieter Gutzen, Winfried Herget, and Hans-Adolf Jacobsen (Bonn: Bouvier, 1992), 195–208; Kemal Gürüz, *Higher Education and International Student Mobility in the Global Knowledge Economy* (Albany: State University of New York Press, 2008); David McCullough, *The Greater Journey: Americans in Paris* (New York: Simon & Schuster, 2011).

8. Daniel Bussey Shumway, "The American Students of the University of Göttingen," *Americana Germanica* 8, nos. 5 and 6 (September–December 1910): 171–254; Paul G. Buchloh, ed., *American Colony of Göttingen. Historical Data Collected Between the Years 1855 and 1888* (Göttingen: Vandenhoek & Ruprecht, 1976); Hertha Marquardt, "Die ersten Amerikanischen Studenten an der Universität Göttingen," in *Göttinger Jahrbuch 1955/56* (Göttingen: Heinz Reise Verlag, 1956), 23–33; John T. Krumpelmann, "The American Students of Heidelberg University 1830–1870," in *Jahrbuch für Americastudien*, ed. Ernst Fraenkel, Hans Galinsky, Eberhard Kessel, Ursula Brumm, and H.-J. Lang, vol. 14 (Heidelberg: Carl Winter Universitätsverlag, 1969), 167–84.

9. For starters, see Anja Werner, "Striving for the Top: German-Trained Southern, Southwestern, and Western University Leaders in the Early 20th Century," in *Education and the USA*, ed. Laurenz Volkmann (Heidelberg: WINTER Universitätsverlag, 2011), 87–103.

10. William Carlos Williams to E. I. Williams, 5 December 1909, Folder 56, and 20 January 1910, Folder 59, Box 2, MS Coll 395, UP Van Pelt.

11. See Knud Krakau, "Einführende Überlegungen zur Entstehung und Wirkung von Bildern, die sich Nationen von sich und anderen machen," in *Deutschland und Amerika. Perzeption und historische Realität*, ed. Willi Paul Adams and Knud Krakau (Berlin: Colloquium Verlag, 1985), 9–10.

12. Lincoln Steffens, *The Autobiography of Lincoln Steffens, Complete in One Volume* (New York: Harcourt, Brace and Company, 1931), 592–97, 644–47. Justin Kaplan, *Lincoln Steffens. A Biography* (New York: Simon and Schuster, 1974).

13. Walter Lippmann, *Public Opinion* (New York: Simon & Schuster, 1965 [1922]), 54–55.

14. Benedict Anderson, *Imagined Communities. Reflections on the Origin and Spread of Nationalism* (London: Verso, 1989 [1983]), 15–6.

15. Konrad Jarausch, "American Students in Germany," in *German Influences on Education in the United States to 1917*, ed. Henry Geitz, Jürgen Heideking, and Jurgen Herbst (Washington, DC: German Historical Institute, and Cambridge: Cambridge University Press, 1995), 201.

16. George Howard Parker, *The World Expands: Recollections of a Zoologist* (Cambridge, MA: Harvard University Press, 1946), 88–89.

17. T. D. Woolsey to Sarah C. Woolsey (Mother), 17 December 1827. Woolsey Family Papers, Group 562, Series I, Box 3, Folder 39, YUL.

18. Hugh Swinton Legaré, *The Writings of Hugh Swinton Legaré ... Prefaced by a Memoir of his Life ... Edited by his Sister,* vol. 1 (Charleston, SC: Burges & James, 1846), 139.

19. Journal, C. Thomas, 28 December 1877. Calvin Thomas Papers, 86180 Aa 2 Ac, Box 3, UM Bentley.

20. Ibid., 6 August 1878.

21. G.H. Parker to Family, 13 December 1891, 24. George Howard Parker Papers, HUG 4674.12, Box 2, HUL Pusey.

22. Shumway, "The American Students of the University of Göttingen," 171–254; also Buchloh, *American Colony of Göttingen.*

23. Eberhard Brüning, *Das Konsulat der Vereinigten Staaten von Amerika zu Leipzig* (Berlin, Akademie Verlag, 1994).

24. Samuel William Johnson, diary, 19 July 1853. Reprinted in Elizabeth A. Osborne, ed., *From the Letter-Files of S. W. Johnson* (New Haven, CT: Yale University Press, 1913), 47.

25. M. C. Weld to Family, 24 July 1853. Lewis Weld Family Papers Group 559, Box 1, Folder 2, YUL.

26. For further information on specific aspects of Leipzig and its larger American colony, see Brüning, *Das Konsulat;* Hartmut Zwahr, Thomas Topfstedt, and Günter Bentele, eds., *Leipzigs Messen 1497–1997: Gestaltwandel, Umbrüche, Neubeginn,* 2 vols (Köln: Böhlau, 1999); Yvonne Wasserloos, *Das Leipziger Konservatorium der Musik im 19. Jahrhundert. Anziehungs- und Ausstrahlungskraft eines Musikpädagogischen Modells auf das internationale Musikleben* (Hildesheim: Olms, 2004). An overview of the history of the University of Leipzig is Konrad Krause, *Alma Mater Lipsiensis. Geschichte der Universität Leipzig von 1409 bis zur Gegenwart* (Leipzig: Universitätsverlag, 2003). See also Amy Fay, *Music-Study in Germany,* 2nd ed., rev. and enl., (Chicago: Jansen, McClurg & Co., 1881) and James N. Retallack, *Saxony in German History: Culture, Society, and Politics, 1830–1933* (Ann Arbor: University of Michigan Press, 2000).

27. I first started doing research on Americans at Leipzig in the context of my PhD dissertation. See Anja Becker, "For the Sake of Old Leipzig Days ... Academic Networks of American Students at a German University, 1781–1914" (PhD dissertation, University of Leipzig, 2006).

28. Slavonic studies and Eastern-European students of Slavic languages have traditionally been of interest at Leipzig. H. Walter, "Schüler Leskiens aus dem Südslawischen Bereich," in *ZfSl* 26, no. 2 (1981): 192–98. Today Leipzig relishes a position as mediator between Eastern and Western Europe. Minka Zlatkeva, "Bulgarische Doktoranden von Karl Bücher," in *Karl Bücher. Leipziger Hochschulschriften 1892–1926,* ed. Erik Koenen and Michael Meyen (Leipzig: Universitätsverlag, 2002), 201–28.

29. E.g., Marita Baumgarten, *Professoren und Universitäten im 19. Jahrhundert* (Göttingen: Vandenhoek & Ruprecht, 1997).

30. George Ticknor, *Life, Letters, and Journals of George Ticknor,* vol. 1 (London: Sampson Low, Marston, Searle, & Rivington, 1876), 107; Eberhard Brüning, "Die Universität Leipzig im 19. Jahrhundert aus amerikanischer Sicht," in *Jahrbuch für Regionalgeschichte und Landeskunde 20, 1995–96* (Stuttgart: Verlag der Sächsischen Akademie der Wissenschaften zu Leipzig in Kommission bei Franz Steiner Verlag, 1996), 101.

31. Anna Ticknor, George Ticknor, Thomas Adam, and Gisela Mettele, *Two Boston Brahmins in Goethe's Germany: The Travel Journals of Anna and George Ticknor* (Lanham: Lexington Books, 2009).

32. Orie William Long, *Literary Pioneers: Early American Explorers of European Culture* (New York: Gordon Press, 1975 [1935]), 26.

33. In his 1968 biography of William E. Dodd, US ambassador to Nazi Germany, Robert Dallek observed that Dodd opted for a Leipzig PhD degree in 1897 even though "it was no longer common for Americans to seek their historical training abroad." Dallek wrote with the hindsight of seven decades that had reversed the academic balance between the America and Europe. In Dodd's day, it was less obvious. Robert Dallek, *Democrat and Diplomat: The Life of William E. Dodd* (New York: Oxford University Press, 1968), 13. Also Fred Arthur Bailey, *William Edward Dodd: The South's Yeoman Scholar* (Charlottesville: University Press of Virginia, 1997).

34. Marquardt, "Die ersten Amerikanischen Studenten," 23–33. Also, Dietrich Goldschmidt, "Historical Interaction between Higher Education in Germany and in the United States," in *German and American Universities*, ed. Ulrich Teichler and Henry Wasser, Werkstadtberichte, vol. 36 (Kassel: Wissenschaftliches Zentrum für Berufs- und Hochschulforschung, Gesamthochschule Kassel, 1992), 13.

35. W. C. Williams to Edgar I. Williams (brother), 17 August 1909. MS Coll 395, Box 2, Folder 50, UP Van Pelt.

36. Exceptions would be Arleen Tuchman, *Science, Medicine, and the State in Germany: The Case of Baden, 1815–1871* (New York: Oxford University Press, 1993) and also Retallack, *Saxony in German History.*

37. Karl-Heinz Jeismann, "American Observations Concerning the Prussian Educational System in the Nineteenth Century," in Geitz et al., *German Influences*, 21. My emphasis.

38. Konrad H. Jarausch, *Students, Society, and Politics in Imperial Germany: The Rise of Academic Illiberalism* (Princeton, NJ: Princeton University Press, 1982), 336.

39. James C. Albisetti, "German Influence on the Higher Education of American Women, 1865–1914," in Geitz et al., *German Influences*, 227–44. As to Leipzig specifically: Anja Becker, *"How Daring She Was! The Female American Colony at Leipzig University, 1877–1914,"* in *Taking Up Space. New Approaches to American History*, mosaic 21, ed. Anke Ortlepp and Christoph Ribbat (Trier: Wissenschaftlicher Verlag Trier, 2004): 31–46; Sonja Brentjes and Karl-Heinz Schlote, "Zum Frauenstudium an der Universität Leipzig in der Zeit von 1870 bis 1910," in *Jahrbuch für Regionalgeschichte und Landeskunde 19* (Weimar: Verlag Herrmann Böhlaus Nachfolger, 1993/94), 57–75; Renate Drucker, "Zur Vorgeschichte des Frauenstudiums an der Universität Leipzig. Aktenbericht," in *Vom Mittelalter zur Neuzeit*, ed. Hellmut Kretzschmar (Berlin: Rütten & Loening, 1956), 280.

40. Sandra L. Singer, *Adventures Abroad: North American Women at German-Speaking Universities, 1868–1915,* Contributions in Women's Studies 201 (Westport, CT: Praeger, 2003).

41. Carl Diehl, "Innocents Abroad: American Students in German Universities, 1810–1870," *History of Education Quarterly* 16, no. 3 (Fall 1976): 321–41.

42. C. Thomas, unfinished, typed autobiography, ca. 1919, 16. Calvin Thomas Papers, 86180 Aa 2 Ac, Box 1, UM Bentley.

43. Josephine Bontecou met Lincoln Steffens in 1890 attending lectures by Wilhelm Wundt. A decade later, Elfrieda Hochbaum met Paul Russell Pope in the lecture hall of Eduard Sievers. Josephine Bontecou Steffens, *Letitia Berkeley, A.M.* (New York: A. Stokes Company, 1899); Elfrieda Hochbaum, *Burning Arrows* (Boston: Bruce Humphries Publishers, 1963). Another contemporary Leipzig novel discussing the experiences of English-speaking students there is Henry Handel Richardson, *Maurice Guest* (1908; London: Virago, 1981).

Chapter 1

MOVEMENT AND THE HISTORY OF HIGHER EDUCATION

Educational Dynamics

EDUCATION IS A dynamic phenomenon. It evolves over time in response to a given society's changing needs. It evolves in contact with others, when students, faculty, and administrators move on to learned institutions elsewhere. Finally, it evolves as people exchange ideas about how to define the world. The history of education is therefore movement in a *temporal,* a *spatial,* and a *subject-related* sense.

As a starting point, let me therefore revisit existing scholarship on the history of American higher education and US student migration abroad, whereby I will focus on the college and university level even if at times I simply speak of education. My main goal is to highlight interrelated transatlantic, regional, and disciplinary educational dynamics over time. To do so, I first establish five phases of development in nineteenth-century US student migration abroad that I link with educational reform movements in the United States. I then add another layer by connecting these phases with wars and revolutions on both sides of the Atlantic in the course of time to illustrate to what extent education developments and military conflicts are intertwined.

I will subsequently focus on movement in space by reevaluating student migration abroad from regional perspectives, such as by revisiting the place the South held in the history of US higher education generally and in the history of US student migration specifically. Indeed, to be a little provocative, one could actually argue that the South (rather than New England) was essential in laying the foundations for the late-nineteenth-century US educational mainstream, whereby student migration played a noteworthy role. The section on regional perspectives mainly aims at illustrating that it would be a rewarding undertaking to evaluate different US regions on an equal par for their position in and contributions to American higher education.

Finally, I will explore disciplinary dynamics. My main interest in this regard is a reevaluation of the ideal of "German science," which has sometimes been too narrowly applied to natural sciences exclusively. For instance, an awareness of linguistic subtleties helps to install the humanities in the picture of the scientific revolution. Establishing the humanities as scientific, in turn, can help us appreciate the role of, for example, the South in educational history better. After all, what I feel tempted to call "scienticity" became a major current in academia in the twentieth century. If the humanities can be considered scientific in the 1800s, they consequently become a symbol of the latest trends in the creation of knowledge, which, in turn, attributes scientific thinking to US regions that in the late nineteenth century did not have the resources to finance the expensive but necessary apparatuses for *natural*-scientific inquiries.

Student migration ideally illustrates the interconnectedness of these various movements. In search of the best possible education, students travel quite literally away from home. They also travel through time, for in the course of an educational journey, time passes and life changes more or less noticeably, not just for the students encountering a foreign culture, but also for the people back home. Students traveling abroad consequently never quite return to the place they left behind, a phenomenon that becomes more apparent the longer they stay away. The simultaneous movements through space and time lead to a gradual evolution of new scholarly and scientific disciplines, for one might start out on the transatlantic journey an organic chemist and end it a physical chemist thriving on the latest discoveries made while in Europe. One might start out a classicist and, in Europe, suddenly find oneself a comparative linguist tackling modern languages and unwittingly moving away from the field of expertise of one's mentor back home.

Five Phases of Educational Reform and Student Migration, 1760s–1914

Five phases of educational reform and student migration may be discerned up to 1914 that coincided with (or were framed by) wars, military conflicts, and revolutions on both sides of the Atlantic. Moreover, the success or failure of reform initiatives corresponded directly to the intensity of student migration. That is, greater student numbers abroad would result in a greater openness towards foreign education, thus resulting in a wider consensus with regard to a necessity to reorganize the creation of knowledge at home. Hence, reform attempts were more likely to succeed.

American student migration to German universities changed its direction and intensity over the decades, illustrating that the phenomenon was carried by many, not just one German institution. Taking the four universities that I examined in the context of this study as examples, the following picture may be derived: The first phase of US student migration lasted roughly from the 1760s to 1810. Very few North American students traveled to the German countries back then; Halle is noteworthy for having aroused the earliest interest. The second phase from 1810 to 1830 experienced a first small wave of students at German universities, most notably at Göttingen. The third phase from ca. 1830 to the US Civil War witnessed an increase in US student enrollment in German universities, with Heidelberg now being the most prominent attraction. In the fourth phase, from 1865 to ca. 1898, US enrollment at German universities soared, with Leipzig taking the lead. Finally, starting in the late 1890s, US student numbers at all four German universities began to decline gradually until the outbreak of World War I. Of course, the US student bodies at other universities such as in Berlin and Munich would add even more refinement to this picture.

These five phase in US student migration abroad may be linked to different stages in reforming American higher education. Following the onset of a steadier stream of "educational pilgrims" from the United States at German universities in the 1810s, the 1820s witnessed a few reform initiatives with the opening of Thomas Jefferson's University of Virginia in 1825, Ticknor's unsuccessful reform attempts at Harvard, and the 1828 Yale Report. These various activities were far from identical. Theodore Dwight Woolsey, a future Yale president who had studied at the Universities of Paris, Leipzig, Berlin, and Bonn, for once, had different ideas than Jefferson and Ticknor. Whereas the latter two attempted something quite foreign from existing mainstream US ideals, Woolsey preferred the "American system" with a little of the German "grafted on."[1] The difference lay in creating and preserving a US identity in higher education rather than accepting what a few men who had traveled abroad proclaimed to be wonderful foreign notions. Only when student migration increased in numbers did the public consensus open up to concepts from abroad—not as a blueprint, but as an inspiration.

The years between 1840 and the US Civil War witnessed increased reform activity, including the creation of scientific schools at Harvard (Lawrence Scientific School, 1846) and Yale (Sheffield Scientific School, 1847).[2] During this transitional phase, Americans began opening up towards new concepts. A milestone in the development was the first Morrill Land Grant Act of 1862—passed in the middle of a war that tried the nation. The 1862 act paved the way for the founding of new colleges and universities. It emphasized agricultural and mechanical education, that is, instruction in applied sciences. A second such act was passed in 1890. Both acts also preceded significant shifts in US student migration abroad by only a few years—the 1862 act was followed by a notable increase around 1870, the 1890 act by an eventual decline after 1898. The first act reflected a realization that the educational needs of society were changing and that new models were needed. The second act may be interpreted as a desire to consolidate educational transformations at home.

With growing US student numbers exposed to education abroad since the mid-nineteenth century, reform mindedness grew as well, which, in its turn, may reflect that era's reform mindedness generally (alternatively, the increased exposure to foreign cultures and education may have prompted reform activities also in other spheres of society). US students abroad realized that the German universities differed considerably in organization, methods, and outcome from what was then offered at US colleges. For instance, in 1857, Philip Schaff announced that US colleges were unfit to confer higher degrees. Even though they "claimed and exercised" academic privileges, they were preparatory schools comparable to the German gymnasium rather than to the German university. Cambridge, New Haven, and Charlottesville came "nearer the European idea," but they too left much to be desired.[3]

Rather than a search for German education, the educational pilgrimage abroad, consequently, became a focused search for new approaches to be implemented in America. More criticisms of US higher education were heard after the Civil War. James Morgan Hart observed in his 1874 guidebook on German universities that the incomes of Harvard and Yale compared to that of Leipzig. But both colleges "would be slow in provoking a comparison between themselves and Leipsic."[4] He cautioned his readers that the "higher education of the German universities is the best in the world. Yet Americans should beware of entering upon it before they are fully ripe, before they know what to take and what to leave."[5]

Late-nineteenth-century Americans longed to have exceptional education that would appeal to the world. Simultaneously, US student migration abroad experienced a heyday that coincided and overlapped with US progressivism. With notable military victories in the international realm (i.e., the war of 1898), the United States began consolidating its role as a "City on a Hill," a cultural discourse that has been part of US self-identification since, in 1630, John Winthrop preached his famous sermon "A Model of Christian Charity" aboard the *Arabella* on his way to New England. The idea has also found its way into historiography on higher education: the University of Virginia has been styled a Southern "village on a hill,"[6] and Don DeLillo created a "college on the hill" in his 1985 novel *White Noise*.

In the post–Civil War era, wealthy industrialists contributed to the changing US educational landscape by offering large monetary gifts to found new institutions of higher learning or to transform existing ones, including Cornell (1868), Vanderbilt (1873), Johns Hopkins (1876), and Tulane (1884).[7] By the late 1890s, the situation had much improved, although wealthy magnates continued to invest into higher learning—Rice Institute (1908), Emory (1914), and the 1920s gift that turned Trinity College into Duke University are examples. The first of these waves of new institutions began sending students off to German universities in the 1870s and 1880s. The young US universities thus contributed to the diversification of the student body abroad by diversifying academic backgrounds also in terms of region. Indeed, several of the new and transformed universities were located in the South, Southwest, and West of the United States and often were run by and staffed with German-trained leaders and faculty.[8]

A growth in student numbers at US institutions of higher education is evident since at least 1900, that is, the time when US student bodies at German universities began to diminish. But while student numbers in the United States increased, the percentage of college-aged youngsters—as Laurence Veysey pointed out—did not show a similar increase, which implies that a larger percentage of the population now opted for a higher education. They now obviously found opportunity at home.[9] Interest in German universities began to drop around 1900 as the US educational landscape was becoming more appealing also thanks to the numerous well-trained US alumni of German-speaking universities.

Transatlantic Dynamics: Linking War and Education in America and Europe

As the previous section insinuates, educational history intersects with military history on both sides of the Atlantic, for military history helps to explain when and why educational reforms—and thus cultural transformations—picked up speed or stagnated. Wars, upheavals, revolutions—all of them leave a crucial imprint on the educational landscape indirectly but also directly. Wars are movement. Wars move societies painfully in various ways once all diplomatic means of communication fail.[10] Besides the metaphorical movement, wars move people quite literally as soldiers and refugees. People on the move are likely to pick up new ideas. Wars can prevent people from moving, or encourage them to do so. It happens directly when regions are devastated. But other regions benefit indirectly—if eager students cannot find education in their devastated hometown, they will move elsewhere. Thanks to migrations, the history of one region thus continues to be written elsewhere, a phenomenon that is particularly intriguing when migrants return home, which was often the case with US students in Germany.

The period of interest to this monograph spans some 140 years, including several wars and revolutions that occurred simultaneously on both sides of the Atlantic, causing educational stagnation in one place and progress in another. North American student migration to the European mainland picked up speed after the 1776 American Revolution and lasted throughout the nineteenth century until a rupture occurred with the 1898 Spanish American War and certainly with World War I, which put at least temporarily a full stop to American interest in German education. Even if eventually in the twentieth—the American—century Americans began turning to German learning once again, their interest never again rose to the levels of the nineteenth century.

The moments of different military conflicts and civil unrest between 1776 and 1914 match changes in the intensity of both educational reform activities and student migration in the United States. Again, five periods may be discerned: (1) The American Revolutionary War on the one hand and the Napoleonic Wars as well as the War of 1812 on the other frame an early period with the United States emerging as an international actor also on the educational front. (2) By the time of the Mexican War (1846–1848), and the 1848 revolutions in Europe, US student migration had increased to more noticeable numbers. (Natural-)scientific education was beginning to arouse more significant—that is, more institutional—interest. (3) The US Civil War, the Austro-Prussian War of 1866, and the Franco-German War of 1870/71 mark the onset of a heyday of US student migration to German-speaking universities, a phenomenon that was accompanied by growing activity in reorganizing and even reinventing US higher education. (4) With the Spanish-American-Cuban-Philippine War of 1898, US student numbers at German universities started to decline while reform activity continued back home. (5) World War I marked the closing point of the "German chapter" in US higher education. Let me now elaborate on these five periods.

Frederick Rudolph started off his 1962 history of the American college and university with the observation that by the time of the American Revolution, the English colonies in the New World featured nine colleges styled after Oxford and Cambridge.[11] Up to 1776, a close relationship had existed between the North American colonies and Great Britain also in the academic realm. The American struggle for independence from the British crown, however, meant a turning point also in educational history and thus in the history of student migrations. That is, as another expression of the newly won independence, the American Revolution (which Europeans call a War of Independence) began turning North Americans, who had traditionally gone to Great Britain for their higher education, to the European mainland.

Until the late eighteenth century, Great Britain had been the first choice of young Americans to further their education.[12] Back then, the largest group of North American students abroad comprised Southerners headed for the British Inns of Court.[13] Eighteenth-century students in the North American colonies—many of them at home in the South—"completed" their education in England and Scotland, the latter being then a notable center of the Enlightenment.[14] But the Declaration of Independence brought about a symbolic turning point. Replacing Edinburgh as an academic first choice, Paris became a US favorite. In 1781, for example, John Foulke of Philadelphia initially went to Paris, where he met Benjamin Franklin, and subsequently to Leipzig.[15] Henry Dwight observed in the 1820s that until very recently, US students had communicated with Europe mainly through Great Britain, implying that a different era had dawned by the time of the 1820s.[16]

While there are earlier examples, it was not until after 1815 that German universities seriously started to attract US students.[17] At that time—and following military losses—German education was reorienting and reforming, which could not fail to arouse interest in North America. When George Ticknor, in 1815, moved from Harvard to Göttingen, the Vienna Congress was reorganizing Europe after the Napoleonic Wars, and the War of 1812 between Great Britain and the United States was ending. Both France and England had just witnessed defeat as Ticknor, determined to move abroad for educational purposes, embarked for the German countries. He visited Berlin, where only in 1810 a new university had been founded, a project that has been interpreted as an act of educational revenge against France for the Prussian losses in the battlefield early on during Napoleon's military campaigns (see also chapter 4).[18]

Charles Franklin Thwing observed in 1928 that in the 1810s, "America was coming to national and academic self-consciousness."[19] He argued that accumulating wealth and physical comfort resulted in a broadened way of thinking. A national culture was beginning to sprout. Assistance from the outside was needed. Thwing concluded that the German countries were the solution, whereby the absence or presence of reform mindedness in Great Britain and German countries, respectively, certainly influenced US students' decisions as well besides victories and losses on battlefields.

While contributing to stimulating interest in German universities in the first place, war also coincided with the decline of US interest in German universities. World War I may be interpreted as an eruption of conflicts that had accumulated in the course of the nineteenth century; but, in fact, as regards

US student numbers in Germany, their decline had begun already around 1900 while total student numbers at German universities simultaneously continued to rise notably (see also chapter 2). One may link the decline in US student numbers abroad to a maturation of the US educational system. After all, a century of student migration—and particularly student migration since the US Civil War—had resulted also in bustling reform activity in the United States. But even if since the late 1860s reform-minded administrators, faculty, and boards of trust had created new research institutions like Johns Hopkins and reformed others such as Harvard, the question arises as to why the turn of the century would be the point in time to halt and reverse trends in US student migration.

Declining interest in German education overlaps with the "splendid little war" of 1898 between the United States and Spain over the Philippines and Cuba (the Spanish call it *el desastre*), which lasted but three months and left the United States in sweeping victory. The United States had matured into a world power that was no longer occupied with an internal frontier.[20] With heightened nationalist sentiments generally in Western civilizations around the turn of the twentieth century (such as the notorious Dreyfus Affair in France[21]), the United States felt victory in 1898 as a boost in national self-confidence, personified by future president Theodore Roosevelt and his Rough Riders.[22] The United States had triumphantly entered the scene as a global power and no longer needed foreign educational aid.

A letter by Edward Washburn Hopkins, a philological student in Germany during the late 1870s and early 1880s, to his former Leipzig professor Ernst Windisch discussed the war and then proceeded to express sympathy with Germany while actually threatening that if in conflict with US goals, Germany would become an enemy. Hopkins wrote on 23 October 1898, from New Haven: "For myself I believe in Ethnic decline, that a race, representing perhaps several nations, dies like an individual, and I believe that Italy, Spain, and France are all moribund, as they are all of one race. There comes now the Teutonic age, the more reason why Germany should be with us and not against us, but if against us, so much the worse for Germany."[23] It was, incidentally, the last letter from Hopkins to Windisch that has been preserved, though Windisch lived for another twenty years.

Regional Dynamics: The South in the History of US Higher Education

It was also a war that strikingly affected the way in which educational prestige has been accorded different US regions. More specifically, the Civil War left an imprint on how historians interpreted the role of the South in the history of American higher education even before 1860. In 1999, Roger Geiger pointed out that earlier historians, such as Richard Hofstadter, portrayed Southern higher education in a negative light. Geiger undertook to remedy the problem with a monograph on Southern higher education, which, however, focused on the twentieth century.[24] John R. Thelin as well set out to reconsider the South in the history of US higher education.[25] More recent publications acknowledge Thomas Jefferson's role. In 2004, Jennings Wagoner observed that even though Harvard president Charles W. Eliot is "typically given credit as being the father of the elective system," Eliot himself recognized Jefferson as the one who first implemented it.[26] Jefferson in turn had actually credited the College of William and Mary with employing a system of free election in late 1821.[27] In 1998 and again in 2009, Arthur M. Cohen acknowledged that Jefferson had introduced "the" university idea.[28]

I would like to add outside perspectives to draw even more attention to the emerging regional sensitivity in historiography. Let me start by reflecting on the picture as it was established in traditional literature on both US higher education and student migration abroad. The significance of this overview lies in the fact that—to simplify it a little—whereas Southern educational history is typically discussed in the context of regional studies, Northeastern educational history is taken as representative for the entire nation. Once there is a greater awareness of this discrepancy, new possibilities for scholarship open up that would allow us to establish Western, Midwestern, Southern, and Northeastern contexts side by side as a multitude of educational concepts that over time contributed in more or less open ways to the American educational mainstream.

The regional turn in scholarship occurred sometime around the turn of the twenty-first century. Publications from the 1990s on American education prior to the Civil War still enhance the image of the South as educationally backward while the Northern Puritans are described as having been on a mission to "civilize" the non-Puritan "wilderness" ever since their arrival in Massachusetts Bay.[29] Although this civilizing referred, above all, to "civilizing the Indians," it may be argued that it also holds true for how the South was treated in the history of higher education.[30] For instance, in 1994, George Marsden marveled that in 1636 "only six years after their settlement in the Massachusetts wilderness the Puritans established what soon became a reputable college. Higher education was for them a high priority in civilization building."[31] Marsden then created a Southern Other that lacked a similar commitment to civilization building and therefore was automatically educationally inferior: "By establishing a college so early (in the Southern colonies it took a century to do the same) the Puritans laid the foundation for New England's dominance in American higher education for the next three centuries."[32] But the question should rather be *why* Southern higher education was institutionalized so much later, and whether the reason for that could be found in the make up of the colony. Moreover, one wonders if *un*-institutionalized study especially in the South should not be added to the picture besides an inquiry into slave-owning Southern planters sending their sons to Europe for an education.

Marsden's not-so-subtle language is revealing. He claimed that the North had positively "dominated" US higher education since the founding of Harvard College in 1636. The idea of "dominance" pertains, however, to the language of colonization, implying that education can serve as a tool of subjugation. Thus, the language of colonization and dominance insinuates that the educationally superior North would have to educate the South in order to establish national standards. That we find repeated instances of such a language until the very recent past not just in historiography on American higher learning suggests that it was considered an unquestioned consensus, which takes us into the realm of generalizations and simplifications. Both help us avoid dealing with sensitive questions such as how someone could be a slave owner and a scholar at the same time and as such still contribute to the well-being of the nation (Jefferson being a most prominent case in point). Another question would be to what extent the knowledge of enslaved Africans could be considered a part of American education even if it was passed on orally and appears to have little in common with Western (European) educational traditions. Does leaving out such questions mean to repress aspects of the collective memory?

The focus on Northern educational patronizing is the more ironic as an early application of the outspoken New England mission of civilizing a wilderness in the context of college building can be found in Southern historiography. In his history of the University of Georgia, *College Life in the Old South* (1928), E. Merton Coulter chose "A University in the Wilderness" as a chapter heading. Coulter implied that in contrast to wilderness, "civilization" meant education as it was envisioned by the frontiersmen. He applied a "New England theme" to the history of higher education in the South when he alluded to Samuel Danforth's *A Brief Recognition of New-England[']s Errand Into the Wilderness* (1670), a case of Puritan exceptionalism that explored the question of how New England distinguished itself from other colonies—through religion. The idea of an *Errand into the Wilderness* became central to American Studies and culminated in Perry Miller's 1956 book by that title. But while the theme of civilizing the wilderness was adopted into national *American* historiography on higher education, the South, although it had early on applied the idea to education, was not.

The South as an example of educational exceptionalism is a foreign entity in US history. To give another example, in 1932, Donald Tewksbury had the Southern college disappear in a westward-moving frontier, that is, the South didn't even exist for him but was subsumed in the abstract concept of a western frontier. As civilization moved westward, the new frontier college is said to have developed dependency on Eastern mother colleges, which implies a static Northeastern dominance.[33] But although early Princeton presidents tended to be Yale graduates, no one ever speaks of a Princeton dependency on the New Haven mother college.[34] Such warnings only occur when region becomes a sensitive reflection of a national trauma. Princeton and Yale today both form part of the educational trinity alongside Harvard, and all of them are located in the Northeast. Once we look South, however, influences from other colleges become an issue: Tewksbury warned his readers that "too great an emphasis" on the impressive "local and independent character of many of the western ventures in college-building" would be a "real misinterpretation of the facts. There is a larger pattern involved which reveals a close dependence of the frontier college on the resources of the older communities in the east."[35] Interestingly, when Donald Robert Come cited Tewksbury later on, he omitted the reference to local independence altogether. The picture was simplified, removing Southern educational identity and stressing plain materialistic dependence on the North instead.[36]

Negative references to the South remain with the reader subconsciously especially when they occur in works that devote little attention to Southern educational specifics. In his introduction, Laurence Veysey referred to the South but once, citing an 1891 proposal to abolish the University of South Carolina. Without context, it leaves the impression that in the South a general disinterest in education prevailed. Veysey also accorded the University of Virginia a single footnote in which he cited Daniel Coit Gilman—without comment—as having been "influenced by the model of the University of Virginia."[37] Rudolph merely observed that the "Virginia experience was a remarkable deviation from the normal American pattern" adding that Jefferson's university was "rediscovered" in the "1860's and 1870's."[38] He listed institutions that spread the university movement in the South (Vanderbilt since 1893, Tulane, Duke, and Emory) but did not elaborate.[39] Christopher Lucas spoke of the "Virginia experiment" without explaining what he meant by that.[40] All of these references acknowledge Southern education but in contrast to the recent works I cited in the beginning of this section, they are even less explicit in pointing out that the South actually contributed to the American educational mainstream.

Borders can be redrawn quite arbitrarily in scholarship according to the necessities to uphold an argument such as Southern educational inferiority. The borders of the South continue to be flexible depending on what we are talking about. Maryland had been part of the Old South, but not of the Reconstruction South—Old South and New South geographically do not match. Destruction during the war plays into that. But wartime destruction is only one of many factors giving the South its identity today. The implication for higher education is that Johns Hopkins University in Baltimore, Maryland, founded in 1876, has not usually been advertised as a Southern institution, which is the more remarkable considering that Johns Hopkins is generally regarded the first real US university and thus a model of how to educate the nation.[41] Baltimore's racial make-up clearly marks it as Southern, though.[42] When the first true American research university is discussed, its regional identity is not explicitly part of it.

The example once again points to shifting priorities in historiography over time. In fact, Johns Hopkins increasingly became neutral with regard to its regional identity in twentieth-century scholarship. Peter Novick observed that rather than being Southern, Johns Hopkins as well as its eminent German-trained historian Herbert Baxter Adams had merely Southern ties.[43] By contrast, back in 1888, Adams had been appointed by the US Commissioner of Education to write a history of the University of Virginia. He stressed a sisterhood of the two institutions, observing that the "first professor for the Johns Hopkins University, in Baltimore, was obtained from the University of Virginia, and the first professor for Jefferson's original institution was sought in Baltimore,"[44] which places Johns Hopkins in the tradition of Jefferson's university.

The South also left its imprint on student migration to Germany. Already in 1947, Mary Bynum Pierson observed that "there is evidence that many Southerners attended ... [German universities] within the last half of the nineteenth century, and some returned to their native region to work and contribute to its educational advancement."[45] She provided a list of sixty-four Southerners, including four women.[46] Moreover, considering that New England was accorded a central role in student migration, it is ironic that two of the better-known late-nineteenth-century commentators on German universities (besides W.E.B. Du Bois) were Samuel Clemens (Mark Twain, Heidelberg 1878), who had been born in Florida but grew up in Missouri, and the future muckraker Joseph Lincoln Steffens, a Californian who studied in Berlin, Heidelberg, Leipzig, and Paris around 1890.[47] Both had a great sense of humor. While, however, their accounts make for enjoyable reading matter, they cannot be taken as representative of the typical US student in Germany, as neither of them had an academic career in mind.[48] Their objectives and expectations differed from those of the chemists, biologists, philologists, and historians who meant to study scientific methods in preparation for teaching and research careers back home, and who would contribute to changing the academic landscape of the United States.[49]

There is even more to Southern student migration. To apply Toni Morrison's concept of an unspoken African-American presence,[50] a Southern and also a Western presence may be detected in older scholarship on student migration so heavily focused on New England: Scholars have styled "educational pilgrims" in Europe up to the Civil War as "innocents abroad"[51] without elaborating on the concept's implications. The idea may be traced to Twain's 1869 *Innocents Abroad; or, The New Pilgrim's Progress,* with which the Southern humorist made fun of a popular New England founding myth. The "new pilgrim" alluded to an old tradition of viewing early immigration to New England as the cradle of North American identity. According to Twain, in the nineteenth century, a new American began innocently to explore the Old World. The idea of innocence abroad simultaneously may be seen as Twain's critical comment on the unpreparedness of the new pilgrims for a new Old World. Curiously, while the idea of the innocent educational pilgrim caught on among historians of higher education, Twain's satirical irreverence did not.

Instead, it appears that the Southern educational pilgrim has little autonomy in historiography. In 1965, nearly two decades after Pierson, John T. Krumpelmann discussed early-nineteenth-century Southern educational pilgrims in the German countries. He treated the subject from the vantage point of Orie William Long's *Literary Pioneers* (1935), which focused on the Harvard pioneers abroad in the late 1810s. Krumpelmann intended to integrate US educational history by pointing out that his Southern travelers had Northern credentials as they had studied at Harvard or—in the case of Basil Lanneau Gildersleeve—had been "awarded an honorary degree by that university."[52] One might conclude that Southern scholars were true scholars as long as Harvard recognized their academic accomplishments, which, once again, points to the assumed necessity of pressing a Northern stamp on Southern education.[53]

Krumpelmann seriously grappled with that issue. But even though he pointed out a "scholarly tradition that prevailed in the aristocratic circles of the old South [and] made formal learning a desirable goal for its post-Revolutionary youth,"[54] he lapsed back into pointing to Northern preeminence: "The fact that German universities then began to attract Southern students away from the previously visited British institutions was due at least in part to the influence which Harvard University and its 'Literary Pioneers' exerted both directly and through the founder of the University of Virginia, Thomas Jefferson, on ambitious young intellectuals of the Southern States."[55] While Krumpelmann acknowledged late-eighteenth-century Southern sophistication, he insinuated the necessity of Northern guidance to redirect Southern educational pilgrims to Germany, denying the Southerner intellectual independence. The idea was legitimized by the notion that Ticknor's Harvard used Jefferson as a medium to educate the South. Did the much younger Northerner educate the South through the sage of Monticello? Is it realistic to assume that a 24-year-old would speak through the aged author of the Declaration of Independence and third president of the United States?

In mid-1815, John Adams wrote to Jefferson from New England that the "Universities in Protestant Germany have at present the Vogue and the Ton in their favour."[56] Jefferson, however, had seen a necessity to procure professors for his new university from Europe as early as in 1800. Ticknor had visited and befriended Jefferson right *before* his 1815 trip to Göttingen. Jefferson sent Ticknor his concept of a university to be established in Virginia while the young man was still in Europe.[57] Did Ticknor bring Göttingen to Harvard, or did he learn to appreciate Jefferson's ideas while in far-away Europe exposed to foreign education? If so, Ticknor used a European matrix to develop educational ideals for the New World that would eventually (half a century later) be implemented on a larger scale. The ideas, though, did not simply reflect German learning but also Jeffersonian ideas.

Jefferson was likely as much an inspiration to young Ticknor as was the University of Göttingen. Western Enlightenment had influenced Jefferson's thinking; education had always been a concern to him.[58] But Ticknor turned down Jefferson's offer of a professorship at the new institution in Charlottesville and thus turned down the opportunity to cooperate in creating a new type of educational establishment in the young United States. He thus also turned down an opportunity to educate the South under Jefferson's tutelage. In the 1820s, Ticknor was firmly established at Harvard and preferred his native New England to educational experimenting in the South. He thus preferred transforming the establishment to creating something entirely new. Left alone at Harvard, Ticknor pretty much failed back then.

The University of Virginia opened in 1825 with a faculty of eight, five of them young Europeans (mainly of British extraction).[59] Jefferson's ideas resembled those that Ticknor would (unsuccessfully) promote at Harvard during the 1820s.[60] Evidently, back then the desirability of electives and seminar-style teaching on a larger scale was less obvious than it is, with hindsight, today. Both Ticknor and Jefferson had experienced foreign educational concepts from close up. Both were ahead of their times in trying to implement them back home. US society needed more substantial student migration—and thus more exposure to foreign education—before it would open up to such ideas. Curiously, it would be Ticknor's nephew—the famous Harvard president in the final decades of the nineteenth century, Charles W. Eliot (president from 1869 to 1909)—who would have a breakthrough with Jefferson's concepts after the Civil War.[61]

Ticknor's reform frustrations in the 1820s have been discussed in terms of a conservative Harvard hindering a progressive Ticknor from successfully effecting changes;[62] he resigned his professorship in May of 1835 and left for a tour of Europe.[63] That does not mean, however, that only Ticknor called for change. It simply means that different ideas prevailed. The 1828 Yale Report is a case in point.[64] Theodore Dwight Woolsey, a future Yale president, had just returned from his European student days when the report was written.[65] According to Veysey, two decades later, during Woolsey's administration at Yale, "emphasis upon science, history, and economy had declined"; English and Scottish philosophers—rather than Immanuel Kant and Georg Friedrich Wilhelm Hegel—were held in high esteem even though Woolsey had studied in German universities. Veysey also referred to the atmosphere in Woolsey's classroom as "chilly and forbidding."[66] Then again, "carefully segregated" scientific schools were founded at Yale and Harvard that nurtured future academic reformers, but Veysey did not elaborate.[67] He did admit that Yale "was a complicated case;" it had granted a first PhD degree in the United States in 1861, and "it was not until a decade later, when [Noah] Porter was chosen president, that it turned decisively in a conservative direction."[68]

Could we view Yale as a progressive educational institution during the first half of the nineteenth century? It incorporated foreign learning and attempted to adapt to contemporary educational necessities.[69] Woolsey was elected president in 1846, the year when the first scientific school was established in the United States. The future reform president Daniel Coit Gilman of Johns Hopkins referred to his alma mater Yale in the 1850s and 1860s as an important influence in the making of himself as an educational leader. In fact, he also spent some time studying in Germany and, upon his return to Yale, promoted adapting the German PhD degree to the necessities of US higher education. He thus successfully initiated a future standard in US academia. While Gilman in some respects placed himself in a Yale tradition, as a graduate student he nonetheless decided against following up exactly in Woolsey's footsteps, a phenomenon that is not exceptional in disciple-teacher relationships: new generations try out new directions, which Gilman did when he built up Johns Hopkins University, an undertaking that allowed him to further develop ideas with which he had first experimented at Yale.[70]

Woolsey was an advocate of an educational system that served the needs of his day. As he was returning from Europe, the 1828 Yale Report noted, among other things, that "attentive observation" should be given to "the literary institutions in Europe; and by the earnest spirit of inquiry which is now so prevalent, on the subject of education."[71] The Yale faculty furthermore expounded "with no small surprise" that "[we] occasionally hear the suggestion, that our system is unalterable."[72] Indeed, education needs to be "adapted to the spirit and wants of the age." They concluded to promote scholarship as a means to discipline the mental faculties.[73] Students were to receive "such a proportion between the different branches of literature and science as to form in the student a proper balance of character."[74] It is an early manifesto against the idea of regarding the humanities as inferior to the natural sciences, which came to be prevalent in the twentieth century. The humanities—and, in this case, more specifically the classics—provide systematic platforms to pose ethical questions about life.

Ideas similar to those of the Yale Report may be traced in the South back then such as at Randolph-Macon College,[75] and, as the century progressed, persisted though not necessarily as an educational mainstream. Rather, some ideas became minor in terms of the attention accorded them in public. Woolsey's successor as president of Yale, Noah Porter, wanted the college to teach students to think rather than to impart special knowledge.[76] It is a striking contrast to the ideal of utility, which, according to Veysey, became central later in the nineteenth century. At the same time, it reflects an observation that Charles Franklin Thwing made in 1897: "The college is to make the thinker," he noted, "American life needs the thinker more than it needs the scholar; for the thinker will take the old truth and apply it to the new conditions of the present and the future."[77] When Stephen Olin of Randolph-Macon College in Virginia remarked in 1834 with regard to college courses that their "utility in relation to the business of life is an important but secondary and inferior consideration,"[78] he simply reflected on an existing concept that was yet to become popular.

Disciplinary Dynamics: Revisiting the Ideal of "German Science"

Another concept was gaining in popularity quickly: the idea of a "scientific spirit," which was closely linked to the nineteenth-century German university ideal. But the English term *science* back then also embraced the humanities, which is why evidence of a scientific revolution may be traced across the nation also in economically weaker regions. Linguistic sensitivity with regard to etymological changes can consequently enrich historical interpretations. For instance, Novick observed that German *eigentlich*—nowadays typically translated as "really" or "actually"—in the nineteenth century could be understood to mean "essentially." A historical interpretation thus shifts from the concrete to more metaphorical realms.[79]

Likewise, the meaning of nineteenth-century "science" changes a historical interpretation if applied in its contemporary sense to past contexts. David Lindberg provided eight different descriptions of the term *science*, though none of them was an etymological explanation.[80] Thelin pointed out that the meanings of "science" or "scientific" varied according to time and place. In the late nineteenth century, for "an endeavor or an organization to be 'scientific' meant that it was disciplined, ordered, and systematic—in other words, that it adhered to the principles of 'scientific management.' Science used in this sense connoted efficiency, effectiveness, and accountability."[81] In recent editions on Jefferson and education, his usage of the term is actually translated as "knowledge" or "branches of knowledge."[82]

Translations between German and English present an additional hurdle but are inevitable when discussing US student migration to German universities. Indeed, whereas English "science" was reduced in common usage to "natural science" in the twentieth century, German *Wissenschaft* has kept its broader meaning. The German term literally translates more neutrally as "creation of knowledge." According to Merriam-Webster's dictionary, the etymological root of "science," the Latin verb *scire,* simply means "to know." "Science," in some of its earliest usages documented in the Oxford English Dictionary, was not just knowledge as opposed to belief, opinion, or ignorance; it was "knowledge acquired by study; acquaintance with or mastery of *any* department of learning." When excluding the humanities from "science," it implies that they do not play a role in acquiring knowledge through study.[83] To this day, English "science" actually carries a host of different meanings of which "natural science" is merely a particularly prevalent one—in British English "science" has denoted "natural science" since the 1860s, but it is not clear when this usage became dominant.[84]

In the past, dividing lines between today's branches of knowledge were less clearly drawn than one might think. For example, mathematics is related to the classics—many mathematical discoveries were made in ancient Greece. An activity of the mind rather than an experimental science, mathematics is also an analytical tool for natural sciences. Experimental psychology grew out of philosophical *and* physiological roots; physiology is a basic medical science. Psychology is consequently situated somewhere between the elusive *Geist* (mind) and observable manifestations of nature. Philology often overlapped with theology, which, in turn, overlapped with philosophy in its narrower sense but also with psychology and textual analysis as exercised today in linguistics and literary scholarship. German *Philologie* covers a variety of disciplines ranging from the classics to modern languages, including comparative linguistics.

In the US South, a scientific spirit was reflected in a considerable appreciation of the Classics—many Southern educational pilgrims in Germany would embark on philological careers.[85] But the South must not be linked to philological scholarship exclusively. To the contrary, as John Boles pointed out, at Rice Institute, in the early days, "science and engineering seemed more applicable to the 'problems [of] ... a new and rapidly developing country.' ... But this limitation was intended to be only temporary."[86] Moreover, Thelin presented evidence of Southern pre–Civil War openness towards technical education. While he observed that "Southern congressmen led the opposition" to federal involvement in investments "in advanced technical education," he also pointed out that their "objections pertained not so much to scientific and technical education as to the precedent of federal projects intruding on state's rights."[87] Dan Frost noted that many ex-Confederates became involved in higher education after the Civil War; they saw scientific curricula as a way to advance the South.[88]

Already the Yale Report had "insisted" on the "undeniable fact" that "Classical learning is interwoven with every literary discussion."[89] This may be seen as a conservative holding on to older forms of the creation of knowledge. The Yale Report makes it clear, however, that this should instead be interpreted as not allowing new fields of the creation of knowledge to replace but rather to supplement and possibly to transform older ones. The Classics continued to appeal in the late nineteenth century, although students now also began increasingly to turn to natural sciences as well as to modern languages, which provided them with the thrills of newness. It was not an easy transition. In the mid-1920s, the Nobel Prize–winning physical chemist Wilhelm Ostwald remembered that after his arrival at the University of Leipzig in 1887, he had refused to regard the natural sciences as inferior to older scholastic disciplines, suggesting that at that time the natural sciences were still struggling for equal prestige with the humanities.[90]

Against this background, one needs to reexamine how historiography has dealt with the idea of the scientific spirit in the context of US student migration to German universities. For example, Veysey claimed that the "larger, almost contemplative implications of *Wissenschaft* were missed by the Americans."[91] Novick argued along similar lines.[92] But what exactly did Veysey and Novick understand the term *science* to mean? In the end, maybe it was not the nineteenth-century US student who missed the larger implications of the term *Wissenschaft* but the twentieth-century historian who missed the larger implications of the term *science*.

"Science" became a synonym for "natural science" in twentieth-century institutionalized learning. If consciously or not, through his biographer Alex Haley, the civil rights icon el-Hajj Malik el-Shabazz (better known as Malcolm X) also expounded provocative views on sciences far from the mid-twentieth-century mainstream. Malcolm X thought that philology was a "tough science." He was self-educated, having begun to read voraciously while in prison in the late 1940s, where he also studied the "science of etymology."[93] Malcolm X was much closer to nineteenth-century scientific thinking, because he had *not* been trained in a contemporary institution of higher education (neither had his biographer, for Haley had dropped out of college early on). Malcolm X was thus free to use terminology in its nineteenth-century meaning rather than follow the prescribed standards of the formal education of his day. Incidentally, Malcolm X had refused a formal education in protest to the Jim Crowism of the Midwest and New England (rather than the South) in the early twentieth century.

The nineteenth-century "scientific method" also embraced the humanities, which, in turn, were open to apply to philology, for example, concepts from evolutionary theories and biology.[94] The humanities also resorted to new (natural-)scientific methods and concepts in order to study literature, language, and history. They posited that the natural and cultural sciences functioned on the basis of the same underlying principles. The evolutionary approach to linguistics focused on family trees of languages and basic laws that could be applied to all tongues once they had been reconstructed from a mother language.[95] It came to blossom in Germany in the 1870s, a little over a decade after Charles Darwin's 1859 *The Origin of Species,* in which language was also discussed.[96] In 1903, the German-trained historian and future ambassador to Nazi Germany, William Dodd, remarked that as objects of study in historical science, human beings could be classified just as plants are classified in biology, which brings to mind the scientific novels by the French writers Honoré de Balzac and Emile Zola that attempted to classify human beings into a number of different types.[97]

While scientists of the humanities were willing to make use of new methods that were borrowed from the natural sciences, they ultimately failed as scientific methods—meaning exact observation, experimentation, and comparison rather than speculation—apparently do not encompass the entire spectrum of human knowledge satisfactorily.[98] Indeed, it should not be concluded that German science was concerned with classifications and systematization exclusively, that it was, in short, "nothing more than counting nails."[99] At Leipzig, Georg Curtius "first brought two great sciences into a mutually helpful relation to one another," by which he was actually referring to grammar and literature.[100] He welcomed students—including quite a few illustrious women—from across the United States, not simply from the Northeast and maybe the Midwest. He also nursed a number of disciples from the South. One of them was James Hampton Kirkland. Just like Curtius, Kirkland refused to get lost in scientific detail. He called for the study of structure in combination with larger philosophical questions. As a chancellor of Vanderbilt University, Kirkland promoted the idea of studying for one's personal and intellectual benefit rather than for academic prestige and a career. Reflective of the 1828 Yale Report, this idea is now becoming a more widely valued ideal again.[101]

Summary

Recent scholarship on the history of American higher education is moving into new directions as it is developing a greater awareness of regional diversity. The result is a greater openness toward acknowledging, for example,

Southern contributions to the national educational mainstream, such as the fact that Thomas Jefferson actually introduced educational concepts that would be popularized only decades into the future. By incorporating the experiences of those who studied abroad, such regional diversity can be emphasized even further. For instance, US student migration abroad also occurred in the eighteenth century, but it was directed at Great Britain rather than Germany, and Southerners formed a considerable part of it.

The subject of student migration also adds other aspects to the picture, such as by sharpening the historians' awareness of the changing meaning of terminologies over time. Hence, the nineteenth-century idea of "science" should not be mistaken for the term's twentieth-century understanding as referring mainly to "natural science." The fact that, for example, studies on Jefferson's educational concepts translate the term "science" from older English to contemporary English usage is reflective of the notion that linguistic meanings are not static. Yet another layer is added as student migration to foreign countries also implies translation issues. An example would be the question of how to convey the idea of nineteenth-century German *Wissenschaft* to nineteenth- as opposed to twentieth-century English-speaking audiences.

Finally, student migration illustrates to what extent wars can impact educational developments. The American Revolution and the Civil War, but also the Napoleonic Wars in Europe and wars fought in the context of German unification, all more or less directly influenced US student migration abroad as well as educational reform activities in so far as they either brought promising developments to a halt or actually boosted attempts to improve education in a specific locality. All in all, straddling the period from the American Revolution to World War I, I discovered five phases of reform activity and student migration abroad, each of which was roughly framed by military conflicts on both sides of the Atlantic.

Notes

1. T. D. Woolsey to Sarah D. Woolsey (Sister), 21 April 1828. Woolsey Family Papers, Group 562, Series I, Box 3, Folder 42, YUL.
2. Roger Geiger, "Introduction," and "The Rise and Fall of Useful Knowledge: Higher Education for Science, Agriculture, and the Mechanic Arts, 1850–1875," in *The American College in the Nineteenth Century*, ed. Roger Geiger (Nashville: Vanderbilt University Press, 2000), 26, 155–56.

3. Philip Schaff, *Germany; Its Universities, Theology, and Religion* (Philadelphia: Lindsay and Blakiston/New York: Sheldon, Blakeman & Co., 1857), 36–37.

4. James Morgan Hart, *German Universities: A Narrative of Personal Experience* (New York: G. P. Putnam's Sons, 1874 [reprinted London: Routledge/Thoemmes Press, 1994]), 345–46.

5. Hart, *German Universities*, 393.

6. Harold Hellenbrand, *The Unfinished Revolution: Education and Politics in the Thought of Thomas Jefferson* (Newark: University of Delaware Press and London/Toronto: Associated University Press, 1990), 141–69.

7. On Cornell, Andrew D. White, *Autobiography*, vol. 1 (New York: The Century Co., 1906), 287–376. On Johns Hopkins, see Fabian Franklin, *The Life of Daniel Coit Gilman* (New York: Dodd, Mead and Co., 1910), 179–218.

8. For example, Anja Werner, "Striving for the Top: German-Trained Southern, Southwestern, and Western University Leaders in the Early 20th Century," in *Education and the USA*, ed. Laurenz Volkmann (Heidelberg: WINTER Universitätsverlag, 2011), 87–103; Anja Becker, "Southern Academic Ambitions Meet German Scholarship: The Leipzig Networks of Vanderbilt University's James H. Kirkland in the Late Nineteenth Century," *Journal of Southern History* 74, no. 4 (November 2008): 855–86; John B. Boles, *University Builder: Edgar Odell Lovett and the Founding of the Rice Institute* (Baton Rouge: Louisiana State University Press, 2007).

9. E.g., enrollment at the University of Colorado in Boulder increased more than tenfold between 1897 and 1931. Laurence R. Veysey, *The Emergence of the American University* (Chicago: University of Chicago Press, 1965), 1–2. Obituary, 25 Oct [1947?], HUG 300 Charles Carlton Ayer '89, HUL—Pusey.

10. War happens after diplomacy fails. The reference is, of course, to Carl von Clausewitz, *On War*, translated from the German (London: Penguin Books, 2007 [1832]). Also, Philip Windsor, *Strategic Thinking: An Introduction and Farewell*, ed. Mats R. Berdal and Spyros Economides (Boulder, CO: Lynne Rienner Publishers, 2002), 23.

11. Frederick Rudolph, *The American College & University. A History* (Athens/London: University of Georgia Press, 1990 [1962]), 3.

12. Regarding the medical profession, see Thomas Neville Bonner, *American Doctors in German Universities. A Chapter in International Intellectual Relations* (Lincoln: University of Nebraska Press, 1963), 4; Whitfield J. Bell, Jr., "Philadelphia Medical Students in Europe, 1750–1800," *Pennsylvania Magazine of History and Biography* 67, no. 1 (January 1943): 1–29.

13. J. G. de Roulhac Hamilton, "Southern Members of the Inns of Court," *North Carolina Historical Review* 10, no. 4 (October 1933): 273–86.

14. As regards Scottish Enlightenment, see Alexander Broadie, *The Scottish Enlightenment: The Historical Age of the Historical Nation* (Edinburgh: Birlinn, 2001/2007); James Buchan, *Crowded with Genius: The Scottish Enlightenment: Edinburgh's Moment of the Mind* (New York: HarperCollins, 2003/2004); Douglas Sloan, *The Scottish Enlightenment and the American College Ideal* (New York: Teachers College Press of Columbia University, 1971); Robert David Anderson, *Education and Opportunity in Victorian Scotland: Schools and Universities* (Edinburgh: Edinburgh University Press, 1983/1989).

15. Bonner, *American Doctors and German Universities*, 4–5, 16–17; Marcel H. Bickel, *Die Entwicklung zur experimentellen Pharmakologie 1790–1850. Wegbereiter von Rudolf Buchheim* (Basel: Schwabe & Co. AG Verlag, 2000), 37; Jurgen Herbst, *The German Historical School in American Scholarship* (Ithaca, NY: Cornell University Press, 1965), vii.

16. Henry E. Dwight, *Travels in the North of Germany, in the Years 1825 and 1826* (New York: G. & C. & H. Carvill, 1829), iii.

17. Henry A. Pochman challenged the idea of an assumed ignorance of German learning before 1815 in *German Culture in America: Philosophical and Literary Influences, 1600–1900* (Madison: University of Wisconsin Press, 1957), 20.

18. Alexander von Humboldt's older brother Wilhelm was essential for the Berlin university project. Another example of an educational revenge would be the build-up of the University of Leipzig, which gained momentum after the Saxons had lost sovereignty to Prussia in the 1866 Prussian-Austrian war (see chapter 4).

19. Charles Franklin Thwing, *The American and the German University* (New York: Macmillan, 1928), 4–6.

20. E.g., see John Whiteclay Chambers II, *The Tyranny of Change: America in the Progressive Era, 1890–1920*, 2nd ed. (New Brunswick, NJ: Rutgers University Press, 2001), 6. Wilbur R. Jacobs, *The Historical World of Frederick Jackson Turner. With Selections from His Correspondence* (New Haven, CT: Yale University Press, 1968), 1–5. Frederick Jackson Turner, "The Significance of the Frontier in American History," in *The Frontier in American History* (New York: Henry Holt, 1920 [1893]).

21. See e.g., Joseph Reinach and Pierre Vidal-Naquet, *Histoire de l'affaire Dreyfus*, Bouquins (Paris: Éditions Robert Laffont, 2006 [1900]); Philippe Oriol, *L'affaire du capitaine Dreyfus, 1894–1897* (Paris: Stock, 2008).

22. Theodore Roosevelt, *Rough Riders* (1899). Also Gail Bederman, *Manliness & Civilization: A Cultural History of Gender and Race in the United States, 1880–1917* (Chicago: University of Chicago Press, 1995), 170–215.

23. E. W. Hopkins to E. Windisch, 23 October 1898. NA Windisch 2.247.7, LUA. As regards German attitudes toward the 1898 war, see Markus M. Hugo, "'Uncle Sam I Cannot Stand, for Spain I Have No Sympathy': An Analysis of Discourse About the Spanish-American War in Imperial Germany, 1898–1899," in *European Perceptions of the Spanish-American War of 1898*, ed. Sylvia L. Hilton and Steve J. S. Ickringill (Bern: Peter Lang, 1999), 71–91.

24. Roger Geiger, "Southern Higher Education in the 20th Century. Introduction to Volume 19. A Special Issue of the *History of Higher Education*. Editor's Introduction," *History of Higher Education Annual* (1999): 7–24

25. John R. Thelin, *A History of American Higher Education* (Baltimore: Johns Hopkins University Press, 2004).

26. Jennings L. Wagoner, Jr., *Jefferson and Education* (Charlottesville, VA: Thomas Jefferson Foundation; Chapel Hill, NC: Distributed by University of North Carolina Press, 2004), 139. Wagoner quotes Charles W. Eliot, "Address at Southwestern Association of Northern Colleges, San Antonio," *San Antonio Express*, February 27, 1909, clipping, Eliot Papers, Box 273, HUL.

27. Wagoner, *Jefferson and Education*, 160 n.191, Thomas Jefferson to Francis Wayles Eppes, 17 November 1821. Wagoner cited Edwin M. Betts and James A. Bear, Jr., eds., *The Family Letters of Thomas Jefferson* (Columbia: University of Missouri Press, 1966), 441.

28. Arthur M. Cohen and Carrie B. Kisker, *The Shaping of American Higher Education: Emergence and Growth of the Contemporary System*, 2nd ed. (San Francisco: Jossey-Bass, John Wiley & Sons, 2009), 112.

29. Arthur M. Cohen, *The Shaping of American Higher Education: Emergence and Growth of the Contemporary System* (San Francisco: Jossey-Bass, John Wiley & Sons, 1998), 18. Cohen cites Martin Trow, "American Higher Education—Past, Present and Future," *Studies in Higher Education* 14, no. 1 (1989): 5–22.

30. Cohen, *Shaping of American Higher Education*, 19.

31. George M. Marsden, *The Soul of the American University: From Protestant Establishment to Established Nonbelief* (New York: Oxford University Press, 1994), 33.
32. Ibid., 33.
33. In the case of the University of Georgia, Northerners (Yale graduates) were civilizing a Southern wilderness. In his novel *A Fool's Errand* (1879), in turn, Albion Winegar Tourgée undermined the idea of the North's errand into the Southern (moral) post–Civil War wilderness, suggesting that the North did not *really* reach the South and thus could not leave an imprint on the defeated former enemy. Donald G. Tewksbury, *The Founding of American Colleges and Universities Before the Civil War: With Particular Reference to the Religious Influences Bearing Upon the College Movement* (New York: Archon Books, 1965 [1932]), 1–29, 14; E. Merton Coulter, *College Life in the Old South: As Seen at the University of Georgia* (Athens: Brown Thrasher Books/University of Georgia Press, 1983 [1928]), 3; Donald Robert Come, "The Influence of Princeton on Higher Education in the South before 1825," *William and Mary Quarterly* (3rd ser.) 2, no. 4 (October 1945): 359–96.
34. Come, "The Influence of Princeton," 361.
35. Tewksbury, *Founding of American Colleges*, 9.
36. Come, "The Influence of Princeton," 359. Failures of Southern and Western colleges might be explained by a lack of understanding for the local traditions and problems on the part of ambitious northeasterners.
37. Veysey, *Emergence of the American University*, 15, 160 n.122.
38. Rudolph, *American College & University*, 127.
39. Rudolph, *American College & University*, 348.
40. Christopher J. Lucas, *American Higher Education: A History*, 2nd ed. (New York: Palgrave, Macmillan, 2006), 132.
41. Cohen actually named Cornell (1869) *and* Johns Hopkins the first US universities. Cohen, *Shaping of American Higher Education*, 104.
42. Gertrude S. Williams and Jo Ann Robinson, *Education as My Agenda: Gertrude Williams, Race, and the Baltimore Public Schools*, Palgrave Studies in Oral History (New York: Palgrave Macmillan, 2005); Hilary J. Moss, *Schooling Citizens: The Struggle for African American Education in Antebellum America* (Chicago: University of Chicago Press, 2009).
43. Peter Novick, *That Noble Dream: The "Objectivity Question" and the American Historical Profession* (Cambridge: Cambridge University Press, 1988), 78. Raymond J. Cunningham, "The German Historical World of Herbert Baxter Adams: 1874–1876," *Journal of American History* 68, no. 2 (September 1981): 261–75.
44. Herbert B. Adams, *Thomas Jefferson and the University of Virginia* (Washington: Government Printing Office, 1888), 106.
45. Mary Bynum Pierson, *Graduate Work in the South, published under the sponsorship of The Conference of Deans of Southern Graduate Schools* (Chapel Hill: University of North Carolina Press, 1947), 41.
46. Pierson, *Graduate Work in the South*, 43–53. An examination of the US student body of the University of Leipzig revealed that at least 225 of about 1,530 US citizens who registered there between 1781 and 1914 hailed from the South. The number was likely even higher, as not all students could be traced. See chapter 3.
47. Lincoln Steffens, *The Autobiography of Lincoln Steffens, Complete in One Volume* (New York: Harcourt, Brace and Company, 1931); Justin Kaplan, *Lincoln Steffens. A Biography* (New York: Simon and Schuster, 1974).
48. Steffens was unusual in studying for the sake of learning rather than preparing for an academic career in the United States. L. Steffens to Frederick M. Willis, 4 January 1890, in

Ella Winter and Granville Hicks, eds., *The Letters of Lincoln Steffens,* vol. 1 (New York: Harcourt, Brace and Company, 1938), 39.

49. The majority of US students abroad focused on academic careers; the University of Leipzig alone produced some thirty university presidents, including presidents of Yale, Bryn Mawr, Berkeley, Rice, Vanderbilt, Tulane, Randolph-Macon, and the Southern Baptist Seminary in Louisville, Kentucky. Anja Becker, "For the Sake of Old Leipzig Days ... Academic Networks of American Students at a German University, 1781–1914" (PhD dissertation, University of Leipzig, 2006).

50. Toni Morrison, *Playing in the Dark: Whiteness and the Literary Imagination* (London: Picador, 1993), x.

51. Paul Nash, "Innocents Abroad: American Students at British Universities in the Early Nineteenth Century," *History of Education Quarterly* 1, no. 2 (June 1961): 32–44; Carl Diehl, "Innocents Abroad: American Students in German Universities, 1810–1870," *History of Education Quarterly* 16, no. 3 (Fall 1976): 321–41. A recent example is Jonathan Zimmerman, *Innocents Abroad: American Teachers in the American Century* (Cambridge, MA: Harvard University Press, 2006).

52. John T. Krumpelmann, *Southern Scholars in Goethe's Germany* (Chapel Hill: University of North Carolina Press, 1965), 1.

53. Krumpelmann himself was a case in point. Born in New Orleans in 1892, he attended Tulane, obtained a Harvard PhD degree in 1924, and embarked as a Harvard traveling fellow for Europe. In 1938, he returned to the Deep South as Professor of German at the Louisiana State University in Baton Rouge. Carl Hammer, Jr., "John T. Krumpelmann," in *Studies in German Literature,* ed. Carl Hammer, Jr. (Baton Rouge: Louisiana State University Press, 1963), xiii–xv.

54. Krumpelmann, *Southern Scholars,* xi.

55. Ibid.

56. J. Adams to T. Jefferson, 19 June 1815. Reprinted in Lester J. Cappon, ed., *The Adams-Jefferson Letters: The Complete Correspondence between Thomas Jefferson and John Adams* (Chapel Hill: University of North Carolina Press, 1959), 444.

57. George Ticknor, *Life, Letters, and Journals of George Ticknor,* vol. 2 (London: Sampson Low, Marston, Searle, & Rivington, 1876), 120, 126.

58. Hellenbrand, *The Unfinished Revolution,* 15, 39, 66–67.

59. Ibid., 93–99. Virginia cherished educational "progressivism" even after Jefferson's death. For example, in 1839, on request of Governor David Campbell, Benjamin Mosby Smith, who had recently returned from studying at Halle "where he had made observations on the schools" prepared a report and a plan for a public school system in Virginia. The Prussian model was to provide inspiration. Charles William Dabney, *Universal Education in the South,* vol. 1 (Chapel Hill: University of North Carolina Press, 1936), 76.

60. Ticknor, *Life, Letters, and Journals,* vol. 2, 120, 126.

61. Henry James (eldest son of Harvard philosopher William James), *Charles W. Eliot* (Boston/New York: Houghton Mifflin Company, 1930), 31.

62. Orie William Long, *Literary Pioneers: Early American Explorers of European Culture* (New York: Gordon Press, 1975 [1935]), 54.

63. Ibid. See also Ticknor, *Life, Letters, and Journals,* vol. 2.

64. David B. Potts, *Liberal Education for a Land of Colleges: Yale's Reports of 1828* (New York: Palgrave Macmillan, 2010).

65. Peter Dobkin Hall, "Noah Porter Writ Large? Reflections on the Modernization of American Education and Its Crisis," in Geiger, *The American College,* 197, further sources 331n4; David B. Potts, "Curriculum and Enrollment: Assessing the Popularity of Antebellum Colleges," in Geiger, *The American College,* 39–40; James Turner and Paul Ber-

nard, "The German Model and the Graduate School: The University of Michigan and the Origin Myth of the American University," in Geiger, *The American College,* 224; Louise L. Stevenson, *Scholarly Means to Evangelical Ends: The New Haven Scholars and the Transformation of Higher Learning in America, 1830–1890* (Baltimore: Johns Hopkins University Press, 1986), 16–17, 31.

66. Veysey, *Emergence of the American University,* 8.

67. Ibid., 10.

68. Ibid., 50.

69. See also Brooks Mather Kelley, *Yale: A History* (New Haven, CT: Yale University Press, 1974). Lester F. Goodchild and Margaret M. Miller also point out Yale's leading role in introducing American graduate education in their "The American Doctorate and Dissertation: Six Development Stages" in *Rethinking the Dissertation Process: Tackling Personal and Institutional Obstacles,* ed. Lester F. Goodchild, Kathy E. Green, Elinor Katz, and Raymond C. Kluever (San Francisco: Jossey-Bass Publishers, 1997), 17–32 (here 19–20).

70. Daniel Coit Gilman, *The Launching of a University* (New York: Dodd, Mead & Company, 1906), 4. Concerning Gilman's role in introducing the PhD degree to America, see Francesco Cordasco, *The Shaping of American Graduate Education: Daniel Coit Gilman and the Protean Ph.D.* (Totowa, NJ: Rowman and Littlefield, 1973); Goodchild and Miller, "The American Doctorate and Dissertation," 17–32 (here 19–20). As regards the German PhD degree, see also chapter 8.

71. *Reports on the Course of Instruction in Yale College* (New Haven, CT: Hezekiah Hower, 1828), 5. Available at http://www.yale.edu/yale300/collectiblesandpublications/special-documents/Historical_Documents/1828_curriculum.pdf.

72. Ibid., 5.

73. Stevenson, *Scholarly Means to Evangelical Ends,* 16–17, 31.

74. *Reports on the Course of Instruction in Yale College,* 7–8.

75. Stephen Olin, *Inaugural Address,* 5 March 1834, 4, 5. Quoted in James Edward Scanlon, *Randolph-Macon College: A Southern History. 1825–1967* (Charlottesville: University of Virginia Press, 1983), 55.

76. Marsden, *Soul of the American University,* 125.

77. Charles Franklin Thwing, *The College of the Future: An Address Delivered at the Commencement of Miami University, June 7th, 1897* (Cleveland, OH: Williams Publishing and Electric Co., 1897), 7.

78. Olin, *Inaugural Address,* 5 March 1834, 6, quoted in Scanlon, *Randolph-Macon College,* 429n58.

79. Novick, *That Noble Dream,* 25, 28.

80. David C. Lindberg, *The Beginnings of Western Science: The European Scientific Tradition in Philosophical, Religious, and Institutional Contexts, 600 B.C. to A.D. 1450* (Chicago: University of Chicago Press, 1992), 1–4.

81. Thelin, *History of American Higher Education,* 114.

82. Wagoner, *Jefferson and Education,* 53. Dumas Malone, *Jefferson & His Time,* vol. 6, *The Sage of Monticello* (Charlottesville: University of Virginia Press, 1981), 235.

83. Anja Becker, "Crossing Disciplinary Boundaries," *Our hemisphere—Nuetro hemisferio. A Newsletter of the Center for the Americas at Vanderbilt* (Fall 2007).

84. Stefan Collini, "Introduction," in C. P. Snow, *The Two Cultures* (Cambridge: Cambridge University Press, 1998), xi. Snow first delivered his essay as a lecture in 1959.

85. Until the 1950s the leading department at the University of Mississippi was the Classics department. John Hardin Best, "Education in the Forming of the American South," in *Essays in Twentieth-Century Southern Education: Exceptionalism and Its Limits,* ed. Wayne

J. Urban (New York: Garland Publishing, 1999), 14–5. An earlier edition was published in *History of Education Quarterly* 36, no. 1 (Spring 1996): 39–51.

86. John B. Boles, *A University So Conceived: A Brief History of Rice*, 3rd rev. and exp. ed. (Houston: Rice University, 2006), 11. See also President's Papers E.O. Lovett, Rice Fondren.

87. North Carolina sent a delegation on a tour of New York, Connecticut, Massachusetts, and Rhode Island in the summer of 1851. It was found that little communication existed among Northern institutions of higher learning as regarded innovations and developments in applied science. Thelin, *History of American Higher Education*, 81.

88. Southerners realized that the South had lost the Civil War because it "lagged behind" the North in terms of scientific advances and instruction. Some believed that the 1870 war between Germany and France had been won by the German universities. Dan R. Frost, *Thinking Confederates: Academia and the Idea of Progress in the New South* (Knoxville: University of Tennessee Press, 2000), 48.

89. *Reports on the Course of Instruction in Yale College*, Part II: "Liberal Education and the Classical Curriculum," 35. Available at http://collegiateway.org/reading/yale-report-1828/curriculum.

90. Wilhelm Ostwald, *Lebenslinien. Eine Selbstbiographie*, vol. 2 (Berlin: Klasing & Co., 1926–27), 106.

91. Veysey, *Emergence of the American University*, 127.

92. Novick, *That Noble Dream*, 24, 37.

93. Alex Haley, "Epilogue," *The Autobiography of Malcolm X as Told to Alex Haley* (New York: Ballantine Books, 1992 [1964]), 393, 416.

94. In 1867, the German linguist August Leskien was asked at Göttingen whether his line of thinking might not be considered "a branch of physiology." E. Eichler, "August Leskiens Wirken für die Slawistik," *ZfSl* 26, no. 2 (1981): 171. Leskien urged Charles Rockwell Lanman, one of his US students, "to get as many of the really needed books of science *as I can.*" C. R. Lanman to Aunt, 7 November 1875 and 14 May 1876. C. R. Lanman Papers, HUG 4510.67, Letters from Europe, vol. 3, HUL Pusey. Emphasis in the original.

95. Eveline Einhauser, *Die Junggrammatiker. Ein Problem für die Sprachwissenschaftsgeschichtsschreibung* (Trier: WTV, 1989), 3; Conrad Bursian, *Geschichte der classischen Philologie in Deutschland von den Anfängen bis zur Gegenwart* (München and Leipzig: Oldenbourg, 1883), 971–1007; Rudolf Růžička, "Historie und Historizität der Junggrammatiker," *Sitzungsberichte der Sächsischen Akademie der Wissenschaften zu Leipzig* 119, no. 3 (Berlin: Akademie Verlag, 1977), 5, 6.

96. Robert J. Richards, "The Linguistic Creation of Man: Charles Darwin, August Schleicher, Ernst Haeckel, and the Missing Link in Nineteenth-Century Evolutionary Theory," in *Experimenting in Tongues: Studies in Science and Language*, ed. Matthias Doerres (Stanford, CA: Stanford University Press, 2002); Robert J. Richards, *The Romantic Conception of Life: Science and Philosophy in the Age of Goethe* (Chicago: University of Chicago Press, 2002/2004).

97. William E. Dodd, "Karl Lamprecht and Kulturgeschichte," *Popular Science Monthly* 63 (September 1903): 419–20; Lowry Price Ware, "The Academic Career of William E. Dodd," (PhD dissertation, University of South Carolina, 1956), 16. Novick, *That Noble Dream*, 40–41, referred to Flaubert and Zola. Balzac was inspired by the Prussian scholar-scientist and America-traveler Alexander von Humboldt. See Charles Dédéyan in *L'Année balzacienne*, ed. Michel Lichtle, Nouvelle serie, 18 (Paris: PUF, 1997).

98. Ottmar Ette, *ÜberLebenswissen. Die Aufgabe der Philologie* (Berlin: Kadmos, 2004), introduction.

99. Edwin Mims, *Chancellor Kirkland of Vanderbilt* (Nashville: Vanderbilt University Press 1940), 48. The Leipzig scholar Georg Curtius "never lost himself in details"; he observed linguistic peculiarities without losing sight of a text's meaning and aesthetic beauty. A. S. Wilkins, "Georg Curtius. Eine Charakteristik by E. Windisch," *Classical Review* 1, no. 9 (November 1887): 263. In Thomas A. Sebeok, *Portraits of Linguists. A Biographical Source for the History of Western Linguistics, 1746–1963*, vol. 1, *From Sir William Jones to Karl Brugmann* (Bristol, UK: Thoemmes Press, 2002 [1966]); Ernst Windisch, *Georg Curtius. Eine Charakteristik* (Berlin: Verlag von S. Calvary & Co., 1887). Cited in Becker, "Southern Academic Ambitions."

100. Wilkins, "Georg Curtius," 263. Windisch, *Georg Curtius*.

101. Mims, *Chancellor Kirkland*, 82–83. Also, Margot Adler, "Some Students Look for Hidden-Gem Colleges," *Morning Edition*, 22 February 2007, NPR. Available at http://www.npr.org/templates/story/story.php?storyId=7384194. Accessed 22 Feb 2007. While a graduate student at Johns Hopkins in 1876, Walter Hines Page complained that the German-type scholars there "can make dictionaries but can no more appreciate the soul beauties of literature than a piano manufacturer can appreciate Wagner." Kirkland would be an example to the contrary. See also the letters he sent to his mother while at Leipzig: James Hampton Kirkland Papers, VU SCUA. W. H. Page to Sarah Jasper, 15 October 1976. Reprinted in Burton J. Hendrick, *The Training of an American: The Earlier Life and Letters of Walter H. Page 1855–1913* (Boston and New York: Houghton Mifflin Company, 1928), 75.

Chapter 2

US STUDENT NUMBERS AT GÖTTINGEN, HALLE, HEIDELBERG, AND LEIPZIG

The Challenges of Numbers

IN THIS CHAPTER, I establish American student numbers at four important German universities in comparison with the total student numbers there from the late eighteenth century until World War I. In addition to that, I discuss US students' backgrounds as derived from the Leipzig register, including the socioeconomic status of their parents, their religious affiliations, and their ages upon their first enrollments. While I collected the data for the Universities of Halle and Leipzig at the respective university archives, for the comparison with the Universities of Göttingen and Heidelberg I relied on published lists with the names and registration information of American students there—mainly the 1910 list of American students at Göttingen by Daniel Bussey Shumway and the 1969 list of American students at Heidelberg by John T. Krumpelmann.[1]

I thus add to our existing picture of American student migration to German universities substantial archival and statistical information about two universities—Leipzig and Halle. In doing so, I put available data on Göttingen and Heidelberg in perspective and, in a close reading of the data, trace fluctuations in American attendance at all four universities over prolonged periods of time. My approach represents a first comprehensive, comparative approach to the phenomenon of nineteenth-century US student migration to German universities covering the entire long nineteenth century (for instance, Carl Diehl merely focused on the decades up to 1870[2]). Against such

---

Notes for this section begin on page 71.

a statistical background, I will in subsequent chapters not only portray an American colony based on biographical research, but I will also illustrate to what extent the German and American academe were intertwined through something that might best be termed old boys networks that connected German professors with their American disciples.

Revisiting Existing Scholarship

Most of the published materials on US student migration to German universities are either selective or rather specific by focusing on individual aspects of the German experience and its impact on American education or by stressing a given student category or even group (I discuss different US students groups in chapter 3). As a result, many of our assumptions about the allure of the German universities are based on rough estimates rather than facts. Of course, there exist valuable studies with statistical undercurrents,[3] but they tend to focus on the German university as such, not so much on the dynamics of their US student bodies in comparison.[4]

Most historians who tackled the numerical problems of American student bodies in Germany did not work with actual student lists extracted from the archives but analyzed nineteenth-century statistics or presented estimates. They thus found a variety of ways to trace tendencies despite a lack of concrete data. Hertha Marquardt in 1956 and Paul Buchloh twenty years later refined and corrected Shumway's list of American students at Göttingen, thus adding many valuable details and background information.[5] Apart from that, scholarship often quoted numbers from sources that did not always provide references. Such sources included accounts by German-trained Americans that might reflect general trends but were based on subjective impressions. Let me provide a few examples in the following, whereby I will focus on historiography on higher education and how it integrated the topic of US student migration to German universities.

One of the most influential historians in the field, Laurence Veysey, was likely also the most elaborate in incorporating student migration abroad. He was quite perceptive in analyzing a US interest in German universities in his path-breaking 1965 *The Emergence of the American University.* His conclusions generally correspond with my archival findings, which I will discuss below. Veysey analyzed contemporary publications authored by American students abroad, which reflected a changing interest in German education. He determined that an increasing number of such sources (though of a varying quality) appeared in the 1870s, most notably James Morgan Hart's 1874 *German Universities.* Veysey proceeded to claim that *intellectually*—explicitly not in numbers—the 1880s represented the "high point of American interest in the German university," a claim that he backs with the observation that US publications back then "commonly voiced enthusiastic, uncritical approval."[6] Veysey also traced a disillusionment with the German university in the 1890s, from which he correctly deduced that German and US academic circles had lost contact well before World War I.[7]

The idea of uncritical approval, though, strikes me as somewhat contrary to the idea of an intellectual heyday. Indeed, as my statistics below illustrate, at least at Leipzig US student numbers actually decreased somewhat in the 1880s, suggesting that while people might have talked about German universities, they did not necessarily study there with the same fervor as in the previous decade. The 1870s had been a very fruitful period for Leipzig Americans. US student numbers exploded again in the 1890s, turning it into a fashion fad to study at Leipzig then. Hence, the publication of enthusiastic articles about German universities in the 1880s might thus actually reflect the intellectual appeal of the 1870s and prepare the increased US student numbers of the 1890s.

Veysey claimed that "The numerical peak of American study in Germany was reached in 1895–96, when 517 Americans were officially matriculated at German institutions."[8] Judging from my own archival research, I would agree that the mid-1890s saw indeed the heaviest enrollment. But Veysey did not provide a reference. How did he obtain such a specific number? And did it include German-speaking universities like the ones in Strasburg and Breslau (Wrocław), or did it refer exclusively to universities that were part of the German academic world in the 1960s?

Numbers remain a murky element in other studies as well, and few authors accorded US student migration to Germany as much cohesive space as did Veysey. John Thelin devoted an entire subchapter to "Discussions and Debates about the Character of a Modern University," which also relied on accounts of Americans who had studied in Europe.[9] But he did not address the subject of student migration directly and consequently did not provide any numbers. Arthur M. Cohen and Carrie B. Kisker mentioned in the 2009 second edition of *The Shaping of American Higher Education* that "only a few hundred American students had traveled to German universities by 1850."[10] They added subsequently that "Beginning in the first quarter of the century a number of American college graduates went to Germany for further study."[11] Finally, they observed that the idea of "converting colleges to universities can be traced to the men who had been influenced by direct contact with higher education in Germany. George Ticknor was earliest," being followed up by "Daniel Gilman, Andrew White, Charles Eliot, Theodore Woolsey, and G. Stanley Hall."[12] Their influencing Johns Hopkins, Cornell, Harvard, Yale, and Clark, respectively, "stand out." According to Cohen and Kisker, others, of course, also went.

Cohen and Kisker refrained from presenting more precise numbers. Numbers would be necessary to analyze especially the period from 1870 to 1914, when student migration to German universities surpassed everything witnessed in the previous decades. Numbers accompanied by biographical research would reveal that not simply a few future East Coast and Midwestern university presidents went to Germany. They would prove that future Southern and Western administrators and educators were among those who traveled to German universities for further education. An examination of numbers would give us a more exact idea of how many thousands of Americans registered in German universities.

A statistical analysis paired with a biographical approach would help us define the often-cited "German educational model." Few studies on the history of American higher education fail to mention the idea, but for the most part, authors then either quickly move on without exploring the concept any further, or they merely focus on a specific aspect. For instance, Frederick Rudolph merely observed in 1962 that the "collegiate tradition in the United States could not find new inspiration in the spirit of the German university without some loss to the collegiate way."[13] Veysey culminated his paragraph on increasing interest in German universities during the 1870s with a quote from an 1879 article by G. Stanley Hall containing the fuzzy announcement, "The influence of German modes of thought in America is very great and is probably increasing."[14] But what exactly was that influence? How can we approach it and track down its meanings?

Veysey at least pointed out that there was not "a" German university experience but that it could have a host of different meanings.[15] Indeed, in different studies I find different ideas on the German impact: the introduction and transformation of the PhD degree, a focus on scientific research methods (also simply on pure research), intellectual societies, specialization, an awareness of broader contexts, the introduction of the seminar teaching method, and academic freedom such as by introducing electives. Obviously, some of these ideas such as specialization versus a contemplation of broader contexts might appear somewhat contradictory, although they simultaneously could well be considered as complimentary sides of one coin.

Moreover, while historians tend to mention earlier student migration in earlier chapters, they typically discuss the subject in the context of the transformation of American colleges into universities during the 1860s and 1870s (and, as I pointed out in chapter 1, they are likely to focus on a few well-known examples from the Northeast and Midwest). Rudolph might be an exception. He devoted more space to George Ticknor than to the German influences later in the century.[16] Considering that most studies refer to German models in occasional, isolated paragraphs, the readers may find subtle hints at best that imply a long tradition of student migration to Germany. But the phenomenon is not explored including its beginnings in the eighteenth century, and long-term transformations consequently are absent from the monographs. Considerable US student migration thus appears almost out of nowhere around 1870 and, after a few decades, subsides again. I would argue, however, that the earlier developments need to be included in the analysis as a precondition for later developments thanks to academic networking that encouraged US students to follow their mentors' examples by traveling to Germany.

Veysey accorded the subject of "The Lure of the German University" a separate subchapter, in which he focused his analysis on the foreign institutions' intellectual attraction.[17] Later studies did not devote so much time to the German influence at all and, by reducing the subject to a paragraph here and there or even less, they also reduced the diversity of the German experience and influence. In his brief chapter on universities, Lewis Perry in 1984 merely pointed out that in post–Civil War America, universities transformed following "no single blueprint."[18] He added that the customs of the German universities, which were "widely praised as models," were modified. The German influence subsequently was linked to the introduction and transformation of the PhD degree. Taken together, without mentioning student migrations, Perry discussed the transformation of American higher education as a phenomenon happening in its own right. Something similar may be observed in Thelin's monograph, which he prudently named *A History of American Higher Education* rather than claiming it to be *the* ultimate account. He mentioned a "German ideal," which he qualified as "advanced scholarship, professors as experts, doctoral programs with graduate students, and a hierarchy of study."[19] He did tie the idea mainly to Johns Hopkins University. But even if many US institutions of higher learning could not compare with Johns Hopkins on the whole, they might have achieved desirable advances in at least some respects. A few men, like Vanderbilt's second chancellor James Kirkland, certainly aspired to more, which illustrates the importance of studying biographies in addition to statistics.[20]

Two more points strike me as vital though somewhat neglected in existing literature on American higher education. First, the idea that in spite of the German lure, nineteenth-century higher education continued also to thrive on British college traditions. Cohen and Kisker, for example, point out that as colleges were being transformed into universities, the "treatment of undergraduates followed the British form of residential colleges. Graduate study and research was adopted from the German universities."[21] Thelin briefly mused about Andrew White and a vision of "Oxford and Cambridge transplanted to upstate New York."[22] Veysey even dropped the remark that the "painstaking 'German method,' perhaps tacitly joined to an empirical philosophy more British than German (though England was hardly ever mentioned in this connection), became linked in many American minds with the main cause of academic reform at home."[23] Unfortunately, I have not yet come across a profound analysis that would present German and British influences on American education not as a succession of but as concurrent influences.

Second, the available studies do not put enough emphasis on the diversity of American colonies abroad. American students included representatives of all possible fields of study. But these students differed greatly in their expectations and motivations. Some were graduate students, others already advanced in age. Some wanted a teaching career in schools or in colleges and universities, others would become administrators, yet others never embarked on careers in education at all, which brings us to the concept of what the Germans call *Bildungsbürger*, that is, persons interested in knowledge and education without being professionally occupied with either. That, in turn, brings us to the question of the larger American presence in the different university towns—the families, travelers on the grand tour, professional artists who lived, worked, and studied in Europe in considerable numbers. Often the categories overlapped, such as when students were accompanied by family members or entire families.

David McCullough depicted the diversity of a single American colony in Europe including also ambitious women and African Americans. In his very readable *The Greater Journey* (2011), he discussed Americans in Paris in the course of the nineteenth century. His numbers are vague, though, and he switched from comprising students to referring to all Americans in town. He observed, "Between 1830 and 1860 nearly seven hundred Americans came to Paris to study medicine."[24] Regrettably, I was unable to procure a copy of the book that McCullough quoted to check the reference. As I will show in chapter 3, taking women as an example, US students' impressions of the number of their compatriots at the foreign university could be quite arbitrary. Other numbers cannot clearly be attributed to a specific source. For instance, McCullough described how circa the 1870s Paris was filling up with Americans. There were now "more than 4,000" living in the city.[25] He also spoke of an "estimated 13,000 Americans in Paris, mostly tourists," by the time of the Franco-German war, adding that of the "4,500" Americans who were part of the American colony in town, almost all would leave.[26] Eventually, he pointed out that by the mid-1880s, "American medical students in Paris now numbered relatively few."[27] These last examples suggest that for a lack of more reliable published sources, numbers were likely based on subjective, contemporary accounts.

Different Student Statuses

A comparative, statistical examination of US student bodies at several German universities requires first of all that one discern the different student categories at the universities in question, and how they were recorded. There were typically three different categories—regularly registered students, auditors or hearers, and visitors. Older published US student lists tend to point out which of these student categories were included. But discrepancies cannot be entirely excluded as every university had its own specifics in recording the different student categories in its registration records and published directories. While all data that I present in the following will consequently have to be taken with caution, the numbers nonetheless represent very close approximations rather than vague estimates of the actual situation. If information is uncertain or unreliable, such as in the case with hearer records at the University of Leipzig, I explicitly point out the uncertainties.

Before I delve into presenting and discussing my data in more detail, let me briefly describe my sources and discuss to what extent the different student categories are relevant for my analysis. The data that I collected for Halle and Leipzig are based on the handwritten registration records (*Matrikel*) and printed student and faculty directories (*Personalverzeichnisse*), whereby the register contains handwritten information about each student including his name, fatherland, place of birth, place of previous education, religion, age, and field of study. The directories, in turn, which were printed for each semester, list the students in alphabetical order and also include information on when a student registered. The directories furthermore contain statistics on the student body more generally.[28] The two sources are not identical, as sometimes students registered so late in the semester that their names do not appear in the directories. At both Halle and Leipzig, statistics from the directories do not distinguish between US students and other foreign students until the late nineteenth century.

Newly registered students made up the largest percentage. Fewer students stayed for several semesters; if they did, they were likely to pursue a degree. I therefore base my subsequent considerations on newly registered Americans per term rather than on the total US student body. It would have been a rather challenging task to identify all the students who stayed for more than just one semester. One would have to look up each student in a succession of directories until their names are no longer listed, which would have been very time consuming. By contrast, the Halle register also included a note on when a student left, which was not the case at Leipzig.

Besides registered students, there are two more categories of student status. The two categories of auditors (then called "hearers" by native English speakers in a literal translation of the German *Gasthörer*) and visitors comprise students who studied at a university without having enrolled there; auditors signed a "hearer list," visitors did not, but particularly in earlier years, the distinction is not always evident. After the 1860s, the hearer/visitor status allowed women, who could not officially register in Germany before 1900, to have a German university experience in spite of all.[29]

Visitors make up the most elusive group. They were more likely to be advanced in age and did not register or place their names in the auditor lists even though they studied with German professors for up to several semesters, of which their correspondence gives proof. They are usually traced by chance in secondary literature on the history of certain disciplines or in the letters and journals of their contemporaries. Some of the more illustrious educational pilgrims never registered, such as Julius Hawley Seelye, a future president of Amherst College, who studied at Halle in 1852/53.[30]

Hearers and visitors at German universities are particularly challenging to research. At Leipzig, hearers were statistically recorded in the student directories starting only with the 1859 spring term. A hearer list was not introduced until 1873,[31] containing for the most part merely names and cities of origin without references to nationality. But, for example, a student from Manchester might be a British or a US national. At Halle, hearer numbers were added to student statistics starting already in 1836. US hearer numbers there are available from the fall term 1867/68 onwards. Shumway marked different student statuses in his 1910 list of US students at Göttingen, which allowed me to pick regularly matriculated students. Krumpelmann's 1969 list contains only regularly matriculated US students at Heidelberg.

For US students—both men and at some institutions women as well—it was possible to earn a German PhD degree without having registered. Caspar René Gregory, for instance, traveled to Europe in 1873 after six years at the Princeton Theological Seminary. His name was not found in the Leipzig student directories even though he submitted a dissertation there in 1876.[32] He had, however, placed his name in the hearer list on 29 October 1873 as number 23.[33] Some students would change their status from "regular" to "hearer" when preparing their dissertations, as did Guy Tawney, a student of psychology, who had registered at Leipzig in late 1894 and was a hearer during the 1896 spring term, in which year he earned his PhD degree.[34]

US Student Numbers Abroad I: Statistical Overview

In 1928, Charles Franklin Thwing observed that "somewhat less than one thousand" US students had studied at Leipzig in the "one hundred years which have passed since [Edward] Everett, [George] Ticknor, [George] Bancroft, and [Joseph Green] Cogswell took their degrees at Göttingen,"[35] that is, since the 1810s. He did not indicate where he got that number. I found more than 1,700 entries from US students in the Leipzig register between 1781 and 1914, the overwhelming majority of whom enrolled between circa 1866 and 1914. Subtracting multiple enrollments, we have 1,530 individuals, including two women. The numbers correspond to 336 students at

Halle-Wittenberg between 1769 and 1914 or 319 without multiple enrollments, also including two women.

I compared my actual Leipzig number with Thwing's Leipzig number
and Shumway's Göttingen number, of which Thwing must have been aware.
According to Thwing, Leipzig attracted the overall same number of US
students or maybe even less than Göttingen. That is not true. Not counting multiple enrollments, US students at Göttingen numbered only about
two-thirds of all of Leipzig's newly enrolled US students. By the late nineteenth century, Leipzig was the bigger university and had considerably more
students. Shumway lists the names of some 1,235 Americans at Göttingen
between 1782 and 1910 (including Shumway himself). Some 261 names
on Shumway's list including several women were not found in the Göttingen register;[36] they must have been hearers or visitors. The number of
regularly matriculated students, including also a few women, consequently
totals about 974. Considering that Shumway compiled his list in 1910, his
numbers correspond to roughly 1,460 US students at Leipzig between 1781
and the 1910 spring term and 303 US students at Halle (Table 1).

Table 1

Total New US Enrollments at Halle, Göttingen, and Leipzig			
University	Time Period	New US Enrollments	New US Enrollments up to 1910
Halle	1769–1914	319	303
Göttingen	1782–1910	974	974
Leipzig	1781–1914	1,530	1,460

This first comparison insinuates that Göttingen benefitted indeed from
its early-nineteenth-century reputation as a magnet for US students well into
the twentieth century, when Thwing published his study on American and
German universities. In other words, a few individuals such as Ticknor and
Shumway were so successful in vocalizing their Göttingen experience that in
the minds of many, Göttingen became the epitome of the nineteenth-century
German university town to host an American colony. Of course, there is
truth in Göttingen's special status especially as Göttingen Americans were so
successful in promoting their German alma mater. But a long-term examination and comparisons with other universities are nonetheless necessary.

As suggested already in chapter 1, German universities complemented
one another in attracting US students in the course of time. A comparison of
the actual US student numbers at the four universities Göttingen, Halle, Heidelberg, and Leipzig can serve to illustrate the idea. The general tendencies
at all four institutions under review were rather similar. After the arrival of

the earliest pioneers in the late eighteenth century, from a US point of view, comparatively little happened in the first half of the nineteenth century, although the 1830s and 1840s witnessed a small but notable presence of US students at all four institutions. During the years from 1850 to 1870, the US presence became much more pronounced, but it did not really take off until the early 1870s when US student numbers virtually exploded. Decline set in around the turn of the twentieth century.

The differences lie in detail. During each of these time periods, a different German university was of greatest appeal to US students. For example, for the years from 1830 to 1870, Heidelberg took the lead—Krumpelmann traced 320 Heidelberg Americans during this period. The number corresponds to only 196 new US enrollments at Göttingen, 51 at Halle, and 43 at Leipzig. Heidelberg had evidently bypassed Göttingen in appeal to US students by the 1830s. At the same time, Leipzig and Halle were of considerably less importance than either of the other two. This balance would, however, change yet again. In spite of the similar student numbers at Halle and Leipzig by midcentury, the appeal of both universities would come to differ significantly during the next few decades, with Leipzig taking a lead by far. Göttingen in the 1810s and 1820s is clearly only one episode of the story. Table 2 provides an idea of US student numbers at the four German universities to the extent to which data is available.

Whereas in my chapter 1 I discussed five overlapping periods in the history of US higher education and the history of US student migration to European institutions of higher learning that were framed by wars and revolutions on either side of Atlantic, I chose slightly different time frames for Table 2 simply because the available data for Heidelberg merely covers the period 1830 to 1870. It seemed more reasonable to compare Heidelberg's American student body during this time period with the American student bodies at the other three universities. General tendencies that roughly correspond with the trends I outlined in chapter 1 may nonetheless be discerned. In the table, I highlighted the respective university that appeared to have attracted most US students during a specific time period.

Table 2

New US Enrollments per Semester				
University	1769–1815	1815–1830	1830–1870	1870–1898	1898–1910
Göttingen	3	22	193	552	204
Heidelberg	xxxxxxx	xxxxxxx	320	xxxxxxx	xxxxxxx
Halle	5	1	51	169	74
Leipzig	3	1	43	1,084	329

The different German universities obviously experienced different hey-days as regarded their American student populations in the course of the nineteenth century. Put differently, universities apparently transform over time, and these transformations may be measured by closely observing the developments of student bodies (or specific sections thereof).

It may be concluded that Göttingen's and Halle's US student populations grew much more steadily in the course of the nineteenth century than that of Leipzig, whereby Halle maintained the overall smallest American student body. Leipzig, in turn, quite literally experienced an enrollment explosion around 1870.[37] While it had one-fourth of Göttingen's American student population in the four decades until 1870, it welcomed about twice as many US students in the three decades thereafter. Leipzig maintained its lead into the twentieth century. Regarding the early years, it may be observed that student migration before 1815 was minuscule. It never really gained momentum until the 1830s. One wonders why Krumpelmann chose 1830 to 1870 as the timeframe for his list of American students at Heidelberg. My guess is that student migration there prior to 1830 was insignificant if nonexistent, while after 1870 it might have experienced a rise similar to that at the other three German universities.

The numbers may not simply be added up to obtain the larger picture of total US student migration to German universities. After all, many students registered at two or even more institutions of higher learning while abroad. There is consequently much overlapping between the student bodies of the individual German universities. To obtain the total number, lists of American students at all German-speaking universities would have to be obtained and the trajectories of each student be checked simply to find out if they studied at other German universities. While the result of such an undertaking would be intriguing, it might simply be too labor intensive at this point (although university archives are beginning to transcribe their registers to make them available online).

US Student Numbers Abroad II: Developments over Time

In the following, let me provide a more detailed analysis of the US student numbers as presented in Table 2. To illustrate my findings better, I prepared Figure 1, which reflects developments at all four institutions within the large group of new enrollments rather than the institutions' entire US student bodies in a given semester. In addition to that, Figure 2 illustrates the differences in total and newly enrolled US student numbers at Halle and Leipzig based on both the registers and statistics in the directories.

Already in the nearly half a century before Ticknor's celebrated departure, a handful of students from the New World had registered at German-speaking universities, whereby Halle and Leipzig (rather than Göttingen exclusively) had aroused their interest.[38] It happened at a time when the British Isles were still the favored destination of American students—subjects from the colonies returned for their advanced education. The phenomenon may be qualified even further by focusing on Scotland. In the late eighteenth and early nineteenth centuries, Edinburgh alone produced various natural-philosophical journals, also providing English translations of, for example, the writings of the influential scholar and scientist Alexander von Humboldt. Americans from the South preferred to go to Great Britain at that time, where they studied law above all, albeit not exclusively.[39]

The early Scottish-Southern connection raises the question to what extent North American student migration to Europe was tied to kinship rather than to scholastic appeal. At least in the early period, it might have played a role, although Scotland, of course, was a notable center of the Enlightenment and thus emanated intellectual appeal. My own archival research as regards American students at German universities revealed that the earliest students were indeed more likely to be of a German extraction—recent immigrants sent their sons back to the German countries for their education. This was no longer the case one hundred years later with much larger US student crowds abroad. Alternatively, one might argue that there had always been a tendency for some people of Germanic roots to send their offspring back to the Old World for a German education. But with increasing academic appeal of the German universities, heritage became insignificant for many Americans who simply wanted to obtain what was then reputedly the best possible education. It is, however, difficult to determine students' ethnicity merely on the basis of the not completely reliable registration information at German universities.[40] In fact, foreign names were on occasion Germanized, turning a "John" into a "Johannes," or a "William August Smith" into a "Wilhelm August Schmidt."[41]

When searching for causes for an educational pilgrimage to Europe, it needs to be kept in mind that the earliest American students in Germany amounted to a mere handful, whereas one hundred years later hundreds would roam German universities at a time. The first two North American students at Halle were brothers of German descent. In March 1769, Fridrich August Conrad Mühlenberg enrolled, followed in October by Gotthilf Henric Ernest Mühlenberg. Both studied theology. They were sons of the preacher Heinrich (or Henry) Melchior Mühlenberg (1711–1787) of Philadelphia, a native of Halle who had immigrated to Pennsylvania in 1742. He sent three of his four sons back to Halle in 1763. They returned in 1770.[42] The Mühlenberg brothers were followed up at Halle in the 1770s by

Carolus Fridericus Gustavus Holtze, also of Philadelphia, in October 1774; Egidius Gottlib Vogt in March 1778; and Johannes Henricus Boode in April 1784. The latter two merely stated that they were "Americans" but did not specify their native state or city. That Holtze, just like the Mühlenbergs, was a native of Philadelphia emphasizes the importance of that city as an intellectual center in Benjamin Franklin's day.[43] It is also possible that Holtze knew the Mühlenbergs.

The early Halle-Philadelphia connection beats both Göttingen and Leipzig by more than a decade. The first North American student at Leipzig was another native of Philadelphia, John Foulke, a medical student who registered in October 1781. Foulke traveled to Leipzig directly from Paris, where he had enjoyed the hospitality of none other than Benjamin Franklin and his grandson Temple. Upon his arrival in Leipzig, Foulke sent letters to both men, also commenting on the university, which did not appeal to him much.[44] Only in 1782 did a first North American student finally matriculate at Göttingen. He was a math student by the name of Frederick C. White. In 1792, a second US student, Daniel Müller of New York (?), registered at Leipzig. He was followed at Göttingen in 1800 by Philip Tidyman of Charleston.[45] The identity of a third representative from the US at Leipzig in 1807, John Morton Johnson, also from Philadelphia, could not be confirmed. Another doubtful case is the one of a US student who, according to Shumway, had enrolled at Göttingen in the previous year.[46]

In the first half of the nineteenth century when, from US perspectives, Göttingen, Heidelberg, and even Halle flourished, Leipzig was hardly of interest at all. At Halle, I traced sixteen students who registered between 1826 and 1850, a number that corresponds to the one given in a 1915 article by Karl Diehl.[47] At Leipzig, however, between 1807 and 1852, only two US students enrolled:[48] Theodore Dwight Woolsey in December 1827, and, in January 1840, Arthur Payson of Boston. Woolsey, like Foulke, had traveled from Paris to Leipzig. A future president of Yale, he was a cousin of Henry Dwight, who was a son of former Yale President Timothy Dwight[49] and author of a travel book on the German countries.[50] It may be suspected that Henry Dwight's opinions had had an impact on Woolsey's choice of Leipzig. After all, Dwight had provided him with at least one letter of introduction to a Leipzig professor.[51] Woolsey also studied in Berlin and Bonn. Seventeen-year-old Payson opted for *cameralia,* a kind of predecessor of business studies. Since 1838, he had attended the Institution de Bellerive in Vevey,[52] Switzerland, a famous school for boys from affluent backgrounds. Many foreigners including numerous US citizens would send their sons there in the course of the following decades. The school had been founded in 1836 by Edouard Sillig of Saxony, who might have pointed out the Saxon University of Leipzig.

Considering the attention the Harvard-Göttingen connection of the 1810s and 1820s was accorded in historiography, it is noteworthy that Woolsey was a Yale rather than a Harvard graduate and that during his formative years, Payson had been exiled from educational establishments in his native country. Payson was not in line with general trends in US student migration, which might also be explained by the fact that he had spent most of his young life in Europe. His father John Larkin Payson was US Consul in Messina from 1827 to 1845.[53] Payson embarked on a career in business rather than opting for academia. In the first half of the nineteenth century, nothing comparable to the Philadelphia-Halle or the Harvard-Göttingen connection may be traced at Leipzig, though the foundation of a Yale-Leipzig connection was established in the person of a future Yale president. Indeed, when US interest in Leipzig awakened in the early 1850s during Woolsey's Yale presidency, Yale graduates were among the first to spread the news.

By midcentury, in the 1840s, Heidelberg attracted considerably more US students than Göttingen. Leipzig, by contrast, between 1830 and 1850 basically did not play a role at all, disregarding Payson and a few US visitors in the 1840s, who heralded subsequent Leipzig popularity among US students.[54] The revolutionary year 1848 was accompanied by a general drop in US student numbers. But already by the early 1850s, all four institutions featured more or less slowly increasing US student populations. The one at Göttingen steadily grew for the next two decades. The one at Heidelberg did so, too, but by the 1860s had even more clearly surpassed Göttingen in attracting North Americans. Unfortunately, no post-1870 data is available for Heidelberg at this point. It may be assumed that the rising tendency continued for some time, possibly with a temporary decline due to the 1870/71 war between Germany and France, for Heidelberg, in contrast to Leipzig, was close to the battlegrounds and thus more directly affected than universities in Eastern German states such as Saxony.

By midcentury, the situations at both Halle and Leipzig began to diverge. Halle did experience a notable peak in US student numbers by the late 1850s, but with the outbreak of the US Civil War, numbers there dropped. In the late 1860s, only one or two new enrollments per semester are on record. No rising tendency is evident until the early 1870s; stagnation or steadiness would be closer to the truth. Leipzig lingered on until about the mid-1860s. In the late 1860s, however, almost overnight, US student numbers there skyrocketed. While in the 1860s, between none and four Americans had registered at Leipzig per semester, by 1873, numbers fluctuated between around 15 in the spring terms and from 21 to 40 in the fall terms. These fluctuations between fall and spring reflected the fact that Leipzig was preferred in the fall. Many Americans opted for a Southern German university such as

Heidelberg or Freiburg i./Br. as preferable places for the spring semesters on account of the lovely Southern German countryside. In terms of new enrollments, Leipzig thus quite suddenly took the lead over Göttingen and Halle by far. The rise in US student numbers at Göttingen during the early 1870s is notably steeper than the one observed during the previous two decades, but it is less pronounced than the one at Leipzig. Halle in turn, in spite of a little peak in the mid-1870s, maintained a comparatively steady but low attraction to US students.

Only by the late 1880s did the number of new enrollments at Halle begin to increase; a decline did not set in until the early 1900s. Decline at Leipzig had already commenced in the late 1890s. While at Leipzig, new enrollments per semester had been back to the single digits in the 1880s, the 1890s witnessed registration numbers that ranged from a low of 10 in the spring term of 1892 to a high of 44 in the fall term of 1896/97 (not counting multiple enrollments). At Halle, fluctuations were less pronounced, ranging in the 1890s from 1 to 11 per term. Göttingen, in turn, experienced a high of 22 new enrollments in the fall term 1895/96 and a low of 3 during the spring terms 1893 and 1899. Fluctuations between fall and spring semesters are less pronounced at either Halle and Göttingen.

Some fluctuations in numbers appear to be complementary, though. That is, one German university's temporary losses in US students coincided with increases at another—a close examination of US students' subject-choices in combination with German professorial recruitments might help explain this phenomenon (see chapters 4 and 5). Leipzig experienced a temporary drop in new US enrollments around 1881 followed by a similar setback at Göttingen around 1883. At about the same time, Halle's US enrollments temporarily increased. Similarly, when new US enrollments at Leipzig briefly dropped yet again, those at Göttingen went up. In the early 1890s, the phenomenon may be observed in reverse: Leipzig rose, Göttingen declined.

A considerable increase in hearer numbers at Göttingen in the course of the 1890s might be attributed to the arrival of women. Basing the number of US women at Göttingen during the 1890s on Shumway is, however, not completely reliable, as he often listed only initials rather than first and middle names (although it appears that he tended to spell out female first names, thus inadvertently Othering them). I discuss female hearers in more detail in chapter 3.

At all three institutions, the late 1890s witnessed an all-time high followed by a significant drop in numbers around 1898 with only a few exceptions that may be explained by analyzing specific academic disciplines and their changing appeal. As we have seen, the war against Spain over Cuba and the Philippines also marked the turning point in the development of US student migration to these three German universities. Until World War I, the number of new US enrollments steadily diminished, although a few curious countertendencies may be observed as well (without the numbers ever going up again to the apex of the 1890s). Leipzig experienced a little peak around 1910 following the creation of Karl Lamprecht's Institute of Universal History. Göttingen numbers went up at around the same time and then broke off (the year 1910 marks the publication of the Shumway list). Halle, however, witnessed a steady downward tendency at this point, although numbers there rose again immediately before the outbreak of World War I.

Comparison: Total Student Numbers

To get a better idea of the meaning of the ups and downs of US student numbers at individual German institutions, I compared the developments with those of total student numbers. Statistics are available for the Universities of Halle and Leipzig for the period from 1850 to 1914 (Figures 3–5). It is more difficult to obtain a statistical idea of earlier periods as for example at Leipzig statistics were not preserved for every year in the early nineteenth century.[55]

My most intriguing finding is that at both Leipzig and Halle, total student numbers after 1900 continued to rise, while US student numbers decreased. Reasons for this phenomenon are likely also found on the US rather than on the German side exclusively. The main difference between the two German universities is that in comparison with Leipzig, Halle's total student population caught the train of dramatically rising numbers a few years later and never grew quite as substantially as Leipzig, an observation that mirrors my conclusions about US student numbers.

Statistics since 1850 reveal that developments in US student numbers match trends in total student numbers until about the turn of the twentieth century. Moreover, observations regarding total student numbers might be corroborated with the tendencies in total hearer numbers. The one significant difference is that while mirroring trends in total numbers, hearer numbers tend to precede tendencies in regular student numbers by a few semesters. It appears that visitors and hearers checked out the university first before a tidal wave of regularly matriculated students set in—or not, depending on what the pioneering hearers reported (see also chapters 4 and 5).

Since midcentury, Leipzig had grown steadily with differing degrees of intensity, eventually more than quintupling its student body. Leipzig's total student numbers amounted to less than 1,000 in the early 1850s but slowly rose in the next two decades. In the early 1870s, joining the enrollment explosion at German universities, Leipzig's student numbers rose steeply, soon passing the 3,000 mark. Numbers remained quite stable until the early

1890s, when another period of growth began that lasted until the outbreak of World War I. In the two semesters before the Great War, Leipzig had an overall student population of over 5,300, whereas Halle with more than 2,800 students in the last peaceful fall term had still not reached the 3,000 mark.

Halle's student population of the 1850s totaled about two hundred students less than Leipzig. The number increased steadily but slowly until the late 1860s. Halle also joined in the enrollment explosion of 1870, but it did so in a much less pronounced fashion than Leipzig. A decline to once again fewer than one thousand students followed at Halle, while Leipzig simultaneously was possibly the number one German university for a few years during the mid-1870s. Only in the late 1870s did Halle's total student numbers pick up again. They remained somewhat stable during the 1880s, and, in the 1890s, began steadily to increase until World War I.

US Students' Backgrounds

Regional Origins and Socioeconomic Backgrounds

US student bodies abroad may be further dissected by examining students' regional origins, socioeconomic backgrounds, ages upon first enrollment, religion, fields of study, and previous education as represented in the university registers (see also chapter 5). Information on regional backgrounds was gleaned from the category "place of birth" in the Halle and Leipzig registers. Fortunately, most students provided a state besides the name of a town or city. Student directories merely copied the information from the register, sometimes introducing mistakes. When Arthur Mitchell Little of Fort Wayne, Indiana, registered at Leipzig in November 1887, the student directories indicated that he hailed from the state of "Iud." Andrew Cunningham McLaughlin complained in 1893 that the "Rector insisted on spelling Beardstown Pettytown [and] of course did not ask me where I lived but only where I was born."[56]

The regional backgrounds of US students at Halle and Leipzig overall show similar general tendencies (Figures 6–9), but they differ in details. Most students hailed from the Northeast, followed by the Midwest/West and the South/Southwest. Both German universities also welcomed a small but notable number of foreign-born US students—that is, immigrants mainly from German and other European counties, but also sons of US missionaries and businessmen in Asia and South America. At both institutions, the regional backgrounds of a number of students could not be determined. Then again, the percentages of students from the various US regions differed. On the whole, Halle attracted more Northeasterners—they made up nearly one-half of the entire US student body there. Leipzig, in turn, attracted a comparatively larger number of Southerners. Comparatively more US students remain unidentified at Leipzig with its much larger US student body.

But these numbers need to be qualified by analyzing them according to developments over time. The period prior to 1870 was studied more intensely in the past. If, however, we take the findings for the years from 1815 to 1870 as representative of the entire long nineteenth century, we will ultimately get a distorted picture. To examine the degree to which regional backgrounds changed over time, I broke up the data into narrower time frames. I decided on five periods, chosen loosely by decades: the late eighteenth century until 1865, 1866 until 1879, 1880–1889, 1890–1899, and 1900–1914. While these categories might appear arbitrary, they still allow us to indicate changes over time. They also show that depending on a chosen time frame, the resulting interpretation can differ considerably. Moreover, during the earliest period only a few students registered at these German universities, while after the US Civil War numbers went into the hundreds. If, therefore, an earlier period shows a substantial portion of Southerners, this translates into only a few individuals compared to later decades (Figures 8 and 9).

In contrast to the situation at the smaller Halle, at Leipzig family and national ties were a minor motivation for student migration. Taken together, only about 80 Leipzig Americans were foreign born (with varying degrees of certainty). Almost half were of German descent, while some ten students were born in the British Commonwealth as natives of Great Britain and Canada. I also traced a few persons born in Ireland. Various European countries were cited once or twice as places of birth. Japan, Costa Rica, India, Mexico, Peru, Persia, and Turkey also sent students to Leipzig who explicitly pointed out their US citizenship.

The socioeconomic backgrounds of foreign-born US students are telling. US students born in the Near East and Far East sprang from missionary families. Students connected with South America, by contrast, had merchants and landowners as fathers, that is, people who were inclined to make their fortune in business. Finally, the European-born students tended to represent various socioeconomic backgrounds, including blue collar. Their fathers were workers, teachers, clergymen, or, as in the case of the Morgenthaus, families searching for a new business start in the Promised Land. Julius Caesar Morgenthau was a Jewish American of German extraction. He was born in Mannheim in 1858, the son of a well-to-do businessman. In 1866, after considerable financial losses, the family moved to America.[57] Julius's brother Henry, who would father Franklin D. Roosevelt's secretary of the treasury, and their brother-in-law William Ehrich enabled Julius Caesar to work towards a PhD degree in archaeology at Leipzig, which he accomplished in 1886.[58]

Information on "father's profession" provides a basis for general conclusions regarding socioeconomic backgrounds (Figures 10 and 11). The overall picture suggests that students came from solid, middle-class backgrounds, whereby trade and commerce played the largest roles, followed by farming, religion, education, law, and medicine. I grouped my findings into five main categories: business, clergy, agriculture, learned profession, and "other," including a variety of blue- and white-collar professions that were cited but a handful of times.

At Leipzig, students who enrolled more than once added ambiguity to their fathers' respective occupations. For once, a tendency to move from a specific job description to a more general term such as "merchant" or "businessman" may be observed. For example, August Martin Bierwirth upgraded his father from a *Fleischermeister* (butcher) in 1869 to a more neutral *Kaufmann* (merchant) in 1871. Similarly, Charles Homer Holzwarth switched from *Klempner* (plumber) in 1906 to "businessman" in 1908. It may be suspected that "merchant" was applied indiscriminately. The same trend may be suspected with regard to agriculture. In 1895, Samuel Hefelbower referred to his father as a "farmer." Seven years later, he had become a *Gutsbesitzer* (landowner). The exact size and status of the farm is open to speculation. Sometimes multiple enrollments provided a specification of fathers' professions, such as in the case of Marvin Beeson, who in 1911 stated that his father was a college president. Two years later, he added that his father was the president of a women's college in Meridian, Mississippi.

Halle and Leipzig alumni and their fathers included notable members of US society. Among the fathers of US students at Halle were three presidents of institutions of higher learning: James Burrill Angell of the University of Michigan in Ann Arbor, the "Cancellarius" of New York University Henry MacCracken, and Amherst's Julius Hawley Seelye. Two superintendents from New York (Alexander Bird) and Arkansas (Thomas Futrall) were traced. Thomas's son John C. Futrall, who registered at Halle in October 1899, would serve as president of the University of Arkansas. Among the fathers of Halle alumni were also the president of a preparatory school, Francis Blakeslee; the dean of New York University, Joseph French Johnson; a librarian; and several professors and teachers. At least thirty future university presidents were traced at Leipzig, ranging from Yale to Berkeley, and also including Vanderbilt and Rice.[59]

An examination of fathers' professions over time reveals changes in students' socioeconomic backgrounds. A new, middle-class elite was emerging in the three decades following the Civil War. Late-nineteenth-century US students in Europe were not exclusively the sons of "Boston Brahmins" or "Southern aristocracy." There were, of course, students who represented New England elite, such as Henry Pickering Bowditch of Boston at Leipzig in 1869, who was a nephew of Paris-trained Henry Ingersoll Bowditch.[60] Eva Channing, a hearer at Leipzig in 1879, was the daughter of William Francis Channing, who was William Ellery Channing's son.[61] Wilder Dwight Bancroft,[62] grandson of the historian and pioneering educational pilgrim George Bancroft, matriculated at the Saxon university in 1890. Similarly, during the late 1850s and 1860s, when US student numbers at Leipzig were comparatively low, a number of sons of Southern "landowners" opted for the Saxon university. For instance, 10-year-old Wymberly De Renne of Georgia was sent to Europe during the Civil War. He stayed until 1873, the final two years studying at the University of Leipzig.[63]

Examples of family enrollments help detect trends of upward mobility. Eric Hobsbawm pointed out the "real test of schools and universities as socializers ... for those who were climbing up the social ladder, not for those who had already arrived at the top."[64] A case in point was economist John Maynard Keynes and his paternal ancestors—while his father was a "Cambridge don," his grandfather had been a "nonconformist Salisbury gardener."[65] Another example connected Halle and Leipzig: the Seelyes. Seelye Senior studied at Halle in 1852/53.[66] By the time he had become president of Amherst College, his son was ready for higher education. William James Seelye registered at Halle in May 1882. In the following fall term, he was a hearer at Leipzig. Upon his return to the United States, he embarked on a career as a professor of Greek and a clergyman. The grandfather, Seth Seelye, had been a storekeeper, merchant, farmer, and deacon in his day.

Religion

Neither at Leipzig nor at Halle was religion recorded in the late eighteenth century. It was not until the early nineteenth century that registration information became more detailed. The category yielded the most homogenous results; overall, religion appears not to have played a decisive part in choosing a German university. Multiple enrollments furthermore suggest that—as was the case with father's profession—students sometimes noted a specific faith, and, on other occasions, chose a broader categorization like "Protestant" or "Evangelical." This appears to have been dependent on previous entries. If on a page in the registration book the immediately preceding students had registered as "*evangelisch,*" subsequent US students were likely to do the same. The same holds true for "Protestant." Just as "merchants" covered a wide range of paternal professions, "Protestantism" was apparently a conveniently broad category to cover a multitude of religious denominations.

Whereas it is difficult to determine exact numbers as some students made use of questionable abbreviations, once again general tendencies may be observed. More than 1,370 of the 1,530 Leipzig Americans claimed to be either generally Protestant (ca. 1,020) or—in considerably smaller numbers and sometimes in combination with Protestantism—Lutheran, Presbyterian, Methodist, Episcopalian, Baptist, Reformed, Unitarian, Congregational, American or Anglican or English Church. At Halle, the picture looks quite similar. The vast majority was Protestant: 146 students noted that they were *evangelisch,* another 93 enrolled as Protestants. At Halle, I also counted 4 Catholics and 1 "Roman Catholic (American Branch)," 5 Baptists, a Christian and a reformed Christian, about 4 Congregationalists, 9 Episcopalians and/or Methodists, 7 Lutherans, a Mennonite, 5 Presbyterians, 8 members of the Reformed Church, and 4 Unitarians. Nearly 20 cases remain uncertain. Only some 30 Catholics registered at Leipzig, 5 of whom specified their faith as Roman Catholic. Upon his second enrollment, 1 of 3 Universalists switched to the Catholic faith.

At Halle, there registered also two Mormons, three Jewish students, a free thinker, and two students who stated that they did not have a religion at all. The Jewish Halle Americans were Leo Rowe, who spent the spring term 1890 there, as well as Harry E. Kohn and Walter Weyl, both of whom registered in June 1893. All three of them enrolled in the philosophical faculty and had previously been affiliated with the University of Pennsylvania in Philadelphia. The latter institution was also linked to Jewish American life at Leipzig: Morris Jastrow had registered at the Saxon university in April 1884. Upon his return to Philadelphia, he worked successively at his American alma mater, the University of Pennsylvania, as Lecturer in Semitic Languages, Professor of Arabic and Rabbinical Literature, and Assistant Librarian. His brother Joseph Jastrow made a name for himself in psychology; Morris had worked with the father of experimental psychology, Wilhelm Wundt, while at Leipzig.

Thirty US students at Leipzig were Jewish, although one Jewish American decided to drop his religion when he registered a second time. Julius Caesar Morgenthau enrolled as Jewish in October 1882. But when he returned two years later, he stated that he was *confessionslos,* that is, he did not practice a specific faith, which either suggests that he did not feel connected to his religion or that he wanted to avoid falling prey to anti-Semitism. Twelve Jewish American students registered during the 1870s and another twelve during the 1880s. While the 1890s witnessed the largest number of US students, only one Jewish American was among them. A few more registered after the turn of the century. Jews were predominantly the sons of merchants and bankers, but three sons of clergymen and a teacher may also be found. Of the one-third of the Jewish students who were identified, almost half (or one-sixth overall) embraced university careers. Jewish students tended to study medicine and law above all.[67]

In one instance, a US student was expelled for his religious activism. Many US students did practice their faith on a regular basis at one of the German churches in town or at an official American Church.[68] But students at German universities were under the jurisdiction of the institution. They were required not to make any political statements, a fact that was reflected in the statutes of the official American Students Club at the University of Leipzig.[69] Religious activism outside the university could backfire as well, especially when associated with what might have struck authorities as an American sect. In April 1904, 34-year-old Andrew B. Christenson of Manti, Utah, registered at Halle, openly stating that he was a Mormon. He had also studied at the University of Michigan in Ann Arbor and at Berlin. A note next to his name observed with reference to a ministerial decree from 26 April 1853 that the police had affected Christenson's expulsion from both the city limits of Halle and the state of Prussia on 26 July 1904 "because he appeared as a speaker at a public event of the Mormon brethren in Hannover."[70] This did not end his university career. After all, Germany has historically been a conglomerate of more or less independent states, kingdoms, and principalities. Christensen registered at Leipzig in late 1910, by then aged forty-one. He gave his religion as Protestant this time rather than admitting to the Mormon faith. He had taught in Salt Lake City before his second German venture but chose not to disclose this information to Leipzig authorities upon enrollment, preferring instead to associate himself with the University of Chicago.

In another instance, a foreign-born Jewish American was quite shrewd in creating himself, albeit not without benefit to US academe. Elvin Morton Jellinek[71] enrolled at Leipzig in November 1911 and again in 1913. He registered as a Hungarian even though he had been born in New York the son of Jewish-Hungarian immigrants. In 1939, he embarked on a career as an alcohol scientist. Later a professor at Yale, he devoted a good portion of his academic life to the subject of alcoholism. He died of a heart attack at Stanford in 1963. Jellinek's resume contains a few rather doubtful points, such as the claim that he earned a PhD degree from Leipzig in 1935. No evidence was discovered at the Leipzig University Archives (LUA) to support the notion that he stayed at Leipzig in the mid-1930s. Nor had he earned a Leipzig PhD degree in the 1910s. Jellinek apparently worked as the "Director" of the "Biometric Laboratory and Associate Director of Research, Memorial Foundation for Neuro-endocrine Research" in Worcester, Massachusetts, from 1931 to 1939. Could he have devoted himself to two commitments on both sides of the Atlantic simultaneously, also considering that his Jewish faith would *not* have been a small obstacle in Nazi Germany of the 1930s? The option of a background check by US officials was obstructed first by World War II and thereafter by the fact that Leipzig disappeared "behind" the Iron Curtain in the late 1940s. Still, his work in alcohol studies was path breaking and—"at least he was *interesting!*"[72]

Age

US students' ages upon their first enrollment at Halle and Leipzig indicate that they tended to turn to bigger and more prestigious institutions before moving on to less-well-known, smaller ones. Moreover, the numbers suggest that US students first completed their college educations at home before embarking for Europe. They might even have spent a few years in the new graduate schools before opting for a transatlantic educational journey. In contrast to German students, who typically proceeded from a German *Gymnasium* (grammar school) to a university at the age of eighteen, US students tended to be a little older.

The majority of US students in Halle and Leipzig were in their twenties, although a close comparison shows that students at Halle were even older. While US students at Leipzig peaked at 22 and 24 years of age, those at Halle did so between the ages of 23 and 25 (Figures 12–14). One might interpret this as evidence of the fact that Leipzig was chosen over Halle in the first instance, that is, for fall terms (US students tended to leave for Germany in the summer rather than in winter) and for first years abroad, while Halle was chosen as a second choice if a student decided to stay for more than one or two semesters.

An explanation for US students' higher ages is the fact that it was common after a college or even as early as after a high school education to teach at a high school or to head such a school for a few years before obtaining further education. Occasionally, such a step was brought about by necessity. For instance, after his graduation from the University of Michigan at Ann Arbor in 1874, Calvin Thomas needed to earn money before he could travel to Leipzig. In fact, according to his unpublished 1919 memoirs, when he held his first job teaching in a high school, he formed the plan of studying abroad, for which the money that he had earned through teaching would be a necessary resource.[73] Besides saving money for a European trip, teaching at a secondary school also provided an opportunity to gather experience and to pursue independent studies by the by.

At both German institutions, US students appear to have grown older upon first enrollment in the course of the century, a clear indication of the fact that educational paths were lengthening. More specifically, this prolongation of education seems to have been cemented between the 1880s and the early 1900s (Figures 12–14). Two explanations come to mind: Financial crises or generally a continuing push on the part of lower-middle-class people for higher education during the 1890s might have resulted in longer periods of saving money before a trip. Then again, as the educational scene in the United States was changing rapidly, educational pilgrims' increasing ages might mean that US students were beginning to spend more time in the nascent US graduate schools.

Ages upon first enrollment ranged from 16 to 63 at Leipzig and from 16 to 46 at Halle. The considerable number of 30- and 40-year-olds at both institutions indicates that not simply graduate students but also younger faculty as well as middle-aged educational travelers, including *Bildungsbürger* and older faculty on sabbatical leave, sought to further their education at the two German universities. A noteworthy number of students were well advanced in age when they first registered. Then again, some US students proceeded to Germany as soon as they had graduated from high school. Andrew Stewart is a case in point. He was twenty years old when he registered at Leipzig to study chemistry in 1887. He had completed high school in his native Washington, DC, but had not attended college there. He earned a Leipzig PhD degree in 1895.

The age curve at Leipzig suggests that every few years faculty went on sabbatical leave to a German university, either one where they had studied before and had befriended professors, or another where meanwhile a new authority had embarked on promising new scientific-scholarly adventures. The University of Michigan at Ann Arbor under the presidency of James Burrill Angel was particularly eager to provide its faculty with an opportunity for further training at Leipzig, including Angel's son-in-law, the historian Andrew McLaughlin, in the 1893/94 fall term. He enjoyed the company of his Ann Arbor colleagues Volney Morgan Spalding, a 44-year-old botanist, and Ernst Voss, a Germanic scholar, aged thirty-three. Likewise, 37-year-old George Thomas White Patrick, who had already been involved in establishing a psychological laboratory at the University of Iowa when he traveled to Leipzig in the spring of 1894, was joined there by his older sister Mary Mills Patrick, the president of the American Girls' College in Constantinople (Istanbul). Both heard Wilhelm Wundt's lectures.[74]

Some US students were advance in age because they had been prevented from completing their education earlier. Henry Pickering Bowditch had fought in the US Civil War after graduating from Harvard. Only after the conflict did he go to Europe for further study.[75] He never matriculated at Leipzig but stayed as a visitor for two years. He was thirty-one years old when he returned to the United States. Likewise, Dan Frost noted that former Confederates cherished studies in Germany.[76]

At both German institutions the youngest and the oldest American students enrolled after the turn of the twentieth century, which suggests that by 1900 German universities were popular to an extent that virtually everybody in the United States wanted to have a share of them. The youngest student at Leipzig was 16-year-old Theodore Schmidt, enrolling in October 1900. The son of a clerk at a fire insurance company in Indianapolis, Indiana, Schmidt was accompanied by his 18-year-old brother John Lorence Schmidt. Both studied philology. The oldest student was James Stephen Lemon, who, curiously, registered twice in 1903, once in January and a second time in May. He was born in Utica, New York; studied philosophy; and had been to Munich before. His deceased father had been a merchant. The youngest US student at Halle, Walter Haupt, was also accompanied by an older sibling, 18-year-old Ilse Haupt, shortly before the outbreak of World War I. They were grandchildren of Halle's Johannes Conrad. The oldest student at Halle was 46-year-old Seth K. Gifford, who registered in October 1901. He had studied at the University of Munich in the mid-1880s.

In one instance, a father registered alongside his sons at Leipzig as he had missed the chance to do so in his youth. Fifty-four-year-old Augustus Hart Carrier remembered in 1891: "My two sons matriculated in the University and I, who wished that I might have had an inside view of German University life, saw no reason why I might not matriculate with them. And so it happened that an American father and his two sons, to the surprise if not perplexity of the University officials, were enrolled together upon the University register."[77] All three of them registered in October 1885, although 22-year-old Charles Frederick Carrier registered on the 15th and his brother, 27-year-old Augustus Stiles Carrier, and their father followed up only on the 30th. The mother, Susan Ann, a former acting principal of the Wheeling Female Seminary in Virginia, and August Stiles's new wife were part of their company. There is no evidence that the women attempted to attend classes as well. Carrier Senior was a preacher and a manufacturer's son. His older son became a professor of Hebrew, the younger a lawyer.

Summary

US student numbers at nineteenth-century German universities are hard to come by. Even if one resorts to a systematic analysis of archival records and published student and faculty lists, the results turn out to be very close approximations on account of discrepancies between the different sources. Moreover, the documents will never be entirely conclusive as regards the questions of whether all students were correctly identified as Americans and whether they had indeed studied there during the semester in which they had registered.

Such uncertainties notwithstanding, archival research is fruitful. Until recently, only two lists of American students were available—one for Göttingen and one for Heidelberg, whereby the later list only includes students between 1830 and 1870. Numbers that were not derived from these resources tend to be shady in their origins. That is, they too often contain inconclusive references when a number is cited, or, if references are given, they often lead us to a personal account by a contemporary American, at which point the question usually will have to remain unanswered where the person obtained that number.

I compiled lists of American students at the Universities of Halle and Leipzig from the respective university records. When compared with the two available lists of American students at Göttingen and Heidelberg, it can be inferred that American student bodies at German universities rose steadily in the course of the nineteenth century, following trends in total student numbers. With the turn of the twentieth century, however, the developments diverged—whereas the total student bodies at Halle and Leipzig continued to grow until the outbreak of World War I, American student numbers began to decline.

Even though the same general trends in US student numbers may be observed at all four universities in question (to the extent to which statistical materials are available), differences may nonetheless be traced. The US student bodies at the four universities did not grow or decline with the same intensity. In fact, each university experienced more or less pronounced heydays and also downfalls in attracting US students. They even complemented one another—a decline at one institution showed a corresponding rise at another and vice versa. I will explore reasons for that in chapter 5.

Besides comparing developments in student bodies at different universities, statistical insights may also be derived by examining one such student body more thoroughly. An examination of the US student body at Leipzig (and at Halle for comparison) reveals that US students' socioeconomic backgrounds became more diverse, a question that I will explore further in chapter 3. Moreover, with increasing student migration, Germanic ancestry became less traceable. At times of more intense student migration, Americans obviously chose a German university for academic rather than family reasons. Family connections were more apparent in the eighteenth century, when German universities were hardly a destination for American students. In terms of religion, the American student bodies at Halle and Leipzig presented themselves as particularly homogenous. Both Halle and Leipzig are located in predominantly Protestant German states, which, for a predominantly Protestant country like the United States at that time, evidently did not present an obstacle.

Finally, it may be observed that in the course of the nineteenth century, American students grew older upon their first enrollment abroad. The finding insinuates that students studied longer and probably began spending more time at US educational institutions before traveling to Germany. In addition to that, at both Halle and Leipzig a fair number of US students who were already advanced in age could be traced, which suggests that not simply graduate students in our contemporary sense registered at German universities but also well-established US faculty members besides educational travelers who might simply have been interested in higher learning. The age range becomes more diverse after the turn of the twentieth century. In combination with the fact that American student numbers abroad were then slowly declining, the diversifying age range might mean that the heyday of elite students had passed. Now virtually anybody tried to obtain a German higher education.

Notes

1. Daniel Bussey Shumway, "The American Students of the University of Göttingen," *Americana Germanica* 8, nos. 5 and 6 (September–December 1910): 171–254; John T. Krumpelmann, "The American Students of Heidelberg University 1830–1870," in *Jahrbuch für Americastudien*, ed. Ernst Fraenkel, Hans Galinsky, Eberhard Kessel, Ursula Brumm, and H.-J. Lang, vol. 14 (Heidelberg: Carl Winter Universitätsverlag, 1969), 167–84. See also Hertha Marquardt, "Die ersten Amerikanischen Studenten an der Universität Göttingen," in *Göttinger Jahrbuch 1955/56* (Göttingen: Heinz Reise Verlag, 1956), 23–33.
2. Carl Diehl, *American and German Scholarship, 1770–1870* (New Haven, CT: Yale University Press, 1978).
3. Konrad H. Jarausch, *Students, Society, and Politics in Imperial Germany: The Rise of Academic Illiberalism* (Princeton, NJ: Princeton University Press, 1982), 23; Konrad Jarausch, *Deutsche Studenten, 1800–1970* (Frankfurt a./M.: Suhrkamp, 1984); Charles E. McClelland, *State, Society, and University in Germany 1700–1914* (Cambridge: University Press, 1980), 240–41.
4. Konrad Jarausch also undertook a statistical survey of Göttingen: "American Students in Germany" in *German Influences on Education in the United States to 1917*, ed. Henry Geitz, Jürgen Heideking, and Jurgen Herbst (Washington, DC: German Historical Institute, and Cambridge: Cambridge University Press, 1995); Jarausch, *Students, Society, and Politics*.
5. Marquardt, "Die ersten Amerikanischen Studenten"; Paul G. Buchloh, ed., *American Colony of Göttingen. Historical Data Collected Between the Years 1855 and 1888* (Göttingen: Vandenhoek & Ruprecht, 1976).
6. Laurence R. Veysey, *The Emergence of the American University* (Chicago: University of Chicago Press, 1965), 129.
7. Ibid., 131.
8. Ibid., 130.
9. John R. Thelin, *A History of American Higher Education* (Baltimore: Johns Hopkins University Press, 2004), 87–90.
10. Arthur M. Cohen and Carrie B. Kisker, *The Shaping of American Higher Education: Emergence and Growth of the Contemporary System*, 2nd ed. (San Francisco: Jossey-Bass, John Wiley & Sons, 2009), 70.

11. Ibid., 79.
12. Ibid., 112. Following quote ibid.
13. Frederick Rudolph, *The American College & University. A History* (Athens/London: University of Georgia Press, 1990 [1962]), 272.
14. G. Stanley Hall, "Philosophy in the United States," *Popular Science Monthly* 1 (1879), no page number given, quoted in Veysey, *Emergence of the American University*, 129.
15. Veysey, *Emergence of the American University*, 132.
16. Rudolph, *American College & University*, 118–20.
17. Veysey, *Emergence of the American University*, 126. In a footnote following this observation, he based his understanding of the German academic scene greatly on "conversations with Fritz K. Ringer," who was then working on a study in this area. Veysey likely referred to Fritz K. Ringer, *The Decline of the German Mandarins: The German Academic Community, 1890–1933* (Cambridge, MA: Harvard University Press), 1969. Ringer had authored a PhD dissertation on "The German Universities and the Crisis of Learning, 1918–1932," Harvard University, 1960. In a 1979 article, Ringer voiced similar thoughts. Fritz K. Ringer, "The German Academic Community," in *The Organization of Knowledge in Modern America, 1860–1920*, ed. Alexandra Oleson and John Voss (Baltimore: Johns Hopkins University Press, 1979): 409–29, here especially 409–10.
18. Lewis Perry, *Intellectual Life in America: A History* (Chicago: University of Chicago Press, 1989), 281, 283. Following quote ibid.
19. Thelin, *A History of American Higher Education*, 104.
20. See Anja Becker, "Southern Academic Ambitions Meet German Scholarship: The Leipzig Networks of Vanderbilt University's James H. Kirkland in the Late Nineteenth Century," *Journal of Southern History* 74, no. 4 (November 2008): 855–86; Anja Werner, "Striving for the Top: German-Trained Southern, Southwestern, and Western University Leaders in the Early 20th Century," in *Education and the USA*, ed. Laurenz Volkmann (Heidelberg: WINTER Universitätsverlag, 2011), 87–103.
21. Cohen and Kisker, *Shaping of American Higher Education*, 122.
22. Thelin, *A History of American Higher Education*, 118.
23. Veysey, *Emergence of the American University*, 127.
24. David McCullough, *The Greater Journey: Americans in Paris* (New York: Simon & Schuster, 2011), 132. He quoted Jonathan Mason Warren, John Collins Warren, and Russell M. Jones, *The Parisian Education of an American Surgeon: Letters of Jonathan Mason Warren, 1832–1835* (Philadelphia: American Philosophical Society, 1978), 2.
25. McCullough, *Greater Journey*, 250–51.
26. Ibid., 264.
27. Ibid., 425. The information must have been derived from Oliver Wendell Holmes, *One Hundred Days in Europe*, Works vol. 10 (Boston: Houghton, Mifflin, 1891), 175.
28. Leipzig Matrikel 1781–1914, Rektor M, M11, microfilm 583; M12–M29, microfilms 600/95–604/95; M30, 584; M31–M51, microfilms 631–635; M44–M44a, microfilms 1337; M52–67, microfilms 679–683, Leipzig University Archives (LUA). Matrikel, 1769–1914, Halle University Archives. The Leipzig student and faculty directories (*Personalverzeichnisse*) are available online: http://www.ub.uni-leipzig.de/.
29. Anja Becker, "*How Daring She Was!* The Female American Colony at Leipzig University, 1877–1914," in *Taking Up Space. New Approaches to American History*, mosaic 21, ed. Anke Ortlepp and Christoph Ribbat (Trier: Wissenschaftlicher Verlag Trier, 2004), 31–46.
30. *Amherst College Biographical Record*, Centennial Edition (1821–1921)—Julius Hawley Seeley [Online]. http://www.amherst.edu/~rjyanco94/genealogy/acbiorecord/1849.ht

ml#seelye-jh. Access Date: 19 August 2006; Thomas LeDuc, *Piety and Intellect at Amherst College, 1865–1912* (New York: Columbia University Press, 1946).

31. Leipzig hearer lists, LUA.

32. Caspar René Gregory, "Gregoire. The Priest and the Revolutionist," (Dissertation, Leipzig: 1876).

33. Leipzig hearer lists, LUA.

34. Guy A. Tawney, "Die Wahrnehmung zweier Punkte mittels des Tastsinns, mit Rücksicht auf die Frage der Uebung und die Entstehung der Vexirfehler," (Dissertation, Leipzig: Wilhelm Engelmann, 1897).

35. Charles Franklin Thwing, *The American and the German University* (New York: Macmillan, 1928), 40.

36. Shumway, "The American Students," 186 [general numbers], 175, 232, 250 [women].

37. As to the phenomenon of the enrollment explosion, see Jarausch, *Students, Society, and Politics,* 23; Jarausch, *Deutsche Studenten*; McClelland, *State, Society, and University in Germany,* 240–41.

38. Already in 1957 Henry Pochmann had pointed out that the significance of the Göttingen pioneers in the 1810s might have been exaggerated. Pochmann, *German Culture in America: Philosophical and Literary Influences, 1600–1900* (Madison: University of Wisconsin Press, 1957), 20.

39. J. G. de Roulhac Hamilton, "Southern Members of the Inns of Court," *North Carolina Historical Review* 10, no. 4 (October 1933): 273–86.

40. Mary Bynum Pierson, *Graduate Work in the South, published under the sponsorship of The Conference of Deans of Southern Graduate Schools* (Chapel Hill: University of North Carolina Press, 1947), references Johannes Conrad: "Records of registration at German universities were not very accurate in detail." See Johannes Conrad, *The German Universities for the Last Fifty Years,* trans. John Hutchinson, with a preface by Ambassador James Bryce (Glasgow: David Bryce and Son, 1885).

41. See Leipzig Matrikel, entry for John Foulk of Philadelphia on 4 October 1781 and William August Smith on 23 October 1894, LUA. Also, Anja Becker, "For the Sake of Old Leipzig Days ... Academic Networks of American Students at a German University, 1781–1914" (PhD dissertation, University of Leipzig, 2006).

42. Information on the Mühlenbergs is available in the Halle University archives and in the Franckeschen Stiftungen <archiv@francke-halle.de>. Pochmann, *German Culture in America,* 43. Jurgen Herbst, *The German Historical School in American Scholarship* (Ithaca, NY: Cornell University Press, 1965), 13–14. A descendant of Mühlenberg, William Augustus Muhlenberg in the 1830s ran a preparatory school for boys in College Point, NY. One of his students was Wymberly De Renne's father, who would study at Leipzig from 1871 to 1873. William Harris Bragg, *De Renne: Three Generations of a Georgia Family* (Athens: University of Georgia Press, 1999), 11.

43. Whitfield J. Bell, Jr., "Philadelphia Medical Students in Europe, 1750–1800," *Pennsylvania Magazine of History and Biography* 67, no. 1 (January 1943): 1–29.

44. J. Foulke to B. Franklin, 12 October 1781. Benjamin Franklin Papers, BF85, vol. 23, Folio 11, Hays Calendar II, 400, APS. J. Foulke to W. T. Franklin, 1 October 1781, ibid., vol. 103 Folio 106, Hays Calendar IV, 62. Franklin had visited Göttingen in 1766. Marquardt, "Die ersten Amerikanischen Studenten."

45. Shumway, "The American Students of the University of Göttingen," 186, 172. Marquardt, "Die ersten Amerikanischen Studenten," 24.

46. Shumway, "The American Students," 199. Marquardt, "Die ersten Amerikanischen Studenten," 24 n. 4.

47. Herbst, *German Historical School*, 13–4. Herbst cites Karl Diehl, "Johannes Konrad," in *Jahrbücher für Nationalökonomie und Statistik*, CIV, 3rd Series, 49 (June 1915): 753.

48. Thwing mentioned as much without giving names. Thwing, *The American and the German University*, 42.

49. John T. Krumpelmann, *Southern Scholars in Goethe's Germany* (Chapel Hill: University of North Carolina Press, 1965), 26. Louise L. Stevenson, *Scholarly Means to Evangelical Ends: The New Haven Scholars and the Transformation of Higher Learning in America, 1830–1890* (Baltimore: Johns Hopkins University Press, 1986), 14.

50. Henry E. Dwight, *Travels in the North of Germany, in the Years 1825 and 1826* (New York: G. & C. & H. Carvill, 1829).

51. On 17 December 1827, Woolsey told his mother: "I have seen also Prof. Heinroth [to] whom H. Dwight gave me a letter and who has received me with great kindness. Other acquaintances I shall soon form from letters which I have brought with me to respectable merchants and bankers." T. D. Woolsey to Sarah C. Woolsey, 17 December 1827. Woolsey Family Papers, Group 562, Series I, Box 3, Folder 39, YUL.

52. Student lists and A. Scheiterberg, *Bellerive. Institution Sillig 1836–1892. Souvenir du Jubilé du 15 Juillet 1886*, 2nd ed. (Vevey: Imprimerie Alph. Recordon, 1892). Available at the Vevey Community Archives, Vevey, Switzerland.

53. Appointment Papers and Letters of Recommendation, Record Group 59, General Records of the Department of State, NARA.

54. Becker, "For the Sake of Old Leipzig Days."

55. See also Franz Eulenburg, *Die Frequenz der deutschen Universitäten von ihrer Gründung bis zur Gegenwart* (Leipzig: Teubner 1904; Reprinted by Akademie Verlag Berlin, 1994); Marita Baumgarten, *Professoren und Universitäten im 19. Jahrhundert* (Göttingen: Vandenhoek & Ruprecht, 1997).

56. Journal, A. C. McLaughlin, 25 October 1893. A. C. McLaughlin Papers, 85536Aa2, Box 1, UM Bentley.

57. Henry Morgenthau III, *Mostly Morgenthaus: A Family History* (New York: Ticknor & Fields, 1991), 37, 45, 75–76.

58. Julius C. Morgenthau, "Ueber den Zusammenhang der Bilder auf Griechischen Vasen," (Dissertation, Leipzig: Bär & Hermann, 1886), 89–90.

59. Becker, "For the Sake of Old Leipzig Days," chapter 7.

60. Vincent Y. Bowditch, *Life and Correspondence of Henry Ingersoll Bowditch*, vol. 2 (Freeport, NY: Books for Libraries Press, 1902), 14. See also Walter B. Cannon, "Henry Pickering Bowditch, Physiologist," in *Science* 87, no. 2265 (27 May 1938): 471–78; C. S. Minot, "Henry Pickering Bowditch," *Science* 33, no. 851 (21 April 1911): 598–601.

61. James C. Albisetti, "German Influence on the Higher Education of American Women, 1865–1914," in *German Influences on Education in the United States to 1917*, ed. Henry Geitz, Jürgen Heideking, and Jurgen Herbst (Washington, DC: German Historical Institute, and Cambridge: Cambridge University Press, 1995), 243. He refers to the *National Cyclopedia of American Biography*, vol. 23, 284–85.

62. See for example C. W. Mason, "Wilder Dwight Bancroft 1867–1953," *Journal of the American Chemical Society* 76, no. 10 (26 May 1954): 2601–2.

63. Bragg, *De Renne*, 103.

64. Eric Hobsbawm, *The Age of Empire* (New York: Vintage Books, 1987), 177.

65. After having obtained his PhD degree in psychology at Leipzig, James McKeen Cattell moved on to England. From Cambridge he wrote on 8 June 1888, "I took Mrs. Keynes and her little boy and a young guest out boating this afternoon." The little boy was the future distinguished economist. J. M. Cattell to Parents, 8 June 1888, reprinted in Sokal, ed., *An Education in Psychology*, 297.

66. Amherst College Biographical Record—Julius Hawley Seeley [Online]. LeDuc, *Piety and Intellect*, 42.

67. Anja Becker and Tobias Brinkmann, "Transatlantische Bildungsmigration: Amerikanisch-jüdische Stundenten an der Universität Leipzig 1872 bis 1914," in *Bausteine einer jüdischen Geschichte der Universität Leipzig im Auftrag des Simon-Dubnow-Instituts für Jüdische Geschichte und Kultur an der Universität Leipzig*, ed. Stephan Wendehorst, Leipziger Beiträge zur Jüdischen Geschichte und Kultur, ed. Dan Diner, vol. 4 (Leipzig: Universitätsverlag, 2006), 61–98. See also Keith H. Pickus, *Constructing Modern Identities: Jewish University Students in Germany; 1815–1914* (Detroit: Wayne State University Press, 1999); Andrew R. Heinze, *Jews and the American Soul: Human Nature in the Twentieth Century* (Princeton, NJ: Princeton University Press, 2004).

68. On churchgoing in Leipzig, see Becker, "For the Sake of Old Leipzig Days."

69. Ibid. Verzeichnis der Verbindungen, WS 1891/92, Rep. II/XVI/II, Nr. 17, microfilm 488/94, 0205, LUA.

70. Matrikel Halle, University Archives Halle. My translation, original: "weil er in einer öffentlichen Veranstaltung der Mormonengemeinde in Hannover als Redner aufgetreten ist."

71. Ron Roizen, "Ranes Report: Roizen's Alcohol News & Editorial Service. RR #11: Jellinek's Phantom Doctorate." http://www.roizen.com/ron/jellinek-pres.htm. Access Date: 13 January 2005. Also, Ron Roizen, "E.M. Jellinek and All That! A Brief Look Back at the Origins of Post-Repeal Alcohol Science in the United States." http://www.roizen.com/ron/jellinek-pres.htm. Access Date: 13 January 2005.

72. Roizen, "E.M. Jellinek and All That!" Emphasis in original.

73. C. Thomas, unfinished, typed Autobiography, c. 1919, 14–15. C. Thomas Papers, 86180 Aa 2 Ac, Box 1, UM Bentley.

74. G.T.W. Patrick, *An Autobiography* (Iowa City: University of Iowa Press, 1947). Mary Mills Patrick, *Under Five Sultans* (London: Williams and Norgate, 1930), 182. G.T.W. Patrick in "In Memory of Wilhelm Wundt," *Psychological Review* 28, no. 3 (May 1921): 171. Edward T. James, Janet W. James, and Paul Boyer, eds, *Notable American Women: A Biographical Dictionary, 1607–1950,* vol. 3 (Cambridge, MA: Belknap Press of Harvard University Press, 1971), 25–26. Sandra L. Singer, *Adventures Abroad: North American Women at German-Speaking Universities, 1868–1915,* Contributions in Women's Studies 201 (Westport, CT: Praeger, 2003), 145.

75. David L. Crandall, "From Roxbury to Richmond: The Military Career of Henry P. Bowditch." *The Physiologist* 32, no. 4 (1989): 88–95. Walter B. Cannon, "Henry Pickering Bowditch," in *Biographical Memoirs of the National Academy of Sciences,* vol. 17 (1922), 183–86, reprinted in *The Life and Writings of Henry Pickering Bowditch,* vol. 1 (New York: Arno Press, 1980).

76. Dan R. Frost, *Thinking Confederates: Academia and the Idea of Progress in the New South* (Knoxville: University of Tennessee Press, 2000), xi–xii, 39, 48, 70, 110.

77. *A History of the Yale Class of 1851, for Forty Years. Mainly by Themselves* (Boston: Alfred Mudge & Son, no. 24 Franklin Street, 1893), 53. Ybb 1851, vol. 2, Augustus Hart Carrier '51, YUL.

Chapter 3

THE GERMAN UNIVERSITY, MASCULINITY, AND "THE OTHER"

White Men vs. the Other?

THE PURPOSE OF this chapter is to discuss the experiences of white, able-bodied, heterosexual men—the target group of the nineteenth-century German university—on an equal par with those of African-American men, homosexuals, US women, and a few hearing-impaired and blind Americans, focusing specifically on their efforts to access the German university. No data on African-American women is available at this point for the universities that I examined in the context of this study. African-American women nonetheless also registered at German-speaking universities after the US Civil War.

My goal in this chapter is to highlight obstacles (or the absence of obstacles) that representatives of various US student groups encountered when entering a German university such as Leipzig. Obstacles arise from rules, organizational structures, and customs on both sides of the Atlantic. My notion of obstacles is therefore a sophisticated cobweb of German and American prejudices, some of which were institutionalized at the German institution, while others merely reflected social customs. The American Students Club at the University of Leipzig illustrates the point. Academic clubs were run according to German university statutes, which meant that only regularly registered students could join, a practice that excluded female auditors even if they were Americans. Members of the American Students Club thus adopted (or had to adopt) the much more pronounced discrimination against women in the realm of higher education in Germany. Moreover, the fact

---

that the club was an *American* club led to an exclusion of African-American students, a custom brought over from the United States. In Germany, no customary exclusion on account of race existed, as so few non-Caucasians tried to enter German universities that they were typically not perceived a threat to the establishment.

As may be derived from these introductory observations and from the statistics presented in chapter 2, the growing student bodies of the nineteenth century (both at home and abroad) were marked by an increasing diversification not just as regarded socioeconomic backgrounds, but also as regarded ethnicity, gender, and physical ability. Much energy has in recent years been devoted to minority studies, creating a body of alternative histories that typically appear in separate publications. Mainstream historiography thus continues at least implicitly to focus on the history of white, able-bodied, heterosexual men, creating what I feel tempted to term a segregated, more or less hierarchical historiography without truly challenging the notion of traditionally white, male perspectives of the past.

Of course, it is vital to continue constructing alternative histories that focus on the perspectives of different groups in US history. Additionally, however, a new mainstream historiography is now surfacing that successfully interweaves the different perspectives as equally valid components of the past. By discussing the experiences of different groups within society in a comparative approach rather than zooming in on only one at a time, a much more multifaceted picture may be constructed that would allow us to draw conclusions for one group by examining another. In other words, women's history or black history are not alternative histories. They form not simply part of the grander national narrative but in various ways also interact with one another and certainly with white men, which is why their perspectives are equally valid and desirable.

An examination of the US student body at a German university is particularly well suited to exemplify the idea of interwoven historical narratives, especially if we examine the period after the US Civil War and German unification in 1871 when the student bodies on both sides of the Atlantic grew and diversified significantly. I suggest to start by first identifying different groups among the US student body in Germany through their interaction with German realities, and then (in the following chapters), include different perspectives in the narrative to the extent to which it is possible. Unfortunately, minority group voices are few, which makes it twice as important to describe these groups in relation.

Existing scholarship offers detailed knowledge of different US minority groups at German-speaking universities. But one may erroneously conclude from these materials that minority student migration abroad was considerable and thriving. Then again, we basically do not know anything about the by far largest group of US students at German-speaking universities in the second half of the nineteenth century: white, able-bodied, heterosexual men. Studies explore white American men abroad up to the 1870s, when their numbers virtually exploded. No thorough research exists, though, on the period thereafter. Ironically, because of the interest in separate, alternative histories, by now quite a few excellent publications are available on white American women studying at German-speaking universities. We even have first works on African Americans and deaf Americans joining in the nineteenth-century student migration abroad after the US Civil War. At Leipzig, however, by the late 1870s, more than three thousand male students counterbalanced some ten female auditors. These women led isolated lives encountering numerous restrictions that were intended to exclude them from the German university experience. As regards US students at Leipzig specifically, four US women faced some one hundred of their male fellow-countrymen (exact student numbers are hard to come by because of an unknown number of male auditors, visitors, and long-term students). Let us start from there.

But before discussing the specifics of each US student group in detail, let me point out one striking similarity: US students—no matter with what section of the population they identified—shared a notable reform mindedness with regard to education in the United States. The idea can best be described as a search for a new *Americanness* on the part of representatives of an ambitious young nation striving for the top in the global power game. Constructing such *Americanness* required an Other, which, however, varied depending on which group we examine. For American white men, the Other was the (male) German student. For white American women, it was men— not as a generic group but as an old American type compared to the possibility of a new, improved, Europeanized American man. Even though gender restrictions in education were more pronounced in the German countries, US women, ironically, expected the German educational matrix to produce a feministically more advanced male American. Something similar may be observed in the case of African-American men, who found the German experience to be a revelation as to what race relations could be like at home. To them, it was of secondary importance that the feeling of equality, which they experienced in Germany, was *not* rooted in a deeply felt sense of racial equality on the part of the Germans—it did not matter *why* Germans gave African Americans a feeling of equality. It mattered that they did.

It is consequently worthwhile to ask what exactly the different groups of US students in German universities understood by *Americanness* from the perspective of their own shared group experience within US culture, and to what degree these concepts might have changed in the course of time. In terms of education, Americanness referred to the specific aspect of education that they planned to change upon their return, which, incidentally, reflected their self-identification (that is, their belonging to a specific group of US students) both from experience and necessity while abroad. It is little surprising, then, that—once they had returned home—African Americans would not just turn to improving black education but to fighting for racial equality, whereas white women would focus on issues of coeducation and women's colleges combined with support of the suffragette movement. Homosexuals, in turn, for the chilling climate with regard to sexual codes on either side of the Atlantic, would keep a low profile. Last but not least, disabled Americans would blend in easily with the crowds as long as they aspired to and kept up with able-bodied standards, which were, of course, set up by the able-bodied mainstream and increasingly reflected a German scientific (rather than cultural) ideal.

Matriculation Procedures for White, Able-Bodied, American Men

While white, able-bodied American men wrote critically about the organization and standards of higher education at home and in Germany—thus self-identifying as reform-minded Americans—they were also particularly intrigued by ritualistic aspects of the German university experience. Maybe that was because, in contrast to their female counterparts, their previous education hardly mattered when entering a German university. Their matriculation at a German university was a mere formality. After all, they were the only distinctive American students group that had unrestricted access to all aspects of German university life.

American men observed rituals such as the registration procedures with a mixture of admiration, excitement, curiosity, boredom, and ironic distance. In its rituals, the German university revealed itself not simply an academic institution of systematic and profound higher learning but also an inherently gendered space intended to forge "real" men. Interestingly, the accounts of American men concerning their admission are quite similar. They emphasized and mirrored the ritualistic aspects of the experience, which often culminated in the handshake with the head of the German university as an impressive symbolic act of entering a special *brother*hood. But as a group, they did not entirely succumb to the experience. Instead, they stressed the tediousness of the overall procedure and even made fun of it.

The following examples reflect to what extent American men felt drawn into the German university rituals while at the same time attempting to keep a distance—be it by humor or boredom—in spite of their undeniable fascination with the procedures. Such a distance was necessary to hold up one's own American identity. The idea of keeping a distance is certainly a phenomenon that may also be traced among other American students groups, albeit for different reasons. White women or African-American men experienced distance on account of existing exclusionary practices. White American men thus had their own small dilemma. They could feel part of the German university experience to a much greater extent than other Americans. But in the end, they were foreigners who had come to Germany because of educational opportunities there that could not (yet) be obtained at home.

In 1874, James Morgan Hart reflected a common perception of the German university as an epitome of masculinity. He started off neutrally advertising the relaxed attitude of the Germans towards administrative matters. He observed that "you proceed to the secretary's office and deposit there your 'documents' entitling you to admission,"[1] whereby "in the case of a foreigner, the utmost liberality is displayed." Explaining this openness toward foreigners, Hart unwittingly implied—as was certainly the custom of his day—that he was speaking of *male* foreigners, for "I doubt whether any German university would refuse to admit any foreign candidate who *showed by his size and bearing that he was really a young man* able to look after himself, and *not a mere boy*." He concluded, "the Germans know perfectly well that they can afford to be liberal toward foreigners. They take it for granted that when a young *man* puts himself to the trouble and expense of a visit to Germany, the chances are that he means to do well."

German university authorities expected foreign students to excel, whereby the fact that a foreigner was *male* made extensive background checks and entrance examinations unnecessary. But to American men, this was almost a bit offensive as it downplayed the effectiveness of US colleges, whose educational merits apparently did not matter to German university authorities. Although Hart acknowledged that Prussian authorities were stricter than those elsewhere in Germany, a diploma or bachelor's degree usually sufficed besides a passport and a "manly" bearing. While there was a decree at Leipzig stating that foreign students had to give proof of an adequate previous education,[2] Lincoln Steffens complained how little it actually mattered: "all I had to have to enter the German and the French universities was my American citizenship, which I was born with."[3] When James R. Angell registered in Berlin in the fall of 1892, he quipped, "The police evidently do not suspect my revolutionary antecedents and have accepted me into citizenship without a murmur."[4] He added that matriculation was "an awfully tedious process" that involved exchanging his passport for a student card for the duration of his stay in town as a university student.

For American men, registration was an important step, a sort of initiation to be recorded with due respect, though not without mixed feelings. The handshake with the rector—the head of the university—was a first ritual with which the passage from citizenship to student status and thus to acknowledged masculinity was completed. US students rarely failed to record it. It insinuated their appreciation for the ritualistic aspects of German university life as an example of male bonding. For instance, during his first semester at Leipzig, Thomas Day Seymour kept a diary with concise entries on striking incidents. On 26 October 1870, he described the matriculation procedures somewhat in detail: "Went this morning to 'inscribirt lassen' [to register]—Received our first papers, left our passport, paid our fees, inscribed our names and residences. PM. Went at 3. Recorded our full names, residences, birth places, country, age, religion, profession of father, where previous education was received, our lander [countries of origin] etc. Signed a promise to be good. Received the handschlag [handshake] of the Rector."[5] The final statement referring to the handshake brings to mind the picture of a man being knighted or else receiving an exclusive honor.

In spite of ever-increasing student numbers in the late nineteenth century, matriculation procedures remained essentially the same, the biggest challenge being how to keep them efficient. By the 1890s, enrollment meant a wait of several hours, and the different stages of the registration process occasionally took several days. Writing to his mother and sisters in December 1891, George H. Parker mildly poked fun at it all, observing that he merely "presented myself, told my mother's middle name, my sisters' ages how much I could eat, etc., etc., paid 21 marks and went home a poorer but no wiser man."[6] Several days later, he attended the official matriculation ceremony, to which he established an ironic distance by claiming that in a long speech he now was told "what I ought to have for a middle name to my mother, what my sisters' ages ought to be and how much I ought to eat." Once again, the handshake with the Rector was accorded its ritualistic significance—it simultaneously figured as a climax (if not anticlimax) of his brief account: "My name was called out, I received a hand shake from the rector, a large piece of paper and my student's card and thus became a member of this famed University." The choice of words of Leipzig as a "famed University" suggests a question on Parker's part: how could this university be so renowned if a student merely had to present irrelevant information (rather than educational credentials) in order to register?

Andrew McLaughlin recorded the matriculation procedures much more elaborately in his journal on 25 October 1893, giving a detailed description that speaks volumes about the tediousness of the procedure. He observed the matriculation procedures together with a friend from the University of Michigan, Ernst Voss, who had already registered together with yet another Michigan man, Volney Morgan Spalding. By the time of their Leipzig student ventures, McLaughlin, Voss, and Spalding had already embarked on teaching careers at the University of Michigan. They were on sabbatical rather than being students.

McLaughlin's account is less jocular and more indirect in its comments on German university culture. He focused in greater detail on the long wait and the fact that he was repeatedly asked to provide the same basic information about his background and intentions. McLaughlin had presented himself at 9AM only to find "so many people waiting that Herr V. [Mr. Voss] must go to his Vorlesung [lecture]."[7] They tried again two hours later and waited until 1PM. McLaughlin proceeded to describing the bureaucracy involved in the procedure: "At the University such student as he appears is given a card with a number showing his chance of getting in to the Rector. The fiedelle [clerk] takes down your name. + your fach [subject] +c—and then when you are allowed into the room you are shown into the Rector[']s private room who takes down the same information + so it goes on." Having moved on to the Quaestor (treasurer), he had to wait yet again until 3PM to pay the 21 Mark registration fee.

At this point, he was finally ready to attend the actual matriculation ceremony together with Voss. "The Rector made a little speech inviting us all to emulate the example of good King Albert of Saxony, who replied to the compliment of the Kaiser by the phrase I did only my duty. Each student was then given his little students card + his large paper, shook hands with the Rector as a pledge of good behavior + as admission to the brotherhood + then marched out—or waited longer as he chose." The handshake with the rector appeared here as an acceptance of a type of honor code, personalizing the relationship between student and German university. McLaughlin and Voss did not stay but went directly from the registration ceremony to a beer hall to have official ritual followed by a more informal one—the beer drinking: "found the Münchner [Munich beer] ausgezeichnet [excellent]—," he concluded.

After 1900, for US men determined to enter the University of Leipzig, enrollment had not changed. Only the wait and bureaucratic build-up seemed to have increased, for general student numbers were on the rise again. Arthur B. Lamb exclaimed to his family in late 1904, "Matriculation is a very tedious process."[8] Like McLaughlin, he described the procedure in greater detail, stressing the long wait and the repetitiveness: "I had first to go and secure a so called Anmeldungs-Karte or presentation ticket, which told me when to present myself and credentials for examination. My time was some two hours later, at twelve o'clock. I was on hand at this appointed hour, but had to wait some half hour before my time came. I was then asked a number of questions, about my age, religion, birthplace etc. etc. (father's name business etc.), my pass port and diploma were examined and put on file—by the so called Richter, or Judge of the University. He then sent me to the Secretary, who repeated many of the questions, had me sign my name in several places—and in turn sent me to the Treasurer, to whom I paid my fee of 21 marks—(after answering another long series of questions). I was then told to return at 3.45" to be matriculated." Thus ended the first part of the procedure.

Lamb then moved on to describing the actual matriculation ceremony, starting out by observing that "The ceremony of matriculations is gone thru with but two or three hours a week, and so, when I arrived, I found myself one of a bulk [*sic*] of 2–300." His patience was tried some more as he had to wait yet again finally to hear the rector's speech: "After interminable waiting His Serene Magnificense, the Rector of the University, appeared—gave a swift and forceful speech of admonition and advice, and then handed out our matriculation certificates one at a time, calling our names, and shook hands with us, the hand shakes signifying our promise to abide by all the rules and regulations of the Univ. and to endeavour to do her honour by our scholarly attainments." Interestingly, Lamb interpreted the significance of the handshake rather than merely highlighting it. Moreover, as was the case with McLaughlin's description, Lamb's interpretation of the Rector's handshake as an honorable agreement is reminiscent of the honor code still extant for example at universities in the US South today.

As the Rector of the University of Leipzig was elected for merely one year, the ceremony during which the office and responsibility was passed on to his successor was also an event of interest to the curious US student, although it was less often mentioned, matriculation being the prime event in a US student career in Germany. Charles Rockwell Lanman's matriculation had nearly coincided with the last day of the outgoing Rector's term of office, which might explain why the change in university leadership aroused his interest to a greater degree than the matriculation procedures. A rector was typically a faculty member. His one-year term started with the new semester each fall term. Lanman wrote on 31 October 1875, "This morning I went to the University hall, and saw the new Rector, Prof. [Johannes] Overbeck, invested in the insignia of his office."[9] Fascinatingly, Lanman does not fail to sneak in a reference to his handshake with the rector the previous day "Rector [Gustav Adolf Ludwig] Baur, who gave me his hand yesterday, along with the other young men who were matriculated, first gave an account of his stewardship for the past year." Noteworthy is furthermore Lanman's fascination with the symbols of power of the German rector: "[Bauer] then administered the oath of office to Rector Overbeck, and put on the velvet mantle, embroidered with gold, and an immense great chain of gold about his neck; and gave him the seal and key and other insignia of office."

Fewer sources are available about leaving the university. Obviously, the significant event was admission, not departure, which is a curious contrast to the marvelous graduation ceremonies at US colleges and universities today, something almost unheard of in contemporary Germany. Maybe by the end of a stay abroad back then a student's mind was already set on the next stage of the European venture—either a journey, a stay at another European university, or the return home. George Lincoln Burr, who had spent the 1884/85 fall term at Leipzig, is somewhat exceptional as he apparently described but the final days of his stay. On 3 March 1885, he had bought presents, said good-bye to friends, attended final lectures, and gone "To University *Richter* [judge] for my exmatriculation."[10] He added at the bottom of the page that the weather that day was "Gloomy + unpleasant + rainy." In February 1894, McLaughlin also described a meeting with the university judge: "I received a notice at the Fruhstück [breakfast] to come to Univ + change cards or be called before the Univ Gericht [court]. As I didn't want to be hingerichtet [a pun meaning to get into trouble] I went in the Nachmittag [afternoon] + paid 50 pfennig for a new yellow card."[11] It is not clear why he did that; he had arrived in the previous fall for one term only and was about to leave.

African-American Men

Like the most famous African-American student in Germany, W.E.B. Du Bois, who studied in Berlin in the mid-1890s,[12] the African-American Richard R. Wright, Jr., found a new quality of Americanness in Berlin and Leipzig. This quality was rooted in his realization that a black and white racial hierarchy was a specific construct of US culture, an outgrowth of a long history of slavery and segregation. Still, he decided to return home rather than stay in a less racially charged climate. Of course, racial issues existed and exist in Germany, but they are expressed in constellations different from the black-and-white dichotomy that is so central to US history—anti-Semitism would be an example. African Americans abroad saw the relations between white and black in Germany as an inspiration and encouragement to return to their homeland and be active to advance their people. They were just as reform minded as their white fellow countrymen studying abroad. Merely their priorities naturally differed.[13]

Only two African Americans have been traced to date who studied at Leipzig and Halle. Gilbert Haven Jones is known to have studied in Göttingen, Berlin, Leipzig, Halle, and Jena between 1907 and 1909, earning a PhD degree from the latter institution.[14] He was not traced at Halle and Leipzig, where he might have visited or studied as an auditor rather than registering as a regular student. Richard R. Wright., Jr., of Cuthbert, Georgia, in turn, enrolled at Leipzig on 26 April 1904. He was the son of the president of Georgia State College (later Savannah State College), which institution he had entered in 1892. After his graduation in 1898, he opted for the University of Chicago in his first venture outside the "black curtain." He also spent a semester at Berlin, just as his role model Du Bois had done a decade before. Wright studied theology and, in 1911, earned a PhD degree from the University of Pennsylvania, where he had worked with Du Bois. According to his autobiography, his future career found him, among other things, a social worker, president of Wilberforce University, bishop, and "Negro" activist.[15]

It would be desirable to examine to what extent a white American establishment controlled black student migration abroad through the allocation of fellowship funds. After all, the European student experiences of African Americans have not yet been examined in a comprehensive, in-depth study.[16] Just like Du Bois,[17] Wright was prevented from staying in Germany for a lack of funds; he had hoped to spend another year at Bonn. Even though a PhD degree from the University of Pennsylvania or Harvard, where Du Bois had earned his degree, would nowadays be considered rather prestigious, it should be kept in mind that according to a general consensus around the turn of the twentieth century, German institutions of higher education back then were still viewed as the most renowned in the world. To gain access to these universities meant to gain access to the ultimate heights of (white) learning. DuBois and Wright had both had support from whites at least to some degree in order to realize their European student ventures. Wright had earned money before his trip; his family and a kind dean also supported him.[18]

Both Wright and Du Bois pointed out that African Americans experienced a less racially charged climate in Germany.[19] More important, they became aware of the deferential role that had been forced upon blacks in the United States. Wright described it succinctly in his memoirs, pointing out little details such as his comportment towards white Germans (both men and women), which to him highlighted race relations in the United States as they were being taken for granted there. At the same time that he became aware of the problem, he began developing a self-consciousness and self-confidence to overcome it. By not acting in the accustomed white-and-black pattern, Germany "cured" him from looking down on himself as a second-class citizen. He remembered:

> Study in Germany was epoch-making in my life. I associated with students, men and women, who knew little or nothing about American race prejudice, who, while curious about my color, never looked down upon it.... I never knew that I walked about a foot behind my white companions, all unconsciously. Germany cured that and I learned to walk abreast. I had a habit of not speaking categorically, of putting a deferential inflection in my voice, and evading questions, of stopping what I was saying as soon as a white person interrupted. These and a dozen other little things were habitual, but noticed by German young men who

teased me about them, never knowing about their cultural roots. Young women students invited me to concerts, theatre, sports, etc., not hanging back for me to make the suggestion, as was done in America.[20]

One must concede, however, that the equality that Wright experienced in Germany to some extent might be explained by a curiosity for the exotic: "The barbers argued for an opportunity to cut my hair and shave me, without charge. Germans invited me to sit in train compartments with them, join them in all sorts of celebrations, etc. I was even asked to join the White-Black Club, whose purpose was to encourage intermarriage between Germans and Africans." Then again, Wright avoided fellow countrymen in Europe as if to temporarily disconnect himself from his roots better to understand the European ways: "I made it a point not to look up Americans and not to speak English." He was not an official member of Leipzig's American Students Club.

In short, for Wright, one vital benefit of the German venture was the fact that he "forgot American prejudice, for even the Americans in Germany treated me as a human being." It was little surprising, then, that he yearned to return to the United States in order to turn the American Dream into one that could be dreamed also by "persons of color": "While Germany showed me how one gentleman should treat another, and heightened in my mind the knowledge of the things I should contend for, I never felt like deserting America, believing that some day America's eyes would open. Her conscience awaken, I came back with greater determination to help make her a great country of freedom and equality." Wright saw his German venture as an opportunity to look at his native land from "the outside," that is, from abroad. He established a distance to the United States that went beyond a mere geographical distance and that allowed him to develop a clearer vision of what was wrong at home, and how it should be changed.

Gay American Men

Homosexuality was quite a different story. The fact that back then it was unspeakable on both sides of the Atlantic would explain why in contrast to black men—or, as we will see below, "manly" white university women—homosexuals or "effeminate men" kept a low profile rather than announcing stratagems to struggle for equal rights in terms of sexual freedom.

Homosexuality was a criminal offense. The case of 33-year-old Peter Harry Thomson of Davenport, Iowa, gives proof of that. He enrolled at Leipzig on 27 October 1908 to study philology. The son of a lecturer had previously been affiliated with the University of Nebraska. What happened to him is described in a police report dated 7 December 1908 and preserved in a folder at the LUA on students' indecent behavior toward women (!) of a questionable reputation.[21] It is the only entry in the voluminous folder involving a US student.

In early December 1908, Thomson had approached young Heinrich Hertel in the restroom of a restaurant in the street Elisen Strasse and suggested to retire to the Hotel Stadt Nürnberg and engage in "abnormal fornication" (*widernatürliche Unzucht*), although it may be suspected that Thomson had phrased his proposal differently. Hertel initially consented, but he proceeded to report the case to a police officer. Thomson cooperated with the authorities. He was given a warning for the time being. As students were under the jurisdiction of the university, the case was forwarded to the university judge, Dr. Meltzer, along with a recommendation to expel Thomson from Saxony. Meltzer consented to the suggested course of action on the very same day. The American Students Club of Leipzig, of which Thomson was a member, did not get involved.[22] Thomson's future fate is not known.

Another episode illustrates that in spite of a strict gender line in late Victorian America, the borders between homosexual behavior in our modern sense and affectionate same-sex friendships were fuzzy and open to interpretation. The future muckraker Lincoln Steffens roomed at Leipzig with his German buddy Johann Friedrich Krudewolf. They were inseparable.[23] But there is a twist to Steffen's relations with Krudewolf. The German was of ill health and died already in 1894. Of moderate wealth, he left all of his possessions to Steffens, who, after successful speculation at Wall Street, was thus enabled to lead the life of a Bohemian for the rest of his days. Krudewolf's motives are not clear. Apparently, a homosexual attraction on his part was the decisive factor,[24] of which Steffens claimed to have been unaware. In November 1932, Steffens wrote to a fellow US student at Leipzig back in 1890, Harlow Gale: "Do I understand that you thought that Johann and I had some sort of sex relationship! We didn't have, you know. It never occurred to me that our affection might look like that to anyone."[25] Steffens' case is particularly fascinating, for he would marry a much older woman whom he had met in a Leipzig lecture hall. His views were generally somewhat subversive from a white male perspective (see also below section on deaf Americans).

White US Women

Besides white men, white women constituted the most sizeable American student group abroad, albeit a much smaller one. Enough material is available at this point to sketch this group at Leipzig in more detail. The most important distinction between female and male students at a German-speaking university in the late nineteenth century was that women were only allowed to enter with a special status or as *Gasthörer* (hearer), whereas men embodied the regularly registered student. Within the German university, US women thus formed a tiny, doubly foreign group on account of their gender and nationality, whereby, interestingly, in the early days, German authorities were more comfortable with admitting foreign women. It was only after women had been granted regular student status at German-speaking universities in the first decade of the twentieth century that German authorities underwent a nationalist shift, now favoring German over foreign women. For these reasons, it makes sense to focus on three major points with regard to American women at Leipzig: their struggles to be admitted as hearers and eventually as regular students as well as their interaction with male fellow students (which corresponds to a search for a new Americanness abroad).

German universities began admitting women as regular students between 1900 and 1910.[26] They were the last in Europe to do so, with institutions in the German South pioneering the development. By contrast, the university in Zurich had admitted women since 1864.[27] US women had enrolled there since 1868.[28] It should be pointed out, though, that since the mid-1870s German universities admitted women as hearers and sometimes even conferred degrees to them. Leipzig was then of particular interest to female hearers from the United States, even though a few other German universities distinguished themselves by allowing American women to pioneer as students and even graduates.[29] A first US woman, Rebecca Rice, entered Heidelberg as a hearer in 1873.[30] At Göttingen, Margaret A. Maltby was awarded a PhD degree in physics in 1896. She had entered the university as a hearer in 1893. The first woman to enroll there as a regular student, Ruth G. Wood, registered in 1908.[31]

Until 1906, women were not permitted to register as regular students in Leipzig, that is, not significantly earlier or later than elsewhere in the country. Nonetheless, between 1906 and 1914 only two US women enrolled at the Saxon university, Mathilde Margarethe Lange from New York, who matriculated thrice in October 1910, 1911, and 1912 to study mathematics and natural sciences, and Laura Emilie Mau from Young America, Minnesota, who registered in November 1913 at the age of thirty-four. Little information is available about them except that Mau unsuccessfully tried to earn a PhD degree.[32]

Between the 1870s, when women were first permitted to hear lectures, and 1910, when all German universities admitted women as regular students,[33] a nationalist shift occurred in Germany. While in the 1870s, foreign women rather than German women had been granted the hearer status (albeit in small numbers), after 1900 the *German* University of Leipzig opened up to *German* women rather than to female foreigners. The nationalist shift might have occurred because of increasing Russian student numbers at Leipzig.[34] For female foreigners it was now advantageous to be of German stock. Lange and Mau were cases in point. Lange's apparently German name must have reassured the authorities. Mau, in turn, was admitted explicitly because she struck the authorities as German. The fact that the maiden name of the wife of one of Leipzig's star professors, Wilhelm Wundt, was Sophie Mau probably had helped to establish her Germanic roots.[35] That L. E. Mau held an AM degree from Columbia University was interpreted in her favor; yet, it ranked secondary in importance.

Likewise, only two women with a US connection registered at Halle after 1900. They were Annie M. Hannah (born Macgregor) in 1908 and Ilse Haupt in 1913, the US granddaughter of Halle's famed economist Johannes Conrad.[36] Hannah registered alongside her husband Neilson C. Hannah of Schenectady, New York, on 6 November 1908; a penciled note next to their names at the registrar's points out that they were a married couple. Both enrolled in the theological and philosophical faculties. Neilson was twenty-eight years old, the son of the farmer Neilson Campbell. Scottish by birth, Annie was twenty-nine years old, the daughter of the teacher George Macgregor from Glasgow. She had previously attended the University of Glasgow. Both Hannahs left the University of Halle in July 1909. Eighteen-year-old Haupt was a native of Cincinnati, Ohio. She registered on 30 October 1913 in the philosophical faculty, having previously attended a Cincinnati high school. She was traveling with her brother, 16-year-old Walter Haupt, who had registered already on 17 October 1913 to study natural sciences. Their father Hans was a pastor. They left Halle in August 1914, World War I cutting short their German student venture.

Before 1906, three periods of developments regarding female hearers at the University of Leipzig may be discerned. The first lasted through the 1870s until the clash of 1879, when the Saxon ministry of education in Dresden decided that the female inroads at the University of Leipzig would have to be stopped. At least six US women had entered the university as hearers until then. The second period, to which I like to refer as "the dark ages," lasted through the 1880s until the mid-1890s. No female hearers were officially accepted. But there are numerous indications that US women studied at Leipzig then in spite of all, even advertising Leipzig opportunities for women in US journals. Finally, the third phase lasted until 1906. It is characterized by the fact that Saxon authorities now grudgingly started to readmit women, for the number of women trying to obtain a higher education was now ever increasing.

An exact estimate of Leipzig's total US female hearer numbers is hardly possible; numbers that are given in the student directories are not reliable as these directories were printed before all women's applications for the hearer status were decided. Then again, between 1879 and 1896, when women were not officially admitted as hearers, no information is available at all at the LUA regarding female students. An impression of Leipzig's female American student colony may be obtained by combining LUA sources with additional materials such as references to female US students in Germany in contemporary articles in *The Nation* and in *The Atlantic Monthly* or in primary and secondary sources by and about other students.[37]

Up to now I have collected references to a few dozen US women who audited or hoped to audit lectures at Leipzig between 1877 and 1914. The apparently largest group of female hearers second only to Russian women comprised US women and women who had received an undergraduate education in the United States. At least six US women entered Leipzig until 1879, several more between 1883 and 1896, and an even larger number between 1897 and 1914.

Female hearer numbers vary even for periods that are recorded in the LUA. According to Sonja Brentjes and Karl-Heinz Schlote, between the 1873/74 fall term and the 1882 spring term, 24 women—four of them from the US—heard lectures at Leipzig. By contrast, Renate Drucker mentioned 34 female hearers up to the 1879/80 fall term, four of them from the United States: Eva Channing of Boston, Harriet Parker of Iowa, M. Carey Thomas, a future president of Bryn Mawr College, and her travel companion Mary ("Mamie") Gwinn of Baltimore. Channing arrived in the spring of 1879; the others joined her in the fall of that year. Parker stayed for one semester. Thomas was determined to earn a German PhD degree, but neither Leipzig nor Göttingen would examine her. She left with Gwinn for Zurich in the spring of 1882 and received her degree summa cum laude. Channing had left Leipzig a semester earlier.[38]

Remarkably, Channing voiced her surprise as to how easy it had been for her to put her name on record as a hearer at Leipzig. As was the case with some of the male US students, her passport rather than her previous education had sufficed as an entrance ticket to the university. This was, however, to change as the number of prospective female students rose to a threatening ten in late 1879 (as compared to some three thousand male students), after which period more hurdles were established to prevent what was apparently perceived as a threatening female takeover of the German university.[39]

The four women knew one another during their sojourn at Leipzig. Thomas referred to both Parker and Channing in her letters.[40] But the women apparently did not know all female students. Once she had learned that she would be allowed to stay in 1879 but that no further women were to be admitted, Thomas commented: "How glad I am that we came this year—next year would probably have been too late. It rather adds to one's glory to be one of the thirteen women in all, I think, who have studied at Leipzig."[41] The LUA lists ten female students during the 1879 fall term alone.[42]

Thomas had heard about Channing through the US envoy in Berlin, Andrew D. White, the founding president of Cornell, where Thomas had earned her undergraduate degree. White supplied Thomas with letters of recommendation to Leipzig professors. Her parents permitted her to go when Gwinn decided to accompany her. Gwinn fought hard with her parents over the issue. Her strategy involved fits of fever that she aroused by sheer will power. Rather than watch her destroy her health, Gwinn's parents eventually consented.[43]

Many sources concentrate on these four pioneering US women at Leipzig, but at least two more entered the university as hearers even before Channing, whom James Albisetti supposed to have been the first female US hearer at Leipzig.[44] The reason for this might be that the folders on female hearers in the 1870s at the LUA do not mention early women who simply placed their names in the Leipzig hearer lists and apparently did not stay long enough to cause unease among officials. The hearer lists are, however, a difficult source, because they offer names and places at best, making it rather difficult to identify a person.

A search of the hearer-lists revealed a "Miss Ida Köhler" of St. Louis and a "Miss Hulda Stallo" of Cincinnati, Ohio, as hearers number 114 and 115, respectively, in the fall of 1877/78.[45] Both were also students of the Leipzig Conservatory. No information concerning Köhler and Stallo was found in the LUA folders regarding female students. I. Köhler and H. Stallo probably heard lectures during one term only. Had they stayed longer, they might have been mentioned in connection with the éclat of late 1879 when officials at the Saxon ministry of education in Dresden objected to the university authorities' admitting ten female hearers.[46]

It is likely that both Köhler and Stallo were of German extraction, although little is known about Köhler. She was possibly related to 18-year-old Oscar C. Köhler of Fort Madison in Iowa, who had registered at Leipzig in April 1876 to study natural sciences. Especially the early US women in Leipzig often traveled with siblings or parents. In 1888, I. Köhler married the German immigrant Adolph Priester in Iowa. She would give birth to three sons.[47]

Stallo was from a prominent German-American family in Cincinnati. The writer Friedrich Bodenstedt visited them in 1880 and noted that the head of the family was Judge John Bernhard Stallo. A grown son and three daughters, the oldest named Hulda, completed the family. Hulda was a tall woman who played the piano exceedingly well and loved outings in her buggy together with Bodenstedt (she drove). For several years the family had resided in Leipzig, where Hulda had studied at the conservatory[48] and also ventured to the university. Walter Stallo of Cincinnati, son of a "Jurist" (lawyer), had registered on 29 May 1876, at the age of twenty-four, to study medicine. W. Stallo was an atheist; a liberal family attitude might account for their thoroughly educating their daughters. Andrew D. White observed that in the 1880s, Judge Stallo was the US minister in Rome.[49] As White had supported both Channing and Thomas at Leipzig, one may wonder if he had not found out about opportunities for women there through the Stallos. But for the time being, this will have to be left to speculation.

In 1883, a year after Thomas and Gwinn had left for Zurich, another US woman, Elizabeth H. Denio, took advantage of Leipzig opportunities. Denio had been a professor of German and Art History at Wellesley College since 1876. Not only did she stay at Leipzig (and in 1883 also in Berlin) for extended periods between 1883 and 1886, but she supposedly studied under as many as ten different Leipzig professors. In 1889, she actually led a group of Wellesley students to Leipzig. One member of the group wrote an enthusiastic, if somewhat flowery, letter to her classmates back home describing her experiences. Ironically, in 1896 Denio was fired for her antiquated style of teaching. She proceeded to obtain a PhD degree from Heidelberg in 1898 and in 1917 ended her career at the University of Rochester.[50]

Denio was no exception in studying at Leipzig when officially not even female hearers were admitted. James McKeen Cattell remembered that during his Leipzig student days from 1883 to 1886, the psychologist Wilhelm Wundt admitted a US woman to his lectures. She was not identified, but perhaps she was Myra L. Hopkins of San Francisco. Like Stallo and Köhler in 1877, Hopkins was affiliated with the conservatory, but she became interested in psychology and acquainted with Cattell. Cattell mentioned Hopkins in an 1885 letter to his parents, stating that she participated in one of his experiments.[51] But she cannot positively be identified as the woman in Wundt's lecture hall whom Cattell remembered later in his life. Another explanation is possible. Abby Leach, a professor of Greek and Latin at Vassar College, in 1886/87 studied the classics at Leipzig. She had previously studied at the "Harvard Annex" for women (Radcliffe) and at Johns Hopkins University. Albisetti remarked that the future psychologist Mary Whiton Calkins might have joined her; but the latter's stay at Leipzig was never verified. Cattell's future wife Josephine Owen was also a student at the conservatory who joined his efforts in experimental psychology. She was, however, British.[52] The identity of the female psychology student from the US in the 1880s will have to remain obscure for now.

More certain are the cases of a few US women who traveled to Leipzig between 1889 and 1895 as hearers or visitors. Many of them were interested in teaching careers. Some female students eventually got married and subsequently gave up their professional careers. But this did not mean that they gave up learning or intellectual activity. Josephine Bontecou [Steffens] wrote a novel, published in 1899. From her husband Lincoln Steffen's published writings it can be discerned that even though she was a strong and determined woman, she expected him to be the provider and never seriously challenged that role. Likewise, Leipzig-trained Helen Thomas [Flexner], M. C. Thomas's youngest sister, gave up her career as an English teacher at Bryn Mawr College to marry Simon Flexner, a student of Leipzig-trained William Welch and brother of the medical reformer Abraham Flexner.[53]

It may be assumed that there were more female US students at Leipzig. Isabelle Bronk, in a letter to *The Nation*, referred to eight women there in the fall of 1890/91, six of them Americans. Bronk knew approximately the same number of female students at Leipzig as Channing had known roughly a decade before. But that does not mean that eight women were the exact number for the 1890/91 fall term. Was female US attendance the same in the early 1890s as it had been in 1879? One source mentioned twenty American and English women who audited lectures at Leipzig in 1892,[54] suggesting that the female population might have been much higher during the dark ages than is known to date. Then again, in 1894 an unidentified person from California who had "recently" studied at Leipzig recalled the presence of "four women" who had "given satisfactory evidence of [their] ability and desire to pursue post graduate study."[55]

Statistical data is available for the period from spring term 1900 to spring term 1908. On average, about six US women stayed per semester. Considering that Bronk had mentioned six female Americans in 1890, it may be concluded that, in spite of some fluctuation, no significant growth in the number of female US students at Leipzig may be observed after the turn of the century, except for a peak of up to eleven women from the US between the 1904/05 fall term and the 1906 spring term. This pre-1906 peak is remarkable, because in 1906 women were allowed to enter Leipzig as regular students for the first time. But, as noted before, only two US women took advantage of this opportunity. Similar to what may be observed for their fellow country*men*, US women after 1900 might not have shown a growing interest in Leipzig. By contrast, the total number of all female hearers steadily rose after 1900 (Figure 15).[56]

That female US student numbers at Leipzig did not skyrocket after the university had opened up to them might be explained by the fact that in the final decades of the nineteenth century, the opening of women's colleges, female annexes, and coeducational universities in the United States had greatly improved the educational infrastructure for women. US institutions also provided jobs for administrators and faculty, both male and female. The New World had thus become much more progressive than Germany in terms of women's education. One might argue that the long refusal to acknowledge the intellectual potential of half of the population contributed to the decline of inflexible, masculine German universities.

Two female hearers at Leipzig, Josephine Bontecou and Elfrieda Hochbaum suggested in autobiographical novels that they would not associate with fellow country*men* in Europe unless they encountered a new type of US man with a peculiar understanding of European ways. They both met their future husbands in a Leipzig lecture hall. Around 1890, Bontecou and Lincoln Steffens were both attending the lectures of the experimental psychologist Wilhelm Wundt. They would secretly get married in London before returning to America. Their marriage was somewhat unconventional, as she was ten years his senior. She died in 1909, disappointed with her inability to conceive and the failure of her literary efforts. Steffens would marry again; his second wife Ella Winter was much younger. They had a son when he was well advanced in age.[57] At the turn of the century, the German American Hochbaum of Chicago attended the lectures of Eduard Sievers, who was notorious for not admitting women to his classes.[58] She met Paul Russell Pope there, who would become a professor of German at Cornell University. They were not married until 1904 after both had earned a PhD degree—Pope at Leipzig and Hochbaum, for a lack of opportunity in Germany, at Cornell. She taught at a small college until her wedding and later became a writer and active suffragette. The couple had two children.[59]

Bontecou's novel *Letitia Berkeley, A.M.* was published in 1899. It starts out in a Henry Jamesean universe, but soon Letitia escapes stuffy New York society and moves to Paris, where she studies medicine also in an attempt to understand and connect with her body. At the same time, she associates with Eastern European anarchists, thus departing from Henry James's well-trodden path. Letitia's desire to acquire knowledge about the functions of the female body becomes an open act of resistance as she thereby undermines the prescribed norms of society that withholds knowledge of physicality from females, especially scientific knowledge. In contrast to Bontecou, Letitia chooses not to support the institution of marriage. As the novel was published several years after Bontecou's student days in Europe, it may be assumed that the author might have become disillusioned with her married life in spite (or because?) of her somewhat unconventional husband.

Unconventionality is the binding element between the woman-student and her lover abroad. When Bontecou's fictional alter ego Letitia Berkeley gets to know a US student in Paris, he tells her about his futile attempts to meet her in the usual gathering places, thus highlighting both their unwillingness to be part of the American colony: "I have tried to get myself introduced in the usual way … but I have not been able to make sure even of your name till to-day … though I have martyred myself attending American festivities and American churches."[60] They instantly strike a bond as they discover their mutual dislike for mingling with US student crowds abroad. The American is modeled after Steffens, and their romance is relocated from Leipzig to Paris, where Bontecou and Steffens spent some time before getting married. Interestingly, Steffens was an alumnus of the University of California in Berkeley. The female protagonist's longing for education is thus intricately intertwined with the author's real-life husband's educational journey.

Just like Letitia Berkeley, Hochbaum's fictional reincarnation Hilda Brandt openly resists partaking in American colony life at the German university town. Hochbaum's autobiographical novel was posthumously published in 1963. Its title *Burning Arrows* alongside the protagonist's last name "Brandt" ("fire") reflects determination fed by desire. When Hilda is invited by her US neighbor at a Leipzig bed and breakfast to come along to the American Church, she declines:

> "I'm going to the American Church, *Fräulein*," Mr. Burton said.
>
> "I'm not," she answered.
>
> "It's a good place to meet Americans."
>
> "I'm studying Europe."[61]

When Hilda meets her future husband, she is not sure of his nationality at first—he seems neither German nor American but displays characteristics that appear to combine the best of both peoples. Likewise, Letitia, while recognizing her suitor instantly to be an American, also quickly learns that something about his approach to life is different. Both protagonists thus realize that they have come across a new American man who dares falling in love with a woman who is no less educated and ambitious than himself.[62]

Like the African-American Wright, the two US woman-writers sought distance from US culture. They searched and to some degree found new US identities in Europe. In their novels, distance to the United States and the European-American alternative is played out in the personal sphere, that is, in the ambitious woman-student's romantic involvement with a fellow countryman who distanced himself from late Victorian American culture.

Deaf and Blind Americans

While women could succeed if they persisted, a disability such as blindness or a hearing impairment[63] did not obstruct admission to a German university in any notable way. The blind and deaf were "real" *men* and *women*—as long as they agreed to play by able-bodied standards. German educational and scientific models nonetheless affected US women differently than the deaf. Women fought hard to gain access to German universities—the latter eventually had to give in to their strength in numbers. With regard to deaf education, however, the late-nineteenth-century appeal of German education might have backfired. Germans favored teaching the deaf a spoken language (oral method) rather than resorting to a nationally signed language (sign method), as was done at the oldest US school for the deaf in Hartford, Connecticut, where American Sign Language (ASL) was developed based on the French system.

During the nineteenth century—somewhat correspondingly with increasing enthusiasm for German education and science throughout the century—a shift occurred in the United States in favor of oral education. Hearing advocates of deaf education began to advertise the oral method more widely. One of their best-known representatives was Alexander Graham Bell, whose invention of the telephone was a side-product to his experimentations with teaching methods for the deaf. Both Bell's mother and wife were hearing impaired.[64] If, as James Mark Baldwin, a Leipzig student of psychology in the 1880s, observed in his post–World War I memoirs, "German scholarship had become a fetich [sic],"[65] one may wonder whether the oral method gained wider acceptance in the United States simply because it was German.[66] Indeed, while some early Leipzig Americans stood for promoting sign language, later generations of hearing-impaired Leipzig Americans resorted to vocal speech. The struggle between the oral and sign systems is reflected in the fact that US representatives of both systems visited Leipzig especially during the 1840s, but a predominance of the oral system may be traced among Leipzig Americans thereafter. The subject would have to be studied more thoroughly—my following observations can only be a beginning.

The several US visitors in Leipzig who represented deaf education up to the 1850s not only stood for the struggle between the two systems of how to teach the hearing impaired. They incidentally also appear to have paved the way for American interest in the University of Leipzig. For, as I observed in chapter 2, a notable increase in visitors at Leipzig tended to precede an increase in actual student numbers there. After especially the 1840s had witnessed numerous American teachers of the deaf in town, the following two decades saw an increase in student numbers spearheaded by Yale graduates who may have been linked to deaf American networks. While it is challenging to trace US visitors at Leipzig's school for the deaf in the second half of the nineteenth century, deaf and also blind students now registered at the university as students. In other words, after the 1850s, Americans no longer came to Leipzig to study teaching methods for the deaf. Rather, deaf and blind Americans came to study the latest scientific models.

When in 1853 the Yale graduate Mason Cogswell Weld arrived with his travel companion Samuel Johnson, it marked the onset of Leipzig's rise in favor with US educational pilgrims. But how had Weld and Johnson found out about Leipzig in the first place? Through the Leipzig-trained Yale president Woolsey? Or maybe through a deaf network with Weld's father Lewis at its center? Leipzig, after all, is the home of the oldest German institution for educating the deaf founded shortly after a French school had been sponsored in Paris. Frederick Augustus, elector of Saxony, had invited Samuel Heinicke to Leipzig for that purpose. The school opened with nine pupils on 14 April 1778.[67] While contrary to Heinicke's initial hopes, it never became a part of the university, from its founding until 1878 the school was under university supervision, meaning that one or two overseers—university professors—would annually examine it and report to the ministry of education in Dresden. They would push or oppose matters of concern to the school's director.

The earliest known American student in Leipzig, John Foulke, visited the school in the third year of its existence and almost immediately after his arrival in town. He reported to Benjamin Franklin on 12 October 1781: "There is a school at Leipsic where the unhappy muets [mutes, i.e., the deaf] of both sexes & all ages are taught to write[,] speak & read—similar to those of Paris & Edinburgh, I was shown there by a friend."[68] The fact that Foulke referred to similar institutions in Paris and Edinburgh suggests that he had looked into this issue before. A medical doctor by training, he might have had a professional interest.

There are more connections between deaf education in Leipzig and North America. Mason Weld's father Lewis was the principal of the first US asylum for the deaf at Hartford, Connecticut. He visited the Heinicke School in 1844. For the Cogswell-Welds, it was a family mission to teach the deaf on the basis of sign language rather than by lip reading and vocal speech. Mason Weld's maternal aunt, Alice, born in 1805, had lost her sense of hearing after an illness in her early life. Her condition had aroused the interest of a neighbor, Thomas Gallaudet, who in 1817 set up the first US school for the deaf together with Alice's father, Mason Fitch Cogswell, and the deaf Frenchman Laurent Clerc. They laid the foundations for ASL. Gallaudet's son Edward Miner Gallaudet continued his father's work after he became the first president of Gallaudet University in Washington, DC, the only university for the deaf. Lewis Weld married Alice's hearing sister Mary, thus extending his professional connection with the Hartford school into personal realms. Lewis Weld and Thomas Gallaudet had both graduated from Yale.[69]

It is not known whether Lewis Weld visited the University of Leipzig during his 1844 stay in town, and if so to what extent he planted the idea in his son's head of enrolling there. Still, through his father, Mason had obtained an idea of educational opportunities at Leipzig. Mason hinted at his father's familiarity with the town in one of his letters: "Leipzig you know Father is a pleasant place."[70] In the fall following Mason's arrival, Lewis, in failing health, visited his son. As father and son embarked on a journey through the German countries, they visit schools for the deaf. Early in November 1853, Mason wrote to his mother and sisters back home: "In the evening we went to Frankfurt on/Main. Here we visited the D. + D. School and were most kindly received and even affectionately by the Director."[71] "D. + D." referred to "Deaf and Dumb." Mason accompanied his father during the visit, thus displaying his family loyalty to the cause of deaf education.[72]

During the 1840s, American advocates of both the oral and the sign methods traveled to Leipzig and visited the Heinicke school, which suggests that by then the debates as regarded teaching approaches for the deaf were in full swing. The main purpose of Lewis Weld's 1844 trip had been to visit institutions and gather information about different approaches to the education of the deaf. He wanted to refute Horace Mann's claims on the desirability of oral education rather than teaching sign language. Mann himself had visited the Leipzig school for the deaf together with Mary Mann on 27 July 1843. The following year, Lewis Weld, Thomas A. Thacher of Yale, and George Day, a philologist of New York, signed the school's guest book. Two more US visitors had placed their names in the guest book already in 1841— Dr. John P. Hiester of Philadelphia and Charles Peters of New York.[73]

While no other US visitors were traced in the guest book at an earlier or later period, that does not mean that others did not visit during the 1840s. In his 1854 publication about a stay in Leipzig, N. Parker Willis referred to a visit at the school that must have occurred in 1845. Willis was impressed with the institution and devoted four pages of his rather brief account of Leipzig to the school. He had been accompanied by Mann's friend Dr. Vogel, his brother (who was a student at the Leipzig Conservatory), and a Dr. Bartlett of Philadelphia. Bartlett was likely David Bartlett, a Yale alumnus, who had learned ASL from none other than Laurent Clerc. In 1852, Bartlett opened a private school in New York that admitted deaf children aged four and a half to seven alongside their hearing siblings when possible. He used sign language, written English, and the manual alphabet in his teaching. While the school did not last long (Bartlett eventually rejoined the staff of the Hartford school), his idea of lowering the admission age of deaf students to schools for the hearing impaired eventually became a standard. Before his school, the admission age had been ten to twelve years.[74]

By the second half of the nineteenth century, increasing enthusiasm for empirical science was turning deafness into a condition that could be studied and possibly remedied with scientific methods. Viewing deafness as a medical condition rather than a form of cultural diversity objectified the deaf as it created dependence on the scientific evaluations of hearing experts. An example from the 1870s illustrates the idea. While working on his dissertation at Harvard in 1878, G. Stanley Hall contacted Leipzig's experimental psychologist Wilhelm Wundt regarding Laura Bridgman, the first blind and deaf person to have been educated successfully in the United States. Bridgman had lost her hearing and sight as a toddler and lived in an asylum in Boston.[75] Wundt was curious. He wondered about "her remembrance of light & color."[76] Hall, in turn, regarded the nearly 50-year-old Laura as an object of scientific study, referring to her as "it" at some point, even though she had helped teach a deaf and blind friend to read and had published autobiographical writings. Hall informed Wundt that "by learning her language, making her trifling presents, &c" he tried "to gain her confidence, besides measuring *its* sensibilities of skin, tongue & nostrils as far as my own competency & the physiological apparatus at my disposal made it possible."

After the US Civil War, American students in Leipzig showed no traceable interest in the local school for the deaf. Instead, among the ever-increasing and diversifying student body at the University of Leipzig, we now find a few disabled students. The most interesting observation one can make about them as a group is that they apparently fit into the able-bodied student crowds without causing friction. They were mainly hearing-impaired students, but a blind student also registered: Franz Joseph Dohmen was twenty-four years old when he enrolled for a first time in October 1898 to study mathematics. He had lost his eyesight after a serious illness as a child. It is a curious irony that his father was an eye specialist; he was deceased by the time his son registered at Leipzig. Having attended a school for blind children in the early 1880s, Dohmen obtained a bachelor's degree from the University of Texas in his native Austin. He also studied in Greifswald. In 1905, he earned a Leipzig PhD degree. He was a member of the American Students Club and the Mathematical Society. A reference to his impaired vision may be found in the vita that was attached to his PhD dissertation.[77] George William Heimrod, in turn, registered at Leipzig as a chemical student in 1901. The Harvard-trained future associate member of the Rockefeller Institute for Medical Research in New York would lose his eyesight in 1909.

Two hearing-impaired men and a woman from North America may be traced as students at Leipzig since the late 1860s. One of the men and the woman had lost their hearing after they had acquired vocal speech. Possibly also because of that they seemed to have adjusted well enough to the hearing world. The second man, who had been born profoundly deaf, and who registered at Leipzig as late as in 1914, apparently had a harder time fitting in.

As early as in 1867, 25-year-old Gideon Emmet Moore traveled to Germany to further his education. He had been fond of music in his boyhood, but by the time he was eighteen years old, he was totally deaf. As a child,

Moore had attended above-mentioned "Mr. Bartlett's School for Young Deaf-Mute Children" where deaf and hearing children learned both sign language and vocal speech. Moore graduated with honors from the Yale Sheffield Scientific School in 1861, his interests being chemistry, metallurgy, and mineralogy. Mason Weld's travel companion at Leipzig in the early 1850s, Sam Johnson, might have known Moore. After all, by the time Moore studied chemistry at Yale in the 1860s, Johnson held a chair in chemistry there. Besides, through his travel companion's father Lewis Weld, Johnson must have been well aware of the Hartford school and more generally of attempts to educate the deaf since at least the early 1850s. As suggested before, Yale graduates played a key role in early deaf education in America.

Having completed his Yale education, Moore embarked on a European tour. He first stopped at Wiesbaden and then moved on to Heidelberg, where he received a PhD degree summa cum laude, thus becoming the first deaf American on record to obtain that degree.[78] He subsequently went to Leipzig and Berlin for further studies. On 29 June 1870, he registered at the Saxon university to study chemistry. He "acquired a very perfect command of the German language and carried on spoken conversation with marvelous propriety and facility."[79] The fact that in 1872 he married an Austrian might have helped. Documents at the Heidelberg University Archives do not mention unusual circumstances in connection with his oral exams.[80]

In the spring of 1894, 24-year-old Helen Thomas spent a semester at Leipzig together with her lifelong friend Lucy Donnelly. Ever since the death of her mother a few years prior to her German student venture, Helen's health and particularly her sense of hearing had begun to fail. That she received a higher education in Germany is the more remarkable as she arrived during the "dark ages" when not even female hearers were officially admitted at Leipzig. Once she had arrived in 1894, she consulted a specialist and achieved a temporary improvement. However, she remained nearly deaf for the rest of her life. Both Thomas and Donnelly had previously studied at Bryn Mawr College, where Helen's oldest sister, Leipzig-trained M. Carey Thomas, was about to become the first female president. In a way, Helen had been destined to follow in her sister's footsteps. During Carey's Leipzig student days, their parents had visited her. Nine-year-old Helen had been part of the company as she had refused to be left alone in America.[81]

Donnelly helped H. Thomas in hearing everyday life while at Leipzig. Helen wrote to Carey, Lucy "stands between me and the world.... When I am with her, I hardly realize I am deaf, but without her I am helpless."[82] Both studied philology. It may be assumed that they went to lectures together and that Helen made use of Lucy's notes. That in spite of a few setbacks a hearing impairment was not the end of the world is evident from the following statement: "I dare say that after all it is my fate to be deaf, and I must put up with it, and it has certain advantages too, eliminates much of the commonplace and the tiresome in life, as well as much joy."[83] Thomas returned to the United States and for some time taught English at Bryn Mawr College, as did Lucy. But while Lucy stayed on the faculty for the rest of her life, Helen married Simon Flexner. One of their two sons, James Thomas Flexner, became a historian and published with *An American Saga* a history of the unlikely romance between his Jewish father and hearing-impaired Quaker mother.

The case of 26-year-old George Draper Osgood differs from Moore's and Thomas's on account of his having been born deaf. He was one of four US students who registered at Leipzig in 1914 after the onset of World War I. Having been educated in the oral method, he followed conversations by lip reading. Moreover, he usually had his pockets stuffed with paper for writing short messages. At Harvard, he paid fellow students to copy lecture notes for him. A member of the Harvard class of 1912, he was an athletic champion and rather hot tempered.[84] Complaints about him included insubordination as well as unacceptably loud noise from his dormitory room. One of his Harvard professors, who had acquired the manual alphabet to facilitate communication with him, noted with surprise that Osgood was not familiar with it.

Little is known about Osgood's experiences at Leipzig. He studied chemistry. His correspondence with the noted physical chemist Wilhelm Ostwald comprised seven of Osgood's and six of Ostwald's letters between the fall of 1913 and winter of 1915. Osgood visited Ostwald at his retirement retreat *Energie* in Grossbothen near Leipzig in mid-July 1914.[85] On 16 February 1915, Osgood informed Oswald with much regret that he had to return to America, expressing his hope that Oswald would publish him. Nothing is known about Osgood's future fate. According to a 1937 Harvard class report, he had been ill for many years by then.[86]

The reference to illness might have been a euphemism for mental illness, the beginnings of which may be traced back to his Leipzig student days. Then again, it is difficult to determine whether Osgood was indeed mentally ill or possibly the victim of discrimination as a result of his Otherness and his somewhat stormy temper. He might have been perceived as un-American on account of what he referred to as his philosophical ideas. In February 1914, Osgood wrote to Ostwald, who had wide-ranging interests outside his own discipline:

> You will understand that a philosopher who busies himself with space and time and strange smells and things like that will not get on very well with lickspittle timeservers of Mammon who think the difference of 1/2 inch in a collar a matter almost of life and death. You know the atmosphere of these practical Ameri-

cans around here by personal experience I am sure. It is useless to tell them that there are more practical and worthier things in life than talking about the stock market all the time.... I absolutely despise that point of view as an end of life in itself.[87]

As a student in Berlin, the future muckraker Lincoln Steffens had also grappled with the stereotype of the "practical" US student. In 1890, he complained that his fellow countrymen did not adopt enough German academic culture. He was "a conundrum to my fellow-students from America," for "they do not understand why I am studying such a subject as philosophy" since "I am not going to become a professor or teacher."[88] He observed that most of them studied ultimately to be able to make a living. The "idea that there is any other motive seems never to occur to them." Steffens, of course, was a potential Other for several reasons, such as his homoerotic relationship with a German and marriage to a considerably older woman.

On 2 February 1914, Osgood remarked that he was on troubled terms with his family. He told Ostwald that he was "very glad to receive your letter for it simplifies a situation that was pretty thick." He continued to explain that things were complicated:

> I have long since become weary of the ideas of some of my family and their associates; they are equally tired of reflecting that I am queer by their lights. I do not care; I go my way and keep my thought for those who can understand.... I went to the doctor, as I wrote you ... ; it took him three hours to understand that anyone could possibly think I was not responsible for myself. He gave me a clean bill; it dawned on the practical people gradually in the course of six weeks that they had blundered badly. Relations have been extremely unpleasant ever since; I have had to stay so as to let things blow over. A split is always most unfortunate, and must be handled so as not to become irreparable. Things have mended in the last two weeks, however, and I can now take things into my own hands.[89]

Ostwald was willing to publish Osgood's chemical theories. He advised him, however, to be less vocal about his philosophical ideas. In another letter, Ostwald cautiously suggested that Osgood's at times haughty manners might be the cause of some of his problems. He furthermore insinuated that not all people whom Osgood had met at Harvard might have intended to cause him trouble.[90] Ostwald's letters became more cautious over time, which suggests that Osgood was indeed—to put it cautiously—a difficult character. The question remains to what extent Osgood's life could have been different if he had had the option of sign language early in his life, which would have allowed him to communicate with people in the same situation as him and thereby spared him some isolation.

Summary

No matter which American student group in Germany is examined, they typically felt a distance from German academic culture on at least one or even more levels. For white American men, who enjoyed all privileges accorded to German university students, this distance was rooted in the fact that they could not find the same educational opportunities at home, which is why they especially observed the rituals of the German university with a mixture of feelings including fascination and humor. African-American men, in turn, in their interaction with Germans experienced the American race problem in much more clarity simply by not being faced with it. Homosexuals fared badly when outed. They therefore cannot be traced as an activist group.

Women curiously expected from the—in gender terms—more conservative German customs that they would turn American men into a more progressive lot. This resonated well with the self-perception of American men, who, as will be made even more apparent in the following chapters, were indeed very much reform minded (as least as regarded general educational progress in the United States). American women at German universities were furthermore headstrong. With their determination they helped open German universities to women generally.

Finally, like homosexuals, the blind and hearing impaired did not really perceive of themselves as one specific group of the population—likely mainly because there were so few of them studying in Leipzig at different times, but also because disability, and especially a hearing impairment, became increasingly coded in scientific terms, making it desirable to do one's best to blend in with the able-bodied mainstream rather than being singled out as an imperfect or even defective human being.

Notes

1. James Morgan Hart, *German Universities: A Narrative of Personal Experience* (New York: G. P. Putnam's Sons, 1874 [reprinted London: Routledge/Thoemmes Press, 1994]), 36–37. The following two quotes ibid. My emphasis.
2. *Immatrikulations und Disziplinar-Ordnung für die Studierenden der Universität Leipzig vom 8. März 1903* (Leipzig: Alexander Edelmann, 1903), § 13, 9.
3. Lincoln Steffens, *The Autobiography of Lincoln Steffens, Complete in One Volume* (New York: Harcourt, Brace and Company, 1931), 133.

4. J. R. Angell (Berlin) to J. B. Angell (Father), 6 November 1892. J. R. Angell Papers, 85605 Aa 1, J.R. Angell Letters 1880–1945, UM Bentley.

5. Diary, T. D. Seymour, Wednesday, 26 October 1870. Seymour Family Papers, Box 25, Folder 200, YUL. Also: "Today I was matriculated as student of the University. The ceremony is rather formidable, though not oppressive. I had to present my diploma from the University of Michigan, and also my passport.... I received my collegienbuch, Gesetzbuch, Student Karte Certificate of Matriculation in Latin, and two or three circulars containing advertisements." Journal, C. Thomas, 15 October 1877. C. Thomas Papers, 86180 Aa 2 Ac, Box 3, UM Bentley.

6. Parker to Family, 13 December 1891. G. H. Parke Papers, HUG 4674.12, HUL Pusey. Following quotes ibid.

7. Journal, A. C. McLaughlin, 25 October 1893. A.C. McLaughlin Papers, 85536Aa2 Box 1, UM Bentley. Following quotes ibid.

8. A. B. Lamb to Family, n. d. [2nd week after arrival]. A. B. Lamb Papers, HUG 4508.50, Box 2, HUL Pusey. Following quotes ibid.

9. C. R. Lanman to Aunt, 31 October 1875. Lanman Papers, HUG 4510.67, Letters from Europe, vol. 3, HUL Pusey. Following quotes ibid. On Lanman, see Walter Eugene Clark, "Charles Rockwell Lanman, 1850–1941*," *Journal of the Oriental Society* 61, no. 3 (September 1941): 191–92; Franklin Edgerton, "Charles Rockwell Lanman," in *The American Philosophical Society Yearbook 1941*, 1 January–31 December 1941 (Philadelphia: 1942), 348–86.

10. Diary, G. L. Burr, 1 March 1885 to 9 March 1885. George Lincoln Burr Papers, 14/17/22 Box 25, Cornell Kroch. Emphasis in original.

11. Journal, A. C. McLaughlin, 12 February 1894. A. C. McLaughlin Papers, 85536Aa2, Box 1, UM Bentley.

12. Kenneth Barkin, "W.E.B. Du Bois' Love Affair with Imperial Germany," *German Studies Review* 28 (May 2005): 284–302.

13. William Wells Brown, *The American Fugitive in Europe Sketches of Places and People Abroad* (Boston: John P. Jewett and Co, 1855). Available online from Academic Affairs Library, University of North Carolina at Chapel Hill, 2000, http://docsouth.unc.edu/neh/brown55/brown55.sgml; William Henry Ferris, *[The Black Man in America and Beyond the Seas: Advertising Prospectus for a Book of This Title, with Extracts from It on P. 16–36]* (New Haven, CT: 1912); Black History Month, *The Role of Afro-American Churches in Economic, Political and Social Development at Home and Abroad* (Columbia: University of Missouri–Columbia, 1989); Joseph J. Reid, "Minority Student Participation in International Study Abroad Programs: A Family Perspective" (Master's thesis, East Carolina University, 1995); Ernest Dunn, *Survey of the Black Experience in America and Abroad* (Dubuque, IA: Kendall/Hunt, 1996).

14. George Yancy, "In the Spirit of the A.M.E. Church: Gilbert Haven Jones as an Early Black Philosopher and Educator," *A.M.E. Church Review* 68, no. 388 (2002): 43–57; reprinted in *The American Philosophical Association Newsletter on Philosophy and the Black Experience* 2, no. 2 (Spring 2003): 42–48.

15. One Wright's life, see Richard R. Wright, Jr., *87 Years behind the Black Curtain: An Autobiography* (Philadelphia: Rare Book Company, 1965); Corey D. B. Walker, "'Of the Coming of John [and Jane]': African American Intellectuals in Europe, 1888–1938," *American Studies Quarterly* 47, no. 1 (2002): 7–22.

16. An overview of available references will be provided in a forthcoming article: Anja Werner, "Convenient Partnerships? African American Civil Rights Leaders and the East German Dictatorship" [working title]. In *Anywhere But Here! Black Intellectuals—The Atlantic*

World and Beyond, ed. Kendahl Radcliffe, Jennifer Scott, and Anja Werner (University of Mississippi Press, forthcoming).

17. As to Du Bois's trip to Europe, see for example Herbert Aptheker, ed., *The Correspondence of W.E.B. Du Bois. Selections 1877–1934*, vol. 1, (Amherst: University of Massachusetts Press, 1973–78), xxiii–xxv, 3–29. W.E.B. Du Bois, *The Autobiography of W.E.B. Du Bois; a Soliloquy on Viewing My Life from the Last Decade of Its First Century* (New York: International Publishers, 1968), 154–82.

18. Wright, *87 Years Behind the Black Curtain*, 44. On Du Bois's lack of funding, see, D. C. Gilman to W.E.B. Du Bois, 13 April 1894, in Aptheker, *The Correspondence of W.E.B. Du Bois*, vol. 1, 29.

19. See Du Bois, *The Autobiography*, 159–60.

20. Wright, *87 Years Behind the Black Curtain*, 46–47. Following quotes ibid.

21. Acta, [Un]sittlichen Verkehr Studi[ren]der mit Frauenpersonen betr., Universitäts-Gericht, 1893 bis 1914, Rep. II/IV, Nr. 55a, 390–91, LUA.

22. Thomson was listed as a member in the 1908/09 fall term. Student. Körperschaften W.S. 1908/09, Rep. II/XVI/II, Nr. 6 Bd. 23, microfilm 479/94, 0191 [9], LUA.

23. Justin Kaplan, *Lincoln Steffens. A Biography* (New York: Simon and Schuster, 1974), 40; Steffens, *The Autobiography*, 146–47.

24. Steffens, *The Autobiography*, 140, 146ff., 292ff., 303ff.. Kaplan, *Lincoln Steffens*, 40, 42–43, 71–72, 93, 163. L. Steffens to H. Gale, 13 January 1895, reprinted in Ella Winter and Granville Hicks, eds., *The Letters of Lincoln Steffens*, vol. 1 (New York: Harcourt, Brace and Company, 1938), 110.

25. L. Steffens to H. Gale, 12 November 1932, Hicks, *Letters of Lincoln Steffens*, vol. 2, 932.

26. Patricia M. Mazón, *Gender and the Modern Research University: The Admission of Women to German Higher Education, 1865–1914* (Stanford, CA: Stanford University Press, 2003).

27. See e.g., Hiltrud Häntzschel and Hadumod Bußmann, eds., *Bedrohlich gescheit. Ein Jahrhundert Frauen und Wissenschaft in Bayern* (München: Verlag C. H. Beck, 1997), 343; Lothar Mertens, *Vernachlässigte Töchter der Alma Mater*, Sozialwissenschaftliche Schriften, Heft 20 (Berlin: Duncker & Humblot, 1991), 20, 29. As to other European countries, see Sandra L. Singer, *Adventures Abroad: North American Women at German-Speaking Universities, 1868–1915*, Contributions in Women's Studies 201 (Westport, CT: Praeger, 2003), 6. Also, Anonymous, "Higher Education for Women in Germany.—I.," *The Nation* 44, no. 1274 (28 November 1890): 426.

28. Singer, *Adventures Abroad*, 27. Thomas Neville Bonner, *To the Ends of the Earth: Women's Search for Education in Medicine* (Cambridge, MA: Harvard University Press, 1992), 41–44.

29. Anja Becker, "*How Daring She Was!* The Female American Colony at Leipzig University, 1877–1914," in *Taking Up Space. New Approaches to American History*, mosaic 21, ed. Anke Ortlepp and Christoph Ribbat (Trier: Wissenschaftlicher Verlag Trier, 2004), 31–46. Also, Anja Becker, "For the Sake of Old Leipzig Days ... Academic Networks of American Students at a German University, 1781–1914" (PhD dissertation, University of Leipzig, 2006).

30. James C. Albisetti, "German Influence on the Higher Education of American Women, 1865–1914," in *German Influences on Education in the United States to 1917*, ed. Henry Geitz, Jürgen Heideking, and Jurgen Herbst (Washington, DC: German Historical Institute, and Cambridge: Cambridge University Press, 1995), 243; G. Stanley Hall, *Life and Confessions of a Psychologist* (New York/London: D. Appleton and Company, 1924), 202.

31. Daniel Bussey Shumway, "The American Students of the University of Göttingen," *Americana Germanica* 8, nos. 5 and 6 (September–December 1910): 171–254, 186 [general], 175, 232, 250 [women].

32. On 10 April 1906, the *Königlich Sächsisches Ministerium des Kultus und öffentlichen Unterrichts* (Royal Ministry of Culture and Public Education) in Dresden decreed that starting with the spring term of 1906, women would be admitted as regular students at Leipzig. Acta, die Immatrikulation weiblicher Studierender betr. (1906–?), Rep. II/IV, Nr. 67, microfilm 434, 0041 [7], LUA. Patricia Mazón, "Die Auswahl der 'besseren Elemente.' Ausländische und jüdische Studentinnen und die Zulassung von Frauen an deutschen Universitäten 1890–1909," in *Jahrbuch für Universitätsgeschichte*, ed. Rüdiger vom Bruch, trans. Axel Fair-Schulz, vol. 5 (Stuttgart: Franz Steiner Verlag, 2002), 185, 196. Singer, *Adventures Abroad*, 149–50. She quoted exclusively from the LUA.

33. See e.g., Häntzschel and Bußmann, *Bedrohlich gescheit*, 343.

34. Siegfried Hoyer, "Studenten aus dem zaristischen Russland an der Universität Leipzig 1870/1914," in *Recht—Idee—Geschichte. Beiträge zur Rechts- und Ideengeschichte*, ed. Heiner Lück and Bernd Schildt (Köln/Weimar/Wien: Böhlau Verlag, 2000), 431–49.

35. Immatrikulations-Kommission (Leipzig) to Ministerium (Dresden), 13 November 1913. Acta, die Immatrikulation weiblicher, 0137 [91], LUA. Sophie Wundt was the daughter of theology professor Heinrich Mau in Kiel. Marita Baumgarten, *Professoren und Universitäten im 19. Jahrhundert* (Göttingen: Vandenhoek & Ruprecht, 1997), 97; Georg Lamberti, *Wilhelm Maximilian Wundt (1832–1920)* (Bonn: Deutscher Psychologen Verlag, 1995), 88.

36. See Gregory R. Zieren, "From Halle to Harvard: Johannes Conrad as Transatlantic Mediator of Economic Thought," in *Tangenten: Literatur und Geschichte*, ed. Martin Meyer, Gabrielle Spengemann, and Wolf Kindermann (Munster: Lit Verlag, 1996). The name Haupt is missing from the article. Greg told me about the Haupt-Conrad connection during one of our exchanges between Clarksville and Nashville, TN.

37. Liselotte Buchheim, "Als die ersten Medizinerinnen in Leipzig promoviert wurden," *Wissenschaftliche Zeitschrift der Karl-Marx-Universität Leipzig* 6 (1956/57): 366. For experiences of US women in Leipzig, see Becker, "*How Daring She Was!*"

38. Sonja Brentjes and Karl-Heinz Schlote, "Zum Frauenstudium an der Universität Leipzig in der Zeit von 1870 bis 1910," in *Jahrbuch für Regionalgeschichte und Landeskunde* 19 (Weimar: Verlag Herrmann Böhlaus Nachfolger, 1993/94), 64. Renate Drucker, "Zur Vorgeschichte des Frauenstudiums an der Universität Leipzig. Aktenbericht," in *Vom Mittelalter zur Neuzeit*, ed. Hellmut Kretzschmar (Berlin: Rütten & Loening, 1956), 281 n.5. Albisetti, "German Influence," 243. Also, Leipzig hearer lists: GAXM1 to GAXM4, microfilm 502/94, LUA. Spring 1879 [0075] (only Channing), fall 1879/80 [0076, 0077] (all four), spring 1880 [0081] (Gwinn, Thomas), fall 1880/81 [0085] (only Channing), spring 1881 [0090] (Channing, Gwinn, Thomas), fall 1881/82 [0094] (Channing, Gwinn, Thomas), spring 1882 [0098] (Gwinn, Thomas). See also Acten des akademischen Senates der Universität LEIPZIG die Zulassung Hörer weiblichen Geschlechts zu den academischen Vorlesungen betr., 6 December 1873, Rep. II/IV, Nr. 35, LUA.

39. Eva Channing, "The Contributors' Club," *The Atlantic Monthly. A Magazine of Literature, Science, Art, and Politics* 44 (December 1879): 788. The case is described in more detail in Becker, "*How Daring She Was.*"

40. M. C. Thomas to Mother, 15 November 1879 and 20 November 1879. Reprinted in Marjorie Housepian Dobkin, ed., *The Making of a Feminist: Early Journals of M. Carey Thomas* (Kent, OH: Kent State University Press, 1979), 198, 202.

41. M. C. Thomas to Father, 29 February 1880, ibid., 213.

42. Ministerium to Immatrikulations-Kommission, Universität Leipzig, 6 December 1879. Acten des akademischen Senates der Universität Leipzig die Zulassung Hörer weiblichen Geschlechts zu den academischen Vorlesungen betr., Rep. II/IV, Nr. 35, 7, LUA.

43. Edith Finch, *Carey Thomas of Bryn Mawr* (New York/London: Harper & Brothers, 1947), 88. M. C. Thomas to Mother, 2 October 1879, reprinted in Dobkin, *Making of a Feminist*, 188. Helen Lefkowitz Horowitz, *The Power and Passion of M. Carey Thomas* (New York: Alfred A. Knopf, 1994), 110. Dobkin, *Making of a Feminist*, 156.

44. Albisetti, "German Influence," 243. James C. Albisetti, *Schooling German Girls and Women: Secondary Education in the Nineteenth Century* (Princeton, NJ: Princeton University Press, 1988), 122–23. Bonner, *To the Ends of the Earth*, 104. Singer, *Adventures Abroad*, 56–60.

45. Hearer lists, GAXM1 to GAXM4, microfilm 502/94, 0060, LUA.

46. Ministerium (Dresden) to Immatrikulations-Kommission (Leipzig), 9 October 1879. Acten des akademischen Senates der Universität LEIPZIG, Rep. II/IV, Nr. 35, LUA; 7. M. C. Thomas to Mother, 7 February 1880, in Dobkin, *The Making of a Feminist*, 208. Becker, "For the Sake of Old Leipzig Days." Regarding the Conservatory, see Yvonne Wasserloos, *Das Leipziger Konservatorium der Musik im 19. Jahrhundert. Anziehungs- und Ausstrahlungskraft eines Musikpädagogischen Modells auf das internationale Musikleben* (Hildesheim: Olms, 2004).

47. Harry E. Downer, *History of Davenport and Scott County*, vol. 2 (Chicago: S. J. Clarke Publishing Co., 1910) Available online at http://www.celticcousins.net/scott/1910vol2bi os25.htm [7 May 2006].

48. Friedrich Bodenstedt, *Vom Atlantischen zum Stillen Ozean* (Leipzig: Brockhaus, 1882), 209, 212–13, 222.

49. Andrew D. White, *Autobiography* (New York: The Century Co., 1906), vol. 1, 569 and vol. 2, 420.

50. Singer, *Adventures Abroad*, 163–65.

51. Bird T. Baldwin, ed., "In Memory of Wilhelm Wundt," in *Psychological Review* 28 (May 1921): 157. Reprinted in Wolfgang G. Bringmann and Ryan D. Tweney, eds., *Wundt Studies* (Toronto: C. J. Hochgrefe, 1980), 280–308; J. M. Cattell to Parents, 17 March 1885. Reprinted in Michael M. Sokal, ed., *An Education in Psychology: James McKeen Cattell's Journal and Letters from Germany and England, 1880–1888* (Cambridge, MA: MIT Press, 1981), 164.

52. Albisetti, *Schooling German Girls and Women*, 223; Mary Whiton Calkins, "Autobiographical Sketch," in *A History of Psychology in Autobiography*, vol. 1, ed. Carl Murchison (Worcester, MA: Clark University Press, 1930), 31–62. As to Leach, see Edward T. James, Janet W. James, and Paul Boyer, eds, *Notable American Women: A Biographical Dictionary, 1607–1950*, vol. 2 (Cambridge, MA: Belknap Press of Harvard University Press, 1971), 379–80. Sokal, *An Education in Psychology*, 363 [index].

53. On Steffens as the provider, see e.g., Kaplan, *Lincoln Steffens*, 54. Also, Steffens, *The Autobiography*. M. C. Thomas had been involved in obtaining funding for the Johns Hopkins Medical School under the condition that it would admit women. S. Flexner's younger brother Abraham Flexner published a famous report on the state of American medical education and a study about universities. Abraham Flexner with a new introduction by Clark Kerr, *Universities. American. English. German* (London: Oxford University Press, 1968 [1930]). Also, Abraham Flexner, *The American College; a Criticism* (New York: Century Co., 1908); *Medical Education in the United States and Canada; a Report to the Carnegie Foundation for the Advancement of Teaching* (New York, 1910); *Medical Education in Europe; a Report to the Carnegie Foundation for the Advancement of Teaching*

(New York, 1912); "The German Side of Medical Education," *The Atlantic Monthly* 62 (1913): 654–55. See also Thomas Neville Bonner, *American Doctors in German Universities. A Chapter in International Intellectual Relations* (Lincoln: University of Nebraska Press, 1963), 58.

54. Isabelle Bronk, "Women at the University of Leipzig," *The Nation. A Weekly Journal Devoted to Politics, Literature, Science & Arts* 51, no. 1329 (18 December 1890): 481; Channing, "The Contributors' Club," 789; H. Kersten, *Die Frau und das Universitätsstudium* (Stuttgart, 1892). Quoted in Albisetti, *Schooling German Girls and Women*, 224 n.62.

55. Student, "Women at the German Universities," in *The Nation* 58, no. 1498 (15 March 1894): 193.

56. See statistics in *Personalverzeichnisse* Leipzig, http://www.ub.uni-leipzig.de/. Also, Acta, Zulassung weiblicher Personen zum Besuche von Vorlesungen an der Universität Leipzig betr. (1900), Rep. II/IV, Nr. 60 Bd. 1, microfilm 428, 0341; Bde. 2–5, microfilm 429; and Bd. 6, microfilm 430, LUA; Akten der Universität Leipzig betreffend: "Hörerinnen" (1907–18), Rep. II/IV, Nr. 60 Bd. 6., microfilm 430, LUA. Mazón, "Die Auswahl der 'besseren Elemente'," 195. Shumway noted a similar decline in attendance on the part of US students at Göttingen. Shumway, "The American Students of the University of Göttingen."

57. See Steffens, *Autobiography;* also Kaplan, *Lincoln Steffens.*

58. Elfrieda Hochbaum, *Burning Arrows* (Boston: Bruce Humphries Publishers, 1963), 320. Drucker, "Zur Vorgeschichte des Frauenstudiums," 288.

59. Graduate Student Folder Mrs. Paul Russell Pope + Faculty Biographical File P. R. Pope, Cornell Kroch.

60. Josephine Bontecou Steffens, *Letitia Berkeley, A.M.* (New York: A. Stokes Company, 1899), 125.

61. Hochbaum, *Burning Arrows,* 250.

62. Hochbaum, *Burning Arrows,* 244, 246, 255. Steffens, *Letitia Berkeley,* 123–27.

63. Regarding disability as an academic discipline, see e.g., Len Barton, *Overcoming Disabling Barriers: 18 Years of Disability and Society* (London: Routledge, 2006); H-Dirksen L. Bauman, *Open Your Eyes: Deaf Studies Talking* (Minneapolis: University of Minnesota Press, 2008); Moshe Barasch, *Blindness: The History of a Mental Image in Western Thought* (New York: Routledge, 2001); Frances A. Koestler, *The Unseen Minority: A Social History of Blindness in the United States* (New York: AFB Press, 2005 [1976]).

64. See e.g., Harlan Lane, *When the Mind Hears. A History of the Deaf* (London: Penguin, 1988), 340, 343.

65. James Mark Baldwin, *Between Two Wars 1861–1921,* vol. 1 (Boston: Stratford Co., Publishers, 1926), 35–36.

66. Leila Frances Monaghan argues along similar lines in her "A World's Eye View: Deaf Cultures in Global Perspective," in *Many Ways to Be Deaf,* ed. Leila Frances Monaghan et al. (Washington, DC: Gallaudet University Press, 2003): 1–24, here 5–6.

67. Lane, *When the Mind Hears,* 102–3.

68. J. Foulke to B. Franklin, 12 October 1781. Franklin Papers, BF85, vol. 23 Folio 11, Hays Calendar II, 400, APS.

69. Lane, *When the Mind Hears.* John Vickrey Van Cleve and Barry A. Crouch, *A Place of Their Own: Creating the Deaf Community in America* (Washington DC: Gallaudet University Press, 1990), 29–46, 155. Biographical Information in the Yale Class Reports of Lewis Weld '18 and Mason Cogswell Weld '52 (Sheffield Scientific School). Also, see Lewis Weld Family Papers, YUL.

70. M. C. Weld, 22 June 1853 [Mason's III Eur, fragment]. L. Weld Family Papers, Group 559, Box 1, Folder 2, YUL.

71. M. C. Weld to Mother and Sisters, 4–5 November 1853, ibid.

72. The Welds were also abolitionists. Mason's brother Lewis volunteered as a white officer in a black regiment during the US Civil War. Joseph T. Glatthaar, *Forged in Battle: The Civil War Alliance of Black Soldiers and White Officers* (Baton Rouge: Louisiana State University Press, 2000), 13, 44, 97.

73. Gästebuch der Samuel-Heinicke-Schule 1803–1852, Spezialbibliothek für Hör- und Sprachschädigung, Samuel-Heinicke-Schule Leipzig, A IV 64,2. As to Lewis Weld's European trip, see Lane, *When the Mind Hears*, 304–9; Van Cleve and Crouch, *A Place of Their Own*, 112.

74. N. Parker Willis, *Rural Letters and Other Records of Thoughts at Leisure* (Auburn/Rochester, NY: Beardsley & Co., 1854), 259–60. Lane, *When the Mind Hears*, 241. Michael Strong, *Language Learning and Deafness* (Cambridge: Cambridge University Press: 1995 [1987]).

75. Dorothy Ross, *G. Stanley Hall: The Psychologist as Prophet* (Chicago: University of Chicago Press, 1972), 70 n., 78, 83; Ernest Freeberg, "'More Important Than a Rabble of Common Kings': Dr. Howe's Education of Laura Bridgman," *History of Education Quarterly* 34, no. 3 (Fall 1994): 305–27.

76. G. S. Hall (Cambridge, MA) to W. Wundt, 7 July [1878]. NA Wundt 1188, LUA. Following quote ibid. My emphasis.

77. Franz Joseph Dohmen, "Darstellung der Berührungstransformationen in Konnexkoordinaten" (Dissertation, Leipzig: B. G. Teubner, 1905).

78. Jack R. Gannon, *Deaf Heritage: A Narrative History of Deaf America* (Silver Spring, MD: National Association of the Deaf, 1981), 7, 399, 439.

79. Obituary Record of Graduates of Yale University Deceased During the Academic Year Ending in June, 1895, Gideon Emmet Moore, 338–39, Yale University Library.

80. The Heidelberg University Archives hold, among others, Moore's Latin curriculum vitae, H-IV-102/72.

81. James Thomas Flexner, *An American Saga: The Story of Helen Thomas & Simon Flexner* (New York: Fordham University Press, 1993), 266, 270, 282–83, 294–96; Helen Thomas Flexner, *A Quaker Childhood* (New Haven, CT: Yale University Press, 1940), 51–73. Flexner, *An American Saga*, 145–46. Horowitz, *The Power and Passion*, 141–42.

82. Flexner, *An American Saga*, 95.

83. Ibid., 96.

84. Articles and correspondence preserved in HUG 300 George Draper Osgood '12, HUL Pusey.

85. G. D. Osgood to W. Ostwald, 21 July 1914. NL Ostwald, 2203, BBAW.

86. Harvard College Class of 1912. Twenty-Fifth Anniversary Report, Sixth Report, June 1937, 551, HUL Pusey.

87. G. D. Osgood to W. Ostwald, 2 February 1914. NL Ostwald 2203, BBAW.

88. L. Steffens (Berlin) to Frederick M. Willis, 4 January 1890, reprinted in Winter and Hicks, *The Letters of Lincoln Steffens*, vol. 1, 39.

89. G. D. Osgood to W. Ostwald, 2 February 1914. NL Ostwald 2203, BBAW.

90. W. Ostwald (Grossbothen) to G. D. Osgood, 23 April 1914 and 9 August 1914, ibid.

Chapter 4

CHOOSING A UNIVERSITY

The Case of Leipzig

The Appeal of Innovation

AFTER HAVING ESTABLISHED the peculiarities in the development of US student numbers at four German universities, and after having elaborated on the increasingly diverse US student body especially at the University of Leipzig, the purpose of this chapter is to flesh out the statistical developments by portraying the University of Leipzig from different American perspectives in the course of the long nineteenth century, which then allows me to infer reasons that explain why US student numbers at Leipzig underwent such dramatic shifts as detailed in chapter 2.

The main reason for opting for a German university—as derived from personal accounts—was the search for innovation. At Leipzig, innovation was carried by collaborations across disciplinary borderlines, a subject that I will introduce here but on which I will elaborate in chapter 5. Based on personal accounts, I discerned four different phases that illustrate Leipzig's changing appeal to US students in their search for innovation. The four phases include the period from the late eighteenth century up to the 1830s, the mid-nineteenth century, Leipzig's heyday in the final three decades of the nineteenth century, and the university's decline in US student numbers since the 1890s.

I opted for four rather than five phases as these phases reflect new developments at Leipzig that are in subsequent years mirrored in the personal accounts of US observers. If, then, so few US students opted for Leipzig prior to 1850s, it also had to do with the fact that it took Leipzig longer than other institutions to adopt aspects of the new German university ideal. Again, military conflicts either halted or triggered the reform and recruitment practices that would shape the university's academic appeal. In unearthing how US students perceived of the specifics at Leipzig, my main interest lies in answering the question of how Americans found out and passed on information about the latest innovative developments (or a lack of and even decline in such developments).

While the earliest US visitors or Leipzig Americans were extremely few in number, their negative or, at best, neutral impressions seemingly overshadowed Leipzig's heyday of the late nineteenth century decades into the future—at least, historiography suggests as much as it continued to focus on Göttingen. Evidently, however, US students increasingly hungered for the most recent, up-to-date reports from their contemporaries as fresh input about the latest scientific and scholarly developments in Europe, which is why since the 1860s they flocked to Leipzig in spite of the earlier negative accounts.

The early North American visitors had formed pronounced opinions of Leipzig *before* actually traveling there—likely simply because information still traveled much slower then than later in the century after the telegraph and steam boat had become familiar institutions. Early North Americans arrived in Leipzig with grand expectations that, when encountering reality, led to a sometimes sobering awakening. Individual scholarly interests and the shiny example of rivaling institutions elsewhere furthermore shaped their opinions. Awareness—or a lack of awareness—of different scholarly traditions additionally impacted the way in which a visitor from the New World depicted a European institution of higher learning in more (or less) favorable terms.

By the late nineteenth century, a time when tendencies everywhere pointed increasingly toward specialization, Leipzig faculty pushed to communicate outside established disciplinary boundaries, which may be viewed as a continuation of Alexander von Humboldt's early-nineteenth-century approach to the production of knowledge rather than a mainstream trend of the immediate future (that is, the early twentieth century). It is, however, representative of scholarly and scientific trends in the early twenty-first century. Obviously, larger educational tendencies come and go in waves, which makes it the more important to keep an eye even on minor tendencies in the past, for they may have been more crucial earlier and may one day flare up again to mainstream importance. In the following, I will first discuss Leipzig's major appeal as rooted in what we would call today interdisciplinary collaborations and subsequently describe the four phases of development.

Interdisciplinary Collaborations at Leipzig

Leipzig's appeal to US students after 1870 may be linked to more or less daring educational choices on the part of the Saxon ministry of education in Dresden dating back to the 1850s, when the build-up of philosophy and medicine laid the foundations for the university's subsequent appeal as a center in natural-scientific but also philological research, branches of knowledge that were not clearly separate then. In fact, the study of modern languages, natural sciences, history, and other subjects all developed within philosophy, that is, one of the traditional four branches (*Fakultäten*) of the German university besides medicine, religion, and law. The Leipzig representatives of these subjects regularly met and talked, thus creating interdisciplinarity.

The main reasons for Leipzig's innovative appeal—or lack thereof—lay in the timing of educational reforms on the part of the Saxon ministry of education and the interrelated issue of warfare, both of which also influenced the university's recruitment policies, which, in turn, stood in direct relation with the presence of US students. As Table 3 suggests, increased and focused recruitment activity tended to precede increased US student enrollments. Put differently, if a university started pouring efforts into its academic outlook, US students were sure to acknowledge it by turning up in larger numbers within only a few years.

Table 3

Number of Professors Newly Recruited to the Leipzig Faculty Who Were Known for Their American Disciples									
before 1820s	1820s	1830s	1840s	1850s	1860s	1870s	1880s	1890s	after 1900
1	3	2	1	3	11	9	17	10	1

While US student numbers in the 1870s and 1890s were notably higher than in the respective previous decade, the 1860s and 1880s had actually witnessed professorial recruitments of interest to the US students of the 1870s and 1890s. At the same time, the 1870s and 1890s experienced—from a US perspective—a decidedly lower recruitment activity, which would also explain the reduced US student numbers of the 1880s and 1900s (see also Appendix 2). Likewise, the slightly increased recruitment activities of the 1820s and 1830s might explain the increased presence of American visitors during the 1840s. Americans thus started taking note of the university and in the following years were rewarded with increased numbers of Leipzig recruitments of interest to them, which was then reflected in a growing American student body.

The relations between recruitments and US student numbers insinuate that Americans were indeed on the lookout for novelty, which could be provided by hiring professors with much promising academic potential, though the numbers and names in Table 3 and Appendix 2 provide even more detail than that. Starting in the late 1880s, and, more noticeably, in the 1890s, newly recruited Leipzig faculty—ranging from the rank of lecturer or *Privatdozent* to full professor—did not stay at Leipzig for the remainder of their careers as had been the case with the celebrated faculty members of the previous decades. By 1900, Leipzig was thus no longer the exclusively final stage in a professor's career. Young academic talent was now called away before reaching their prime. This observation might also have contributed to the then steadily declining US student numbers at Leipzig—the university was either no longer in a position or no longer interested in keeping the most promising young faculty on their payroll, which raises the question if there was any university in Germany that did not witness a decline—or that witnessed a less pronounced decline than Leipzig—in its US student population between 1900 and 1914.

During Leipzig's heyday, scholar-scientists there discussed their approaches across disciplinary boundaries—especially between the humanities and the natural sciences. US students were particularly eager to study under professors who actively promoted this interdisciplinarity in the second half of the nineteenth century, for these professors also happened to be the most innovative faculty members. US students abroad expected cutting-edge science and scholarship. Leipzig's late-nineteenth-century interdisciplinarity provided just that, and it was also, to some extent, a special feature that distinguished the Saxon university from its rival in the north, the University of Berlin.[1] From US perspectives, such a rivalry did not mean that scholars had to choose between two German universities and the approaches for which they stood. They opted for both, if possible, and thus acquired a greater picture of possible forms of the creation of knowledge for the benefit of US education.

The most famous professorial circle was the so-called Leipziger Debattier-Circle around 1900. It is sometimes referred to as Positivisten-Kränzchen, although this latter name has been criticized as inappropriate.[2] I will call it the Leipzig Circle. It was preceded and to some extent overlapped with the Young Grammarians (or Neo-Grammarians) of the 1870s. The aged Greek scholar Georg Curtius had somewhat jokingly nicknamed them thus, for they were young, intended to change the framework of research, and demanded rigorous methods without asking their elders for advice. The name was also attributed to Friedrich Zarncke. Be that as it may, it stuck. The linguistic structuralism of the early twentieth century was rooted in the framework of the Young Grammarians. It was developed both by their critics and followers alike.[3] The diverse and to US students rather appealing group of professors of the Leipzig Circle attempted to find a common language of the natural and the cultural sciences during regular Friday meetings. Besides the psychologist and philosopher Wilhelm Wundt, stable elements of the group included the physical chemist Wilhelm Ostwald and the historian Karl Lamprecht, as well as the geographer Friedrich Ratzel and the economist Karl Bücher. Others may be added, such as the chemist Johannes Wislicenus and the botanist and plant physiologist Wilhelm Pfeffer.[4]

Academic circles added an important component to university life, which contributed to the fruitfulness of discussions as well as to the academic appeal of the professors who participated in them. Such circles provided a friendly yet ambitious and open-minded discussion forum. Their members understood that if the chemistry is right, it can further professional advances.[5] There were more circles.[6] They thrived after the build-up of the Leipzig faculty since the 1850s. The most celebrated professors who joined academic circles also continued to attract students from the New World even after a decline in US student migration to Germany had set in around 1900. Little research has been done on these circles. I cannot fill the gap here, but let me provide a few clues from US perspectives, starting with developments in the early nineteenth century that paved the way and that did not go unnoticed by Americans.

Antiquated Leipzig up to 1830

We get a glimpse of Leipzig between 1780 and 1830 from a handful of young men mainly from the Northeast of the United States. The earliest was John Foulke of Philadelphia, who in late 1781 described the University of Leipzig to no lesser a personality than Benjamin Franklin. More than thirty years later, George Ticknor and his travel companion Edward Everett spent two weeks in town, which Ticknor profusely analyzed in his journals.[7] Finally, in the 1820s, Henry Dwight and his cousin Theodore Dwight Woolsey arrived. Whereas Dwight published his letters home, Woolsey contented himself with private remarks to his sisters and mother about Leipzig and about Dwight's publication. Only Woolsey and Foulke actually enrolled as students. Woolsey would serve—in good family tradition—as president of Yale (1846–1871).[8]

The accounts of Leipzig that these young men left to posterity have a few striking similarities in so far as they seem aware of the university's standing during the Enlightenment. But they also share the assessment that Leipzig could no longer be considered a lighthouse of learning. While, however, they perceived of Leipzig as antiquated especially as its only academic attraction before 1830 appeared to be a scholar of Greek (rather than, for example, of modern languages), they did not uniformly view this focus on an ancient language as a setback. One also finds that depending on their opinions about different German universities, their disciples would or would not follow in their footsteps to Germany. The tendency is particularly pronounced when we look at the Harvard-Göttingen and the Yale-Leipzig connection in this early period. Finally, even though they appear aware of the impact of the region's economic well-being on higher education, they seemed oblivious to the fact that the Napoleonic Wars had devastated greater Leipzig and the state of Saxony to an extent that educational reform had come to a halt. Thus, they were keen young men with clear educational visions who were, however, not always detached enough to evaluate the educational conditions that they encountered abroad in more objective terms.

North Americans expected innovation all over the German countries and were eager to look for it. Indeed, after a year at Göttingen, Ticknor and Everett were impatient to visit other universities. They left on 13 September 1816 "early in the morning with the intention of hastening directly to Leipzig."[9] In anticipation of the trip, Ticknor had enthusiastically described Leipzig as "undoubtedly" one of the "first class" universities.[10] By the 1820s, Dwight praised Leipzig just as liberally, although implying that by then the institution no longer quite lived up to its glorious past, when Leipzig had been "an intellectual Stromboli or perpetual lighthouse to the mind," which for centuries had "poured a flood of intelligence" over Saxony, "rendering this land for ages the intellectual garden of Germany."[11] He concluded that Leipzig's "influence on the world has probably been greater than that of any other institution," disregarding the University of Paris. Dwight thus cautiously prepared his readers for a possible disappointment.

Disappointment indeed awaited the first US visitors in spite of Leipzig's eighteenth-century standing. For Ticknor and Dwight, Leipzig's early-nineteenth-century reputation was rooted in the enlightened eighteenth century, when the idea of freedom of thought had gained momentum in Saxony.[12] Foulke must have traveled to Leipzig for similar reasons. But in his 1781 letter to Franklin, Foulke described Leipzig as antiquated and hardly innovative. "The *coolness* with which science is courted at Leipsic," he remarked, "& a general disposition to a *contentment* in such discoveries as the sons of Science in France or Great Britain may throw into the world, tends to continue *old usages & theories,* & such parts of the school of Leipsic as I have at present acquaintance with appear *much inferior* to that of Paris & *no way superior* to that young seminary [the University of Pennsylvania] which owes its birth to you."[13] The letter was obviously to flatter Franklin. Still, Foulke's Leipzig disenchantment is evident.

Ironically, one of the university's greatest assets in the early nineteenth century—if not the only one when viewed from a US perspective—was Gottfried Hermann, whose expertise as a scholar of ancient Greek actually helped cement the impression that Leipzig was an antiquated institution, because the classics could be perceived as representative of long-standing traditions rather than representing a new discipline.[14] Hermann had studied at Leipzig in the 1780s, in 1794 completed his second doctorate, in 1797 became an associate professor, and in 1803 a full professor. He stood for a philological tradition that focused on a thorough study of individual languages, especially grammar and meter. This strong classical tradition would, in fact, be revived and continued in the 1860s by Georg Curtius and Friedrich Wilhelm Ritschl, the latter being succeeded in 1876 by his student and friend Otto Ribbeck.[15]

North American visitors in Leipzig did take note of the strong tradition in the classics, whereby they did not quite focus on the idea that even a long-established discipline can present new approaches and thus innovation. In the 1820s, Dwight observed that "Leipzig is much more celebrated in classical literature than any other university, but in its professional department, it is equaled by several."[16] As late as in 1857, Philip Schaff observed that Leipzig was "highly distinguished for a large amount of philological and antiquarian learning, and immense literary industry, while in the speculative sciences it occupies only a secondary place, and rarely gives rise to new ideas and systems of thought."[17] According to Schaff, already the Saxon schools made "the language of Cicero …, not only the object, but also the living medium of a thorough instruction," which means that education in Saxony was classic on different levels.

US travelers felt drawn to Hermann but also maintained a distance. In the fall of 1816, Ticknor described Hermann as having "vivacity" and "fire." Hermann "was remarkably voluble—talked of everything—political & literary—publick news & private scandal—among the rest, too, of himself, his nerves, his intentions and even his disposition."[18] After this somewhat creative outburst, however, Ticknor went on to scribble his appreciation of the man in what appears to be almost rehearsed terms: "In short, we saw the man … exactly as he is in his freest hours; and I ~~only~~ learnt by it, to respect & value him the more." In 1844, Theodore Parker was moderately impressed at best—Hermann "talked about America like a book (printed before 1492)."[19] Dwight presented Hermann to an English-speaking audience as "the most distinguished Greek of Germany, as his countrymen style him."[20] In spite of some skepticism about Dwight's book, Woolsey echoed his cousin in repeated and rather flat references to Hermann as the "greatest Greek scholar in the world."[21]

Personal subject preferences had an impact on a visitor's impressions, especially if they were inclined to take one aspect of the university as representative for the whole. Woolsey was less outspokenly critical of Leipzig than either Foulke or Ticknor. But while Foulke was a medical doctor and Ticknor interested in modern languages, Woolsey was a classicist. If Leipzig seemed antiquated as it adhered to lectures in Latin, it did not bother him.[22] Ticknor, in turn, found the past at Leipzig rather than the future. In a twenty-six-page journal entry, he poured out his disappointment. He was appalled by Leipzig's "adherence to old forms and old modes of thinking, which is entirely against the Genius of Germany which despises forms & is fond of novelty."[23] He attempted to be objective by accumulating impressions of different departments. But that made it worse. Facilities generally struck him as in bad shape. The 200-year-old botanical garden only in 1806 had received a gift large enough to start something worthwhile. The observatory was under repair and closed to the visitor. The chemical laboratory with a tradition of barely one hundred years was "not very good."[24] Ticknor left greatly displeased.

The early US visitors in Leipzig would also pass on their impressions. Curiously, a small group of Harvard students followed Ticknor to Göttingen, but no Harvard students registered at Leipzig until the second half of the nineteenth century. In fact, Ticknor had developed such an aversion to Leipzig that when he returned there in the 1830s, both his wife Anna and his friend from European student days—Hugh Swinton Legaré of Charleston, SC—reflected his negative attitude by describing Leipzig as a rather "unsavory" place.[25] By contrast, while no Yale affiliate excepting Woolsey was traced in the Leipzig register between 1810 and 1840, a next generation of Yale students traveled there starting in 1853 with the prospective chemists Mason Cogswell Weld and Samuel William Johnson. (Better-known mid-nineteenth-century Yale graduates in Germany would be Andrew D. White and Daniel C. Gilman, who, however, opted for Berlin.[26]) Had Woolsey influenced their decision? He apparently had not dissuaded them.

Woolsey also differed from his fellow pioneering Leipzig Americans in his more detached view of the German university ideal. Indeed, Woolsey did not expect to find a university ideal abroad: "I prefer the American system with a slight portion of the German grafted on upon it," he wrote.[27] He looked for inspiration for his own and generally for US education. He, too, was of a critical disposition. But he did not praise Leipzig without losing sight of its shortcomings. For instance, Woolsey repeatedly disapproved of Dwight's intention to publish a book about his German travels, confiding to his sister in 1828: "He will not, I suspect see the defects and will not estimate high enough the excellencies of our system."[28] In April he added:

"Henry Dwight ... may have had many opportunities to ~~know~~ learn much about the subject, but I am afraid his vivid mind has not attended to facts and certainly he ought to have been himself in a university which I believe he was not."[29]

The appeal of a university, of course, depends on the well-being of the region. Ticknor was unaware of a larger context that explains Leipzig's old-fashioned appearance in his day. Founded in 1409, Leipzig did not witness any major reform attempts to turn it into a modern university until the early nineteenth century. The feat was not accomplished until 1830. This delay might also be explained with the impact of the Napoleonic Wars, particularly the Battle of Leipzig (now known as the Battle of Nations or *Völkerschlacht*) that ravaged greater Leipzig in 1813, and the 1815 Vienna Congress that considerably reduced Saxony's territory. Reforms had first halted with the defeat of 1806, the battle at fairly nearby Jena and Auerstädt, a sweeping victory for Napoleon. Saxony was forced into alliance with the French until the 1813 Battle of Leipzig. Not until 1818—two years after Ticknor's visit—was the talk of reform taken up again at the university.[30] Leipzig thus did not begin to become more modern and therefore more appealing to educational pilgrims from the United States until later in the nineteenth century when the effects of the battle were no longer immediately felt.

On 18 October 1813, Napoleon I experienced a major defeat in Leipzig that incidentally also devastated the region and thus its educational landscape. Early US visitors were not aware of the battle's direct and indirect educational backlashes, even though they showed a great interest in the battle itself. In 1815, Ticknor had enthusiastically participated in the commemoration festivity at Göttingen.[31] But a year later in Leipzig he realized that the victory had been achieved at the expense of Saxony and was therefore not celebrated there at all.[32] Dwight described Saxony's fate with (com-)passion. Outlining the power politics of nations, he fired away that "A slice of Saxony will enable [Prussia] to digest her dinner [the Rhine Provinces] much better." And even though Saxony "had truth on her side," she pleaded in vain, for "how feeble is the decision of justice, when contrary to that of power." Dwight charged passionately rather than as a neutral outside observer, "Although such conduct as this in miniature, in every part of the civilized world, receives the name of robbery, and is punished in Prussia with death, yet when thus performed by monarchs at wholesale, it is called the administration of justice by the Holy Alliance."[33] These outbursts lend credence to his cousin Woolsey's cautious remark concerning Dwight's vivid mind.

Saxony was unfortunate in her war alliances during the Napoleonic era and paid for them with a notable reduction of her territory. Having traveled from Göttingen through the formerly Saxon regions, Ticknor confided to his journal on 14 September 1816 that for Leipzig's population and the surrounding villages the aftermath of the battle was a burden.[34] He was ambiguous regarding the effects of the battle on opportunities at the university, though. While he imagined that economic hardships accompanying war and its aftermath might affect a region's education, he did not think it through to the end. He went as far as to observe that the university would feel the consequences of the conflict, but only indirectly in lower student numbers, as students in the formerly Saxon regions that had passed to Prussia would now go to the universities in Halle and Berlin. Moreover, "a population of a million cannot keep above 500 students at a time at the university, and Saxony is now reduced to 1,200,000."[35] As events only a few years later would show, Ticknor was mistaken in his bleak assessment of Leipzig's future.

On the Eve of Greatness: The Mid-nineteenth Century

Since the 1830s, things had quietly been changing for the better at Leipzig, which was reflected in construction activity, faculty recruitment practices that were more and more focused on advancing Leipzig's academic prestige thanks to a skilled minister of education who was inaugurated in the aftermath of the 1848 revolution, and also thanks to good fortune—later in the century, Leipzig was remote from battlefields and thus did not face physical destruction as it had in 1813. Besides the classics, chemistry now began to develop into an attractive discipline. Americans did not fail to take note of these developments, thanks to visitors and also a few students from the New World who, after 1850, started arriving as an increasingly steady stream.

For visitors from America, the University of Leipzig started looking more modern and thus more appealing by mid-century. Change was, however, apparent mainly for the insider. With regard to the university buildings, the young US chemist Evan Pugh observed in 1853 that "[t]hey present rather an antiquated appearance in some places on the outside, but I saw none of this in the inside."[36] For Yale-trained Mason C. Weld, in turn, the young look of Leipzig was even more obvious: "There is not much here that is very old and the city has not that very old look that many of the towns we have seen have."[37]

Indeed, new university buildings had been erected since the 1830s and 1840s, although this construction activity was still less considerable than that of the second half of the century.[38] Construction activity certified that scholarship was broadening as well as specializing. It was, in short, on the move. The *Augusteum*—the university's main building—was completed in 1836. In 1837, a zoological museum was instituted and in 1843/44 two chemical laboratories added. In 1846, the library moved from the *Augus-*

teum back to the old site to which two more stories had been added. The Saxon Academy of Sciences was founded in July 1846.

The 1840s also witnessed a number of illustrious US visitors in town; visitors seem to precede regular student waves. One of the visitors was Weld's father, who called on the school for the deaf. When US students began to turn to Leipzig starting in the early 1850s, a noteworthy number of chemists were among them, including Weld, Johnson, and Pugh. Weld and Johnson had both studied at Yale's new Sheffield Scientific School. They sailed from New York in May 1853. (A future Yale president, Noah Porter, and his wife were also aboard.[39]) At Leipzig, they studied under Otto Linné Erdmann.

The foundations of the twentieth-century perception of Leipzig's late-nineteenth-century fame in the natural sciences had been laid in the 1840s with substantial improvements in chemistry above all. The move may be interpreted as a realization that the demand for chemical knowledge was changing. In the early nineteenth century, chemistry had not yet attained the status of a well-defined science even though it aroused a growing interest among students.[40] The late-nineteenth-century Leipzig institute of physical chemistry developed from the chemical professorship that Erdmann held from 1827 until his death in 1869. Erdmann opened a chemical laboratory in 1843/44. Until 1864, he was professor of technical as opposed to organic chemistry, which, however, struck him as degrading. The name of his professorship was therefore changed to plain chemistry. Erdmann was succeeded in 1871 by Gustav Heinrich Wiedemann as a professor of "physical" chemistry rather than "general" or "technical" chemistry. In 1887, Wiedemann gave up physical chemistry for physics. Under Wiedemann's successor Wilhelm Ostwald, the idea of physical chemistry finally took off. Ostwald's US students would come to shape chemical teaching at Harvard, Cornell, Johns Hopkins, MIT, Berkeley, and CalTech, to name just a few.

For the state-directed German universities, the ministers of education/instruction or government representatives who were in a position to influence the educational landscape in the different German states are crucial. Already in the 1820s, Dwight had observed that the skill of Minister Gerlach Adolf von Münchhausen in founding of the University of Göttingen (official opening in 1737) had been the main reason for the promising development of that institution. In the late nineteenth century, Berlin had Friedrich Althoff to thank for its leading educational role.[41] Although developments in chemistry had begun to draw attention to Leipzig since midcentury and thus earlier than in other fields excepting classical philology, in the 1860s the teaching of chemistry also benefited from the scheme of the Saxon government to turn Leipzig into a first-rate university—Freiherr Johann Paul von Falkenstein had a new chemical laboratory built from 1866 to 1868. Von Falkenstein was Saxon minister of education between 1853 and 1871, a period that witnessed increasing interest in Leipzig on the part of US students.[42] He laid the foundation for Leipzig's heyday. His successor Carl Friedrich Wilhelm von Gerber, in turn, occupied the position from 1871 to 1891. Under his "benevolent neglect" the Saxon university began to miss out on the latest scientific developments already in the 1880s.[43]

When after the revolutionary turmoil of 1848 the Saxon minister von Falkenstein entered the scene in 1853, much recruiting and reorganization activity followed almost immediately. With the backing of King Johann of Saxony, Falkenstein set out to build up Leipzig as a rivaling institution to Berlin. Ability became more important than political or religious affiliations, a significant shift in priorities that would contribute to Leipzig's rise.[44] In 1854, Friedrich Zarncke was called as a professor of Germanics. An academic descendent of Leipzig's famed classicist Gottfried Hermann, Zarncke may be considered a link between Leipzig's tradition in the classics and its leading linguistic role since the 1870s also thanks to the Young Grammarians.

Leipzig, a decent second choice by midcentury, now dared calling controversial yet immaculate scholars to her ranks—a fortunate decision. The philologist Zarncke would be as vital to the university's rise as another of Falkenstein's political recruits a decade later: Carl Ludwig, who arrived in March 1865.[45] Ludwig had a radical past and had therefore little hope of being called to a Prussian university in spite of his renown as a physiologist. His activities during the 1848 turmoil stood in the way of professional promotion in Prussia. At Leipzig, he soon not only developed a reputation for his most advanced physiological laboratory but also began influencing recruitments in medicine and in the natural sciences.[46] Moreover, he greatly appealed to a number of US students in various key institutions in the New World during the 1870s. The history of US medicine cannot fully be understood without studying Ludwig's US disciples.[47]

The roots of the Leipzig Circle may be traced back to midcentury and a subsequent general reorientation of scientific thinking also in the context of Charles Darwin's groundbreaking 1859 *The Origin of Species*. New disciplines such as psychology and economy developed that focused on statistical analysis as well as on empirical and experimental rather than on speculative research. Both disciplines—that is, psychology and economy—originated in Leipzig. In the laboratories of Ernst Heinrich Weber and Gustav Theodor Fechner the foundations of experimental psychology, physiology, and pharmacology were cemented by midcentury, while Wilhelm Roscher's work did the same for economy.[48] The philosopher and mathematician Moritz Wilhelm Drobisch, a pioneer in statistics, mediated between the two disciplines. In 1846, Drobisch, Fechner, and Weber were founding members of the Saxon Academy of Sciences.[49]

As the nineteenth century progressed, Saxony's unfortunate military alliances continued with the effect that she became a part of the North German Confederation under Prussian auspices. By the 1860s, however, consequences for the University of Leipzig were not at all devastating. Its remote location with respect to battlefields in the wars of 1866 and 1870/71 added to the institution's attractiveness for US students. In addition to that, US students after the US Civil War began to travel to Europe in larger numbers than ever before, thus contributing to the enrollment explosion at German universities around 1870. With rapidly progressing sciences, Reconstruction at home, and the blessings of industrialization, US men of a greater variety of backgrounds as well as US women no longer were content with the higher education they received at home.

Leipzig's Sudden Heyday

Ironically, the sudden rise of the University of Leipzig around 1870 may at least partly be explained by warfare. During the Austro-Prussian War of 1866, Saxony had again been ally to the losing party. US observers and Leipzig professors (not the historians) described the more complicated political alliances and constellations[50] by simply stating that Saxony ended up becoming a part of Prussia—a defeat that set free resources and ambitions in Saxon's capitol Dresden to gain in the educational sector what had been lost in the battlefield. As James Morgan Hart put it in his 1874 guidebook for US students in Germany, "The Saxon government, relieved from the responsibilities of political action, seems to be devoting its energies and its resources to the promotion of more spiritual interests. The King and his Ministers have now little else to do than to take this indirect and laudable revenge upon Prussia."[51] Likewise, writing in the mid-1920s, Wilhelm Ostwald likened Saxony's educational revenge on Prussia in the 1870s to the Prussian defeat at the hands of Napoleon in 1806.[52] Back then, Prussians had set out to heal their wounded pride by creating in 1809/10 what would become the first modern German research university, today's Humboldt University in Berlin.[53]

US students quickly seized the new opportunities. G. Stanley Hall, who was to become Wilhelm Wundt's first US student in experimental psychology in 1879, ten years before had traveled to Germany a first time to study at Berlin. He was just beginning to ask for additional funding from his financial benefactor Henry Sage and his own family so that he might stay for a Berlin PhD degree when the Franco-German War ended such hopes. In 1878, Hall earned the first PhD degree in psychology ever awarded in the United States. His two Harvard advisers, Henry Pickering Bowditch and William James, had been acquainted with the work of Carl Ludwig and

Wilhelm Wundt since the late 1860s (James) or had studied in Leipzig under Ludwig around 1870 (Bowditch).[54] Hall himself traveled to Leipzig in 1879 to check out both Ludwig and Wundt (see also chapter 5).

The thirty-year-old Bowditch closely followed the Franco-German War while at Leipzig. The US Civil War had interrupted his higher education and had also strengthened his desire of going into research rather than practicing medicine. He had obtained Harvard degrees and subsequently gone to Paris. In the fall of 1869, Bowditch arrived in Leipzig to work with Ludwig.[55] While Bowditch chose Leipzig specifically because Ludwig had been recommended to him, the war of 1870/71 decided the duration of his stay there. In mid-February 1871, he considered moving to Berlin but was reluctant as a change of location always meant a loss of valuable study time when settling down in the new surroundings. More important, however, he learned that Emil DuBois-Raymond's assistant in Berlin was "with the army + things are decidedly out of joint in the laboratory in Berlin[,] at last accounts the whole stock of frogs were frozen together into a solid lump."[56] The war had directly influenced conditions at Berlin, whereas in Leipzig, "[t]here are only about four or five men working in the laboratory here so that one ~~sees~~ has the professor a good deal to oneself, which is of course a great advantage."[57]

But Bowditch was no all-absorbed scholar-scientist who only cared for research opportunities. A lengthy passage on the war itself immediately followed his thoughts about working conditions in Berlin. The letter was addressed to his friend William James, the future Harvard philosopher. Bowditch described the lack of enthusiasm for the war effort on the part of the locals, who struck him as being quite indifferent to propaganda.[58] In light of Saxony's unfortunate military alliance of 1866, the moderate excitement about the 1870/71 war on the part of Saxons makes sense. In a way, it wasn't a Saxon war, and battlefields were far away. For Bowditch, in turn, it brought back memories of the US Civil War: "Internal Commotions in Paris were no doubt calculated upon by the Germans very much in the same way that we at the North counted upon the revolt of the Slaves in the southern states during the war." Craving for "neutral" news reports from England, Bowditch felt a gloomy foreboding regarding future conflicts: "I cannot look upon a great centralized power capable of sending more than a million soldiers into the field in a few weeks time as a very good guarantee for the peace of Europe. There is no doubt that the Germans are getting their tails up in a very decided manner + when they have settled France I am afraid it will be, as the barber says, 'next Gentleman.'" Bowditch did not live to see the next major war, World War I—he died in 1911.

When in 1870, Thomas Day Seymour, a graduate of Western Reserve College in Ohio, traveled to Europe, rumors about the Franco-German War and general incertitude caused him to opt for the more remote Leipzig rather than Berlin. Once settled in Saxony, he realized that the faculty and library offered advantageous conditions for study. He soon reported to his class-mates at Western Reserve: "I have been able to carry out the plan which I made in general before leaving Hudson and of which you all know. The war of last year however lengthened my stay in England and Scotland, which I do not now much regret; and the excited state of feeling in England com-bined with ignorance of the real condition of Germany brought me the latter part of October 1870 to Leipzig and not to Berlin as I had expected."[59] A fu-ture Greek scholar at his alma mater Western Reserve, then at Yale, Seymour spread the news of the emerging academic Mecca: Leipzig.

In a letter to his stepmother in September 1876, William Henry Welch outlined the advantages that Leipzig offered as compared to Strasburg or medical schools in the United States.[60] "In Strassburg I was on the frontier but now I am in the very heart of Germany,"[61] he rejoiced. He moved on to explaining that, "The university of Leipzig is the oldest and largest in Ger-many, having been found in 1409 and now numbering 3000 students. In re-spect of its buildings and laboratories the university is splendidly equipped." While not all facts were correct (Heidelberg is the oldest German university), Leipzig indeed offered both modern laboratories as well as an excellent fac-ulty. Welch took note of that especially with regard to the medical school, whereby he observed that at Leipzig, "body and soul"—that is, buildings as well as professors—were of equally high quality. "There is one part of the city called the medical quarter. Here beside the extensive hospital built on the modern pavilion principle, are large separate buildings for pathological anatomy, normal anatomy, physiology, chemistry etc.[,] subjects[,] many of which with us do not even possess separate rooms in our medical colleges. Strassburg illustrates what a university can accomplish with poor buildings but with good professors, Leipzig seems to combine both soul and body, in its good buildings as well as good professors." Reading such enthusias-tic accounts, one of course always has to keep in mind that, especially in their correspondence with parents, US students felt compelled to explain their choices in German academia in order to assure their elders that neither money nor time were being wasted during the European venture.

By the 1870s, Leipzig no longer struck US visitors as antiquated or as merely subtly modern. Leipzig was now perceived as reflecting the latest sci-entific splendor worthy of being called a true Mecca of learning (or possibly a modern Athens, as early-nineteenth-century US visitors might have done). Welch soon reported to his father William Wickham Welch his expectations as regarded his sojourn in Leipzig: "My aim is to avail myself particularly of such opportunities as can not be replaced by reading books or by the facilities in America; and of such opportunities the most preeminent here are the various practical laboratory courses for which there is no parallel with us."[62] Welch senior was a traditionally trained doctor, that is, one with hardly a scientific foundation. The younger Welch therefore explained the significance of scientific medical training: "It is just as important to know physiology and pathology practically as it is anatomy (by dissections). While therefore I can go over a much less varied range of subjects than attending lectures, I am convinced that I derive far greater profit from confining myself mostly to the laboratories, and taking lectures only when they do not interfere with the former." Welch announced resolutely, "My plan is to spend the mornings with Prof. [Ernst Leberecht] Wagner in pathology and the afternoons with Prof. Ludwig in physiology."

At Wagner's laboratory in Leipzig, Welch met another medical student from the United States, Walter Stallo: "I did not know anyone when I came here and have become acquainted with only one American, a son of Judge Stallo of Cincinnati, with whom I work in the laboratory. But I do not see very much of him and altogether it is rather lonely."[63] Another reference to Stallo further stressed the fact that in spite of a large American colony in town, Welch focused his attention on laboratory work: "There are a good many Americans here but the only acquaintance is Dr. Stallo, son of Judge Stallo of Cincinnati. He is a very pleasant companion in the laboratory."[64] It is not clear what exactly became of W. Stallo. Quite possibly, he practiced medicine.

In Leipzig, Welch also met an old acquaintance from his student days at Yale, which provided him with another opportunity to point out Leipzig's superiority in medical training, "I took a walk with a young man from Tennessee who was in Yale when I was there and has just taken his medical degree here having had his entire medical education here. He has been obliged to study four years and I could not help comparing the thoroughness and extent of his medical knowledge with that of an American graduate."[65] From the description, the Yale acquaintance might have been Fred Coolidge Tallert, who had enrolled at Leipzig on 22 October 1872 to study medicine. Welch returned to the United States in March 1878 after an additional semester in Breslau (Wrocław) and began teaching laboratory courses in New York. In 1884, he was called to Johns Hopkins University to assist in building up its medical school, which opened in the early 1890s.[66]

US students and visitors in the first half of the nineteenth century had professed only cursory interest in Leipzig learning that centered on the Greek scholar Hermann. By 1886, however, the Leipzig professor of Sanskrit and Celtic languages Ernst Windisch realized that while every country had a philological tradition, in late-nineteenth-century Germany new impulses concerning general linguistic theory could be acquired.[67] Starting in the 1860s, the classics had paved the way for innovative linguistics and discussions of grammar in light of Darwin's evolutionary ideas, that is, of language as governed by natural laws. Not one but many philologists now gathered in Leipzig to develop the idea of scientific linguistics. In spite of some skepticism, for many years the Young Grammarians and their followers made Leipzig "the world center of linguistics."[68]

Since the 1870s, comparative philology had attracted students to Leipzig. Sanskrit, Celtic, Old English, Old German, as well as Arabic, Semitic, and Slavic languages all formed part of their curriculum. Furthermore, Greek history, ethnology, archaeology, mathematics, and even music were related fields that linked philology with history, art history, and theology. The most ambitious US students took advantage of the opportunity to benefit from numerous authorities across academic borderlines. On 4 July 1876, Charles Rockwell Lanman, a future Harvard professor of Sanskrit, preferred the gathering of Leipzig scholars to celebrating the US holiday with fellow countrymen, not for a lack of patriotism but to make the most of academic opportunities during his stay in Germany. He joined the pleasant meeting of Leipzig professors and students at the house of the Greek scholar Georg Curtius. Most of them were more or less closely associated with the Young Grammarians. Lanman met "Prof. [August] Leskien, Dr. [Heinrich] Hübschmann, [Hermann] Osthoff, [Adolf] Harnack, [Rudolf] Schoell, [Richard] Wülcker, [Karl] Brugmann & [A.] Funck. The evening was a most agreeable one."[69]

An important figure who would contribute to Leipzig's rise, Curtius left an imprint on philology both in Germany and in the United States that has not yet been examined more thoroughly even though he attracted numerous US students. Curtius was called from Kiel in 1861. His student August Leskien followed him to Leipzig and eventually came to occupy the new chair in Slavonic languages there. Another of Curtius's disciples was Ernst Windisch, who had arrived at the Saxon university as a student in 1863. He returned there in 1877 for the remainder of his career. Windisch and Leskien were close in their professional views. Almost the entire inner circle of the Young Grammarians had heard lectures by Zarncke and Leskien. One of them, Leskien's friend Karl Brugmann, became a central figure of the Young Grammarians himself in the mid-1870s. When Curtius died in 1885, Brugmann succeeded to his chair in the following year. Brugmann was himself succeeded in 1920 by Wilhelm Streitberg, Leskien's son-in-law. Leskien, Windisch, and Brugmann became the three directors of Leipzig's Indo-Germanic Institute—Leskien stood for Slavic and Lithuanian linguistics, Windisch for Sanskrit and Celtic, and Brugmann for Greek and Italic. Another Leipzig breed who was close in his linguistic views, and who would be mentor to several US students, was Eduard Sievers. Sievers had earned his Leipzig PhD degree in 1870. He returned as a professor in 1892. Like Leskien, Sievers approached linguistics innovatively through physiology.[70]

The idea that all branches of knowledge—chemistry just like physics, linguistics, psychology, and history—functioned on the basis of natural laws was also central to the Leipzig Circle. In trying to connect seemingly different disciplines, Leipzig's scholar-scientists antagonized those in Berlin, as they attempted to create methodological bridges between natural and cultural sciences that those in Berlin sought to dismantle.[71] The question remains why the Leipzig approach was eventually considered a failure, why ever-greater specialization and seemingly clearly defined borderlines between disciplines became a major feature of twentieth-century academia. I would argue that it may be explained with a prevailing general tendency back then to specialize into clearly distinct groups, which was also in tune with the fact that Western nations in the age of social Darwinism and survival of the fittest embraced the ideas of nationalism and cultural superiority, which also implied clear borderlines between different groups. The idea would merit a separate study.

Members of the Circle influenced Leipzig's recruitment policy, arranging for their favorite successors to be called, usually a disciple.[72] They were pioneers in their respective fields. In 1869, Ludwig opened a new physiological laboratory that at the time was acknowledged to be the best available in Germany. Ten years later, Wundt opened the first laboratory of experimental psychology. After Ostwald's arrival at Leipzig in 1887, he set up a laboratory of physical chemistry in astonishingly short time. He moved into a new building that allowed him to accommodate more students in early 1898. During the 1870s, Friedrich Ratzel had traveled across North America and was recognized as an authority on American geography even in the United States. Karl Lamprecht developed a cultural and economic (as compared to a political) historiography that corresponded to similar developments in the United States.[73] Wundt, professor of philosophy with a background in medicine and physiology, represents a close link between natural and cultural sciences. In his *Völkerpsychologie* (Social Psychology), he described languages, myths, and customs as products of psychic processes, especially imagination. Ratzel, in turn, established a theory of environmental determination. Tuning in with social Darwinism, he interpreted similar elements in different cultures as proof of migration.[74]

The Leipzig Circle did not come out of nowhere. It needs to be viewed as a part of the Leipzig tradition of the creation of knowledge, a tradition that ever since midcentury had begun attracting students from the "other" side of the Atlantic. The Young Grammarians may also be linked to the Leipzig Circle. After all, Wundt had been called to Leipzig a philosopher rather than an experimental psychologist. He was interested in much more than experimental psychology. After his arrival at Leipzig in 1875, Wundt's first major lecture discussed the psychology of language, with which he joined the debate about phonetic laws.[75] Moreover, Wundt would serve as one of two co-directors (*Mitdirektor*) of the mathematical institute. Mathematics just like psychology was a branch of philosophy about to establish itself as an independent academic discipline—without losing touch with other disciplines. The Leipzig mathematician, philosopher, and psychologist Drobisch already in 1868 had decided to give up his mathematical commitments to concentrate solely on philosophical questions.[76] Despite all that, especially available publications on Wundt's US student focus on his contributions to the individual discipline of psychology without constructing the complexity of his scientific thought that cannot be so easily attributed to one specific field of academic inquiry.

Between 1866 and 1914, US students said surprisingly little about German professors in their letters, journals, and diaries. Their appreciation of a Leipzig professor was expressed in signing up for his classes. If they did mention a professor in letters, the comments usually referred to philologists and their immediate interdisciplinary collaborators. They clearly maintained a critical distance. In 1900, Lane Cooper, a future professor of comparative literature at Cornell, studied under Wülker (Anglicist) and Sievers (Germanist); he was also closely associated with the geographer Ratzel, of whom he was particularly fond.[77] By contrast, the historian Andrew C. McLaughlin was not quite enthused about Ratzel in early 1894, "Heard to day Ratzel— … spoke not like a Saxon but distinctly; evidently a man of self poise and intellect. I had difficulty in reading his face which was very immobile.... He looks to me a man without a very sympathetic nature + consequently perhaps some of the characteristics of his book on America."[78] Lamprecht, in turn, struck McLaughlin as a curiosity: "He begins to speak before he is fairly on the platform + keeps steadily at work for 45 minutes making but little use of notes. Speaking … at least twice as much in an hour as a professor at home."[79] Two months later, he could "understand 2/3 by careful listening."[80]

Attending a course by one of the famed professors did not necessarily provide scholarly excitement. Thomas D. Seymour remarked in November 1870: "Attended the Philological Seminar this morning. Dreadfully dull. Two hours of latin."[81] Lanman simply stated that in "the evening I went to Curtius' grammatical society of which I am a member."[82] Curtius himself left a better impression on him: "Called on Prof. Curtius this afternoon. He spoke German + after the first few minutes I spoke English. He was very freundlich [friendly]." Lanman thought that "Curtius is a *splendid lecturer*";[83] and he was making progress, too: "On Monday evening last, at the grammatical society of Curtius, I spoke and *took part* in the *Discussion* for the first time."[84] He was delighted when the professor referred back to one of his remarks. Then again, "Leskien lectures fast, and his subject is sometimes hard; but I like him."[85]

Leipzig's Decline since the Late 1890s

Where do you go once you have reached the top? Overly self-confident in her ability and strength, Germany waged war in 1914 and lost. In the end, US professors, who in their youth had flocked to German universities to prepare for distinguished academic careers, turned into benefactors to keep those same universities going after war and devastation. But, of course, the story is more complicated than that. While the war of 1870/71 can be seen as a crucial starting point, a belated birth of a German nation, the following decades until the turn of the century witnessed a change in Germany away from a liberal and toward a conservative nationalism.[86] Konrad Jarausch examined this phenomenon specifically concerning the changing atmosphere at German universities in the late nineteenth century.[87] No Jew was likely to be appointed a professor in Germany after 1880.[88] Nationalist sentiments eventually culminated in war, which also sobered up US enthusiasm for German education.

That after 1900 two US Americans taught English at Leipzig may be interpreted as a concern on the part of Saxon authorities and academics to provide high-level language education in the now firmly established English department. Both Americans had previously studied at the Saxon university. They were James Jacob Davies, who first registered in October 1902 and again in 1904, as well as Lehre Dantzler, who matriculated in the fall of 1904, 1908, and 1911. Davies was originally from Great Britain but had moved to the United States before traveling to Leipzig. He studied with Wülker and Sievers. Dantzler had studied at Vanderbilt University during Leipzig-trained James H. Kirkland's administration. He would teach English at the University of Kentucky from 1911 until at least 1941. At Leipzig, he offered a course in English drama in the fall of 1909. One of his students was William Carlos Williams, then an unhappy medical student with a pronounced inclination to write.[89]

A few Leipzig Americans undertook to write their memoirs between 1920 and 1950, that is, after World War I and in some cases during or after World War II. Such documents reveal that reminiscences of Leipzig student days were affected by world politics, by nationalism on both sides of the Atlantic, and by the changing appeal of US and German higher education. The two World Wars entailed bitterness, disbelief, grief, and nostalgia on the part of former US students in Germany.[90] Arthur B. Lamb was a Harvard PhD student when he studied with Ostwald at Leipzig in 1904/05. When the United States entered World War I, he was called from his chemical professorship at Harvard to head a research branch of 150 chemists that had been created by the War Department in Washington, DC. Their task was to work on "defense methods against the increasing number and deadliness of poisonous gases."[91] Ironically, in fighting the Germans, Lamb could well have made use of knowledge acquired in Germany.

This does not mean, however, that Leipzig Americans uniformly supported the US war effort. Some Leipzig alumni never actually faltered in their belief in German high culture. With the outbreak of World War I, Harry Clary Jones, a chemist at Johns Hopkins University, turned into a staunch supporter of the German cause: "I believe that that country," he wrote to Ostwald in early November 1914, "which has done more than *all* others to advance knowledge and culture, will in the end triumph."[92] He had kept up their correspondence ever since his Leipzig student days in 1892. In his one-dimensional appreciation of Germany's intellectual achievements, he saw more US support for her cause than was out there. In his final letter to Ostwald dated 21 October 1915, he rejoiced, "It looks now impossible for the English ever to get through into Constantinople [Istanbul], and this seems to be a crucial point. I hope that the war may end not later than in the spring. If so, we shall give ourselves the pleasure of seeing you next summer."[93] It was not to be. On 9 April 1916, Jones committed suicide, most likely because of professional failure.[94]

After the war, Leipzig alumni in the US set in motion networks to help the Saxon university recover, returning material revenue for former intellectual benefits. In January 1922, Bayard Quincy Morgan of the University of Wisconsin circulated a letter of gratitude that he had received from Leipzig's Eduard Sievers.[95] Morgan had registered at Leipzig in the fall of 1904 and again in 1906. He studied under Sievers, Wülker, and Wundt. By 1922, he was part of a network of Sievers's US students who honored their German professor with a gift that enabled him to publish his latest scholarly undertaking as printing costs were skyrocketing in Germany.[96] Lane Cooper was one of those who donated money for the cause. He also kept in touch with other Leipzig professors and their relatives. As late as in January 1950, Cooper received a letter from Wülker's son, who was then located in Hanover, West Germany, describing a visit to the Leipzig of the early Cold War.[97] Three years before, Wülker's daughter Grete had thanked Cooper for care parcels.[98]

There are more such examples illustrating to what extent the tides had turned since the—for Leipzig—glorious final decades of the nineteenth century: now making the university a recipient of US charity rather than training the New World's brightest minds. In November 1922, a letter was dispatched to Leipzig-trained William Henry Welch at Johns Hopkins. It was written at the Biblical Literature Department of Mount Holyoke College, as a contact person Leipzig-trained Mary I. Hussey was named. It was yet another circular to US Leipzig alumni, both men and women. Signed by Vernon Kellogg of the National Research Council, Alice Hamilton of Harvard,

G. Stanley Hall of Clark, and once again B. Q. Morgan of Wisconsin, the circular asked US citizens "who studied in the University of Leipzig" and who "are presumably still interested in its welfare and in the present generation of students" to support Leipzig; "If you cannot send a large sum, can you not send something."[99]

Summary

Depending on which period a student from the New World registered at Leipzig, they encountered a university that could appear as an especially good or especially bad example of an innovative German institution of higher learning. In the late eighteenth and early nineteenth centuries, a few young man viewed Leipzig as antiquated and complacent, boasting what struck them as a backwardly oriented research focus on ancient cultures. Most, though not all, of the early visitors preferred exploring the new subjects that represented innovative developments of the contemporary curriculum. By midcentury, however, Leipzig had begun to change at least in the eyes of those who cared to take a closer look. The mid-nineteenth-century pioneers actually came from Yale rather than Harvard, which is why it may be suspected that Yale connections—as personified by the Leipzig-trained classicist Woolsey, then president of Yale—might have encouraged students to opt for Leipzig. Yale graduates were obviously not discouraged from giving Leipzig a chance.

In the second half of the nineteenth century, innovation became plainly visible at Leipzig in the form of an appealing faculty that also communicated across disciplinary boundaries, a fact that is evident from the existence of professorial circles, many of whose members had quite a number of US disciples. The larger scientific and scholarly tendencies at the close of the nineteenth and in the course of the twentieth century led, however, to ever-increasing specialization, which was accompanied by ever more clearly cut borderlines between individual disciplines. With hindsight, the Leipzig model of the late nineteenth century was thus interpreted a failure as it did not reflect the mainstream of the twentieth century. It nonetheless did represent an academic current that intrigued many US students and that is beginning to interest scholars and scientists of the early twenty-first century.

The tendency to establish borders was a dominant trend of the late nineteenth century, reflected also in increasing nationalisms in the Western world that eventually led the Germans in a feeling of cultural superiority to wage war. In the end, the University of Leipzig experienced considerable setbacks because of World War I. American Leipzig alumni now paid back their intellectual depth by collecting money to ensure that Leipzig students and faculty could continue on their quest for knowledge. The American alumni's attachment to Leipzig had grown from fond memories of Saxon student days and more or less close mentor-disciple relationships with German professors. I will look more closely into this issue in the following chapter.

Notes

1. Roger Chickering, "Das Leipziger 'Positivisten-Kränzchen' um die Jahrhundertwende," *Kultur und Kulturwissenschaften um 1900 II Idealismus und Positivismus*, ed. Gangolf Hübinger, Rüdiger vom Bruch, and Friedrich Wilhelm Graf (Stuttgart: Franz Steiner Verlag, 1997), 228, 235–36.

2. Elfriede Üner, *Kultur- und Universalgeschichte an der Schwelle der Zeiten. Exemplarische Entwicklungslinien der Leipziger Schule in den deutschen Sozial- und Geschichtswissenschaften* (Leipzig: Karl-Lamprecht-Gesellschaft e.V., 1993), 8–9, 31n13.

3. Theodor Frings, "Eduard Sievers," *Berichte über die Verhandlungen der Sächsischen Akademie der Wissenschaften zu Leipzig. Philologisch-historische Klasse* 85, no. 1 (1933): 28, reprinted in Thomas A. Sebeok, *Portraits of Linguists. A Biographical Source for the History of Western Linguistics, 1746–1963. Vol. 2. From Eduard Sievers to Benjamin Lee Whorf* (Bristol: Thoemmes Press, 2002 [1966]), 1–52. Eveline Einhauser, *Die Junggrammatiker. Ein Problem für die Sprachwissenschaftsgeschichtsschreibung* (Trier: WTV, 1989), 43; Rudolf Růžička, "Historie und Historizität der Junggrammatiker," *Sitzungsberichte der Sächsischen Akademie der Wissenschaften zu Leipzig* 119, no. 3 (Berlin: Akademie Verlag, 1977), 4, 5, 20.

4. Erwin Bünning, *Wilhelm Pfeffer. Apotheker, Chemiker, Botaniker, Physiologe 1845–1920*, Reihe Große Naturforscher Band 37 (Stuttgart: Wissenschaftliche Verlagsgesellschaft mbH, 1975) and "Die Schüler Wilhelm Pfeffers und ihre in den botanischen Instituten zu Tübingen und Leipzig unter seiner Leitung ausgeführten oder auf seine Anregung begonnenen Arbeiten," *Jahrbücher für wissenschaftliche Botanik* 56 (1915): 805–32; Roger Chickering, *Karl Lamprecht: A German Academic Life (1856–1915)* (Atlantic Highlands, NJ: Humanities Press, 1993), 227, 235, 244–45, 295; Luise Schorn-Schütte, *Karl Lamprecht. Kulturgeschichtsschreibung zwischen Wissenschaft und Politik* (Göttingen: Vandenhoek & Ruprecht, 1984), 75, 78–90; Günther Buttmann: *Friedrich Ratzel. Das Leben und Werk eines deutschen Geographen*, Große Naturforscher Band 40 (Stuttgart: Wissenschaftl. Verlagsgesellschaft MBH, 1977), 74, 80; Wilhelm Ostwald, *Lebenslinien. Eine Selbstbiographie*, vol. 2 (Berlin: Klasing & Co., 1926–27), 80–110; Erik Koenen, "Verzeichnis der Hochschulschriften," in *Karl Bücher. Leipziger Hochschulschriften 1892–1926*, ed. Erik Koenen and Michael Meyen (Leipzig: Universitätsverlag, 2002), 51; Beate Wagner-Hasel, *Die Arbeit des Gelehrten: Der Nationalökonom Karl Bücher (1847–1930)* (Frankfurt am Main: Campus, 2011); G. Stanley Hall, *Life and Confessions of a Psychologist* (New York/London: D. Appleton and Company, 1924), 205–06; Konrad Krause, *Alma Mater Lipsiensis. Geschichte der Universität Leipzig von 1409 bis zur Gegenwart* (Leipzig: Universitätsverlag, 2003), 188–89.

5. Ostwald, *Lebenslinien*, vol. 2, 80–82, 101, 91–94, 98–100, 101–2. Schorn-Schütte, *Karl Lamprecht*, 99.

6. Krause, *Alma Mater*, 189. Wilhelm His [Jr.], *Wilhelm His der Anatom. Ein Lebensbild von Wilhelm His* (Berlin/Wien: Urban und Schwarzenberg, 1931).

7. Anna Ticknor, George Ticknor, Thomas Adam, and Gisela Mettele, *Two Boston Brahmins in Goethe's Germany: The Travel Journals of Anna and George Ticknor* (Lanham, MD: Lexington Books, 2009).

8. Other scholarly inclined North Americans had visited Leipzig since ca. 1800. Anja Bekker, "Amerikanistik [American Studies]," in *Geschichte der Universität Leipzig. Band IV: Fakultäten, Institute, Zentrale Einrichtungen (1. Halbband)* [History of the University of Leipzig. Volume IV: Departments, Institutes, Centers (Part 1)], ed. Ulrich von Hehl, Uwe John, and Manfred Rudersdorf (Leipzig: Universitätsverlag, 2009), 12–31. An earlier English version is available at http://americanstudies.uni-leipzig.de/the_leipzig_model/institute_for_american_studies/.

9. Journal, G. Ticknor, 13 September 1816. George and Anna Ticknor, Travel Journals, microfilm W 3275, reel I, vol. I, HUL Lamont.

10. Journal, G. Ticknor, 12 September 1816, ibid.

11. Henry E. Dwight, *Travels in the North of Germany, in the Years 1825 and 1826* (New York: G. & C. & H. Carvill, 1829), 81, 335–36.

12. Günter Mühlpfordt, "Die 'Sächsischen Universitäten' Leipzig, Jena, Halle und Wittenberg als Vorhut der deutschen Aufklärung," in *Wissenschafts- und Universitätsgeschichte in Sachsen im 18. und 19. Jahrhundert*, ed. Karl Czok (Berlin: Akademie-Verlag, 1987), 25; Erich Brandenburg, "Die Universität Leipzig im ersten halben Jahrtausend ihres Bestehens," in *Die Universität Leipzig 1409–1909. Gedenkblätter zum 30. Juli 1909* (Leipzig: Günther, Kirstein & Wendler, 1909), 10.

13. J. Foulke to B. Franklin, [12 ?] October 1781. Franklin Papers, BF85, vol. 103, folio 106, Hays Calendar IV, 62, APS. Thomas Neville Bonner, *American Doctors in German Universities. A Chapter in International Intellectual Relations* (Lincoln: University of Nebraska Press, 1963), 16–17. My emphasis.

14. Eberhard Brüning, "Die Universität Leipzig im 19. Jahrhundert aus amerikanischer Sicht," in *Jahrbuch für Regionalgeschichte und Landeskunde 20, 1995–96* (Stuttgart: Verlag der Sächsischen Akademie der Wissenschaften zu Leipzig in Kommission bei Franz Steiner Verlag, 1996), 108–11.

15. Conrad Bursian, *Geschichte der classischen Philologie in Deutschland von den Anfängen bis zur Gegenwart* (München and Leipzig: Oldenbourg, 1883), 665–67, 812, 840. As to Ribbeck, see Emma Ribbeck, ed., *Otto Ribbeck. Ein Bild seines Lebens aus seinen Briefen 1846–1898* (Stuttgart: Cotta'sche Buchhandlung Nachfolger, 1901). Various Leipzig Americans later in the nineteenth century were involved in the American School of Classical Studies at Athens, Greece. See Louis E. Lord, *A History of the American School of Classical Studies at Athens: 1882–1942* (Cambridge, MA: Harvard University Press, 1947); Anja Becker, "For the Sake of Old Leipzig Days … Academic Networks of American Students at a German University, 1781–1914" (PhD dissertation, University of Leipzig, 2006). Also, John Edwin Sandys, *A History of Classical Scholarship. The Eighteenth Century in Germany, and the Nineteenth Century in Europe and the United States of America*, vol. 3 (Cambridge: Cambridge University Press, 1908).

16. Dwight, *Travels in the North of Germany*, 268.

17. Philip Schaff, *Germany; Its Universities, Theology, and Religion* (Philadelphia: Lindsay and Blakiston/New York: Sheldon, Blakeman & Co., 1857), 79. Following quote ibid.

18. Ticknor mentioned Hermann in his journal on 15, 17, and 18 September and 16 October 1916. Ticknor Travel Journals, microfilm W3275, reel 1, vol. III, HUL Lamont. Following quote ibid.

19. Parker to Dr. Francis, 12 June 1844. Reprinted in John Weiss, *Life and Correspondence of Theodore Parker*, vol. 1 (New York: D. Appelton & Company, 1864), 241.

20. Dwight, *Travels in the North of Germany*, 337.
21. T. D. Woolsey to Mother, 17 December 1827 and to Sister, 3–5 January 1827. Woolsey Family Papers, Group 562 Series I Box 3 Folder 39, YUL.
22. T. D. Woolsey to Laura Johnson (Sister), 3–5 January 1828. Woolsey Family Papers, Group 562, Series I, Box 3, Folder 40, YUL.
23. Journal, G. Ticknor, 18 September 1816. Ticknor Travel Journals, microfilm W 3275, reel 2, vol. 2, HUL Lamont. In his *Travels in the North of Germany*, 332, Dwight agreed that in the German countries the "love of novelty exists."
24. Journal, Ticknor, 18 September 1816. Ticknor Travel Journals, microfilm W3275, reel 2, vol. 2, HUL Lamont.
25. Journal, A. Ticknor, 14 May 1836, ibid., reel 4, vol. 3. Hugh Swinton Legaré, *The Writings of Hugh Swinton Legaré ... Prefaced by a Memoir of his Life ... Edited by his Sister*, vol. 1 (Charleston, SC: Burges & James, 1846), xlvi, 139. See also Ticknor et al, *Two Boston Brahmins in Goethe's Germany*.
26. Glenn C. Altschuler, *Andrew D. White—Educator, Historian, Diplomat* (Ithaca, NY: Cornell University Press, 1979); Fabian Franklin, *The Life of Daniel Coit Gilman* (New York: Dodd, Mead and Co., 1910).
27. T. D. Woolsey to Sarah D. Woolsey, 21 April 1828, ibid., Folder 42.
28. T. D. Woolsey to Sarah D. Woolsey, 31 January 1827 [1828!], ibid.
29. T. D. Woolsey to Sarah D. Woolsey, 21 April 1828, ibid.
30. Hartmut Zwahr, "Von der zweiten Universitätsreform bis zur Reichsgründung, 1830 bis 1870," in *Alma Mater Lipsiensis. Geschichte der Karl-Marx-Universität Leipzig*, ed. Lothar Rathmann (Leipzig: Edition Leipzig, 1984), 141, 142; Marita Baumgarten, *Professoren und Universitäten im 19. Jahrhundert* (Göttingen: Vandenhoek & Ruprecht, 1997), 215; Werner Fläschendräger, "Die Universität vom Ausgang des 18. Jahrhunderts bis zur Universitätsreform von 1830," in *Alma Mater Lipsiensis*, ed. Rathmann, 126–27; Karlheinz Blaschke, "Die Universität Leipzig im Wandel vom Ancien Régime zum bürgerlichen Staat," in *Wissenschafts- und Universitätsgeschichte in Sachsen im 18. und 19. Jahrhundert*, ed. Karl Czok (Berlin: Akademie-Verlag, 1987), 136–37.
31. Journal, Ticknor, 18 October 1815. Ticknor Travel Journals, microfilm W3275, reel 1, vol. 1, HUL Lamont.
32. Journal, Ticknor, 18 October 1816, "Injustice to Saxony," ibid., vol. 3.
33. Dwight, *Travels in the North of Germany*, 341–43.
34. Journal, G. Ticknor, 14 September 1816. Ticknor Travel Journals, microfilm W3275, reel 1, vol. 2, HUL Lamont.
35. Journal, G. Ticknor, 18 September 1816, ibid., vol. 2.
36. Pugh to Editor, 31 October 1853. C. A. Browne, "European Laboratory Experiences of an Early American Agricultural Chemist—Dr. Evan Pugh (1828–1864)," *Journal of Chemical Education* 7, no. 3 (March 1930): 500.
37. M. C. Weld, 22 June 1853 [Mason's III Eur, fragment]. L. Weld Family Papers, Group 559, Box 1, Folder 2, YUL.
38. Rektor and Senat of Leipzig University, eds., *Festschrift zur Feier des 500 Jährigen Bestehens der Universität Leipzig*, vol. 4, part 2 (Leipzig: Verlag von S. Hirzel, 1909), 71, 159; Baumgarten, *Professoren und Universitäten*, 216; Elisabeth Lea und Gerald Wiemers, "Eine Sächsische Gesellschaft der Wissenschaften 'zum Flor und Ruhme unserer Universität,'" in *Wissenschafts- und Universitätsgeschichte in Sachsen im 18. und 19. Jahrhundert*, ed. Karl Czok (Berlin: Akademie-Verlag, 1987), 185–206.
39. M. C. Weld to Parents, 9 May 1853. L. Weld Family Papers, Group 559, Box 1, Folder 2, YUL. Elizabeth A. Osborne, ed., From the Letter-Files of S. W. Johnson (New Haven, CT: Yale University Press, 1913), 39.

40. John W. Servos, *Physical Chemistry from Ostwald to Pauling: The Making of a Science in America* (Princeton, NJ: Princeton University Press, 1990), 8.

41. Dwight, *Travels in the North of Germany*, 58, 77–78; Ralph-Jürgen Lischke, *Friedrich Althoff und sein Beitrag zur Entwicklung des Berliner Wissenschaftssystems an der Wende vom 19. zum 20. Jahrhundert* (Berlin: ERS Verlag, 1991); Bernhard von Brocke, *Wissenschaftsgeschichte und Wissenschaftspolitik im Industriezeitalter: das "System Althoff" in historischer Perspektive* (Hildesheim: Lax, 1991); Baumgarten, *Professoren und Universitäten*, 187; Konrad H. Jarausch, *Students, Society, and Politics in Imperial Germany: The Rise of Academic Illiberalism* (Princeton, NJ: Princeton University Press, 1982).

42. Rektor and Senate, *Festschrift*, vol. 4, part 2, 3–5, 70–72, 85–88; Krause, *Alma Mater Lipsiensis*, 101–2, 118–19, 136–37, 142, 152, 172–75.

43. Wolfgang Tischner, "Das Universitätsjubiläum 1909 zwischen universitärer Selbstvergewisserung und monarchischer Legitimitätsstiftung," *Sachsens Landesuniversität in Monarchie, Republik und Diktatur. Beiträge zur Geschichte der Universität Leipzig vom Kaiserreich bis zur Auflösung des Landes Sachsen 1952*, ed. Ulrich Von Hehl, Beiträge zur Leipziger Universitäts- und Wissenschaftsgeschichte (BLUWiG) A 3, (Leipzig: Evangelische Verlagsanstalt GmbH, 2005), 96; Krause, *Alma Mater Lipsiensis*, 136–37, 152, 169, 204.

44. Baumgarten, *Professoren und Universitäten*, 121.

45. Eduard Sievers, "Zarncke," *Allgemeine Deutsche Biographie*, vol. 44 (Leipzig: Verlag von Duncker & Humblot, 1898), 701, 702, 705; Heinz Schröer, *Carl Ludwig. Begründer der messenden Experimentalphysiologie* (Stuttgart: Wissenschaftliche Verlagsgesellschaft M.B.H., 1967), 71–72; W. Bruce Fye, "Carl Ludwig and the Leipzig Physiological Institute: 'a factory of new knowledge,'" *Circulation* 74, no. 5 (November 1986): 920–28.

46. Schröer, *Carl Ludwig*, 45, 48, 61–62, 72, 74–75. Ostwald, *Lebenslinien*, vol. 2, 83–4.

47. W. Bruce Fye, *The Development of American Physiology: Scientific Medicine in the Nineteenth Century* (Baltimore: Johns Hopkins University Press, 1987).

48. Chickering, "Das Leipziger 'Positivisten-Kränzchen,'" 227–28; W. Eisenberg et al., eds, *Ernst Heinrich Weber*, Heft 6 der Reiher Synergie Syntropie Nichtlineare Systeme (Leipzig: Verlag im Wissenschaftszentrum, 2000); Marcel H. Bickel, *Die Entwicklung zur experimentellen Pharmakologie 1790–1850. Wegbereiter von Rudolf Buchheim* (Basel: Schwabe & Co. AG Verlag, 2000), 94–96; Peter Koslowski, ed., *The Theory of Ethical Economy in the Historical School. Wilhelm Roscher, Lorenz von Stein, Gustav Schmoller, Wilhelm Dilthey and Contemporary Theory* (Berlin: Springer-Verlag, 1995).

49. Walther Neubert-Drobisch, *Moritz Wilhelm Drobisch. Ein Gelehrtenleben* (Leipzig: Dieterich'sche Verlagsbuchhandlung Theodor Weicher, 1902); Gerald Wiemers, "Ernst Heinrich Weber und die Königlich Sächsische Gesellschaft der Wissenschaften zu Leipzig," in *Ernst Heinrich Weber*, Heft 6 der Reiher Synergie Syntropie Nichtlineare Systeme, ed. W. Eisenberg et al. (Leipzig: Verlag im Wissenschaftszentrum, 2000), 31–40.

50. See James N. Retallack, *Saxony in German History: Culture, Society, and Politics, 1830–1933* (Ann Arbor: University of Michigan Press, 2000); Karl Czok, ed., *Geschichte Sachsens* (Weimar: Hermann Böhlaus Nachfolger, 1989).

51. James Morgan Hart, *German Universities: A Narrative of Personal Experience* (New York: G. P. Putnam's Sons, 1874 [reprinted London: Routledge/Thoemmes Press, 1994]), 375.

52. Ostwald, *Lebenslinien*, vol. 2, 83–84.

53. It was only much later named in Wilhelm and Alexander von Humboldt's honor. Charles E. McClelland, *State, Society, and University in Germany 1700–1914* (Cambridge: University Press, 1980), 106, 108–9; David Blackbourn, *The Long Nineteenth Century: A History of Germany, 1780–1918* (New York: Oxford University Press, 1998), 83.

54. Dorothy Ross, G. *Stanley Hall: The Psychologist as Prophet* (Chicago: University of Chicago Press, 1972), 34, 40–41, 79. Hall, *Life and Confessions*, 194–95. W. James (Teplitz, Bohemia) to H. P. Bowditch, 5 May 1868. H. P. Bowditch Papers, H MS c.5.2, Folder 1, HUL Countway [typed copy]. W. James (Berlin) to H. James, Sr. (Father), 5 September 1867. Reprinted in F. O. Matthiessen, *The James Family: A Group Biography. Together with Selections from the Writings of Henry James Senior, William, Henry and Alice James* (New York: Vintage Books, 1974 [1947]), 116.

55. David L. Crandall, "From Roxbury to Richmond: The Military Career of Henry P. Bowditch." *The Physiologist* 32, no. 4 (1989): 88–95. Walter B. Cannon, "Henry Pickering Bowditch, Physiologist," in *Science* 87, no. 2265 (27 May 1938): 183–86.

56. H. P. Bowditch to W. James, 19 February 1871. James Family Papers, bMS 1092.9, items 77–84, Folder 2, HUL Houghton.

57. H. P. Bowditch to W. James, 19 February 1871, ibid.

58. Ibid.

59. T. D. Seymour to Classmates at Western Reserve, 5 November 1871. Seymour Family Papers, Box 21, Folder 153, YUL. As to Thomas, see John Williams White, "Thomas Day Seymour 1848–1907," Memorial Address Given at Yale University on 12 February 1908; published by the Classical Club of Yale University.

60. On the University of Strasburg, see John E. Craig, *Scholarship and Nation Building: The Universities of Strasbourg and Alsatian Society, 1870–1939* (Chicago: University of Chicago Press, 1984).

61. W. H. Welch to Emily Sedgwick Welch, 16 September 1876. Welch Papers, Box 68, Folder 16, JHU med. Subsequent quotes ibid.

62. W. H. Welch to William Wickham Welch (Father), 18 October 1876, ibid., Folder 5. Following quotes ibid.

63. W. H. Welch to Stepmother, 16 September 1876, ibid., Folder 16.

64. W. H. Welch to Father, 18 October 1876, ibid.

65. W. H. Welch to Stepmother, 26 March 1877, ibid.

66. Simon Flexner and James T. Flexner, *William Henry Welch and the Heroic Age of American Medicine* (Baltimore/London: Johns Hopkins University Press, 1993 [1941]), 111, 128–37.

67. Ernst Windisch, "Georg Curtius," in *Biographisches Jahrbuch für Altertumskunde*, vol. 9, (1886), reprinted in Sebeok, *Portraits of Linguists*, vol. 1, 344. Also Windisch, *Georg Curtius*.

68. G. Schlimpert and R. Eckert, "Briefe Leskiens an Karl Brugmann," *ZfSl* 26, no. 2 (1981): 223; G. Schlimpert, "August Leskien im Lichte seiner Briefe an Karl Brugmann," *ZfSl* 26, no. 2 (1981): 218.

69. C. R. Lanman to Aunt, 9 July 1876. C. R. Lanman Papers, HUG 4510.67, Letters from Europe, vol. 3, HUL Pusey. Eveline Einhauser, ed., *Lieber Freund... Die Briefe Hermann Osthoffs an Karl Brugmann, 1875–1904* (Trier: WVT, 1992), 13, 269; Karl Brugmann, "Hermann Osthoff," in *Indogermanische Forschungen* 24 (1909): 219, reprinted in Sebeok, *Portraits of Linguists*, vol. 1, 557.

70. Of course, this is not a complete account of the Young Grammarians. For further reading, see Anja Becker, "Southern Academic Ambitions Meet German Scholarship: The Leipzig Networks of Vanderbilt University's James H. Kirkland in the Late Nineteenth Century," *Journal of Southern History* 74, no. 4 (November 2008): 855–86; Windisch, "Georg Curtius," 342, 344; E. Eichler, "August Leskiens Wirken für die Slawistik," *ZfSl* 26, no. 2 (1981): 169–91. Schlimpert and Eckert, "Briefe Leskiens an Karl Brugmann," 223, 229n48 and 50. Schlimpert, "August Leskien im Lichte seiner Briefe an Karl Brugmann," 216–17. A. Richter, "100 Jahre deutsche Slawistik, Teil VII. Deutsche Slawisten sowie

Vertreter anderer Philologien in ihren Beziehungen zu dem neuen Leipziger Lehrstuhl," *Wissenschaftliche Zeitschrift der TH Magdeburg* 15, no. 5 (1971): 544, 546, 550. Frings, "Eduard Sievers," 1, 3, 27; reprinted in Sebeok, *Portraits of Linguists,* vol. 2, 1–52.

71. Chickering, "Das Leipziger 'Positivisten-Kränzchen,'" 228, 235–36.
72. Ostwald, *Lebenslinien,* vol. 1, 266; vol. 2, 88; Buttmann, *Friedrich Ratzel,* 73, 74, 80, 106, 113; Schorn-Schütte, *Karl Lamprecht,* 75, 78; Wilhelm Wundt, *Erlebtes und Erkanntes* (Stuttgart: Alfred Kröner Verlag, 1920), 283–87; Krause, *Alma Mater,* 180.
73. Schröer, *Carl Ludwig,* 75–76; Wolfgang G. Bringmann, Norma J. Bringmann, and Gustav A. Ungerer, "The Establishment of Wundt's Laboratory: An Archival and Documentary Study," *Wundt Studies,* ed. Wolfgang G. Bringmann and Ryan D. Tweney (Toronto: C. J. Hochgrefe, Inc., 1980), 123–57; Servos, *Physical Chemistry,* 48; Ostwald, *Lebenslinien,* vol. 2, 32–52; Buttmann, *Friedrich Ratzel;* Sam Whimster, "The Significance of Karl Lamprecht and His Work for Contemporary Cultural Studies," in *Karl Lamprecht im Kontext. Ein Kolloquium,* ed. Wolfgang Geier and Harald Homann (Leipzig: Schriften des Instituts für Kulturwissenschaften i. Gr. der Universität Leipzig, 1993), 76–77; Luise Schorn-Schütte, "Kulturgeschichte als Aufklärungswissenschaft. Karl Lamprecht's Bemühungen zur Reform der historischen Bildung im Kontext der internationalen Reformbewegung an der Jahrhundertwende," in *Transformation des Historismus. Wissenschaftsorganisation und Bildungspolitik vor dem Ersten Weltkrieg,* ed. Horst Walter Blank (Waltrop: Hartmut Spenner, 1994), 64–84.
74. Justin Stagl, "Ratzel" and "Wundt," in *Neues Wörterbuch der Völkerkunde,* ed. Walter Hirschberg (Berlin: Dietrich Reimer Verlag, 1988), 392, 527; Buttmann, *Friedrich Ratzel,* 88, 94. Ratzel's theories were perverted during national socialist rule in Germany.
75. Peter Jaritz, *Sprachwissenschaft und Psychologie. Begründungsprobleme der Sprachwissenschaft im ausgehenden 19. und beginnenden 20. Jahrhundert,* Serie OBST, no. 10 (Habilitationsschrift 1988; Osnabrück: Universität, 1990), 100–104.
76. Ibid., 52, 63. As to Drobisch, see also Krause, *Alma Mater Lipsiensis,* 150.
77. See his letters from Leipzig and Berlin, L. Cooper Papers, 14/12/680 Box 18, Cornell Kroch.
78. Journal, A. C. McLaughlin, 27 February 1894. McLaughlin Papers, 85536Aa2, Box 1, UM Bentley. See Friedrich Ratzel, *Die Vereinigten Staaten von Amerika* (München: Oldenbourg, 1878–1880); a second edition was published in 1893 as *Politische Geographie der Vereinigten Staaten von Amerika.* Also, Friedrich Ratzel, *Völkerkunde,* 3 vols (Leipzig: Bibliograph. Institut, 1885, 1886, 1888).
79. Journal, A. C. McLaughlin, 3 November 1893, McLaughlin Papers, 85536Aa2, Box 1, UM Bentley.
80. Journal, A.C. McLaughlin, 31 December 1893, ibid.
81. Diary, T. D. Seymour, Wednesday, 26 November 1870. Seymour Family Papers, Box 25, Folder 200, YUL.
82. C. R. Lanman to Aunt, 7 November 1875. Lanman Papers HUG 4510.67 vol. 3, May 1875 to August 1876, HUL Pusey.
83. C.R. Lanman to Aunt, 31 October 1875, ibid. Emphasis in original.
84. C.R. Lanman to Aunt, 21 November 1875, ibid. Emphasis in original. Following quote ibid.
85. C.R. Lanman to Aunt, 31 October 1875, ibid.
86. Heinrich August Winkler, *Deutsche Geschichte vom Ende des Alten Reiches bis zum Untergang der Weimarer Republik* (Bonn: Bundeszentrale für politische Bildung [Sonderausgabe], 2000), 123, 236, 244–45.
87. Jarausch, *Students Society, and Politics,* 12, 401.
88. Flexner and Flexner, *William Henry Welch,* 140; Winkler, *Deutsche Geschichte.*

89. Becker, "Southern Academic Ambition" and "Amerikanistik."

90. Alice Hamilton, *Exploring the Dangerous Trades* (Boston: Little, Brown and Company, 1943); Lincoln Steffens, *The Autobiography of Lincoln Steffens, Complete in One Volume* (New York: Harcourt, Brace and Company, 1931); James Mark Baldwin, *Between Two Wars 1861–1921*, vol. 1 (Boston: Stratford Co., Publishers, 1926).

91. Newspaper clipping, 2 October 1917, HUG 300 Arthur Becket Lamb A.M. '03, HUL Pusey. As to Lamb, see Frederick G. Keyes, *Arthur Becket Lamb 1880–1952: A Biographical Memoir*, vol. 30 of *Biographical Memoirs*, National Academy of Sciences (New York: Columbia University Press, 1954).

92. H. C. Jones to W. Ostwald, 3 November 1914. NL Ostwald 146/56, BBAW. Emphasis in original.

93. H. C. Jones to W. Ostwald, 21 October 1915, ibid., 146/63.

94. William B. Jensen, "Harry Jones Meets the Famous," *Bulletin for the History of Chemistry* no. 7 (Fall 1990): 26–33. W. Ostwald to Mrs. H. C. Jones, 3 August 1916. NL Ostwald, 146/74, BBAW.

95. Note (accompanying a letter from E. Sievers), B. Q. Morgan to American Leipzig Alumni, 21 December 1921. L. Cooper Papers, 14-12-680, Box 13, Cornell Kroch.

96. E. Sievers probably to B. Q. Morgan, 21 December 1921, ibid.

97. L. Wülker to L. Cooper, 1 Jan. 1950, ibid.

98. Grete Wülker to Lane Cooper, 1947, ibid.

99. Circular, [Mount Holyoke] to W. H. Welch, 29 November 1922. Welch Papers, Box 67, Folder 17, JHU med. At Leipzig, Vernon Kellogg befriended the historian and future US ambassador to Nazi Germany, William E. Dodd. Robert Dallek, *Democrat and Diplomat: The Life of William E. Dodd* (New York: Oxford University Press, 1968), 20, 105.

Chapter 5

TRANSATLANTIC
ACADEMIC NETWORKING

The Idea of German-American Networks in Science and Scholarship

THE ACADEMIC RELATIONSHIPS between US students and professors at Leipzig and Halle are at the center of this chapter. In order to approach the subject systematically, I will first of all examine the preferred fields of study that US students chose upon their enrollment and trace how these subject interests changed over time. As a second step, I will establish US students' routes of study. By this I mean the trajectories from an American university to one or several European universities and back to America with a specific focus on students' specific subject interests. These routes of study would typically involve at least two universities but often more. Leipzig played a central role in the late nineteenth century, for it was then a big university that could afford to offer first-class opportunities in several disciplines, not just in a few as was the case at smaller Halle. My research results in this regard can only be a beginning as the available data to be examined in tracing students' academic trajectories is simply too voluminous.

The examination of US students' subject choices against the background of a university's particularly appealing faculty choices at a given moment in the past allowed me to unearth patterns in transatlantic academic networking. Such patterns in mentor-disciple relationships can be observed regardless of subject matter. In a simplified way, these patterns illustrate that an innovative German professor would attract American students for ten to twenty years before losing his appeal—unless he came up with another innovative approach. My findings insinuate that pioneering American students very systematically benefitted from the expertise of a given German authority first through study and subsequently by sending their own students there for a couple of years. The pioneering Americans' later students, however, would begin looking for new inspiration elsewhere in Germany rather than seeking out the same German authority who had once upon a time inspired their American mentors.

Academic networking based on transatlantic mentor-disciple-relationships played a key role in the transfer of scientific and scholarly methods and approaches across the Atlantic. It did so chiefly in the closing decades of the nineteenth century with a particularly intense student migration to Europe that was fired by substantial reform movements in US academia. As I focus on academic networking rather than on the subject matter of selected disciplines, I decided on a broad definition of the disciple, including anyone who was identified to have been connected academically with a professor of interest here. After all, studying abroad also meant a credentialing oneself, as a result of which even proof of a brief visit to a renowned German professor could be useful on the academic job market in the United States.

Because the rapidly transforming American educational landscape of the nineteenth century offered opportunities for new portions of the population, I will also discuss women's roles in transatlantic academic networking activities. My main motivation in presenting a separate section on women in this context is to highlight the idea that women will have to be integrated in this kind of historiography and not simply be discussed in separate studies, for they indeed played an active role in transatlantic mentor-disciple relationships. The same idea should be examined for other minority groups, an undertaking that I unfortunately cannot accomplish at this point for a lack of further data on, for instance, African-American or disabled Americans at German universities before 1914.

I will close this chapter with a case study on Wilhelm Wundt and his US students, which illustrates that even though much has been published about Wundt, parts of the story are still missing as he is often narrowly defined as an experimental psychologist, whereby the fact is left out that he also influenced a number of disciplines in the humanities such as history and anthropology. The example shows that, as is the case with minority groups among American students abroad, other aspects of the story such as connecting points between different academic disciplines have found little regard in existing historiography due to the fact that often individual disciplines today write their own histories from today's perspective rather than exploring the larger underlying patterns of the developments in the past.

US Students' Faculty Choices at Halle and Leipzig

The examples of Halle and Leipzig illustrate that US students tended to choose a German university because of one or more highly reputed professors with innovative methods.[1] The attraction naturally changed over time as retiring professors were succeeded by others, as a result of which new approaches were introduced that more or less gradually changed a given discipline, even creating new ones in the process. In the long run, US students' overall interests shifted, with the classics making way for modern philology, scientific linguistics, and even natural sciences. Such transformations resulted in a reorganization of the academe, in Germany changing the traditional branches of the creation of knowledge into a structure dominated in the twentieth century by a binary opposition between "exact" (natural) sciences and "more speculative" humanities.[2]

The traditional nineteenth-century German university comprised four branches or schools (*Fakultäten*): theology, law, medicine, and philosophy. In his 1874 guidebook about German universities, James Morgan Hart recommended that US students register in the philosophical faculty.[3] As can be derived from the university registers, US students heeded his advice at both Halle and Leipzig. Students also sometimes chose two *Fakultäten* upon enrollment, such as philosophy and theology. When in the late nineteenth century academia became more specialized, US students increasingly noted more specific subject interests, such as physiology instead of more generally medicine, or they wrote psychology, mathematics, history, or German rather than philosophy. At Halle, the philosophical and theological faculties were especially popular with 206 and 98 students, respectively. Only 13 students registered in the medical school including a prospective dentist, and altogether 6 Halle Americans pursued law. By contrast, at Leipzig, circa 1,100 US students opted for the philosophical faculty, about 165 each for theology and medicine, and 100 for law. Medicine was thus as popular as theology, and the law faculty attracted a number of US students as well (Figures 16 and 17). To complicate matters, at older German institutions such as Leipzig, chemistry and botany had originally been part of the medical faculty, while at more recently founded institutions, they were grouped with the philosophical faculty from the beginning. Sometimes a chair of chemistry existed in both faculties, as was the case at Leipzig.[4]

The philosophical branch gave rise to new structures in the creation of knowledge. It came to cover a broad range of subjects, including what today we would call the humanities, the social sciences, and the natural sciences. But that does not mean that the other three faculties were nothing but reactionary fortresses. At Halle, theology had aroused interest among the earliest North American visitors of the late eighteenth century. Until the

US Civil War, theology was of primary interest there, with a few students opting for philosophy in the 1850s. There were more theologians during the 1870s, a decline during the 1880s, and a newly awakened interest in theology in the 1890s that lasted until the outbreak of World War I.[5] Medical students and students of law were so few at Halle that no arrival patterns can be discerned.

Considering that Leipzig had grown much more significantly than Halle, it may be concluded from US and total student numbers alone that Leipzig played a much larger overall role as an innovator in science and scholarship, whereby the philosophical faculty played a decisive role. At Leipzig, US arrival patterns at the law, theological, and medical faculties taken together do not match the general US enrollment pattern that I described in chapter 2, which suggests that the philosophical faculty had a distinctive impact on the evolution of US student migration—at least in the late nineteenth century. From the perspective of the law, theological, and medical faculties, Leipzig's heyday lasted from 1870 to 1890 rather than to 1900. While after a decrease in the early 1880s total US enrollments increased again until the mid-1890s, the enrollment patterns at the law, theological, and medical faculties show a gradual decline that set in between the mid-1880s and early 1890s. Philosophical disciplines consequently attracted US students longer and began to decline about a decade later than at the other three schools.

From the point of view of numbers, the philosophical branch succeeded the other three in the late nineteenth century as the most popular academic attraction. Only a few isolated individuals studied philosophy at Leipzig between 1850 and 1870. A rising tendency in philosophical enrollments is apparent since the mid-1860s and throughout the 1870s with a peak in the late 1870s, after which numbers fell again until 1882 to reach almost the low level of the late 1860s. While US student numbers decreased in the other three schools around 1880, already in 1882 their numbers in philosophy rose again. The trend continued with a slight setback in 1889 until 1897, after which a decline set in. A small peak may be observed around 1900 and another one around 1905, followed by a small rise in 1907 and a notable one in 1910. After that, numbers dropped. All in all, interest in the philosophical branch did not only soar in the 1890s, but it was higher than interest in the other three during the first decade of the twentieth century.

The majority of students in philosophy studied philology. At Leipzig, at least 320 students opted for classical, Semitic, or modern languages and literatures, or they simply noted "philology" upon registration. About 35 hearers may be added. By contrast, a much smaller group comprised circa 145 regular students and nearly 25 hearers and visitors who studied chemistry, physics, and physical chemistry. Some 105 students and close to 10 hearers and visitors opted for history, economics, political economy, and *cameralia*. Nearly 80 students plus 10 auditors, visitors, and foreigners relevant for future US academia were interested in natural sciences, natural history, geography, geology, and biology. Almost 40 students and 3 visitors and hearers studied mathematics; the same number and close to 20 hearers, visitors, and foreigners were interested in psychology, pedagogy, philosophy in a stricter sense, and related social sciences. Not all fields of study were identified.

These observations also apply to women. Even though their first and foremost concern in choosing a German university was the question of whether they would be admitted, on the whole, women also chose traditionally "more female sciences" such as the fine arts, languages, or "soft" natural sciences such as biology. They had a harder time entering masculine strongholds that provided laws, religious creeds, and an economic basis to society. They did study with particularly renowned faculty at Leipzig when possible, opting for chemistry, history, psychology, geography, and biology besides philology. In other words, they studied disciplines in the philosophical faculty and medicine but not law and religion. Diversification of the student body may consequently be found in the philosophical branch above all.

It has been argued that in the 1870s, Russian women and, since 1908, German women preferred to study mathematics and natural sciences.[6] This statement cannot be taken as universally true. It needs to be qualified by looking at the specific German professors who were willing actively to support female admissions at their universities. Of six pioneering US women at Leipzig in the 1870s, four studied philology when Leipzig was a world center of linguistics; the other two were also affiliated with the Leipzig Conservatory. By contrast, at Göttingen in 1893, the mathematician Felix Klein was inspired by a German professor at the University of Chicago, Heinrich Maschke, to accept US women as PhD candidates. The Americans' success was eventually taken as an argument in favor of admitting German women.[7]

In tracing subject interests and thus the evolution of disciplines, older studies often have either too narrow a time frame, or they focus on only one German university. Contrary to what previous scholars have argued, newly conceived disciplines—and, by implication, particularly innovative and renowned faculty—typically held the greatest appeal to foreign students, which was also reflected in routes of study that establish patterns of subject-related academic travel across the Atlantic (see below).[8] By contrast, Carl Diehl had concluded that most humanities students in German universities studied philology, that is, "classical languages and literatures from a historical point of view."[9] But he merely examined the years up to 1870. By the late nineteenth century, his observation no longer held true. Likewise, in his examination of Göttingen, Konrad Jarausch assumed that US students preferred mathematics and chemistry because they posed the smallest linguistic and cultural barriers.[10]

I would argue differently that mathematics and chemistry represented by Felix Klein and Walter Nernst, respectively, were simply very attractive at Göttingen—and incidentally also at Leipzig, with which university Klein had been affiliated before Göttingen. At Leipzig, Klein was succeeded by his friend Sophus Lie (although they would have a fallout at some point). As regarded chemistry, Nernst and Leipzig's Wilhelm Ostwald were close in their professional views.[11] US students of both fields would travel from Leipzig to Göttingen and vice versa in the 1880s and 1890s (more on such educational trajectories below). Halle was less appealing in either discipline. US students turned to Halle mainly for theology, *cameralia* (a predecessor of economics),[12] and agriculture.

A considerable number of Halle Americans opted for economics or *cameralia*, while only about fifty students explicitly chose *cameralia* at Leipzig. The great interest in economics at Halle may be explained by the fact that "a semester in Johannes Conrad's economics seminar in Halle" was an essential part of the *Wanderjahre* on the part of future US economists and social scientists such as Richard T. Ely, Simon Patten, and Edmund C. James. By the early 1890s, "ten to fifteen Americans were regularly found" in Conrad's seminar.[13] Conrad had started out in agriculture before switching to economy on account of health issues that prevented him from engaging in physical labor. He had been called to Halle from Jena in 1870 and, among other things, published agricultural statistics as well as, in 1884, a book about German universities.[14]

Conrad had started out in agriculture, which was incidentally another subject of great appeal to Halle Americans. German higher agricultural education left an imprint on US agriculture in more than one way. The chemical interests of three early US students at Leipzig in 1853 were fueled by a scientific interest in agriculture, that is, an interest to put theoretical chemical knowledge to a practical use. Mason C. Weld became a scientific agriculturist.[15] Evan Pugh, an agricultural chemist, would become president of the Pennsylvania State College but died untimely already in 1864. He had studied at Göttingen from the spring of 1855 until the spring of 1856 and subsequently enrolled at Heidelberg.[16] Samuel Johnson was professor at Yale's Sheffield Scientific School from 1856 until 1896. From 1877 to 1900, he was director of the Connecticut Agricultural Experiment Station.[17]

Transatlantic Routes of Study

Educational paths of US students across the Atlantic did not remain static but changed depending on whether an academically appealing professor was called elsewhere or whether a new luminary rose to fame at a university that up to then had not been of interest to students with the respective research interests. Moreover, as US students often attended more than just one university while abroad, educational trajectories could comprise several institutions whose professors typically also communicated in various ways—be it by recommending students. Bigger universities such as Leipzig or Harvard excelled in almost all disciplines, whereas smaller institutions like Halle or Vanderbilt focused on a few fields of study that nonetheless could be as prestigious as similar departments at the bigger universities. Depending on the institution's size, contacts between individual universities could occur on many different levels simultaneously.

At Halle and Leipzig, students were asked to disclose their previous education upon registration. At Leipzig, however, the register simply asked where students had been prior to their arrival, which is why some of them merely noted "America" or the name of a town. In the fall of 1885, Charles Frederick Carrier wrote down "Indianapolis" even though he had graduated from Harvard in the previous summer. He was identified because his father and brother, who also registered that fall, were traced at Yale.[18] If students cited Cambridge, New Haven, Ithaca, or Charlottesville, it could mean that they had studied at Harvard, Yale, Cornell, or the University of Virginia. A search for student files at those institutions then yielded a harvest.

Often another German-speaking university was named, which helps us trace other popular institutions for a certain discipline. But it also complicates matters, because one would have to check the US students at all German (if not European) universities to identify each individual or to add all missing details to the picture. It would have exceeded the scope of this one-person research project to double-check names of all 319 Halle and 1,530 Leipzig Americans at other German universities that were listed; quite possibly, looking up a person at one German university might simply have referred me to yet another. Individual examples will consequently have to suffice. For instance, I compared the information that I collected at Halle and Leipzig. While I traced fifteen Leipzig Americans who noted that they had previously studied at Halle, another eighteen Halle Americans had previously studied at Leipzig, more than doubling the number of US students who studied at both institutions. Overall, at both institutions, Harvard and the University of Berlin were most frequently cited; although Leipzig needs to be added to the top three at Halle. At Leipzig, in turn, Göttingen and Heidelberg were among the top four.

Let me provide a few examples for routes of studies of US students in Europe. I already mentioned connections between Leipzig and Göttingen in mathematics and chemistry above. Medical students flocked to Vienna especially if they planned to embark on a career as practitioners; they came to Leipzig for thorough medical training in physiology, and to Berlin for training in bacteriology. Freiburg, Berlin, and Naples besides Leipzig were noted centers for biologists, botanists, and zoologists. Jena was also an attraction for students of biology as Ernst Haeckel was a professor there. Moreover, a lively interaction of professors of philology in Leipzig and Jena existed. But students of languages including Charles R. Lanman and George H. Schodde also turned to Tübingen and Berlin. Students of law and theology had a penchant for Heidelberg, too. Regarding previous education in Europe, while Leipzig Americans also turned to Paris, Oxford, London, Edinburgh, Zurich, Basel, and Vienna, the majority would opt for a German-speaking institutions including Strasburg and Breslau (Wrocław).

Focusing my research on students who had listed an American university in the Leipzig register allowed me to trace those for whom the Saxon university was a first choice in Europe. I refrained from pursuing research about US students who had listed another European university upon registration in Leipzig. A few of these students I nonetheless traced by chance. In the case of Julian Mack, a Jewish student who noted "Berlin" upon enrollment at Leipzig in October 1888, I discovered his connection with Harvard in a biography of him while doing research on Jewish American students.[19] Some students at Leipzig listed "Leipzig" as their place of previous study upon their second or third enrollment, suggesting that they had temporarily disconnected from the university but stayed in town. These instances on occasion indicated the preparation of a PhD thesis, which was the case with Peter Samis Burns, a chemical student who enrolled at Leipzig in June 1889 and again in April 1892. The first time he mentioned Boston, the second time Leipzig as places of previous education. In 1893, he submitted a dissertation revealing that he had been an instructor in chemistry at MIT from 1886 to 1887.[20]

As was the case in Europe, US academia boasted a variety of institutions. I looked up students at the most frequently cited US institutions of higher learning who had referred to their American alma maters upon their registration at Leipzig. They were mainly from the Northeast, as far south as Baltimore, and the Midwest. Harvard was central, taking a lead with at least 150 students and faculty who ventured to Leipzig for further training at some point. Harvard was not immediately but eventually followed by Yale, Princeton, and the University of Michigan at Ann Arbor. These four institutions make up the most often-cited institutions of US higher education to associate with late-nineteenth-century Leipzig learning, whereby Harvard had representatives in virtually all fields of studies and even sent students abroad on a number of traveling fellowships.[21]

This is not to mean, however, that some of the oldest and today most reputable US universities of the late nineteenth century can claim to be the sole players in student migration. Indeed, both Halle and Leipzig attracted students from across the United States, including smaller and lesser-known institutions that obviously also had smaller student bodies and therefore fewer students to travel abroad—be it a solitary representative of the University of Nebraska at Leipzig or Alfred C. Schmitt of Wisconsin, who had obtained his previous education at Albany College in Oregon. One of the earliest Californians to turn to Leipzig in October 1875 was the then nineteen-year-old future Harvard philosopher Josiah Royce, a recent Berkeley graduate.

Students' educational backgrounds shifted over time just like regional backgrounds shifted particularly during the final decades of the nineteenth century. Phrased differently, when in the final three decades of the nineteenth century Leipzig was particularly popular, US students' educational backgrounds there became more diverse.[22] Halle Americans, in turn, had more specific objectives and therefore more specific backgrounds, a conclusion that would be supported by Halle Americans' more focused and selective subject interests.

In fact, different US regions (re-)discovered the blessings of foreign education at different moments in the past and therefore sent their students earlier or later than other regions. Depending on the moment in the course of the nineteenth century when a US institution came in touch with foreign learning, different German-speaking universities were favored by its graduates, faculty, and administrators. For example, Southern scholars were comparatively numerous among Leipzig-trained US historians, and also among linguists. I have elsewhere given an example of an academic network connecting Wofford College in Spartanburg, South Carolina, with Vanderbilt University and Leipzig in the late nineteenth century.[23] This network was philological or rather linguistic and historical in nature, which allowed the faculty and students at the two Southern institutions to benefit from Leipzig learning without having to invest into expensive apparatus that post–Civil War Southern education could not necessarily afford. In German, the saying goes "turn a necessity into an asset," and that is what these Southern scholars appear to have done by focusing on scientific linguistics and the like. But in doing so, they followed academic trends that were particularly pronounced at Leipzig, impressing empirical and scientific method on the study of languages and the past. The Wofford-Vanderbilt-Leipzig connection in the 1870s and 1880s can consequently compare with the Harvard-Göttingen connection of the 1810s and 1820s.

The case of Lane Cooper illustrates a specific US student's route of study as an example of academic networking in philology around 1900. Cooper had received his undergraduate education from Rutgers in 1896 during Leipzig-trained Frank Scott's presidency. He had passed a year of graduate study with Albert Stanburrough Cook at Yale, who had studied at Leipzig in 1878. Cooper obtained a Leipzig PhD in 1901, working with Sievers (Germanics), Wülker (English), and Ratzel (anthropogeography). In the following year, Cooper was made an instructor in English at Cornell while simultaneously Leipzig-trained Paul Pope was hired to teach German there. Like Pope, Cooper became a full professor in 1915. Incidentally, during his German student days, Cooper was in touch with the US ambassador in Berlin, Andrew D. White, the founding president of Cornell.[24]

Cooper's US mentor Cook had followed a very similar educational path a little over two decades before, whereby it is noteworthy that besides the overall prestige of a German university, specific German authorities were of interest above all. Cook had received his BS also from Rutgers in 1872 and a PhD from Jena in 1875, which was then a philological hub close to Leipzig (allowing students to venture there on academic excursions, as Lanman noted, who met Sievers there in the mid-1870s[25]). Cook had enrolled at Leipzig in May 1878. From 1889 to 1921, he was professor of the English language and literature at Yale. According to Cooper, Cook had worked with Sievers in Jena.[26] Hence, as Sievers had moved on to Leipzig by 1900, Leipzig rather than Jena became Cooper's first choice in his quest for a PhD degree.

This particular academic network connected Rutgers, Yale, Leipzig, Jena, and Cornell in the modern languages, that is, English and German. It included pioneering Leipzig Americans—Scott and Cook—who had experienced Leipzig in the 1870s during the heyday of comparative linguistics and the rise of history as a separate field of studies derived from the classics. It was the heyday of the Young Grammarians and a bustling community of US classicists and orientalists, who would also come to influence the next generation of modern philologists. By 1900, the two Leipzig pioneers had moved on to administrative and faculty positions at two East Coast US universities. Their student Cooper met the Leipzig veterans as well as new additions to the Leipzig faculty (such as Sievers, who had left Jena eventually to return to the place of his own student days, Leipzig).[27] At Leipzig in 1900, Cooper coincided with US students who would be his colleagues in the future back in the United States, such as Pope of Cornell.

Patterns in Transatlantic Mentor-Disciple Relationships

My examination of transatlantic professor-disciple-relationships revealed a pattern that seems to hold true, more or less, for all the Leipzig professors whose US students I studied; it is particularly pronounced in the case of Wundt's rather large and comparatively well-researched US student body (see Figure 18). The pattern suggests that the brightest minds in the United States observed a German professor for his potential early on in his career.

They found out about a such a luminary by chance or because they had sought and found advice in European academic circles. Pioneering US disciples turned up basically from the moment a German professor was called to an institution and began building up something new. After 1870, both men and women could be pioneers, such as in the case of Friedrich Ratzel, whose most famous US disciple was Ellen Churchill Semple.[28] The pioneering generation passed on news of the rising academic star in letters to professors, administrators, friends, and family in North America. With a delay of a few semesters, the German professor's US student numbers then rose considerably. After a decade or two at most they began to decline again—unless, of course, the German professor had something new to offer. At the height of a professor's popularity, US students flocked there sometimes merely to be associated with him.[29]

In addition to this basic blueprint, the student pattern of one professor could be amplified by the presence of other professors with related interest as was the case in linguistics or philology (see Figures 19 and 20). When interpreting Figure 19, it needs to be kept in mind that I added up individual professors' US student numbers, as a result of which some students may have been counted more than once. The graph therefore does not show total US student numbers in philology but the student numbers of individual professors, highlighting increased opportunity for a US student when several renowned professors allowed for a subject matter to be inspired by a number of different academic perspectives. When compared with Figure 18, that is, the US students of an individual professor, the main outcome is nonetheless the same: a few students in the beginning, a rise and climax in the course of just a couple of years, and an eventual decline. A difference in the two graphs is rooted in the fact that in the case of linguistics, successive peaks may be observed as several innovative Leipzig professors not only overlapped but also succeeded one another. The pattern thus persisted even though some fields of study were more highly frequented than others. While comparatively few prospective natural scientists from the United States fared well with one or a handful Leipzig professors, the much more numerous US students in philology encountered quite a few eminent linguists among the Leipzig faculty. As a group, the latter's academic attractiveness was upheld much more prominently than what may be observed in the (back then) less well-reputed natural sciences.

A professor could attract pioneering students at different stages in his academic career. That is, as soon as he introduced a new approach or a new take on old problems, he would interest a new generation of US disciples. It could therefore happen that new pioneers arrived fairly late during a university's heyday, focusing on a new aspect in a professor's work or zooming in on an upcoming professorial star. This was the case with Arthur

Amos Noyes, who discovered Leipzig's quite new physical chemist Wilhelm Ostwald as late as in 1888/89. Noyes had initially registered to study organic chemistry but now pioneered as one of Ostwald's earliest PhD candidates in physical chemistry.[30] Wundt's US students furthermore illustrate the point: Wundt was not really frequented notably until the mid-1880s, and then again in the first half of the 1890s. According to Miles A. Tinker's list of Wundt's US students, Wundt lost his appeal in experimental psychology then, but my data shows that he continued to be frequented by US students, attracting a handful per semester once again around 1900, which might also be explained by the fact that he contributed to other disciplines (see Figure 18, also see below).[31]

Ostwald had an inkling of the fact that he might at some point stop being of interest to the most brilliant young students. He decided to retire at the height of his fame, thus escaping what struck him an inevitable fate of threatening obscurity.[32] In his memoirs, he noted that late in his career Carl Ludwig sometimes appeared bitter and then again thoughtful. Ostwald was worried: "I had never seen him like that before and was so worried that afterwards I asked his assistant what had happened. 'Haven't you heard?' he answered, 'this term not a single student signed up for his laboratory. Thinking of the good old days, it's little wonder that he's growing bitter.'"[33] Ostwald was shaken. He realized, however, that the phenomenon was beyond anyone's control, "It was the way of the world, and that's why it was so profoundly tragic."

Physiology had developed in a different direction, as a result of which fewer students were interested in Ludwig's by then well-established methods. While they dutifully listened to his lectures, students now specialized in different academic disciplines and consequently turned to the laboratories of other Leipzig professors, such as the zoologist Rudolf Leuckart and his successor Carl Chun as well as the botanist Wilhelm Pfeffer. They thereby shifted their physiological foci to the plant and animal kingdoms. Ludwig had been on the forefront of the basic medical science of physiology in the 1860s and 1870s.[34] By the time of the 1880s, however, US students began losing interest in his laboratory course, although they continued to frequent his lectures—as did the future Harvard zoologist George Howard Parker, who heard Ludwig lecture in the fall of 1891/92 but did not work in his laboratory. Parker referred to the famous physiologist merely in passing in a letter dated 13 December 1891: "After dinner ... I read and study till about four and then go to Ludwig's lecture on Physiology. This closes at 5 and on the way home I buy my supper."[35] He did not even make special mention of Ludwig in his autobiography.[36] Then again, Ludwig was a part of Parker's curriculum, which reflects Ludwig's earlier standing with a previous generation of US students a decade or two before. Leipzig attracted students of biology above all during the early 1890s, a period that simultaneously witnessed the sad decline in student numbers at Ludwig's laboratory. While Leipzig physiological training in medicine was no longer of primary interest, US students kept arriving at the Saxon university thanks to younger Leipzig authorities who had made a name for themselves by applying physiological methods to plants and animals.

Ostwald resolved never to let happen to him what had happened to Ludwig, which is why he decided to give up laboratory work comparatively early. He increasingly tired of his professorial duties. Gradually, his students Gilbert Newton Lewis and Noyes indeed lost faith in some of his ideas. Ostwald resented the fact that none of Ludwig's students had honored their professor with a biography; but neither would his own US disciples.[37] The most avid Leipzig-American academic networkers, who were also the most gifted students, were busy establishing sciences in the New World. To build a monument to a German professor other than by staying in occasional touch with him did not further that objective and thus was of secondary importance.

According to these findings, a university at its height can keep its status if it manages time and again to call new, promising authorities to the institution to provide new directions for science and scholarship. Such institutions can be of interest internationally in several basic branches of knowledge and serve as innovating centers for more than just a few years. The overall fame of a nineteenth-century university was continuously tested and realigned in relation with the ongoing faculty turnover fueled by the need to fill vacancies occasioned by professors' retirements, deaths, and departures. Departure, it should be added, was a less striking reason for a vacancy in the late nineteenth century with Leipzig being one of the top universities. As Ostwald later reminisced, "Leipzig is the professor's heaven," hence, "you don't get called away from Leipzig."[38] By 1900, however, promising younger faculty would not necessarily stay but accepted calls elsewhere, an indication of the fact that Leipzig was moving past its heyday (see also Appendix 2).

Universities and professors can shift in their academic appeal within only a few years depending on the successes of their research combined with successful related faculty recruitments. Administration is thus a vital part of scientific and scholarly renown by providing the research and teaching conditions for professors and simultaneously succeeding in continuously finding and recruiting promising new talent. The effect of administrative changes can only be witnessed with a delay of a few years. An institution's current standing is consequently not necessarily a reflection of its current leadership, unless this leadership has been in place for at least a decade.

One of the secrets to success is to have a sense of who might be up and coming, and to recruit them or their most promising young disciples—for the latter had proved their mothers' wit by having found out about this particular academic shooting star.[39] US faculty would encourage their students to study under a certain authority abroad, whereas US administrators would be eager to recruit these US students from that authority (see also chapter 8). As a result, we find US researchers, administrators, and students communicating and collaborating in tracking down the most promising German authorities. Of course, the categories of faculty, students, and administrators fluctuated in the course of time with students moving on to becoming professors and even university administrators, thus adding dynamics to the picture in the course of sometimes no more than one or two decades—G. Stanley Hall, a student at Harvard and Leipzig in the 1870s, served as a professor at Johns Hopkins in the 1880s, and, by the end of that decade, was the founding president of Clark University in Massachusetts.

Women's Roles in Academic Networks

As US women—albeit in comparatively tiny numbers—also studied at German universities, they were part of mentor-disciple relationships and thus also of academic networks. An integrated history of nineteenth-century higher education that would incorporate gender has, however, not yet been undertaken. Instead, there is an ongoing excitement to write separate monographs about the first women in German universities. I do not wish to be misunderstood—such studies are needed. But what is the point if no materials are available to compare these few women to their countless male counterparts? The first time I presented this project, a female scholar who had been asked to comment on my work exclaimed: "Not another study about white men!"

Being a woman in academia myself, I am taken aback: Are we exchanging one segregated historiography for another? I take findings from studying women to reconsider what we write about men. I do *not* favor a historiography that features separate sections on women and minority groups, because it upholds existing hierarchies and thus does not truly challenge established mainstream historiography in the field of higher education. Instead, I want to focus on the numerous connecting points between the histories of different groups in society.

While, as I argued in chapter 3, women were a separate group within the masculine German universities, the transatlantic setting allowed them to transcend this gender borderline and, by moving between continents, even entered the realm of elite male education in the United States (see also chapter 8). This does not mean that everything was fine and unproblematic for US university women. It does mean, however, that there was more flexibility between groups than what an exclusively segregated historiography might insinuate.

In light of the criticism I just voiced, this section might appear slightly paradoxical, for it might be perceived as a separate section on women singling them out and thus separating them from the grander narrative. This is not the case. I simply find it necessary to include such a section to raise awareness of how to combine different historiographical narratives. Women were not separate but a part of academic networks. It can be illustrated with examples of male and female US students' paths crossing in the form of letters of recommendations and of career opportunities for men and even for women at historically all-male or all-female colleges, and also at coeducational and coordinated institutions—the former being institutions that admitted both men and women, the latter referring to institutions for men that established a female division, such as Harvard's Radcliffe College, allowing them to admit women but to keep them separate.

Dealing with gender integration in Germany may be compared to ending legal racial segregation in the Southern United States during the 1950s and 1960s. Gender segregation in higher education was, however, subverted in numerous ways back in the nineteenth century. Indeed, the German-speaking universities' long resistance to admitting women ultimately contributed to their decline after 1900, as they had not realized the new intellectual potential—female scholars and scientists—that was being integrated one way or another everywhere else in Europe and in North America. It is an example of not being able to tell future trends on the part of the esteemed German-speaking universities. Sometimes, as in the case of women's admission to higher education, such future trends did not quite correspond to general convictions but rather were derived from necessity. Women in the Midwest of the United States were admitted because the institutions needed every paying customer.[40] Gender integration in Germany and at some of the most prestigious US universities also happened because of outside pressure as expressed in the persistence and increasing numbers of female applicants.

Resistance to gender integration in German academia until 1900 suggests that nineteenth-century education rested on the premise that prestige was masculine—the presence of too many women thus automatically lowered an institution's prestige. That is, top universities could afford to admit a brilliant woman or two, but they would ultimately become alarmed when too many females demanded equal privileges. This also accounts for the invisibility of early female achievements in higher education (once again, the same holds true for racial segregation in US education—individual brilliant African Americans could go far even before the end of slavery, but the broad masses were being kept ignorant). Let me provide a few examples in the following, focusing mainly on more or less visible women in US academia from the perspective of the German student venture of the late nineteenth and early twentieth centuries.[41]

Adding a female dimension to traditional historiography can be revealing. For example, what reports say on the surface, and what other sources tell us about the personal backgrounds of the author, presents something of a discrepancy illustrating that history must not be taken merely at a surface value. One of the milestones in assessing a German element in US higher education is an 1898 report about foreign influences on US education. It was authored by Burke A. Hinsdale, professor of the Science and the Art of Teaching at Ann Arbor.[42] Incidentally, Burke had a daughter, Ellen Clarinda Hinsdale, a graduate of the University of Michigan in French, German, and pedagogy in 1893 (MA). From 1897 to 1931, she was on the Mount Holyoke College faculty. But there is more to it. Ellen studied at Leipzig in 1894/95 and obtained a PhD degree from Göttingen thereafter (it was not yet possible for women at Leipzig). B.A. Hinsdale, a future president of Hiram College, Ohio, published his report a year after his daughter had returned from Europe with a German PhD degree—at a time when only in exceptional cases and with special permission would women be awarded such a degree at a few of the German-speaking universities. Following the famous B.A. Hinsdale report, one finds in the same publication a report on women. To what extent did Ellen Hinsdale provide information about foreign opportunities to her father? Moreover, if she had contributed to her father's report, what to make of the fact that in spite of their sometimes invisible but traceable presence in education, women would be discussed in a separate, segregated chapter?

There are several indications that Leipzig professors more or less grudgingly and even in spite of themselves admitted women to their classes, who thus found an opportunity to become active parts of Leipzig-related US academic networks—albeit as less visible or disadvantaged players. They too may be regarded pioneers, such as, most notably, M. Carey Thomas, a founding member and first female president of Bryn Mawr College in Pennsylvania, which she envisioned as a top research university for women, a sort of "Leipzig in miniature."[43]

Leipzig-trained women in US academia would be just as eager (and sometimes as irreverent) in encouraging their students to seek out European authorities. One of E.C. Hinsdale's students at Mount Holyoke was Eunice Rathbone Goddard, who earned an AB degree from that institution in 1904. In the fall of that year, she traveled to Germany. She wrote to her classmates from Leipzig: "if you feel so inclined you go to the university and watch Herr [Mr.] Professor [Albert] Koester twirl his mustache and [Karl] Von Bahder lecture over his shoulder, because he is afraid of the class, just as Dr. Hinsdale said he did when she was there, and if you are very conscientious you can take notes, but—well, I won't say anything in regard to the lectures, but you ask any of the other Americans who have been there, too, and see what they say."[44] Goddard was writing a class letter, which might account for her tone. Be that as it may, Hinsdale obviously had embroidered her teaching with anecdotes of the quirks of Leipzig professors, thus subtly (or not so subtly) subverting the male world of German academia.

In the 1880s and, even more so, in the 1890s, US botanists and zoologists found inspiration at Leipzig. Sandra Singer pointed out that in the late nineteenth century, botany was deemed particularly appropriate "for both introducing women to science and encouraging feminine behavior. Collecting and identifying plants was to bring women closer to god and nature. This in turn would elevate women's minds, strengthen women's faith and enhance domestic harmony. Botany was so identified with women, that an 1887 article in *Science* actually asked, 'Is Botany a Suitable Study for Men?'"[45] That does not mean, however, that women traveled to Leipzig (or any other university, for that matter) merely to choose a field that was regarded to be particularly suited for them.

Just like their male counterparts, women turned to a German-speaking university for its academically innovative appeal in a specific field of study. The one difference was that, as Edith and Alice Hamilton found out in the mid-1890s, they had to content themselves with going where they would be admitted, which notably reduced their possibilities.[46] On account of such restrictions, their presence at Leipzig is difficult to trace as university sources are hardly available. But outside sources allow us glimpses, such as the following glimpse of male/female chemistry networks. In May 1899, Noyes recommended a woman to Ostwald: "Permit me to introduce to you Dr. Charlotte F. Roberts, Professor of Chemistry in Wellesley College. Dr. Roberts expects to spend considerable time in Leipsic next winter, and is especially desirous of meeting you and of visiting your laboratories. She has made a special study of electrochemistry and is author of a work on the subject."[47] As a woman and as a professor, Roberts may have visited rather than registering as a hearer. When in late 1905 Ostwald stayed at Harvard, he visited Wellesley but was not impressed and certainly not in favor of women's colleges, although his impressions of such institutions in the United States appear to have been rather superficial.[48] All in all, he showed little excitement for female students, and his correspondence with his US disciples, although quite voluminous, gives little evidence of the existence of women chemists.

Case Study: Wilhelm Wundt and His American Disciples

Wilhelm Wundt's career illustrates nicely that a nineteenth-century professor could appeal to a number of students with different scientific and scholarly interests, which is why they cannot simply be claimed by one contemporary academic discipline exclusively. A list with the names of Wundt's 186 PhD students proves the point. Published by Miles A. Tinker in 1980, the list also includes a brief discussion of Wundt's US doctorates. Tinker observed that between 1880 and 1916, the ratio of psychological and philosophical topics was 3 to 2. By contrast, during Wundt's early years at Leipzig (1875–1879), he had supervised mainly philosophical theses, and from 1916 until his death in 1920 psychological ones exclusively. Experimental psychology apparently did not pick up until the early 1880s,[49] but it became more and more central to Wundt's work. Tinker also acknowledged that Wundt was a minor advisor in philosophy, pedagogy, ethics, and anthropology,[50] or, more generally, in the humanities and social sciences.

Indeed, quite a few US students from a variety of backgrounds were *somehow* associated with Wundt, ranging from short visits and listening to his lectures to earning a PhD degree under his supervision. In my attempt to trace the educational affiliations of US students during their stays at Leipzig, I have been able to identify the largest number of students with Wundt, that is, at least fifty showed some interest in his academic offerings. He was therefore indeed most likely the greatest academic attraction Leipzig boasted in the final decades of the nineteenth century. An association with Wundt did not exclusively serve research interests per se. As James R. Angell had confided to his father, the president of the University of Michigan at Ann Arbor, in the spring of 1892 writing from Harvard, "[William] James … lays great stress for me on the mere fact of having had some connection with Wundt's laboratory both as an experience and as a commercial instrument."[51]

Angell's remark illustrates that the German venture was not merely about gaining knowledge in terms of new approaches, methods, and theories—it was also about making connections and credentialing oneself. This observation raises the question of, for example, Wundt's actual impact on US science and scholarship. Considering that Angell merely visited Wundt and still thought a connection with him of importance "as a commercial instrument," it would be advisable not to focus exclusively on those students for whom Wundt was the main advisor—Wundt's interests were too manifold over the years. Of course, it is difficult to determine what impact Wundt had on a student who merely sat in one of his lectures. But isn't there even in the so-called exact sciences always a factor of uncertainty that cannot exactly be pinned down?

Wundt's US students not just from the field of experimental psychology illustrate nicely the arrival pattern in mentor-disciple relationships that I described above. Upon Wundt's arrival at Leipzig in 1875, a pioneering US student turned up in his lectures immediately. He was none other than a youthful Josiah Royce. In the 1875/76 fall term, he took notes on Wundt's "*Logik und Naturforschung*" (logic and natural history) and his "*Anthro-*

pologie" (anthropology).[52] Royce informed the founding president of Johns Hopkins, Daniel C. Gilman, in February 1876:

> In my lectures I have taken most especial interest in *Wundt*, the new member of the philosophic Faculty, formerly Professor at Heidelberg, the author of a prominent work on *Physiological Psychology*, and perhaps the first of the psychologists of Empirical [*sic*] tendencies in Germany at the present time. I am hearing a course from him in Logic. In this more specially philosophic branch he has not yet written much, but he is understood to be a "man with a system," in Metaphysics as well as in Psychology. So in him I have a thoroughly live man, and one who will quite possibly make a powerful impression on the thought of the next decade or so, for he is still in his younger prime.[53]

Wundt had not been called from Heidelberg to Leipzig directly but had spent a year in Zurich in the meantime. But Royce's prediction regarding Wundt's future influence proved correct. Royce stayed at Leipzig for one term only.[54] Even though he "would gladly hear" Wundt for another semester, he moved on to Göttingen, because he had "a strong desire to hear [Rudolph Hermann] *Lotze*," "a professor who seems generally acknowledged as the first in constructive philosophy now living in Germany."[55]

As I showed in my PhD dissertation in more detail, other famous Leipzig professors such as Ludwig, Ostwald, and Curtius, to name just a few, also had one or several early pioneering US disciples who were instrumental in introducing their approaches to one or even more institutions in the United States. Sometimes they would simply leak the news in the United States—as Royce had done by writing to Gilman. Johns Hopkins University would open the following fall, Royce being one of the original fellows. Royce knew Gilman from his undergraduate student days at the University of California at Berkeley, over which Gilman had presided before being called upon to organize the Johns Hopkins University project. Wundt's pioneering US student at Leipzig, Royce would embark on a distinguished career in his own right, though not exactly in the field—experimental psychology—for which Wundt is so well remembered today.

After having sent word of Wundt's coming to Leipzig to the United States, Royce retreated from the scene. No immediate rise in Wundt's US student numbers may be observed. It took another pioneer, G. Stanley Hall, to set off the movement by checking out Wundt's new laboratory of experimental psychology, which was opened in 1879. Hall had earned a first US doctorate in psychology at Harvard under none other than Henry Pickering Bowditch and William James. Through Bowditch, he became familiar with Ludwig's laboratory teachings. James, in turn, had already been aware of Wundt in the late 1860s. Coincidentally, James was another of Royce's fatherly friends besides Gilman. While resting in Bohemia, James had announced to Bowditch on 5 May 1868, "I go to Heidelberg because [Hermann von] Helmholtz is there and a man named Wandt [*sic*] from whom I think I may learn something of the physiology of the senses without too great bodily exertion, and may perhaps apply the knowledge to some use afterwards. The immortal Helmholtz is such an ingrained mathematician that I suppose I shall not profit much by him."[56] The letter is preserved as a typed copy, which might account for "Wandt" as a typo. Yet a fairly unknown young scholar, Wundt was then at Heidelberg working with Helmholtz.[57] Even though Wundt had a background in medicine, James obviously did not consider him an experimentalist—he intended to seek out Wundt for a more theoretical approach to physiology. Only in 1879 did Wundt open at Leipzig what is today acknowledged the first laboratory of experimental psychology. It had taken four years since Wundt's arrival in 1875.[58]

Hall, who had already earned his PhD degree, did not stay very long at Leipzig but during his time there worked with both Wundt and Ludwig, also noting that Wundt's laboratory was only just being organized. Hall returned to the United States to find work eventually at Johns Hopkins University, where an experimentally and scientifically minded Gilman was interested in pursuing the latest trends in hard-core natural science (rather than supporting mere speculative inquiries)—the young philosopher Royce had been sent back to California for the time being, in James's words to sit out the disgrace of youth.[59] Not until the early 1880s would Royce finally be able to join the Harvard faculty, initially filling in for James, who was then on sabbatical leave, visiting, among others, Wundt in Leipzig.

The circle of Wundt's pioneering US disciples can thus be pinned down to the collaboration of a handful of influential professors (Bowditch, James), presidents (Gilman), and promising and enterprising students (Royce, Hall). The pioneering generation demands inclusion of at least two more names: James McKeen Cattell and Lightner Witmer. Cattell, who had encountered Hall at Johns Hopkins, ended up being Wundt's first PhD student in experimental psychology and one of the important figures in introducing Wundt's approaches to psychology in the United States. Cattell arrived at Leipzig in the early 1880s and became a somewhat accidental Wundt student, because he turned to him only as a second choice, his first choice—Lotze at Göttingen, who had already lured Royce away from Wundt—had died before Cattell could start out on a PhD project.[60] Witmer, in turn, was Cattell's student and successor at the University of Pennsylvania in the early 1890s. He deserves credit for the fact that he pioneered in applying Wundt's teachings by establishing a psychological clinic (rather than confining himself to the laboratory exclusively).[61]

But Wundt nonetheless also inspired philosophy and theology, which requires that a discussion of pioneering Wundt students look beyond the realm of what we narrowly define today as psychology. Three of thirteen US disciples on Tinker's list examined a more philosophical subject. They were James Thompson Bixby in 1885, Edward Pace in 1891, and William Harder Squires in 1902. Bixby was Wundt's first PhD student from the United States, even preceding Cattell. He had earned an AB degree from Harvard in 1864 and a Bachelor of Divinity degree from the same institution in 1870. From 1879 to 1883, he had served as a professor of religious philosophy at Meadville Theological School in Pennsylvania. A German CV, which he prepared when applying for his degree at Leipzig, stressed his background in theology. It also listed several publications that reveal Bixby's interest in Darwinism and social Darwinism.[62] The theologian interested in the scientific revolution thus turned to Wundt the philosopher.

Bixby was fortunate not to have opted for a stay at Leipzig right after he had obtained his BD degree in 1870. Another Harvard graduate who did so had turned away in disappointment similar to Ticknor's disillusionment more than half a century before. As a Harvard professor of theology, Francis Greenwood Peabody would apply the methods of the psychological laboratory to theology.[63] But he did not find those methods at Leipzig in the early 1870s. He had obtained a bachelor's from Harvard in 1869 and in the early 1870s, recently married, embarked for Germany. He had difficulty finding a place for the fall term. A "survey of the offerings" at Heidelberg "and the rather chilling receptions by the distinguished Professor [Daniel] Schenkel, drove me to Leipzig."[64] At the Saxon university, however, he "found the prevailing attitude of defensive orthodoxy even more repelling than the arid rationalism of Heidelberg." He ended up in Halle. The writings of a theology professor in Berlin, Otto Pfleiderer, introduced him to the "scientific-historical approach of theological scholars to the phenomena of religion."[65] The "German's application of psychology to the subject of piety" impressed him as "[p]sychology here explained the manifestations of religious feelings in man, and prepared the ground for philosophy and history to begin their respective tasks of interpretation and verification." Wundt came to explore an experimental way to answer questions about human existence a decade later.

Such different beginnings play into Wundt's attraction to US students as a philosopher besides being an innovative experimentalist in psychology. In the 1890s, Wundt's earlier US visitors and disciples were now in place at key institutions, from where their own disciples would soon embark for Leipzig. Taking the more philosophically inclined Americans as an example, when James went on sabbatical leave in 1882/83, also visiting Wundt in Leipzig, Royce was called to Harvard as his substitute. He remained for the rest of his life; his friend the philologist Lanman having joined the Harvard faculty before him. Thus, Royce linked Wundt's philosophy with Harvard, disregarding James, who had been aware of Wundt since the late 1860s. At Harvard, one of Royce's students was Arthur MacDonald, who would move on to Leipzig in the mid-1880s, and from the time of its founding would teach at Clark University for roughly two years. His specialty was criminology. In an autobiographical sketch he related his (from today's point of view, dubious) interest in measuring the heads of certain classes of people such as the young and rich, criminals, and members of Congress. Not much else is known about him.[66]

George Herbert Mead is probably the best known of Royce's students who also studied under Wundt. He had completed his undergraduate education at Oberlin College in 1883. In 1887, he entered Harvard for two reasons—it was alongside Johns Hopkins a prominent intellectual center in the country. But it also was the place where Royce taught, whom Mead would admire for the rest of his life as an excellent academic teacher. Mead did not study with William James; however, he tutored the James children. A year into his stay at Harvard, Mead in spite of Royce decided to specialize in physiological psychology rather than in philosophy. This brought him to Leipzig in the 1888/89 fall term. Curiously, despite his resolve concerning his future career, he enrolled in Wundt's philosophical rather than in his psychological courses. He also heard Max Heinze and Rudolf G. K. Seydel on philosophy. After one term he moved on to Berlin. Mead would join the faculties of the University of Michigan and subsequently of the University of Chicago, at each institution as a colleague of John Dewey.[67]

In keeping with the pattern I observed, US students clustered in Wundt's laboratory and lecture rooms in the early 1890s. Between 1890 and 1893, five prospective American psychologists obtained PhD degrees under Wundt's supervision. The example of the little group suggests how closely knit the early network of US psychologists was, and to what extent American Wundt students assisted one another in furthering their careers. Frank Angell (PhD Leipzig 1891), Edward Pace (1891), Edward Scripture (1891), Edward Titchener (1892, British), and Lightner Witmer (1893) knew one another at Leipzig. In 1890/91 the future muckraker Lincoln Steffens, one of Wundt's numerous US students who did not obtain a degree, associated with their little crowd. Howard Crosby Warren joined them in 1892/93, although he did not earn a Leipzig degree either. Except for Steffens, all of them would embark on academic careers in psychology. Scripture and Pace would establish laboratories at Yale and at the Catholic University in Washington, DC, respectively, already in 1892. Witmer was Cattell's first student at the University of Pennsylvania, where he would succeed him in 1893 and, three years later, opened the first psychological clinic.[68]

Warren had studied at Princeton and would return there for an academic career in psychology. He had received a letter of recommendation to Wundt from Cattell thanks to the help of the Princeton mathematician Henry Burchard Fine, who had befriended Cattell during their student days at Leipzig.[69] At Princeton, Warren was discovered by James Mark Baldwin, a Leipzig student in the mid-1880s who had known Cattell there and who would establish at least three laboratories of experimental psychology in the course of his career—one at Toronto between 1889 and 1893 and a second at his alma mater Princeton between 1893 and 1903. In 1903, Baldwin reopened the Johns Hopkins laboratory that had been closed after Hall's departure in 1887, who moved on to the presidency of Clark. Johns Hopkins was not to become Baldwin's permanent academic home, though. After having been arrested during the raid of a Baltimore brothel, he was dismissed. He subsequently joined the faculty of the University of Mexico, occasionally giving lectures at Harvard, Yale, and at the University of Chicago.[70]

F. Angell was the nephew of the president of the University of Michigan at Ann Arbor, James B. Angell. Having obtained his PhD at Leipzig, he moved on to Cornell, where he established a laboratory. Leaving for a post at Stanford already in 1892, he successfully recommended his Leipzig friend Titchener as his successor. F. Angell also provided his cousin, James R. Angell, with a letter of recommendation to Wundt. In the summer of 1892, though, J. R. Angell did not obtain a place in the overcrowded laboratory. He considered Freiburg to work with the early German Wundt student Hugo Münsterberg, but in the fall of 1892 Münsterberg moved to Harvard, where J. R. Angell had spent the previous year in graduate study. J. R. Angell never registered at Leipzig.[71]

Wundt's psychology was accessible to US women to some degree. Leipzig-trained American men in turn embarked on careers teaching women in psychology. Of Wundt's disciples in the United States, Münsterberg encouraged women at Harvard. Witmer of the University of Pennsylvania in Philadelphia also taught at Bryn Mawr College. Leipzig-trained John Martyn Warbeke spent the better part of his career at Mount Holyoke College teaching psychology. Four US women were identified to have studied with Wundt, three of whom embarked on careers in academia, a fourth became a writer. They were the authoress Josephine Bontecou Steffens in 1890/91,[72] Julia Henrietta Gulliver in 1892/93,[73] Mary Mills Patrick in the spring of 1894,[74] and Grace Neale Dolson in 1897/98.[75]

Summary

In the late nineteenth century, new impulses could be found above all in philosophy in a larger sense. Philosophy represented one of the four branches of the traditional German university that began to break into a new organization of the production of knowledge by the late nineteenth century. Instead of the four faculties of philosophy, medicine, law, and theology, a new order was taking shape then that would find expression in the twentieth-century compartmentalization of academia into the natural and social sciences besides the humanities. Law, religion, and medicine also thrived anew after the turn of the twentieth century in addition to new developments such as business schools. The tendency of the German university to break up the traditional four faculties that led to an ever-increasing specialization was consequently carried mainly by the traditional philosophical branch.

The relationships between US students and German professors reveal underlying patterns that may be applied to different disciplines regardless of subject matter: A new luminary emerges at a German university, of which pioneering US students take note, whereby sometimes they do not even study with the professor but simply report home the developments, as seemed to have been the case with William James and Wilhelm Wundt. For a few years up to around two decades, US students then flock to the German professor before slowly beginning to lose interest, unless, of course, the German professor has something new to offer. The developments suggest that US students indeed looked for innovation, and as soon as a new discipline or approach had been established at a number of US universities, the novelty began wearing off and the next generation of US students sought new impulses.

Women certainly were part of this development (at least as regarded US students in Germany). They too studied preferably with the academically most appealing authorities. Interestingly, though, they were hardly represented among students of law and religious creed, two branches of the production of knowledge that also attracted considerably fewer US men, though, especially in theology, one may also trace innovative streaks, such as the influence of psychological research. It consequently would not be correct to argue that women studied above all subjects that were traditionally regarded more suited for them such as philology or that—to the contrary— they had a preference for subjects such as chemistry and mathematics. Instead, by examining women's fields of study at more than just one German university, it may be concluded that they too chose the best—provided that they would be admitted.

In their search for innovation, US students did not just focus on developments at one foreign university but typically studied at several. One can consequently establish their academic trajectories and thus observe changing centers of learning for specific research interests in the course of time as, of course, a university did not remain static but was always just as appealing as were the professors and research opportunities in the individual departments. No matter how seriously they were focused on studying specific subject matters at a German university, US students would also get in touch with their compatriots in town. As a result, they found ways to engage in numerous networking activities, which I will examine further in chapter 6.

Notes

1. For more detailed case studies than can be presented here, see my dissertation: Anja Becker, "For the Sake of Old Leipzig Days ... Academic Networks of American Students at a German University, 1781–1914" (PhD dissertation, University of Leipzig, 2006). Also, Becker, "Southern Academic Ambitions Meet German Scholarship: The Leipzig Networks of Vanderbilt University's James H. Kirkland in the Late Nineteenth Century," *Journal of Southern History* 74, no. 4 (November 2008): 855–86.

2. As regards fluctuations in enrollments of different academic disciplines, see Hartmut Titze, *Der Akademikerzyklus: historische Untersuchungen über die Wiederkehr von Überfüllung und Mangel in akademischen Karrieren* (Göttingen: Vandenhoeck & Ruprecht, 1990).

3. James Morgan Hart, *German Universities: A Narrative of Personal Experience* (New York: G. P. Putnam's Sons, 1874 [reprinted London: Routledge/Thoemmes Press, 1994]), 48. US students actually read his book: see Journal, C. Thomas, 16 June 1878. Thomas Papers, 86180 Aa 2 Ac, Box 3, UM Bentley. J. M. Cattell to Parents, 29 January 1886, reprinted in Michael M. Sokal, ed., *An Education in Psychology: James McKeen Cattell's Journal and Letters from Germany and England, 1880–1888* (Cambridge, MA: MIT Press, 1981), 202.

4. Marita Baumgarten, *Professoren und Universitäten im 19. Jahrhundert* (Göttingen: Vandenhoek & Ruprecht, 1997), 84. Rektor and Senat of Leipzig University, eds., *Festschrift zur Feier des 500 Jährigen Bestehens der Universität Leipzig*, vol. 4, part 2 (Leipzig: Verlag von S. Hirzel, 1909), 71.

5. An example for a theology student in search of innovation would be Francis Greenwood Peabody. See his *Reminiscences of Present-Day Saints* (Boston and New York: Houghton Mifflin Company, 1927), 69. Jurgen Herbst, "Francis Greenwood Peabody: Harvard's Theologian of the Social Gospel," in *Harvard Theological Review* 5 (1961): 49. Jurgen Herbst, *The German Historical School in American Scholarship* (Ithaca, NY: Cornell University Press, 1965), 94. *The Quinquennial Catalogue of Harvard University 1636–1930* (Cambridge, MA: Harvard University Press), 122, 278, http://pds.lib.harvard.edu/pds/view/6796688. Another example would be Duren James Henderson Ward, a Harvard-trained Canadian with a theological background who matriculated at Leipzig in October 1886 to study Friedrich Ratzel's anthropogeography. He inspired Ellen Churchill Semple to opt for Leipzig in the early 1890s. R. J. Johnson, Derek Gregory, and David M. Smith, eds., *The Dictionary of Human Geography*, 3rd ed. (Cambridge, MA: Blackwell, 1994), 18; Edward T. James, Janet W. James, and Paul Boyer, eds, *Notable American Women: A Biographical Dictionary, 1607–1950*, vol. 3 (Cambridge, MA: Belknap Press of Harvard University Press, 1971), 260–62; Allen D. Bushong, "Semple, Ellen Churchill," *American National Biography Online* (February 2000), http://www.anb.org/articles/14/14–00552

.html. Accessed 4 December 2007; Matt T. Rosenberg, "Ellen Churchill Semple. America's First Influential Female Geographer," http://geography.about.com/library/weekly/aa022301a.htm. Accessed 28 January 2002.

6. Renate Tobies, ed., *Aller Männerkultur zum Trotz. Frauen in Mathematik und Naturwissenschaften* (Frankfurt/New York: Campus Verlag: 1997).

7. Ibid., 7; Renate Tobies, "Mathematikerinnen und ihre Doktorväter," in ibid., 134–36. Sandra L. Singer, *Adventures Abroad: North American Women at German-Speaking Universities, 1868–1915*, Contributions in Women's Studies 201 (Westport, CT: Praeger, 2003), 87.

8. Students generally followed advice; they were flexible in checking out new European opportunities. Becker, "For the Sake of Old Leipzig Days"; Arild Stubhaug, *The Mathematician Sophus Lie: It Was the Audacity of My Thinking*, trans. from the Norwegian by Richard H. Daly (Berlin; New York: Springer, 2002); Elin Strøm, *Sophus Lie 1842–1899* (Oslo: University of Oslo, printed at Godfreds trykkeri, 1992); Herbert Beckert and Horst Schumann, eds., *100 Jahre Mathematisches Seminar der Karl-Marx-Universität Leipzig* (Berlin: VEB Deutscher Verlag der Wissenschaften, 1981); John W. Servos, *Physical Chemistry from Ostwald to Pauling: The Making of a Science in America* (Princeton, NJ: Princeton University Press, 1990); Thomas Neville Bonner, *American Doctors in German Universities. A Chapter in International Intellectual Relations* (Lincoln: University of Nebraska Press, 1963), 32, 69, 105; Simon Flexner and James T. Flexner, *William Henry Welch and the Heroic Age of American Medicine* (Baltimore/London: Johns Hopkins University Press, 1993 [1941]), 138–40; George Howard Parker, *The World Expands: Recollections of a Zoologist* (Cambridge, MA: Harvard University Press, 1946), 82–90, 91–107; C. R. Lanman to Aunt, 26 December 1875. Lanman Papers, HUG 4510.67, Letters from Europe, vol. 3, HUL Pusey; Walter Miller, "Necrology Overbeck," *American Journal of Archaeology* 11, no. 3 (July–September 1896): 361–70; Bernhard Streck, "Wilhelm Maximilian Wundt," in *Hauptwerke der Ethnologie*, ed. Christian F. Feest and Karl-Heinz Kohl (Stuttgart: Alfred Kröner Verlag, 2001), 524–31; Mario Todte, *Georg Voigt (1827–1891). Pionier der historischen Humanismusforschung* (Leipzig: Universitätsverlag, 2004).

9. Carl Diehl, *American and German Scholarship, 1770–1870* (New Haven, CT: Yale University Press, 1978), 3.

10. Konrad Jarausch, "American Students in Germany" in *German Influences on Education in the United States to 1917*, ed. Henry Geitz, Jürgen Heideking, and Jurgen Herbst (Washington, DC: German Historical Institute, and Cambridge: Cambridge University Press, 1995), 208.

11. Servos, *Physical Chemistry*; Karen Hunger Parshall and David E. Rowe, *The Emergence of the American Mathematical Research Community 1876–1900: J. J. Sylvester, Felix Klein, and E. H. Moore* (Providence, RI: American Mathematical Society/London Mathematical Society, 1994); Stubhaug, *The Mathematician Sophus Lie*.

12. Ingomar Bog, "Ist die Kameralistik eine untergegangene Wissenschaft?," in *Berichte zur Wissenschafttsgeschichte*, ed. Fritz Krafft, vol. 4 (Wiesbaden: Akademische Verlagsgesellschaft Athenaion, 1981), 61–72.

13. Daniel T. Rodgers, *Atlantic Crossings: Social Politics in a Progressive Age* (Cambridge, MA: Belknap Press of Harvard University Press, 1998), 62, 84–85.

14. *Meyers Konversationslexikon, 4. Auflage, Bd. 4, (Leipzig/Wien: Verlag des Bibliographischen Instituts, 1885–1892)*; Johannes Conrad, *Das Universitätsstudium in Deutschland während der letzten fünfzig Jahre* (Jena, 1884).

15. L. Weld Family Papers, YUL. Obituary Record of Graduates of Yale University Deceased during the Academic Year Ending in June 1888, no. 8, Series 3, 477–78.

16. C. A. Browne, "European Laboratory Experiences of an Early American Agricultural Chemist—Dr. Evan Pugh (1828–1864)," *Journal of Chemical Education* 7, no. 3 (March 1930): 499–517. Daniel Bussey Shumway, "The American Students of the University of Göttingen," *Americana Germanica* 8, nos. 5 and 6 (September–December 1910): 176, 202. Paul G. Buchloh, ed., *American Colony of Göttingen. Historical Data Collected Between the Years 1855 and 1888* (Göttingen: Vandenhoek & Ruprecht, 1976), 34, 96 John T. Krumpelmann, "The American Students of Heidelberg University 1830–1870," in *Jahrbuch für Americastudien*, ed. Ernst Fraenkel, Hans Galinsky, Eberhard Kessel, Ursula Brumm, and H.-J. Lang, vol. 14 (Heidelberg: Carl Winter Universitätsverlag, 1969), 174.

17. Elizabeth A. Osborne, ed., *From the Letter-Files of S. W. Johnson* (New Haven, CT: Yale University Press, 1913). Johnson probably encouraged his students and associates to travel to Europe. Edward Hopkins Jenkins registered at Leipzig in October 1875. He had studied at the Sheffield Scientific School. Starting in 1876/77, he would be connected with the Connecticut Agricultural Experiment Station.

18. *Quinquennial Catalogue*, 321. Ybb 1851 vol. 2, 53–55, YUL.

19. Anja Becker and Tobias Brinkmann, "Transatlantische Bildungsmigration: Amerikanisch-jüdische Stundenten an der Universität Leipzig 1872 bis 1914," in *Bausteine einer jüdischen Geschichte der Universität Leipzig im Auftrag des Simon-Dubnow-Instituts für Jüdische Geschichte und Kultur an der Universität Leipzig*, ed. Stephan Wendehorst, Leipziger Beiträge zur Jüdischen Geschichte und Kultur, ed. Dan Diner, vol. 4 (Leipzig: Universitätsverlag, 2006). Harry Barnard, *The Forging of an American Jew: The Life and Times of Judge Julian W. Mack* (New York: Herzl Press, 1974); Horace M. Kallen, "Julian William Mack, 1866–1943," *American Jewish Year Book* 46 (18 September 1944 to 7 September 1945): 35–46.

20. P. S. Burns, "Chemisches Verhalten einiger dimolekularen Nitrile," (Dissertation, Leipzig: Johann Ambrosius Barth, 1893).

21. *Harvard Annual Reports*, http://hul.harvard.edu/huarc/refshelf/AnnualReportsCites.htm #tarHarvardPresidents.

22. For a more detailed analysis of educational backgrounds, see Becker, "For the Sake of Old Leipzig Days."

23. Becker, "Southern Academic Ambition."

24. L. Cooper (Berlin) to Father, 3 July 1900. L. Cooper Papers, 14/12/680 Box 18, Cornell Kroch.

25. C. R. Lanman to Aunt, 21 November 1875. Lanman Papers, HUG 4510.67, Letters from Europe, vol. 3, HUL Pusey.

26. L. Cooper (Berlin) to Father, 1 August 1900; to Mother, 17 February 1901. Cooper Papers, 14/12/680, Box 18, Cornell Kroch.

27. Theodor Frings, "Eduard Sievers," *Berichte über die Verhandlungen der Sächsischen Akademie der Wissenschaften zu Leipzig. Philologisch-historische Klasse* 85, no. 1 (1933): 1, 3, 27.

28. See for example Martha Krug Genthe and Ellen Churchill Semple, "Tributes to Friedrich Ratzel," *Bulletin (formerly Journal) of the American Geographical Society of New York* 36 (1904): 550–53; Harriet Grace Wanklyn, *Friedrich Ratzel* (Cambridge: Cambridge University Press, 1961).

29. J. R. Angell to Father, 27 April 1892. J. R. Angell Papers, 85605 Aa 1, UM Bentley; James Mark Baldwin, *Between Two Wars 1861–1921*, vol. 1 (Boston: Stratford Co., Publishers, 1926), 35–36; Alumni File of James Mark Baldwin 1884, Biographical Information, Mudd, Princeton. See also Baldwin's "Autobiography," in *A History of Psychology in Autobiography*, vol. 1, ed. Carl Murchison (Worcester, MA: Clark University Press, 1930), 1–30.

30. A. A. Noyes to H. M. Goodwin, 5 January 1890. H. M. Goodwin Papers, MC 121, Box 1, MIT Archives. See also Becker, "For the Sake of Old Leipzig Days."

31. Miles A. Tinker, "Wundt's Doctorate Students and Their Theses 1875–1920," in *Wundt Studies*, ed. Wolfgang G. Bringmann and Ryan D. Tweney (Toronto: C. J. Hochgrefe, Inc., 1980), 269–79.

32. After his retirement from Leipzig, Ostwald spent a few months at Harvard before settling in his country estate "Energie" [Energy] in Grossbothen near Leipzig. Karl Hansel and Christa Pludra, eds., "Die Vorbereitung des Harvard-Aufenthaltes Wilhelm Ostwalds," *Mitteilungen der Wilhelm-Ostwald-Gesellschaft zu Großbothen e. V.* 6, no. 1 (2001): 27–43.

33. Wilhelm Ostwald, *Lebenslinien. Eine Selbstbiographie*, vol. 2 (Berlin: Klasing & Co., 1926–27), 86–87. My translation, original: "Ich hatte ihn noch nie so gesehen und fragte hernach beunruhigt den Assistenten, was mit ihm geschehen sei. 'Wissen Sie es noch nicht?' war die Antwort, 'in diesem Semester hat sich kein einziger Praktikant für sein Laboratorium gemeldet. Wenn er hierbei an frühere Zeiten denkt, so ist es kein Wunder, daß ihm die Bitterkeit hoch steigt.'" Follwing quote ibid., my translation, original: "Es war ein natürlicher Vorgang, und darin lag seine tiefe Tragik."

34. As to Ludwig's US students, see for example George Rosen, "Carl Ludwig and his American Students," *Bulletin of the Institute of the History of Medicine* (Johns Hopkins University) 4, no. 8 (October 1936): 609–49.

35. G. H. to Family, 13 December 1891. Parker Papers, HUG 4674.12, Box 2, HUL Pusey.

36. Parker, *The World Expands.*

37. Ludwig students in North America published short obituaries upon their Leipzig mentor's death: Frederic S. Lee, "Carl Ludwig," *Science* 1, no. 23 (Friday, 7 June 1895): 630–32; Warren P. Lombard, "The Life and Work of Carl Ludwig," *Science* 44, no. 1133 (15 September 1916): 363–75. As to Ostwald, see Isabell Brückner and Karl Hansel, eds., "Zum Ausscheiden Wilhelm Ostwalds aus der Universitätslaufbahn," *Mitteilungen der Wilhelm-Ostwald-Gesellschaft zu Großbothen e. V.* 6, no. 1 (2001): 45–69. Servos, *Physical Chemistry*, 294. Ostwald, *Lebenslinien*, vol. 2, 87, 88.

38. Ostwald, *Lebenslinien*, vol. 2, 93. My translation, original: "Leipzig ist der Professoren-himmel," hence, "von Leipzig wird man nicht fortberufen."

39. This is particularly well researched in the case of Wilhelm Ostwald. See chapters 6 and 8 as well as Becker, "For the Sake of Old Leipzig Days."

40. Ilse Costas, "Der Zugang von Frauen zu akademischen Karrieren. Ein internationaler Überblick," in *Bedrohlich gescheit. Ein Jahrhundert Frauen und Wissenschaft in Bayern*, ed. Hiltrud Häntzschel and Hadumod Bußmann (München: Verlag C. H. Beck, 1997), 20–21; Ute Frevert, "Die Zukunft der Geschlechterordnung. Diagnosen und Erwartungen an der Jahrhundertwende," in *Das Neue Jahrhundert. Europäische Zeitdiagnosen und Zukunftsentwürfe um 1990*, ed. Ute Frevert (Göttingen: Vandenhoek & Ruprecht, 2000), 178.

41. For additional details, see Becker, "How Daring She Was"; also Becker, "For the Sake of Old Leipzig Days."

42. Burke A. Hinsdale, "Chapter XIII. Notes on the History of Foreign Influence upon Education in the United States," in *United States Bureau of Education. Report of the Commissioner of Education for the Year 1897–98*, vol. 1 (Washington, DC: Government Printing Office, 1899), 591–629.

43. Helen Lefkowitz Horowitz, *The Power and Passion of M. Carey Thomas* (New York: Alfred A. Knopf, 1994), 186.

44. E. R. Goddard to Dear Girls. LD 7096.5 1903 E, 1903 Class Letter no. 2 (1906), Mount Holyoke Coll. Archives.

45. Singer, *Adventures Abroad*, 119; Margaret W. Rossiter, *Women Scientists in America: Struggles and Strategies to 1940* (Baltimore/London: Johns Hopkins University Press, 1982), 61; J.F.A. Adams, "Is Botany a Suitable Study for Young Men?," *Science* 9 (1887): 117–18; Emmanuel D. Rudolph, "How It Developed that Botany Was the Science Thought Most Suitable for Victorian Young Ladies," *Children's Literature* 2 (1973): 92–97.

46. E. Hamilton to J. Hamilton, 23 December 1895. Hamilton Family Papers, MC 278, microfilm 27, Folders 595/96, HUL Schlesinger.

47. A. A. Noyes (Boston) to W. Ostwald, 31 May 1899. NL Ostwald, 153/19, BBAW.

48. Ostwald, *Lebenslinien*, vol. 3, 67.

49. Tinker, "Wundt's Doctorate Students," 278.

50. Ibid., 270.

51. J. R. Angell to Father, 27 April 1892. J.R. Angell Papers, 85605 Aa 1, UM Bentley.

52. Josiah Royce MSS, Box B: Student in Germany Fall 1875 to Summer 1876, Notebooks, Lecture Notes, etc., HUG 1755.5, HUL Pusey.

53. J. Royce to D. C. Gilman, 2 February 1876. Reprinted in *The Letters of Josiah Royce*, ed. John Clendenning (Chicago: University of Chicago Press, 1970), 49. Emphasis in original.

54. He stayed from 19 October 1875 to 15 March 1876 at Leipzig. J. Royce MSS HUG 1755.5, vol. 53, Records of Student Days, University of California and German Universities, HUL Pusey.

55. J. Royce to D. C. Gilman, 2 February 1876, reprinted in Clendenning, *Letters of Josiah Royce*, 49.

56. W. James (Teplitz, Bohemia) to H. P. Bowditch, 5 May 1868. H. P. Bowditch Papers, H MS c.5.2, Folder 1, HUL Countway [typed copy]. Emphasis in original.

57. E.g., G. Stanley Hall, *Die Begründer der Modernen Psychologie (Lotze, Fechner, Helmholtz, Wundt)*, trans. Raymund Schmidt (Leipzig: Felix Meiner Verlag, 1914), 192.

58. Wolfgang G. Bringmann, Norma J. Bringmann, and Gustav A. Ungerer, "The Establishment of Wundt's Laboratory: An Archival and Documentary Study," *Wundt Studies*, ed. Wolfgang G. Bringmann and Ryan D. Tweney (Toronto: C. J. Hochgrefe, Inc., 1980), 123–57.

59. John Clendenning, *The Life and Thought of Josiah Royce*, rev. and exp. ed. (Nashville, TN: Vanderbilt University Press, 1999), 61, 72–75.

60. Sokal, *An Education in Psychology*, 29. Journal, J. M. Cattell (Geneva), 17 August 1881, reprinted ibid., 36. Cattell registered twice at Leipzig; between the two stints, he spent a year at Johns Hopkins, eventually losing his fellowship to John Dewey. The two nonetheless became lifelong friends. George Dykhuizen, *The Life and Mind of John Dewey* (Carbondale: Southern Illinois University Press, 1973); Jay Martin, *The Education of John Dewey: A Biography* (New York: Columbia University Press, 2002).

61. Paul McReynolds, *Lightner Witmer: His Life and Times* (Washington, DC: American Psychological Association, 1997); Robert L. Watson, "Lightner Witmer: 1867–1956," *American Journal of Psychology* 69 (1956): 680–82.

62. J. T. Bixby, CV (draft) for PhD examination. G. L. Burr Papers, 14/17/22, Box 25, Cornell Kroch.

63. Herbst, *German Historical School*, 94. *Quinquennial Catalogue*, 122, 278.

64. Peabody, *Reminiscences of Present-Day Saints*, 69. Herbst, "Francis Greenwood Peabody," 49. Following quote ibid.

65. Herbst, "Francis Greenwood Peabody," 51. Following quote ibid.

66. Arthur MacDonald, "A Short Auto-Biography," *Indian Medical Record* 55 (January 1935): 23–32.

67. Concerning Mead's life, see Hans Joas, *G. H. Mead. A Contemporary Re-Examination of His Thought*, trans. Raymond Meyer (Cambridge, MA: MIT Press, 1997 [1980]).

68. Edward G. Boring, "Edward Bradford Titchener, 1867–1927," *American Journal of Psychology* 38, no. 4 (October 1927): 489–506, here 491; Watson, "Lightner Witmer," 680–82; Alfred C. Raphelson, "Lincoln Steffens at the Leipzig Psychological Institute, 1890–1891," *Journal of the History of the Behavioral Sciences* 3, no. 1 (January 1967): 39; Michael M. Sokal, "Biographical Approach: The Psychological Career of Edward Wheeler Scripture," in *Historiography of Modern Psychology. Aims. Resources. Approaches*, ed. Josef Brozek and Judwig J. Pongratz (Toronto: C. J. Hogrefe, 1980), 257; Samuel W. Fernberger, "The American Psychological Association. A Historical Summary, 1892–1930," *Psychological Bulletin* 29, no. 1 (January 1932): 2. McReynolds, *Lightner Witmer*.

69. Howard Crosby Warren, "Autobiography," *A History of Psychology in Autobiography*, vol. 2, ed. Carl Murchison (Worcester, MA: Clark University Press, 1932): 443–69; Samuel W. Fernberger, "Howard Crosby Warren 1867–1934," *Psychological Bulletin* 31, no. 1 (January 1934): 1–4; H. S. Langfeld, "Howard Crosby Warren: 1867–1934," *American Journal of Psychology* 46, no. 34 (1934): 340–42.

70. Baldwin, *Between Two Wars*, vol. 1, 35–36, 65; Alumni File of James Mark Baldwin 1884, Biographical Information, Mudd, Princeton. See also Baldwin, "Autobiography," 1–30.

71. As to F. Angell recommending Titchener, see Jacob Gould Schurman (President of Cornell), to Edward B. Titchener, 20 June 1892. Edward Bradford Titchener Faculty BIOG. FILE, Cornell Kroch. Also, Unpublished autobiographical sketch, J. R. Angell, January 1936, 9–10. J. R. Angell Papers Group 2, Series II, Box 2, Folder 7a, YUL. As to Angell's frustration of being admitted to the Leipzig laboratory, J. R. Angell to Frank Angell, 4 February 1922, ibid., Box 8, Folder 52.

72. Justin Kaplan, *Lincoln Steffens. A Biography* (New York: Simon and Schuster, 1974), 44–45; see also Lincoln Steffens, *The Autobiography of Lincoln Steffens, Complete in One Volume* (New York: Harcourt, Brace and Company, 1931), 152, 156–58.

73. Singer, *Adventures Abroad*, 151.

74. Mary Mills Patrick, *Under Five Sultans* (London: Williams and Norgate, 1930).

75. Singer, *Adventures Abroad*, 146.

Chapter 6

NETWORKING ACTIVITIES OF LEIPZIG'S AMERICAN COLONY

Formal and Informal Networking

MANY US STUDENTS registered at German universities mainly to advance their professional careers. Especially those who meant to stay in academia worked and studied hard with much focus on the question of how best to employ their time. The academic networking that I described in chapter 5 was certainly an important step toward that goal. But, as the example of the activities of the American colony in Leipzig shows, there was more to it.

In this chapter, I explore different forms of formal and informal networking within American colonies such as the one at Leipzig. Besides US students, the local American colony also embraced resident Americans who were simply visiting or who had opted for Leipzig to do business. Some Americans had taken up lodgings in town for prolonged periods of time. They were therefore in a position to watch several generations of US students pass through and actively interacted with them in various ways.

The formal and informal networking activities of the American colony came in many different facets. Networking served to help students settle down, to meet fellow Americans or other persons of interest in town, and to organize entertainments for the purpose of exchanging information as well as unwinding and smoothing over homesickness. The formal structure of Leipzig's American colony included above all the official American Students Club at the university, of which only regularly registered student could be members. But by all accounts, nonmembers also attended the club meetings,

---

apparently not all of them students. Another more formal form of organization was the American Church, whose organizers were often also actively involved in the affairs of the American Students Club.

Among the more informal networks were private associations with resident families and individuals (not necessarily US citizens), who regularly welcomed Americans in their homes either for evening discussions or Sunday dinners and also on holidays. The American Caspar René Gregory, a professor in the Leipzig theological school, was central to these more informal structures, as was the Knauth family. Both cases are particularly well documented over a prolonged period of time. A form of semiformal networking occurred when US diplomats in Leipzig got involved. I feel tempted to call this form of associating "semiformal" as US consuls were certainly in town on an official, diplomatic mission, but they were also part of more leisurely colony activities. In some cases their associating with US students was welcomed as an opportunity simply to exchange news about America. Then again, US diplomats could also be rather active in promoting US students' careers or helping them get in touch with the university or individual professors. At least twice a US consul in Leipzig was simultaneously also registered as a student in the university.

In the bulk of this chapter, I will discuss these various formal and informal forms of academic networking, whereby the focus will be on more pragmatic aspects such as exchanging information and assisting one another with housing and other practical aspects of the Leipzig venture. Above all else, though, an important aspect of colony activities consisted of simply getting people in touch. Different forms of associating with friends, colleagues, or family members could fuel academic networking, and it is not always easy to draw a clear line. Focusing on academic networking activities and relationships as well as interactions among Americans in Leipzig, I will leave an examination of free-time activities as yet another aspect of the networking in American colony life to chapter 7.

The American Students Club

In 1890, the US presence in Leipzig was so pronounced that the future Harvard zoologist George Howard Parker wrote home, "When I started out for Germany I thought I was leaving America behind but I see about as many Cambridge people here myself as you almost and certainly feel very much at home."[1] It wasn't mere rhetoric. He actually listed fellow countrymen, most of them Harvard graduates, whom he had encountered during a concert: "Gibson who used to room in Divinity Hall; Ayers '90 whom I knew in College; Bancroft with whom I worked in the Chem. Lab. in Cambridge (he is grandson of the historian), Marshall whom I met a[t] Woods Hole and who studies at Univ. Penn. + knows George Ross, etc., etc."[2]

Maybe it was this notable presence in town that finally incited the idea to form an American Students Club at the University of Leipzig, which had happened earlier that year. On 29 January 1890, George Stuart Collins had presented himself to the university authorities with a membership list and the statutes of the new American Students Club.[3] Less than a month later, the news spread to America. On 20 February 1890, Arthur Amos Noyes, a student of chemistry, wrote to his friend Harry Manly Goodwin, who was still working toward his bachelor degree in physics at MIT but would travel to Leipzig soon: "The American students here formed a club last semester ... we have meetings every two weeks."[4] Noyes was listed as a member during the 1890 spring term.[5] But by the time Goodwin enrolled at Leipzig on 15 June 1892, according to the files at the LUA, the club no longer existed. A document written on 13 November 1891 announced that during the meeting on 9 November, the *Verein* (club) had been voted to be postponed "sine die,"[6] that is, it had adjourned without a fixed next meeting. The club thus ceased to exist after barely four semesters.

According to its constitution, this first American Students Club was established for four different purposes, almost all of them geared toward the creation of academic networks.[7] Modeled after German academic clubs and organized according to the university statutes, the American Students Club combined pragmatic academic networking with leisure and distraction, whereby the greatest importance was attributed to the creation of old boys networks especially as regarded the teaching profession. The club intended to provide a forum for its members to discuss topics of interest to teachers and students. It was furthermore to assist its members in getting prospective teachers and faculty into touch with learned institutions and also to help new arrivals settle down at Leipzig. Its fourth purpose was to provide an opportunity for jolly evening gatherings among fellow countrymen. In its first semester, the club had twenty-eight members. Collins was its first patriarch.[8] As only regular students could be members of academic clubs, no women were officially present at the regular meetings that were held in a local *Kneipe* (pub) or hotel.

Long before the club was founded, Americans at Leipzig had gathered to spend their spare time together while abroad. Already in 1827, Theodore Dwight Woolsey did not travel about Europe alone. Shortly after his arrival in Leipzig on 17 December 1827, he wrote to his mother: "I have had however, for the most part excellent spirits and have been not a little comforted by having Mr. Yates with me who intends spending the winter at Leipzig. He is a man of fine and friendly feelings, without very extensive acquirements, whom I should like any where but who I esteem a great acquisition in a strange land."[9] Mr. Yates was not identified. The fact that Woolsey decided against rooming with him not to hinder their progress in German suggests that Yates was also a native English speaker.

In the first place, US students found friends in lecture halls or laboratories and also in subject-related societies, which was especially important in earlier days when few US students traveled to Leipzig. In 1869, the future Harvard physiologist Henry Pickering Bowditch mentioned that he "had joined a club table composed of most of the workers in the laboratory. It is quite an international affair. There are two Germans one Russian one Norwegian one Swiss + one American."[10] This little society was "to meet once a week and to give everyone an opportunity to report anything new or interesting which has fallen under his notice. This will be extremely useful for me as almost all my companions are more experienced than myself in physiological work."[11] Back then, Bowditch was still somewhat isolated as a US student in Leipzig. By contrast, in the next few decades, mingling with fellow students of the same discipline would increasingly also mean to mingle with fellow countrymen.

Throughout the 1870s and 1880s, letters, diaries, and journals give evidence of rich American student life. In 1869, Bowditch had still been an isolated pioneer. By the 1870s, in turn, US student numbers in town had increased to an extent that Leipzig came to feature an American student colony. They were a diverse group with different interests, objectives, and motivations. Some—like Calvin Thomas—concentrated on their scholarly attainments, others were merely after the fun. Thomas remembered later in life (utilizing his personal reform-orthography): "In those days the American colony at Leipzig was strong in men of ability. At least seven of those I knew there afterwards won distinction—some of them great distinction—in their several specialties. Now they ar all gone but one—my Columbia colleag, Edward D. Perry. And there wer others—a motley group some of whom wer just loafing."[12]

When US student numbers reached never-before-heard-of proportions by the early 1890s, an American Students Club came into being and then dissolved again quickly—to meet Americans, special organizational structures were not really necessary. US students studied in all faculties, lived together in pensions, went to the same hotels for dinner or supper, met at the theater or the opera. They rowed on the rivers, played tennis together, and much more. In short, if they desired to meet fellow countrymen, no special platform was needed to make it possible: Americans were all over. According to the US consul in Leipzig, Brainard Henry Warner, Jr., in early 1898 the American colony numbered "about 1500 people."[13] (Unfortunately, I cannot determine how many of them were students in the university as I have only the numbers of new enrollments; exact hearer numbers or numbers of students who stayed more than just one semester are not available at this point.) He added that "[b]esides the regular official routine work, a great deal of my time is taken up by American tourists, residents and students in attendance at the University and the Conservatory."

Consul Warner was a student himself. The 24-year-old Princeton graduate had registered at Leipzig in May 1898 to study law. He was from Washington, DC; his father was a banker. On 21 July 1897 he had been appointed US consul in Leipzig. He served until 1904. His successor was Southard P. Warner, probably his brother, who held the position from 9 August 1904 until 1910, that is, four years before his untimely death. S. Warner was twenty-two years old when he registered at Leipzig in October 1904 to take up *cameralia*. He was also from Washington and had previously studied at Dartmouth. His father was retired. Arthur Becket Lamb, a future Harvard chemist, described S. Warner as "an athletic young fellow."[14] Both Warners were Presbyterians.[15] They personified a close link between the US Consulate and the university.

In the 1900 spring and the 1901/02 fall terms, B. Warner was listed as a member of the Verein amerikanischer Studenten (Association of American Students), which had reappeared in the fall term 1899/1900 with twenty-eight members in the first semester of its existence.[16] The club was reintroduced only when US student numbers in Leipzig began diminishing. Maybe for that very reason, it lasted longer, even though its membership kept declining without US students necessarily taking note of it. For example, Lamb wrote to his family on 6 November 1904: "Last evening, Saturday, I went to the American club meeting. It's held in one of the hotels. About 15 fellows showed up—a rather foul attendance—due it seems to some confusion over the [illegible] of meeting and the fact that it was the first meeting of the year."[17] In fact, for the 1904/05 fall term, only nine members were listed, including Lamb (which shows that more people attended than were listed as members).[18]

The low attendance was symptomatic. In the following semester, the club began admitting students from Great Britain, Canada, South Africa, and New Zealand. It was renamed the American and British Students Club. But the opening to an Anglophone membership did not stop the decline in the long run. A final membership list is available for the 1909 spring term. On 14 December 1909, the last president of the club, Rev. Burtis Mac-Hatton, informed the authorities that the *Verein* no longer existed, though it was hoped to reintroduce it in the 1910 spring term.[19] The plan never materialized.

In the 1911/12 fall term, an Internationaler Studenten-Verein an der Universität Leipzig (International Students Club at the University of Leipzig) was founded. Of the forty-nine founding members, only five were from the

United States, one of whom, Leroy Sheetz, became the first chairman (*erster Vorsitzender*).[20] An attempt to unite international students at Leipzig in one organization, the club ceased to exist with the outbreak of World War I. On 25 November 1914, Herbert A. Beuchel notified the authorities that the club had virtually dissolved as all the members had either joined the army or returned to their native countries (himself excepted).[21]

The American, American-British, and International Students Clubs at Leipzig reflected developments in US arrival patterns. First initiated at a time when the American student colony at Leipzig witnessed an unprecedented peak in numbers, it soon disintegrated. A second attempt was undertaken by the turn of the century. The club lasted longer; however, membership kept declining. The International Students Club illustrated thereafter that there were fewer and fewer US students in town, and that their attempt to create an international educational student association was defeated by the outbreak of the Great War.

In its best days, the American Students Club at Leipzig allowed students to mix career interests with regional patriotism and jolly leisure activities (see also chapter 7). The scheme to get people in touch beyond their Leipzig venture also worked well. For example, Morris Tilley, who was still in Leipzig, kept Lane Cooper, who had already left, informed about mutual friends. In March 1902, Tilley wrote:

> Last night at the American Club ... Stewart was elected Pres. for the summer Semester again.... Abbot sailed from Bremerhafen Saturday with Zalinski for America. Already many of the Colony have started southward. Mrs. Dawson is back from Munich and they are now in *garcon logis* on Simson Strasse. Dawson has not heard from his *Arbeit* [thesis] yet but he hopes to be a spring chicken. I shall be glad to hatch in the summer. Frank Smith is another going to be soon Doctor of Philosophy.[22]

Cooper had arrived at Leipzig in October 1900 and received a PhD degree in 1901. He left later that year. He was a member of the American Students Club in the 1901 spring term and possibly had met Tilley there.[23]

The American Church

Up to World War I, the secular and spiritual leadership of the American colony was often in the hands of a US pastor. An American Church was a prominent feature of American colony life in Europe. At Leipzig, it came into existence long before the American Students Club. It is, however, even less well documented. But it served a similar purpose and to some degree may also be regarded the club's more informal predecessor.

The American Church was typically organized by US students of theology who tended to be older and stayed in Leipzig for extended periods of time. They were likely to be affiliated with theological seminaries or denominational colleges in the United States, Amherst College being the most important one, for it sent those students or rather pastors to Leipzig who would found the American Church there. The pastors became central figures in the American colony and, in the days of American student clubs, also served as the clubs' administrators.

From the beginning, the American Church did not exclusively serve the purpose of worshipping. First and foremost, it provided an opportunity to be among fellow countrymen but also to make acquaintances and thus to network. Lane Cooper wrote to his father from Berlin that he had seen the US ambassador, Andrew D. White, and his wife "on Sunday at the American church."[24] US students in Europe did not shun local services, but attending a German church had a different meaning for them. It served as a means to touch base with German culture. Having assured his family in a June 1853 letter that he had dutifully worshipped, Mason Cogswell Weld drifted off into a detailed description of the German church itself, suggesting that German ways were "curious," a term he frequently used.[25] Weld described what he saw in a detached way that sometimes even produced a comic effect. He had a conspicuous understanding of a "more favored us" as compared to a "curious them." Some forty years later, George H. Parker was similarly detached when talking about German churches, which did not strike him as impressive.[26] Weld was at least impressed with the Germans' commitment, though his description nonetheless also implied incredulity as to whether Germans were *really* as devoted as they seemed to be: "Yet I have not seen so devotional an assembly more than a few times before in my life. During the Singing all the audience sing and the utmost quiet prevails [through] the whole as if each person felt that he was engaging in an act of worship. This is delightful, and the people seem in many of these particulars to act much better up to the true standard of christian duty than many in our more favoured land."[27]

By contrast, Leipzig's American Church allowed US students to be amongst themselves and thus to take a break from the encounter with the foreign culture. The American Church was established in the early 1870s. Regular meetings of US students at Leipzig in the 1870s and 1880s were held in connection with the American Church or by theologians who were either part of or in close touch with the American colony. For example, George Whitefield Manly, who had enrolled in October 1883 to study theology and philosophy, in the vita of his 1885 dissertation mentioned that he had been a member of Franz Delitzsch's "Anglo-American Exegetical Society."[28] The fact that the Leipzig professor gathered his Anglophone students in a separate society suggests that there were quite a few. Manly, the son of a professor of theology, had studied at Georgetown College in Kentucky, followed by a stint at the Southern Theological Seminary in Louisville. Before his arrival in Leipzig, he had been a Baptist pastor. He dedicated his dissertation to the Leipzig philosopher Max Heinze.

The initiator of Leipzig's American Church appears to have been Samuel Ives Curtiss. An Amherst graduate, Curtiss was a student of theology and would later serve as a professor at the Chicago Theological Seminary. He registered at Leipzig in April 1873 and befriended Caspar René Gregory, a fellow countryman who eventually joined Leipzig's theological faculty (see below). The philologist Charles Rockwell Lanman observed that Curtiss was a theological orientalist who hoped to become a professor in the Union Theological Seminary in New York. Curtiss remained in Leipzig at least until 1877. He appears to have left by 1878.[29]

In the 1870s, Curtiss was a central figure in the American colony and held regular meetings in his home. In early October 1877, Calvin Thomas "went to a sort of informal reception at Dr. Curtiss' on West-Strasse. The Americans of Leipzig congregate there hebdomadally on Monday evening. Found it very enjoyable."[30] Curtiss had thus organized an informal American club, for these meetings existed independently of the church. Charles Lanman noted on 7 November 1875: "It is nearly time for me to go to the American chapel, so I must close."[31] A week later, he mentioned a separate visit to Curtiss.[32]

It is noteworthy that several pastors of the American Church were affiliated with Amherst, in the nineteenth century a particularly spiritual institution that had been founded in 1821 "to revive and preserve the faith of the Puritans."[33] Curtiss was succeeded as the pastor of the American Church by John Franklin Genung, previously a student at Union College and at the Rochester Theological Seminary. Genung had worked as a pastor before he enrolled at Leipzig in the fall of 1878 and again two years later. He obtained a PhD degree in 1881. The following year, he embarked on a teaching career at Amherst. By 1906, he had become a professor of literary and biblical interpretation. He had an identical twin brother, who, however, did not study at Leipzig. No information is available as to whether Genung knew Curtiss.

On 20 October 1877, Thomas noted that "at 5 P.M. heard Dr. Curtiss preach at the American chapel."[34] The hour did not change, for in late 1884, Eugene Luzette Mapes would also preach on Sundays at 5 PM in one of Leipzig's schools. Mapes had graduated from Union College (like Genung) and Union Theological Seminary in New York. One may wonder if he had met Curtiss there, who according to Lanman had hoped to be connected with that institution. Mapes stayed in Leipzig until 1885.[35] One of his disciples must have been Ralph Partridge Emilius Thacher, who in the mid-1880s was "quite active in the American church in Leipzig, being constant in attendance Sundays, and engaging actively in the religious discussions on weekday evenings."[36] Thacher had enrolled in October 1884.

At around the same time, another US student, James McKeen Cattell, was aware of the American Church but showed little enthusiasm for it. He wrote to his parents on 19 October 1884, "I was at the American church this afternoon. As I do not know who preached there is no harm in saying that it is a mental and moral injury to me to listen to such stuff."[37] A few lines later he complained that the preacher "evidently owns a dictionary of poetic quotations." He concluded that the man "covers his lack of earnestness and faith, with a veneer of science and culture he does not understand." In contrast to the above-cited churchgoers and pastors, Cattell was neither a theologian nor a philologist. He was an experimental psychologist, which in his case was linked to a pronounced skepticism of religion.

Traces of such skepticism may be found among later Leipzig Americans, particularly those with a natural-scientific background, such as the three botanists and zoologists Volney Morgan Spalding, Joseph Stafford, and Rodney H. True, who were more detached when it came to Leipzig-American religious matters. By the 1890s, with a flourishing US student population, the service at the American Church had become a big affair. Spalding, a zoologist from Ann Arbor, told a lady-friend on 10 December 1893:

> In the afternoon of Sunday I generally attend the American Church, where several hundred people, of various denominations, and no denomination, come together and unite in a common worship. The leader, or pastor, Mr. Edwards, is a man of much ability, working here on a pittance for the good he can do, and the whole organization and its methods and purpose are strikingly like the New Testament Church, with little form, hardly more than the voluntary association of a body of disciples, but as it seems to me a remarkable example of the powerful influence of Christianity in the simple form in which it first took shape.[38]

The episode illustrates that a main purpose of the church was to have an *American* service, rather than a religious service of a particular denomination. The fact that Spalding included even people with "no denomination" stresses the importance of the church as a meeting place for Americans in Europe. Unfortunately, Edwards was not identified. He might have been a 42-year-old philosophy student from London. At Leipzig, Spalding associated with his Ann Arbor colleague, the historian Andrew C. McLaughlin, and his wife Lois Angell McLaughlin. In October 1893, A. C. McLaughlin noted in his journal that they had been to the American service: "Church Thomas Kirche—fine music—selections from St Paul—Church again in the evening. Lois with Mr. Spalding in the American Kirche to hear Mr. Edwards—."[39] In July 1895, Stafford wrote to True, "Pastor Edwards is tolerably well now."[40] It is up to speculation what exactly he meant.

Another religious skeptic at Leipzig was Arthur B. Lamb, a student of chemistry in the 1904/05 fall term. He wrote to his father in early November 1904: "I played tennis this morning as usual, then went to the American Church, which wasn't so usual."[41] The casual remark must have aroused paternal disapproval as Lamb in a follow-up letter roughly a month later set about explaining his religious attitude:

> Father's letter of the 2nd with some very good advice to his impious son arrived yesterday. His surmise that I hadn't been to church but once—because I hadn't mentioned going but once was quite right. I quite agree that the church stands for the better things in life, or certainly many of the better things, but it doesn't mean so much to me personally as it does to many persons, as a help to right living.... You probably will sigh and say that I'll outgrow it—or this—and perhaps I may. I on the other hand will probably go to church next Sunday anyway—and certainly oftener than otherwise.[42]

The letter was written during Christmas time. Lamb felt homesick, which is why he began to frequent church more than he had previously done.

It is not known who was pastor at the American Church in the early twentieth century. But it appears from Lamb's letter that Leipzig's American Church was institutionalized to an extent that involved financial support from the congregation, for Lamb noted that while he had decided not to attend prayer meetings and the choir singing, he did "subscribe toward the support of the church."[43]

The American Church became closely connected with the American Students Club, once it had come into being. Similar to the club, sometime between 1904 and 1909 the American Church changed its name to welcome other native English speakers. In March 1901, Cooper told his mother that there is "a rather flourishing American colony in Leipzig. They hold Church service, have picnics, etc."[44] By 1909, Rev. Burtiss McHatton was president of the American and British Students Club and also in charge of the American-British Church. Born at Morning Sun, Ohio, he had enrolled twice at Leipzig, the first time aged thirty-five in April 1906, the second time in April 1908. He had been a member of the American-British Students Club since the 1908 spring term. In the following semester, he was elected president, a position in which he served for two terms.[45] It is not known when exactly McHatton became pastor of the church.

To sum up, the American Church at Leipzig was established between 1873 and 1875. It appears to have been pretty much a permanent establishment until at least 1909. Although little is known about its pastors, it may be said that they tended to be students either in the theological or in the philosophical branch. They were in their late twenties or mid-thirties. They necessarily spent prolonged periods of time in Leipzig and were central figures of the American colony. Curtiss had previously studied in Bonn, Mapes came directly from New York, McHatton from the University of Wooster. The latter registered twice at Leipzig but apparently did not leave town—he probably continued to preach. Both Curtiss and McHatton had followed their fathers into the ministry, whereas Mapes was the son of an architect, a generally rather unusual profession among the fathers of US students abroad. Genung's father was a carpenter.

A Central Leipzig-American Networker: Caspar René Gregory

Caspar René Gregory (1846–1917) personified a link between the American colony, its church, and the University of Leipzig from the early 1870s until World War I. For some four decades, his fellow countrymen—no matter if students, university presidents, professors, or his academic family relations—gratefully considered him a central figure of American life in Leipzig and turned to him for company, conversation, and contacts.

Gregory was born in Philadelphia. From 1867 until 1873 he studied theology at the Princeton Theological Seminary. In 1873, he came to Leipzig and earned a PhD degree, although he never matriculated. He continued Konstantin von Tischendorf's work, and in the 1883 spring term he was first listed as a lecturer in theology at Leipzig. In the fall of 1890/91, he became assistant professor, and in the 1891 spring term honorary full professor. Gregory declined calls to Cambridge (Massachusetts), Baltimore, and Chicago—that is, apparently to Harvard, Johns Hopkins, and the University of Chicago, some of the most renowned university projects in the United States back then.[46]

What put Gregory in an ideal position for networking (besides his cheerful disposition) was the fact that he was an American on the Leipzig faculty, that he was a theologian and close to the American Church, and that he had interesting academic family ties in the United States. Like Curtiss, Gregory was a central figure of Leipzig's American colony. Americans of various disciplines assembled at his place during leisure hours. On 19 April 1878, Calvin Thomas observed: "Last evening I spent in company with Peirce and Merrill at the rooms of Dr. Gregory where we had also some good 'talk.' Dr. G. is at work on Tischendorf's Greek Testament, has much of Tischendorf's MS."[47] Peirce and Merrill probably referred to Benjamin Osgood Peirce, a Harvard-trained mathematician who would return to that institution, and Samuel Merrill, a philosophy student who had previously studied at Heidelberg. Merrill would enroll at Leipzig in the following fall, whereas Peirce had arrived already a year before.

In the early 1890s, the philologists J. Duncan Spaeth and Thomas Marc Parrott met Gregory:

> It happened that we took our doctor's degree on the same day, and that evening the *Theologen* had a joint Kneipe with the *Philologen*. Dr. Caspar René Gregory of Philadelphia, Tischendorf's successor at Leipzig, made an address welcoming into the ranks of "Leipzig Doctors" his two young fellow-Americans, and I shall never forget the sight of Dr. Parrott in his full dress and white tie (candidates for the Ph.D. degree appeared before their examiners in full dress in broad daylight), making his bow to Dr. Gregory with a huge bouquet of roses in his bossom [sic], which his *Hausfrau* [here: landlady] had dedicated to him in honor of the occasion.[48]

Gregory must have enjoyed seeing many of his fellow countrymen follow up in his footsteps by obtaining a Leipzig PhD degree, but also by relishing fun aspects of the German university experience such as the joyful gatherings of academic club meetings.

Ten years later, Gregory was still an important member of Leipzig's American colony, now also involved in family-related academic networking. Gilbert N. Lewis wrote to his US mentor, the Leipzig-trained Harvard chemist Theodore William Richards, in January 1901: "Please thank Mrs. Richards for her kind letter. In a country where Heimweh [homesickness] is always on the wing and ready to swoop[,] it is cheerful to feel that friends at home are interested in what one is doing here. I see Professor and Mrs. Gregory not infrequently. They were kind enough to invite me to Christmas dinner and I spent an extremely pleasant afternoon there."[49] Richards was related to Gregory by marriage—their wives were sisters.[50] In the fall of 1886, Gregory had wed Lucy Watson Thayer in Cambridge, Massachusetts. She was a daughter of Joseph Henry Thayer of Andover. Gregory had met his future wife when she accompanied her parents on a trip to Germany.[51] Some ten years later, on 14 February 1896, Richards had informed the Leipzig chemist Wilhelm Ostwald that "I am very happy, for my betrothal to a very lovely Cambridge girl, Miss Miriam Thayer, has just recently taken place. Miss Thayer is a sister of Mrs. Professor Gregory of Leipzig, whom perhaps you may know.... I am sure that this will interest Frau [Mrs.] Ostwald. Chemically I am working upon helium now, in the attempt to separate large quantities of it into its components. But Miss Thayer has absorbed most of my spare time recently!"[52] The family ties with the Gregorys would occasionally bring Richards to the Saxon city. He took professional advantage of that, as is evident from the following note to Ostwald posted in the spring of 1907: "I am now on a very brief run to Leipzig to see my relatives there. I wish I could get to Grossbothen, but I am afraid that pleasure must be postponed until June or July, when I shall come again. Can't you find some

business which would bring you to Leipzig to-morrow morning? We might
have a walk together. My Berlin train leaves at noon. I think the Gregorys
have a telephone. Wont [*sic*] you call me up?"[53]

Gregory was also an acquaintance of US ambassador Andrew D. White.
Lane Cooper wrote to his father on 12 November 1900: "Mr. White's letter
to Prof. Gregory, an American and one of the important men in the theological faculty, brought me, I think, an acquaintance of value."[54] In fact,
Cooper's father was no stranger to Gregory, as Lane wrote on 27 April
1900: "Prof. Gregory, when I met him yesterday, spoke pleasantly of having
heard from you."[55] This probably referred to a letter Cooper's father might
have sent. The White-Gregory-Richards connection sooner or later brought
another player into the networking game, White's good friend Daniel C.
Gilman. Richards attempted to introduce Gilman to Ostwald on 20 March
1902: "Permit me to present to you Dr. Gilman, who was, as you know,
President of Johns Hopkins University for twenty five years, and is now
President of the newly founded Carnegie Institution for Research. He has
before him the organization of this great Institution, a problem of unusual
interest, which cannot but enlist your sympathy."[56] Ostwald failed to make
Gilman's acquaintance then and replied with regrets on 28 June 1902 that
he had missed Gilman.[57]

When Gilman visited Leipzig, he enjoyed Gregory's company. The two
men had a glass of wine at *Auerbachs Keller,* the Leipzig restaurant made
famous thanks to the likely best known German-language play, *Faust,* by
Johann Wolfgang von Goethe. From that restaurant, Gilman and Gregory
sent a jolly postcard to Richards. The text of the postcard was printed in
German, only the date and the names had to be filled in. It read: "Certificate: With this I inform you that today on the 26th day of the VIth month
one-thousand-nineteen-hundred-and-two in *Auerbach's Keller at Leipzig* I
thought of you over a bottle of superior wine and drank ... glasses to your
health. I send you my best regards and remain yours truly Caspar René Gregory. D.C. Gilman[.] The signature is certified with this stamp [a stamp]."[58]

Hospitable Families, the Knauths, and US Consuls

North Americans also gathered in the homes of American and English-
speaking German families. In November 1904, Lamb "went to tea at Mr.
Aburne's house. They endeavor to make their home a sort of headquarters
for Leipzig-Americans—and I met many of them—and enjoyed it nicely."[59]
He had met Aburne at a meeting of the American Students Club. Aburne
was from Providence and resided at Leipzig with his wife and family. He did
not register at the university, nor was he a member of the American Students

Club. Similarly, Cooper told his father in March 1901, "We have a number of intelligent young Americans in the University; there are also one or two American families that I have seen occasionally on Sundays."[60]

US students welcomed opportunities to spend a few hours in a surrogate family. Lamb knew several of them. In January 1905, he wrote to an unidentified friend Sam, who must have been connected with Leipzig at some point, "I've made many pleasant acquaintances here, but only one family that I've struck knew you—the Pratts—I must say though they are about the nicest of the lot."[61] Four years before, on 23 December 1901, Morris P. Tilley had informed Lane Cooper, "To-morrow night Mr. and Mrs. Dawson, Myers, Evans, and myself are invited to Mrs. Pratt's for a 7 o'clock Christmas dinner. If you were here you would be one of the fortunate ones."[62] A Henry Pratt from Toledo, then thirty years old, had enrolled in 1888, 1889, and 1891 and been a member of the first American Students Club. But it is not known whether he was related to the Pratts who entertained Leipzig Americans around 1900.

The case of the Knauth family is particularly instructive. Shortly after his arrival in Leipzig, Henry Pickering Bowditch became acquainted with the Knauths, who were fluent in English and desirous to gather Americans in their home. Bowditch told his mother on 3 October 1869: "I was invited last night to take tea with Mrs Knauth & met there quite a number of Americans. The whole family talks very good English particularly the daughter (17 or 18 yrs old I shld say) who was 2 yrs at school in London. Mr. K. is extremely friendly + I shall enjoy going there very much once in a while."[63] A few weeks later, he rejoiced: "I have just been to dine with my friends the Knauths. They are very friendly [+] hospitable people + I enjoy very much going there + talking a little English once in a while."[64] By 14 November, an evening call on the Knauths had become a regular feature in his daily routine: "In the evening I either make a call on the Knauths or go to the theater or stay quietly in my room (the last most frequently)."[65] In the summer of 1870, an opportunity presented itself to pay back the Knauth's kindness: "The son of Mr Knauth the banker, from whose family I have received so much civility, intends to go to America next month on business. I have given him a letter of introduction to Father + if he should present it I hope you will be able to return some of the attentions which his family have shown me."[66] It is not known whether Knauth Junior met the Bowditches in Boston then.

Meanwhile, back in Leipzig, Bowditch was becoming rather fond of the Knauths, particularly the daughter, Selma. The feeling was mutual. When Bowditch was about to return to America in the summer of 1871, the two realized that they would not bear being an ocean apart. The solution was marriage. "At last I have some real news to tell you[!]," Bowditch exulted in a letter to his family dated 17 August 1871, "Nothing less than a new engagement in the family. Miss Selma Knauth to Dr. H. P. Bowditch! What do you think of that? In my letter from Oberammergau I told you that I met the Knauths there. I accompanied them to Munich on my way to Paris. Here I made the discovery that Selma + I were both of us quite unhappy at the idea of separating and—in short we are engaged."[67] Thanks to the Knauths' hospitality, Bowditch found a wife who would accompany him to Massachusetts, and become the mother of their five daughters and two sons.[68]

Like Richards, Bowditch would return to Leipzig because of family ties, jolly memories of his student days, and professional contacts. From 16 to 19 August 1895, Bowditch visited together with his then 22-year-old daughter Ethel. He described the priorities of his visit to his wife: "In the forenoon yesterday I tried to find some of my friends, but all are away except Prof. [Max] Von Frey.... I had a long talk with Salvenmoser, [Carl] Ludwig's devoted attendant for forty years. He seemed to enjoy talking with someone who could appreciate his affection for his beloved master. He led me to Ludwig's grave in the neighboring churchyard where I laid a laurel wreath over the remains of my dear old teacher."[69] The physiologist Ludwig, Bowditch's Leipzig mentor, had died on 23 April 1895. One of the mourners at the funeral had been von Frey, who represented the assistants of the Leipzig Institute of Physiology on the sad occasion.[70]

The story of the Knauth family's association with Leipzig Americans does not end here. Members of the Knauth family were in touch with the American colony long before and after Bowditch became one of their relations. Already in November 1853, Mason C. Weld had met the Knauths thanks to an introductory note that he had obtained with the help of his father. Lewis Weld had been to Leipzig in the 1840s. He visited his son there in the fall of 1853. Mason told his mother: "A few days since I called on Mr Knauth to whom Father had a letter from Mr. Morgan on whom we called together as you know, and he interested me to take dinner with him the next day which I did. Mrs. Knauth speaks beautiful English, and they have lived several years in the United States. Their children speak English also."[71] Bowditch's future wife Selma must have been an infant then. There were several brothers besides her. Mr. Knauth evidently welcomed Weld in an equally winning manner as his family would welcome Bowditch and others in the future. Weld also repeatedly visited Mr. Knauth, insinuating his connection with the small but emerging American colony: "I called again on Mr. Knauth, from him to the club rooms to read the papers now + then. I have made some new acquaintance among the Students and among the Americans here, pleasant ones."[72] Having obtained a new watch, he wrote to his father in late 1853: "I have not seen Mr. Knauth yet to show it to him but will do so tomorrow. I have been at his store but he was out. Some more Americans have come to town to reside but I have not seen them yet."[73]

The Knauths also were known to later US students and stood for contacts with the US Consulate. In 1891/92, Harvard's George Howard Parker boarded with a Fräulein Knauth. Ms. Knauth provided him with a room, breakfast, dinner, heat, and light for 60 Marks a month ($15.00). She owned a pet dog and employed a maid.[74] In November 1890, Lincoln Steffens sent a letter from Leipzig, in which he noted his own address as "care of Knauth, Nachod & Kühne."[75] The name Nachod also stood for hospitality towards Americans. On 8 December 1884, Andrew D. White wrote to George Lincoln Burr: "Should you meet Mr. Nachod, Vice-Consul, please give him my best regards, and tell him that I remember with special pleasure his kindness to me during my last visit to Leipsic."[76] Frederick Nachod had been appointed US vice-consul in Leipzig on 23 July 1880 and vice- and deputy consul on 23 March 1884.[77]

US consuls in Leipzig were in touch with US students, smoothing over homesickness at times. Bowditch, who was the only US student at Ludwig's lab around 1870, rejoiced in meeting the US consul. In October 1869, he wrote, "I went last Sunday to a big dinner given by a club as a semi-annual festivity. We sat four hours at table. Fortunately, I sat next to the American consul who had just returned to Leipzig from a visit home. So I could talk English + get the latest news of my native land."[78] When Thomas Day Seymour reached Leipzig on 21 October 1870, he noted in his diary that together with his travel companion Thomas Harper Bush he went to have dinner with the US consul that evening.[79] Thomas B. McGee was consul from 1869 to 1870. He was succeeded by John H. Stewart, who served from 1870 to 1879.[80]

Family and Friends

More than twenty US students travelled to Leipzig accompanied by their spouses, whereby the personal and educational lives intersected in various ways. Then again, some US students in the late nineteenth and early twentieth centuries turned to Leipzig for higher learning and instead found a spouse, who in some instances shared his—or her—academic interests. James McKeen Cattell met his English wife Josephine Owen, a student of music, in Leipzig. She would collaborate with him also in the professional sphere.[81] The love affairs of Josephine Bontecou and Lincoln Steffens and of Elfrieda Hochbaum and Paul R. Pope also fall into this category. Moreover, a handful of US students actually dedicated their Leipzig dissertations to their wives.[82] US students were generally a little older than their German counterparts. They tended to pursue graduate and postgraduate studies. For the same reason, they were more likely to be married, even though by 1903, the statutes of the University of Leipzig stated that married men were not to be admitted as students. But especially in the case of foreign men, as Hart had noticed already in 1874, rules regarding matriculation were applied quite liberally.[83]

In spite of intellectual co-working, accompanying wives at Leipzig were busy bearing and rearing children. An example would be the McLaughlins. The Ann Arbor historian Andrew C. McLaughlin enrolled at the Saxon university on 25 October 1893. With him were his wife Lois, their toddler son Jamie, and a nanny. On 3 January 1894, McLaughlin made a somewhat cryptic entry into his journal. German words were interspersed as if to stress emotional strain: "Wednesday Jan'y 3rd [4?] Lois took a walk um [at] 5. After ten I was prepared to hold myself in readiness for an excursion. Thermometer had fallen to 8° Fa[h]renheit in honor of the event. Went 1st to Dr who was in Theater—then to nurse + then back to Dr.'s house leaving word to have him call when he came home. At 12:30 he came + and announced to us alles [everything]. Then I had a ride for two hours in the cold after a nurse, whom I had to pull out of the fourth story of the house out in the Vorstadt [suburbs]. At 6 R.H. ML. made his appearance."[84] McLaughlin's typed unpublished autobiography from 1938/39 more explicitly tells of the birth of a baby boy in January 1894 christened Rowland Hazard McLaughlin: "I have always been grateful to Lois for her courage in taking that European trip, when she knew that a second son [penciled: child] would be born during our sojourn in Germany; it required unselfishness and bravery to go, but she rightly said, 'If we don't go now, probably we shall never go.' Rowland was born on a bitterly cold night in Leipzig January 4, 1894."[85] In bitter irony of history, that Leipzig-born member of the Angell-McLaughlin clan died fighting the Germans in World War I.[86]

A letter to McLaughlin's brother-in-law, James R. Angell, as early as in 1892 conveyed Andrew's concerns about traveling with a family: "What do you hear or think about Cholera + its reappearance in Brunswick or Berlin—I am not afraid of it for myself but a baby is not so easy to look after + a whole family is not easy to look after."[87] J. R. Angell was studying in Berlin then. In February 1894, McLaughlin was able to give him more details about the good health of his wife and new son, whom he nicknamed Siegfried with pride in an allusion to Richard Wagner operas and also to victory, which is especially ironic considering the boy's future fate.

> Lois has given you through various sources some idea of our life here. It has been from choice + necessity very uneventful but we have enjoyed it immensely. Lois was so wonderfully well + strong up to the very last moment that Siegfried put in his appearance that she was able to see every thing.... Lois says she is under obligation for your German letter—the effort to read it seems to have

precipitated the coming of Siegfried, for not 24 hours there-after was he on the scene. She seems quite herself again. Perhaps not so strong but she looks quite well again.[88]

The Angell-McLaughlins were not the only extended US family to study at Leipzig. Arthur Mitchell Little and John Cornelius Griggs provide us with another example. Not only were they cousins (Griggs's mother had Little ancestry), but their lives showed a few curious similarities. Both had graduated from Yale with the class of 1889. They had arrived at Leipzig in the fall of 1891, although it was Little's second stint already (he had enrolled a first time in the fall of 1887). Griggs was married in July 1890, his cousin the following year in June. Little's eldest son, Edward Norton Little, born in Washington, DC, in late 1892, must have been conceived while Little was preparing his Leipzig PhD degree; Griggs's first child, Leverett *Saxon* Griggs, as the name suggests, was born in Leipzig in the spring of 1892. For both cousins, the fruitful stay at Leipzig was commemorated in the birth of a son. Leipzig was thus included in the family tree.

A third cousin, Harlow Gale, whose mother was a Griggs, enrolled at Leipzig in October 1890 and again in April 1893. He too had graduated from Yale (in 1885). He was to become a psychologist at the University of Minnesota. Griggs became a professor of music, while Little became a pastor, though he was also interested in music; he wrote a dissertation about Felix Mendelssohn Bartholdy.[89] At Leipzig, Gale befriended Lincoln Steffens, who wrote about him: "I have at last met a really admirable American student here, a Mr. Gale, Yale '85. After his A.B. he entered a theological institute but soon found he couldn't hold to the Faith and went over to philosophy. … One other American I like personally, but the rest are the narrowest of day-laborers in science and lack real culture."[90] The "others" at the Leipzig psychological institute in the early 1890s included some central founding figures of experimental psychology in the United States (see chapter 5). Steffens and Gale corresponded infrequently for the next few decades.[91]

A number of students were accompanied by their siblings—or they had siblings following in their footsteps demonstrating family loyalty to Leipzig.[92] For instance, Theodore William Richards had worked in Ostwald's laboratory in the spring of 1895. In October of that year, his younger brother Herbert Maule Richards arrived in town to study botany with Wilhelm Pfeffer. While no evidence is available to answer the question of whether T. W. Richards had influenced his brother in any other way than by setting an example, such evidence exists in another case. In February 1925, T. W. Richards revived his correspondence with Ostwald to lobby for his son-in-law: "I take pleasure in presenting to you the bearer of this letter, Dr. James Bryant Conant, now Assistant Professor of Chemistry in Harvard University.

We think (although perhaps I ought not to say so, being his father-in-law) that he is one of the ablest young organic chemists in America today."[93] In his attempt to link yet another member of his family to Leipzig, he referred back to the literally good old days before World War I, immediately adding after the introduction of his son-in-law, "It has been many years ago since we have corresponded and many terrible things have happened in the meantime." He closed his letter, "With kind remembrances of old times." The example illustrates that in spite of all, American Leipzig alumni continued to feel attached to their Saxon alma mater even after World War I when US student migration to Germany could no longer compare with that of the prewar period.

Traveling siblings also included sisters: 26-year-old Mitchell Bronk of Manchester, New York, who enrolled on 11 November 1889 to study theology, was possibly a brother of Isabella Bronk.[94] In a letter to *The Nation,* she voiced her humiliation about not being admitted to Leipzig in spite of an equal if not better preparation than "our brothers,"[95] although, of course, the wording might have been mere rhetoric. Only after the turn of the century was it possible for a brother and a sister to register both as regular students. In the fall of 1911, Mathilde Margarete Lange was joined at Leipzig by her younger brother Erwin, who intended to study *cameralia.* Sisters also traveled together. Edith and Alice Hamilton entered the university as hearers in the fall of 1895 to stay for one semester. Another example is that of the Thomas sisters. M. Carey Thomas had been a hearer at Leipzig from 1879 to 1882. Her sister Helen followed up in 1894. Women were also accompanied by their mothers, as was the case with Eva Channing in 1879 and Josephine Bontecou in 1890. Both mothers were divorced.[96]

The majority of students led, however, bachelor lives. They associated with old friends from their American alma mater as well as with new friends whom they had met on the road or to whom they were introduced by way of mutual acquaintances. Sometimes small groups of students travelled to Leipzig together. Associating with fellow countrymen from the same home region or educational institution allowed them to exhibit school spirit or to transfer US college culture to Leipzig, and thus to create a different type of home-atmosphere than was experienced at gatherings of the American Students Club, at the Church, or at the homes of American and Anglophone families.

Michigan provides a telling example about US school spirit in Leipzig. On 2 February 1878, Calvin Thomas, who had earned his Ann Arbor AB in 1874, recounted a conversation in the course of which he had been asked where he was from: "I said Michigan with a certain pride—which is not out of place here in Leipsic, for our University makes us known."[97] Indeed, Ann Arbor men had been a traceable presence at Leipzig ever since it had begun to rise in favor with US students. At Ann Arbor, Thomas had been taught by Leipzig-trained Frank Austin Scott and Martin Luther D'Ooge. On 7 November 1877, Thomas rejoiced over an encounter with three Michigan men at Leipzig:

> Yesterday by chance I ran across three men from Michigan University—one of them my old friend Theodore Johnston, with whom I have smoked many a pleasant pipe in Ann Arbor. I made him a long visit last evening and naturally we had much to talk about. The old "quartette," that used to assemble daily in Johnston's room, smoke the pipe of peace, read the rhythmic Greek and discuss the philosophy of life, has separated. Lane is married and has a boy. Townsend is studying Law at Ann Arbor, and Theodore and myself true to the plan we formed in college, and faithful yet to the bachelor students proclivities are here in Leipzig looking after *höhere Bildung* [higher education]. Well who knows whether one were not happier to mate himself with a "squalid savage" settle down and become a sober plodding citizen?[98]

Theodore Hitchcock Johnston enrolled at Leipzig on 5 November 1877. He had graduated from the University of Michigan with Thomas in 1874. In 1880, he would serve as an instructor in Latin at their alma mater. Not much else is known about him except for the fact that he died in Los Angeles on 29 May 1915. Thomas had had a vague notion that Johnston would turn up at the Saxon university. One of the first things he did after his arrival in early September 1877 was to look for Johnston: "Reached Leipzig ... at 8 this morning. Put up at Sebe's [?] Hotel and set out in a vain search for my classmate T. H. Johnston. Probably he is not in town."[99] It took another two months before they met again.

Yet another journal entry related the story of a new Ann Arbor quartette that formed in Leipzig after the chance meeting of November 1877. On 2 April 1878, Thomas wrote:

> Sunday evening the Michigan men residing in Leipzig met a[t] Johnston's room for a good-bye. There was a quartette of us. G. A. Briggs '75 and Percy Wilson [']75 with Theod. and myself of '74. Briggs and Johnston go to Freiburg in Baden.—are to meet in Weimar on the 10th inst. Wilson will remain here two weeks when he goes to Vienna[,] Prag, and Venice, and ultimately also will bring up at Freiburg. We four Michiganers celebrated with wine, beer, cognac, and cigars, and also more solid refreshments till 3. o'clock a.m. on Monday. It all reminded me of the time when another quartette parted at Ann Arbor some (nearly) four years ago. I felt pretty blue then and bad, also yesterday some experience of *le triste lendemain* ["the unhappy day after," i.e., a hangover]. But it dont [sic] last long and today I find myself decidedly less misanthropic. It may be that we shall meet for a tramp in Switzerland together this Summer, and it may be that we shall not.[100]

They did not.[101]

In the mid-1870s, Charles R. Lanman ran into a few friends in Leipzig. One of them was 25-year-old William J. M. Sloane of Richmond, Ohio, whom he had met in Berlin, and who crossed his path again at the American Chapel in Leipzig shortly after they both had arrived in town in October 1875.[102] In a letter dated 14 November 1875, Lanman introduced yet another friend, George H. Schodde from Pittsburgh, a 21-year-old theology student who had previously studied at Tübingen—like Lanman.[103] Schodde had enrolled at Leipzig already in April 1875 to study theology. He passed his examination at Leipzig in late July 1876.[104]

It was not uncommon to meet kindred souls in one's immediate—that is, academic—surroundings at Leipzig, and thus to find a close friend in a prospective colleague. This adds ambiguity to US student life abroad. It is difficult to separate leisure from scholarly activities and interests. William Henry Welch, who had registered at Leipzig on 14 November 1876, and Franklin Paine Mall, who had done so on 25 October 1885, became lifelong friends. They first met at Carl Ludwig's laboratory in the mid-1880s when Welch returned for a visit. Both eventually joined the medical faculty of Johns Hopkins University. Their liking for one another was so strong that by the turn of the twentieth century, Welch would address the younger Mall as "*Liebes Mäulchen*," a pun in German meaning something like "dear little cheek," signing his letter "*Ihr Ergebenster mit vollster Verachtung*" (devotedly yours with deep disdain).[105]

The association of William Carlos Williams and William J. Kelly, in turn, worked on the basis of a mutual acquaintance and was motivated by practical considerations. In a letter to his younger brother, who was studying architecture in Rome that year, Williams mentioned that he had met Kelly, his brother's friend from MIT student days: "I have found Bill Kelly and rather against your advise [*sic*] I have decided to room with him. We have two rooms opening one into the other in one of which we will sleep using the other as a study. As both of us will be at the University most of the day this ought to be a good arrangement as we will not have a chance to bother each other over much especially as we will be in different departments."[106] Kelly had enrolled on 18 October 1909 right after Williams in order to study chemistry. He was twenty-one years old at that time and one of the few Catholics among the Leipzig Americans. Williams referred to him once more in a letter to his brother in February 1910, "Bill Kelly says youre [*sic*] a lobster not to have written him ages ago."[107] Their association was not particularly close. Williams "didn't have much fun" in Leipzig and on the whole was rather lonely.[108] He befriended his teacher in English drama, Lehre Dantzler, a Vanderbilt graduate.

Housing Matters

Housing was, in fact, an issue that provided opportunities for informal networking in various ways. For once, as was the case with William Carlos Williams and his roommate, Americans would team up for rather pragmatic reasons when searching for a place to stay, resorting at times to distant acquaintances whom they had known in America. Then again, especially with a large US student crowd in town, Americans began frequenting specific bed and breakfasts for several years, obviously passing on information about the place to their fellow countrymen. Indeed, such bed and breakfasts could then become specialized not simply in Americans but in, for example, US students of chemistry and natural sciences. Such a specialization had something to do with the location of a bed and breakfast in proximity to certain laboratories. The housing situation—just like visits to German churches—was furthermore seen as an opportunity to work on one's language skills (sometimes it also turned out to be a hindrance in this regard). Finally, Leipzig was a mercantile city where two major fairs were held annually. Earlier American visitors considered this a nuisance. But in later years, US students could easily turn the demands of the fairs to their advantage by acquiring great lodgings at low prices simply by agreeing to leave their rooms to boarders for the duration of a fair.

Since at least the 1880s some Leipzig pensions were crowded with native English speakers, both to the dismay of serious students of German and to the pleasure of homesick Americans. In 1904, Arthur B. Lamb "found life in Leipzig very pleasant—but have the hardest kind of work getting any thing done[.] Nor am I learning German with any great rapidity. For English speaking people are so ubiquitous that there really isn't much necessity of it."[109] Lamb stayed at a pension in Liebigstrasse 2, first floor. The place was dominated by his fellow countrymen: "There are several Americans and English here, but they are, for the most part, students of several years standing here—and German is spoken at the table."[110] An advantage of the pension was its relative proximity to the laboratory where Lamb intended to work:

> The chief difficulty in getting a suitable room is due to the fact that the phys. chem. Institute is way out in the suburbs of the city, and in a direction away from the better residential districts. My room is *between* the centre of the city and the lab. and about a 15 min.s walk from the latter. It is however, right in the midst of the student district, where the houses tho from a continental standpoint comparably new, from ours are rather old, and hence quite destitute of modern conveniences.

The pension was a favorite with US natural scientists indeed. According to the Leipzig register, the future entomologist Vernon Kellogg stayed there in 1893 and 1897. Edward Zalinski, a student of mineralogy, followed up in 1902. In the summer of 1905, Raymond and Maud Pearl chose to reside at that pension. It had been recommended to them by another couple from across the Atlantic, the Smeatons. William Smeaton was a Canadian who embarked on an academic career at the University of Michigan. Like Lamb, he was a physical chemist. He had worked at Ostwald's physico-chemical laboratory from the fall of 1898/99 to the 1902 spring term.

Just how the Smeatons and the Pearls had met is not clear. The fact that W. Smeaton was a chemist supports Lamb's implication that the place was patronized by English-speaking natural scientists. Pearl was a zoologist. He described the pension to his mother on 23 July 1905:

> Well, we are settled here in Leipzig at last. We got in here yesterday afternoon at 3 o'clock and came here at once in a cab, and engaged a room. It is the place where the Smeatons recommended us to come, and it certainly is a very pleasant homelike place, all things considered. It is only about two blocks from where I shall work. It is a pension much patronized by Americans. Three old maids run it and they are lots of fun. The cooking is good, very fine so far. We are temporarily in a little room about the size of a room at home, but are to have a bigger one about August 1, when a man who is in it moves out. They speak nothing but German, or would not except for us. There are a number of Americans here now, who are all trying to learn German, but today at dinner they talked English nearly all the time. I think we shall like [it] very well after we get a little accustomed in the place.[111]

In a later letter, Raymond noted that in the semester about thirty boarders stayed at the pension. But during the Pearls' stay it was suddenly cleared out when one of the old maids came down with typhoid fever. Pearl revealed this only after they had left Leipzig. They stayed in the deserted place probably for money considerations, for Pearl seemed eternally concerned with expenses. Leipzig struck him as an expensive place to live.[112] But there was a positive aspect about it after all—the empty pension gave them an opportunity to practice German: "We are getting so we can jabber quite a bit of German now, though it is pretty poor. For nearly two weeks now we have been the only ones in the Pension, and so we have to talk German with the Fräulein."[113]

The question of suitable lodgings always touched upon language considerations. Having taken up residence at a pension at Turnerstrasse 17 in August 1883, James Hampton Kirkland, a future chancellor of Vanderbilt University, had only one complaint about his quarters. There were too many "silly Americans who persisted in speaking English, even though some of them had been there for a year."[114] As early as in 1827, the future Yale president Woolsey had decided not to share lodgings with his native English-speaking travel companion.[115] Woolsey was disappointed when he "found it a thing almost unknown to board in a private family, and am obliged to have a room in one place, get my dinners in another and perhaps my supper in a third."[116] It hindered his linguistic progress. By early January, he reported that the situation had not improved:

> You may conceive from the way in which I live that I am in a bad situation for learning the language of conversation with which I am a total stranger. I make the best amends for this that I can by reading and writing it, by talking with a master and with a young student of the University who talks German for my benefit a hour [*sic*] one day and talk English for his own the next. Most of the educated people here can talk French and many English, and until I can converse fluently it is idle to think of going into society to learn German."[117]

Boarding with Leipzig families was becoming easier as time wore on. Calvin Thomas thought staying with a German family attractive for language considerations: "On Thursday last I began to board in a Pension—thus putting an end, temporarily at least to the Ishmaelitish system of nomadic life. I am very well pleased with my situation. German family life is not just like ours—indeed I didn't expect it would be. But one thing is pretty certain. I shall have better opportunities than before for speaking German, and I desire to make all things count in that direction."[118] In 1870, Thomas Day Seymour—subsequently like Woolsey early in his career a professor of Greek at Yale—for the same reason as Woolsey parted with his travel companion, 23-year-old Thomas H. Bush. He explained to a friend back home in late October 1870, "My companion Bush ... from Ann Arbor had a classmate and friends here thro whom we were soon or immediately settled in a couple of large rooms, really almost elegantly furnished, near the University in a first class position."[119] Both Seymour and Bush had registered one after the other on 26 October and roomed together at Ross Strasse 13, third floor, a place that they had evidently found thanks to a Leipzig-Ann Arbor connection. On 11 December, however, Seymour decided to leave "Bachelor-hall life, free and independent tho it is" to stay with a German family, for even though he conceded to have made progress with his German "in sermons, lectures and reading," he found that in conversation he was "not strong."[120] He separated from Bush to focus on the linguistic challenge.

Fairs were a specific feature of the Leipzig experience that affected the housing situation considerably. For the great number of visitors, the prices of hotel rooms skyrocketed—if rooms could be secured at all. Hugh Swinton Legaré complained after his arrival in Leipzig on 29 April 1836 at 8 o'clock PM (only in this journal entry did he point out the time): "I arrived here just now, and, after applying unsuccessfully for lodgings at two hotels, (the town is swarming for the fair,) I established myself for the night at a rather shabby, dirty-looking place, called Stadt-Wien."[121] Legaré's friend from student days, George Ticknor, already in 1816 had observed, "Where a student takes his rooms it is generally on the condition that he shall leave them vacant a month at Easter & Michaelmas, as to be let to some merchant or person who may come to the fairs."[122] It still held true in 1853. Mason Weld, yet uncertain of his plans for the semester break, wrote to his parents, that the "only thing really sure then probably is that during the Messe (Fair) we shall not remain in the city."[123] He had been preoccupied with the issue since at least July: "In September comes the great Messe or fair at which time we will be obliged to leave our room for one month. During this time we shall privat[e]ly travel; whence it is not yet decided—if our friends are then within the bounds of Deutschland [Germany] we may see them, otherwise not."[124] By September, with the fair in full swing, he and Johnson had switched quarters: "The city is now full of strangers probably 20.000 are here attending the Michaelmass fair. The Hotels are of course full and in all just double the annual price is paid.... We have moved our rooms and now have a pleasant lower floor rooms, almost in the country, with very pleasant people, and you can be more pleasantly lodged and accommodated here than in any hotel."[125]

By the late nineteenth century, the fact that students had to vacate rooms for merchants during the fair no longer hindered but served the purpose of higher learning. As Hall observed in 1881, "Hotels double their prices, and excursion-trains run in all directions at reduced rates. Very many poor students take good rooms at very moderate terms on condition of sleeping in an attic or a hall during the fair, while their places are taken by strangers who are charged high prices."[126] It was also a matter of good luck and timing of one's arrival in Leipzig to get a decent deal on room and board. William Welch wrote on 16 September 1876 regarding the Leipzig fair, "They last three weeks, during which time the prices of rooms and of board are doubled, so that I am fortunate in getting settled beforehand."[127]

Summary

Besides interacting with their German professors in preparation for an academic career back home, US students also interacted in various ways with fellow countrymen (and -women) in Leipzig for the duration of their stay. Such interactions were often but not exclusively motivated by pragmatic considerations such as language learning or the necessity to organize aspects of their everyday life in Leipzig. But desire to meet other Americans while abroad also mixed pragmatic concerns with academic curiosity and pleasant leisure-time activities.

Networking activities of the American colony in Leipzig ranged from the formal organization of the American Students Club, which had been initiated comparatively late in the early 1890s for the first time, to meetings with old friends from one's home university. The American Students Club was obviously geared toward academic networking in the sense of aiding one another in advancing teaching careers besides helping newcomers to find their way about Leipzig. But already before the creation of such a formal organization more informal similar associations had existed, such as gatherings at the homes of US students of theology, a phenomenon from which the establishment of the American Church appears to have risen in the early to mid-1870s. Then again, there were simply families—both German and American—who enjoyed inviting students to their homes for the pleasant company and also to celebrate special occasions together. This phenomenon was likely fueled by the fact that occasionally even among students entire families had traveled to Germany, and they enjoyed organizing social events from which the many bachelors benefited who traveled on their own and lodged in bed and breakfasts often with yet a bunch of more single American students.

A particularly useful aspect of the different types of gatherings was the fact that one could meet students from different backgrounds and different fields of study (especially in the late nineteenth century) and also Americans who were in town for purposes other than a higher education. The American colony in its activities thus became a type of little America abroad, where one could get acquainted with compatriots from across the nation. This added yet another aspect to networking—the idea of better getting to know distant parts of the country, which I will discuss in more detail in chapter 7.

Notes

1. G. H. Parker to Family, 13 December 1891. Parker Papers, HUG 4674.12, HUL Pusey.
2. Ibid. The students were future chemist Howard Beers Gibson, Harvard 1888, who had enrolled at Leipzig in the fall of 1891, as well as 23-year-old Charles Carlton Ayer, Harvard 1889, who had arrived a year earlier. Ayer was to become assistant professor of Romance languages at the University of Colorado in Boulder. Wilder Dwight Bancroft, Harvard 1888, was indeed the grandson of George Bancroft, one of the pioneering American students at Göttingen. W. D. Bancroft was twenty-three years old upon his enrollment at Leipzig in the fall of 1890 and intended to study chemistry. William Marshall, a Catholic who had previously studied in Berlin, registered the same day. As Parker noted, Marshall

for a change was not a Harvard graduate. In 1892, Marshall earned a Leipzig PhD under Rudolf Leuckart. Regarding academic interests, he was therefore closest to the future zoologist Parker. Parker mentions more Leipzig Americans in his autobiography, *The World Expands: Recollections of a Zoologist* (Cambridge, MA: Harvard University Press, 1946), 64–5. See related entries and biographical files in *Quinquennial Catalogue of Harvard University 1636–1930* (Cambridge, MA: Harvard University Press) and HUG 300, HUL Pusey. As to W. D. Bancroft, see also Gillispie, Charles Coulston, ed. in chief, *Dictionary of Scientific Biography*, 9 vols (New York: Charles Scribner's Sons, 1970–74); Lilian Handlin, *George Bancroft: The Intellectual as Democrat* (New York: Harper & Row, 1984); Russel B. Nye, *George Bancroft* (New York: Twayne Publishers, 1964). As to Marshall, see K. Wunderlich, *Rudolf Leuckart. Weg und Werk* (Jena: Gustav Fischer Verlag, 1978), 47.

3. Amerikaner-Verein, Rep. II/XVI/III, Nr. 16, microfilm 488/94, 0182, LUA.

4. A. A. Noyes to H. M. Goodwin, 20 February 1890. Harry Manly Goodwin Papers, MC121, Box 1, Correspondence 1888–1891, MIT Archives.

5. Verzeichnis der Verbindungen, S.S. 1890. Rep. II/XVI/II, Nr. 3 Bd. 10, microfilm 474/94, 0097 [7], LUA.

6. Klub der *amerikanischen* und *englischen* Stud., ibid., II/XVI/III, Nr. 16, microfilm 488/94, 0199 [16].

7. Amerikaner-Verein, Rep. II/XVI/III, Nr. 16, microfilm 488/94, 0185 [2], LUA.

8. Verzeichnis der Verbindungen, S.S. 1890, Rep. II/XVI/II, Nr. 3 Bd. 10, microfilm 474/94, 0097 [7], LUA. A student of philology, Collins had registered thrice in October 1885, 1886, and 1890. In 1892, he earned a PhD degree. By the time he became first patriarch, he was twenty-eight years old.

9. T. D. Woolsey to Mother, 17 December 1827. Woolsey Family Papers, Group 562 Series I Box 3 Folder 39, YUL.

10. H. P. Bowditch to Mother, 31 October [1869]. H. P. Bowditch Papers HMS c5.1, HUL Countway. Also, typed excerpt from H. P. Bowditch to Father, 24 October 1869, ibid.

11. H. P. Bowditch to Father, 28 November 1869, typed excerpt, ibid.

12. C. Thomas, unfinished, typed Autobiography, 19–20. Thomas Papers, 86180 Aa 2 Ac, Box 1, UM Bentley. Perry had registered in June 1876. He was to teach Sanskrit and Greek at Columbia University and Barnard College, NY.

13. B. H. Warner, Jr. to William R. Day (Assistant Secretary of State), 7 February 1898. D[i]spatches from US Consuls in Leipzig, 1828–1906, microfilm T-215, roll 11, July 10, 1890-October 16, 1903, NARA. Following quote ibid.

14. A. B. Lamb to Mother, n.d. [winter 1904/05]. A. B. Lamb Papers, HUG 4508.50, Box 2, HUL Pusey.

15. Eberhard Brüning, *Das Konsulat der Vereinigten Staaten von Amerika zu Leipzig* (Berlin, Akademie Verlag, 1994), 19; Card Record Of Appointments Made From 1776 To 1968 (RG 59 Entry A1–798), NARA.

16. American Students' Club, S.S. 1900 + W.S. 1901/02, Rep. II/XVI/II, Nr. 6 Bd. 6, microfilms 476/94 + 477/94, 0497 [10] + 0166 [8], LUA.

17. A. B. Lamb to Family, 6 November 1904. A. B. Lamb Papers, HUG 4508.50, Box 2, HUL Pusey.

18. American Students Club, W.S. 1904/05, Rep. II/XVI/II, Nr. 5 Bd. 6, microfilm 478/94, 0104 [10], LUA.

19. Klub der *amerikanischen* und *englischen* Stud., ibid., Nr. 17, microfilm 488/94, 0209 [8].

20. Student. Körperschaften, S.S. 1909, ibid., Nr. 6 Bd. 24, microfilm 479/94, 0280. S.S. 1911, ibid. Bd. 28, microfilm 480/94, 0149. Sheetz enrolled in 1910, 1911, and 1913, by then aged twenty-five. Sheetz studied history and claimed a connection with the University of

Michigan but was not traced there. A student of philology, Donald Carpenter registered in April 1911. He was a one-time *Beisitzer* (associate); in the fall 1912/13, Mathilde Margarete Lange held the same position. Lange registered in 1910, 1911, and 1912 studying mathematics and natural sciences.

21. Student. Körperschaften, W.S. 1914/15, ibid., Bd. 35, microfilm 481/94, 0405 [54].

22. M. Tilley to L. Cooper, 2 March 1902. L. Cooper Papers, 14/12/680, Box 16, Cornell Kroch. Emphasis in original.

23. A native of Berkeley, Virginia, Tilley, coming from Göttingen, had enrolled in May 1900 and in 1902. He was a club member until the 1902 spring term. A graduate of Brown University, Morton Collins Stewart of Quincy, Illinois, was a student of languages. He enrolled in October 1900 and 1902 and served as club president from the spring 1901 to the spring 1902. He was *Schreiber* (secretary) in the 1902/03 fall. In the 1903/04 fall and 1904 spring terms, he was again first president. Tilley, Frank Abbot, Zalinski, and Dawson all hailed from Virginia. Abbot and Tilley had previously studied at Göttingen. They registered together at Leipzig in May 1900 to study modern languages. In the 1901 spring, Abbot served as *Schriftführer* (secretary). Edward Zalinski studied mineralogy. He enrolled in October 1900 and in May 1902. If he had sailed home before 2 March 1902, he was back two months later. He was a club member from spring 1901 to fall 1903/04. In the fall of 1900, Edgar Dawson arrived coming from Heidelberg. He was a 27-year-old philology student and a club member from fall 1900/01 to spring 1902. A graduate of Harvard and Yale, Frank Clifton Smith of Albany, New York, joined the club with Dawson. He had first enrolled in October 1896 and again in November 1901 and October 1902, by then aged forty. He was a club member until 1901/02 and from the 1903 spring to 1903/04 fall terms. American Students Club, S.S. 1900 to S.S. 1902, Rep. II/XVI/II, Nr. 6 Bde. 6 to 10, microfilms 476/94 + 477/94, LUA. Daniel Bussey Shumway, "The American Students of the University of Göttingen," *Americana Germanica* 8, nos. 5 and 6 (September–December 1910): 241.

24. L. Cooper (Berlin) to Father, 3 July 1900. Cooper Papers, 14/12/680 Box 18, Cornell Kroch.

25. M. C. Weld to Family, 24 July 1853. L. Weld Papers, Box 1, Folder 2, YUL. Emphasis in original.

26. G. H. Parker to Family, 13 December 1891. Parker Papers, HUG 4674.12, HUL Pusey.

27. M. C. Weld to Family, 24 July 1853. Weld Papers, Box 1, Folder 2, YUL. Emphasis in original.

28. George W. Manly, "Contradictions in Locke's Theory of Knowledge," (Dissertation, Leipzig: C. G. Röder, c.1892), 68. As to Delitzsch, see Julius Böhmer, "Das Geheimnis um die Geburt von Franz Delitzsch," *Saat auf Hoffnung* 71, nos. 2 and 3 (1934): 63–75, 110–20; S. R. Driver, "Professor Franz Delitzsch," in *The Expository Times*, vol. 1, ed. J. Hastings (Edinburgh: T. & T. Clark, October 1889–September 1890), 197–201; S.D.F. Salmond, "Franz Delitzsch: The Tribute of a Friend and Pupil," ibid., 201–03; G. Elmslie Troup, "Franz Delitzsch," ibid., 174–77. Owen C. Whitehouse, "Franz Delitzsch—Eregete and Theologian," ibid., 177–79.

29. Amherst College Biographical Record, Centennial Edition (1821–1921)—*Samuel Ives Curtiss* [Online]. 27 Nov 2000. http://www.amherst.edu/~rjyanco/genealogy/acbiorecord /1867.html#curtiss-si [5 Oct 2001]. Siegfried Wagner, *Franz Delitzsch* (Munich: Kaiser, 1978), 117. Samuel Ives Curtiss, *Franz Delitzsch: A Memorial Tribute* (Edinburgh: T. & T. Clark, 1891). C. R. Lanman to Aunt, 26 December 1875. Lanman Papers, HUG 4510.67, Letters from Europe, vol. 3, HUL Pusey.

30. Journal, C. Thomas, 2 October 1877, 141. Thomas Papers, 86180 Aa 2 Ac, Box 3, UM Bentley.

31. C. R. Lanman to Aunt, 7 November 1875. Lanman Papers, HUG 4510.67, Letters from Europe, vol. 3, HUL Pusey.
32. C. R. Lanman to Aunt, 14 November 1875, ibid.
33. Thomas LeDuc, *Piety and Intellect at Amherst College, 1865–1912* (New York: Columbia University Press, 1946), 22, 25.
34. Journal, C. Thomas, 20 October 1877, 150. Thomas Papers, 86180 Aa 2 Ac, Box 3, UM Bentley.
35. He had enrolled at the university a first time in the fall 1882 at the age of thirty-five and again a year later. See Michael M. Sokal, ed., *An Education in Psychology: James McKeen Cattell's Journal and Letters from Germany and England, 1880–1888* (Cambridge, MA: MIT Press, 1981), 129 n.1.
36. Beach, "Harvard Divinity School Necrology 1902–03," HUG 300 Ralph Thacher, HUL Pusey.
37. J. M. Cattell to Parents, 19 October 1884, reprinted in Sokal, *Education in Psychology,* 129. Following quotes ibid.
38. V. M. Spalding to Miss Southworth, 10 December 1893. Volney Morgan Spalding Papers, UM Bentley.
39. Journal, A. C. McLaughlin, Sunday, 29 October 1893. McLaughlin Papers, 85536Aa2, Box 1, UM Bentley.
40. J. Stafford to H. R. True, 14 July 1895, R. H. True Papers, BT763, Series II, Box 8, APS.
41. A. B. Lamb to Family, 6 November 1904. A. B. Lamb Papers, HUG 4508.50, Box 2, HUL Pusey.
42. A. B. Lamb to Family, 13 December 1904, ibid.
43. Ibid.
44. L. Cooper (London) to Mother, 16 March 1901. Cooper Papers, 14/12/680, Box 18, Cornell Kroch.
45. Klub der *amerikanischen* und *englischen* Stud., Rep. II/XVI/III, Nr. 17, microfilm 488/94, 0209 [8], LUA.
46. Karl Josef Friedrich, *Professor Gregory. Amerikaner, Christ, Volksfreund, deutscher Held* (Gotha: Friedrich Andreas Perthes, 1917), 15, 18, 23–25.
47. Journal, C. Thomas, 19 April 1878, 7. C. Thomas Papers, 86180 Aa 2 Ac, Box 3, UM Bentley.
48. J. Duncan Spaeth, "Thomas Marc Parrot," 4, in Faculty File Thomas Marc Parrott '88, PUL Mudd.
49. G. N. Lewis to T. W. Richards, 13 January 1901. T. W. Richards Papers, HUG 1743.1.5, Box 2, HUL Pusey. As to Lewis, see Melvin Calvin, "Gilbert Newton Lewis," in *Proceedings of the Robert A. Welch Foundation. Conferences on Chemical Research,* ed. W. O. Milligan (Houston, TX: 1977), 116–45; W. F. Giauque, "Gilbert Newton Lewis (1875–1946)," in *The American Philosophical Society. Year Book 1946* (Philadelphia: 1947): 317–22; Arthur Lachman, *Borderland of the Unknown: The Life Story of Gilbert Newton Lewis, One of the World's Great Scientists* (New York: Pageant Press, 1955).
50. In a 1901 letter to Richards, Harvard's President Eliot mentioned "your brother-in-law Gregory." Charles W. Eliot to T. W. Richards, 26 August 1901, T. W. Richards Papers, HUG 1743.1.5, Box 2, HUL Pusey. As to Richards, see also E. Bright Wilson, "Theodore William Richards," in *Proceedings,* ed. W. O. Milligan, 106–13.
51. Friedrich, *Professor Gregory,* 26.
52. T. W. Richards (Cambridge) to W. Ostwald, 14 February 1896. NL Ostwald, 106/6, BBAW.
53. T. W. Richards (on the train) to W. Ostwald, 22 April 1907. NL Ostwald, 106/62, BBAW.

54. L. Cooper to Father, 12 November 1900 and 24 September 1900. L. Cooper Papers, 14/12/680, Box 18, Cornell Kroch.

55. L. Cooper to Father, 27 April 1901, ibid.

56. T. W. Richards (Harvard) to W. Ostwald, 20 March 1902. NL Ostwald, 106/31, BBAW.

57. Postcard, W. Ostwald to T. W. Richards, 28 June 1902. T. W. Richards Papers HUG 1743.1.5, HUL Pusey.

58. Postcard, Gilman/Gregory to T. W. Richards, 28 June 1902, ibid. Emphasis in original. "Urkunde: Hiermit thu Euch kund und zu wißen/daß ich unter heutigem/am 26ten Tage des VIten Monats Eintausendneunhundertzwei in Auerbachs Keller zu Leipzig beim Edlen Rebensaft Euer gedencket /und … Glas auf Euer ganz spezielles Wohl geleert hab. Ich send Euch meine herzlichsten Grüsse und erbleibe in Freundschaft. Euer Caspar René Gregory. D. C. Gilman[.] Dieß Unterschrift wird hierdurch beglaubigt [Siegel] und unter Insiegel gelegt."

59. A. B. Lamb to Family, 6 November 1904. Lamb Papers, HUG 4508.50, Box 2, HUL Pusey.

60. L. Cooper to Father, 3 March 1901. Cooper Papers, 14/12/680, Box 18, Cornell Kroch.

61. A. B. Lamb to Sam, 12 January 1904 [1905!]. Lamb Papers, HUG 4508.10, HUL Pusey.

62. M. P. Tilley to Lane Cooper, 23 December 1901. Cooper Papers, 14/12/680, Box 16, Cornell Kroch.

63. H. P. Bowditch to Mother, 3 October 1869. H. P. Bowditch Papers HMS c5.1, HUL Countway.

64. H. P. Bowditch to Mother, 31 October [1869], ibid.

65. H. P. Bowditch to Mother, 14 November [1869], ibid.

66. H. P. Bowditch to Mother, 15 June 1870, ibid.

67. H. P. Bowditch to Mother, 17 August 1871, ibid.

68. Walter B. Cannon, "Henry Pickering Bowditch, Physiologist," in Science 87, no. 2265 (27 May 1938): 194. See also Manfred Bowditch, "Henry Pickering Bowditch. An Intimate Memoir," Physiologist 1, no. 5 (November 1958): 7–11.

69. H. P. Bowditch to Selma Knauth Bowditch, 17 August 1895. Bowditch Papers, H MS c 5.1, HUL Countway.

70. Heinz Schröer, Carl Ludwig. Begründer der messenden Experimentalphysiologie (Stuttgart: Wissenschaftliche Verlagsgesellschaft M.B.H., 1967), 94, 217 n. 93.

71. M. C. Weld to Mother, 22 November 1853. L. Weld Family Papers, Group 559, Box 1, YUL.

72. M. C. Weld to Father, 5 December 1853, ibid.

73. M. C. Weld to Father, 18 November 1853, ibid.

74. G. H. Parker to Family, 13 December 1891. Parker Papers, HUG 4674.12, Box 2, HUL Pusey.

75. L. Steffens to Frederick M. Willis, 1 November 1890, reprinted in Ella Winter and Granville Hicks, eds., The Letters of Lincoln Steffens, vol. 1 (New York: Harcourt, Brace and Company, 1938), 51.

76. A. D. White (Cornell) to G. L. Burr (Leipzig), 8 December 1884. White Papers, 1/2/2, Box 46, Cornell Kroch.

77. Card Record Of Appointments Made From 1776 To 1968 (RG 59 Entry A1–798), NARA.

78. H. P. Bowditch to Mother, 31 October [1869]. H. P. Bowditch Papers HMS c5.1, HUL Countway.

79. Diary, T. D. Seymour, 21 October 1870. Seymour Family Papers, Group 440, Box 25, Folder 200, Series VII, YUL.

80. Brüning, Das Konsulat, 19.

81. Sokal, *An Education in Psychology*, 363 [index].

82. Mattoon Monroe Curtis, a pastor and student of philosophy in early 1888, mentioned in his dissertation that he had been married since 1884. Mattoon Monroe Curtis, "An Outline of Locke's Ethical Philosophy" (Dissertation, Leipzig: Gustav Fock, 1890). See also Ernst C. Meyer, "Wahlamt und Vorwahl in den Vereinigten Staaten von Nord-Amerika" (Dissertation, Leipzig: R. Voigtlander, 1908); Conrad Kubler, "Beitrag zur Chemie der Condurangorinde" (Dissertation, Weida i. Th.: Thomas & Hubert, 1908); Jonathan Hildner, "Untersuchungen über die Syntax der Konditionalsätze bei Burchard Waldis. Ein Beitrag zur Grammatik des Frühnhd" (Dissertation, Leipzig: August Hoffmann, 1899).

83. *Immatrikulations und Disziplinar-Ordnung*, 11 [§ 18]. Concerning matriculation procedures, "in the case of a foreigner, the utmost liberality is displayed." James Morgan Hart, *German Universities: A Narrative of Personal Experience* (New York: G. P. Putnam's Sons, 1874 [reprinted London: Routledge/Thoemmes Press, 1994]), 36–37. See also John T. Krumpelmann, "The American Students of Heidelberg University 1830–1870," in *Jahrbuch für Americastudien*, ed. Ernst Fraenkel, Hans Galinsky, Eberhard Kessel, Ursula Brumm, and H.-J. Lang, vol. 14 (Heidelberg: Carl Winter Universitätsverlag, 1969), 169.

84. Journal, A. C. McLaughlin, 3 January 1894, 34. McLaughlin Papers, 855 36 Aa 2, Box 1, UM Bentley.

85. A. C. McLaughlin, autobiographical sketch, 32–3, ibid.

86. Shirley W. Smith, *James Burrill Angell: An American Influence* (Ann Arbor: University of Michigan Press, 1954), 62 n.5, 318.

87. A. C. McLaughlin (Ann Arbor) to J. R. Angell, [1892]. J. R. Angell Papers, Group 2, Series II, Box 8, Folder 55, YUL.

88. A. C. McLaughlin to J. R. Angell, 13 February 1893 [1894!], ibid.

89. Arthur M. Little, "Mendelssohn's Music to the Antigone of Sophocles" (Dissertation, Washington, DC: Gibson Brothers, 1893).

90. L. Steffens to Frederick M. Willis, 29 January 1891, reprinted in Winter and Hicks, *Letters of Lincoln Steffens*, vol. 1, 59.

91. See Alfred C. Raphelson, "Lincoln Steffens at the Leipzig Psychological Institute, 1890–1891," *Journal of the History of the Behavioral Sciences* 3, no. 1 (January 1967): 38–42. Another case in point is the Carrier clan. See *A History of the Yale Class of 1851*, 53 and Ybb 1851, vol. 2, Augustus Hart Carrier '51, YUL.

92. The five Fritschel brothers (?) of Iowa, who studied at Leipzig between 1877 and 1891, provide us with another example. Geo. J. Fritschel to C. R. Gregory, 28 (?) September 1911. Gregory Papers, a box marked MS 0994, MS 0995, MS 0996 (letters to Gregory), LUL Albertina—Sondersammlung. Dr. William Roba, Eastern Iowa Community College, provided me with materials about St. Sebald.

93. T. W. Richards to W. Ostwald, 1 February 1925. NL Ostwald, 106/72, BBAW. Following quotes ibid.

94. Isabelle Bronk, "Women at the University of Leipzig," *The Nation. A Weekly Journal Devoted to Politics, Literature, Science & Arts* 51, no. 1329 (18 December 1890): 480–81. Written at Leipzig on 24 November 1890.

95. Ibid., 481. David Y. Cooper, "Detlev Wulf Bronk," *American National Biography*, ed. John A. Garraty and Mark C. Carnes (New York/Oxford: Oxford University Press, 1999).

96. As to Channing, see M. C. Thomas to Mother, 20 November 1879, reprinted in Marjorie Housepian Dobkin, ed., *The Making of a Feminist: Early Journals of M. Carey Thomas* (Kent, OH: Kent State University Press, 1979), 202. As to Bontecou, see Justin Kaplan, *Lincoln Steffens. A Biography* (New York: Simon and Schuster, 1974)s, 45–46.

97. C. Thomas to Miss Davis, 2 February 1878. Thomas Papers, 86180 Aa 2 Ac, Box 1, UM Bentley.

98. Journal, C. Thomas, 7 November 1877, ibid., Box 3. Emphasis in original.
99. Journal, C. Thomas, 6 September 1877, ibid.
100. Journal, C. Thomas, 2 April 1878, ibid. Emphasis in original.
101. Percy Ripley Wilson and George A. Briggs had enrolled immediately after Johnston on 5 November 1877, both studying philosophy. Like Thomas, all three originally came from the Midwest: Wilson was born at Athens, Ohio; Briggs at PawPaw, Michigan; and Johnston at L'Anse, Michigan. Wilson passed away a lawyer in Los Angeles, California, in 1909, where he had lived since 1882 probably in touch with Johnston. Briggs died already in 1882 in his native PawPaw. Necrology Files Percy Ripley Wilson, George Allen Briggs, and Theodore Hitchcock Johnston, UM Bentley.
102. C. R. Lanman to Aunt, 24 October 1875. Lanman Papers, HUG 4510.67, Letters from Europe, vol. 3, HUL Pusey. Lanman mentioned him in his diary on 9, 12, 18, 23, 26 January; 5 February; and 26 July 1876, ibid., HUG 4510.5, Diaries pre-1881, no. 11 and 13, 29 December 1875 to 11 February 1876, Box 1.
103. C. R. Lanman to Aunt, 14 November 1875, ibid., HUG 4510.67, Letters from Europe, vol. 3.
104. Lanman mentioned him in his diary on 19, 31 January; 11 February; and 26 July 1876, ibid., HUG 4510.5, Diaries pre-1881, no. 11 and 13, Box 1.
105. For example, letter [typed copy], W. H. Welch to F. P. Mall, 5 April 1901 and 8 April 1902. Welch Papers, Box 36, Folder 25, JHU med.
106. W. C. Williams to Edgar I. Williams (Brother), 20 September 1909. MS Coll 395, Box 2, Folder 51, UP Van Pelt.
107. W. C. Williams to E. I. Williams, 20 February 1910, ibid.
108. William Carlos Williams, *The Autobiography of William Carlos Williams* (1948), 109–12.
109. A. B. Lamb to Sam, 12 January 1904 [1905!]. Lamb Papers, HUG 4508.10, HUL Pusey.
110. A. B. Lamb to Family, 17 October 1904, ibid., HUG 4508.50, Box 2. Following quote ibid. Emphasis in original.
111. R. Pearl to Mrs. Frank Pearl, 23 July 1905. R. Pearl Papers, B:P312, Series II Personal Correspondence, APS.
112. R. Pearl to Mrs. Frank Pearl, 21 August 1905, 3 September 1905, 18 September 1905, ibid.
113. R. Pearl to Mrs. Frank Pearl, 12 August 1905, ibid.
114. Edwin Mims, *Chancellor Kirkland of Vanderbilt* (Nashville: Vanderbilt University Press 1940), 45. See also the Kirkland Papers at Vanderbilt University's Special Collections.
115. T. D. Woolsey to Mother, 17 December 1827. Woolsey Family Papers, Group 562 Series I Box 3 Folder 39, YUL.
116. T. D. Woolsey to Mother, 17 December 1827, ibid. It still held true by 1881. From Berlin, Henry Alfred Todd wrote to his parents: "To my disappointment I found no family boarding-house for students advertised. They [added: students] all take their meals at restaurants, which is not the way for me to learn German. I discovered, however, a private boarding-house so delightfully located that I felt almost certain it would be full of Americans." Henry Alfred Todd (Berlin) to Parents, 27 March 1881. A. W. Dulles Papers, Todd Family Correspondence, Box 117, Folder 8, PUL Mudd. Todd would be the father-in-law of Allen Welsh Dulles, whose father, Allen Macy Dulles, had been Todd's Princeton acquaintance and a student at Leipzig in 1879/80. In her autobiography, A. M. Dulles's daughter Eleanor Lansing Dulles only mentioned that her father had studied in Göttingen. She omitted Leipzig in her book written in the midst of the Cold

War: Eleanor Lansing Dulles, *Chances of a Lifetime: A Memoir* (Englewood Cliffs, NJ: Prentice-Hall, Inc., 1980).

117. T. D. Woolsey to Sister, 3–5 January 1828. Woolsey Family Papers, Group 562 Series I Box 3 Folder 39, YUL.

118. Journal, C. Thomas, 8 October 1877. Thomas Papers, 86180 Aa 2 Ac, Box 3, UM Bentley.

119. T. D. Seymour referred to his "companion Bush" from "Ann Arbor" in a Leipzig letter to Philo, 30 October 1870. Seymour Family Papers, Box 21, Folder 153, YUL.

120. T. D. Seymour to Philo, 4 December/11. December 1870, ibid.

121. Hugh Swinton Legaré, *The Writings of Hugh Swinton Legaré ... Prefaced by a Memoir of his Life ... Edited by his Sister,* vol. 1 (Charleston, SC: Burges & James, 1846), 137.

122. Journal, G. Ticknor, 18 September 1816. Microfilm W3275, reel 1, vol. II, HUL Lamont.

123. M. C. Weld to Parents, 1 Aug 1853. L. Weld Family Papers, Group 559, Box 1, Folder 2, YUL.

124. M. C. Weld to Parents, 24 July 1853, ibid.

125. M. C. Weld to Father, 22 September 1853, ibid.

126. G. Stanley Hall, *Aspects of German Culture* (Boston: James R. Osgood and Company, 1881), 75.

127. W. H. Welch to Emily Sedgwick Welch, 16 September 1876. Welch Papers, Box 68, Folder 16, JHU med.

Chapter 7

FORGING AMERICAN CULTURE ABROAD

Approaching a Foreign Culture

THIS CHAPTER TRACES American perceptions of German student life and culture, focusing on the question of what US students found worthwhile to be adopted in order to advance the state of affairs in America. After all, besides their scientific and scholarly quests as well as active involvement in Leipzig's American colony, US students also tried to get to the bottom of the German experience by observing German culture and student life, which they would subsequently mix with their own customs and activities. One could say that they were adjusting aspects of American culture in direct contact with the foreign culture. As increasingly large numbers of US students returned from Europe by the late nineteenth century, the elements of German (academic) culture, which they more or less consciously embraced, would stand a greater chance of being accepted into US society at large.

Language is a good example to illustrate what was happening, for as Americans were becoming more fluent in German, some would begin to communicate by incorporating German in their English as needed. In doing so, US students adopted their favorite slices of Germany, whereby the outcome was nonetheless genuinely American as the vast majority of US educational pilgrims were not just conscious of but also proud of their American identity. Their eagerness to identify, choose, and take on aspects of German culture was motivated by a desire to advance America's standing in the world. With regard to German culture, US students nonetheless often remained outside observers who followed with a certain emotional detachment what was happening in Germany and at the German university.

They discussed aspects of the foreign student culture and developed clear opinions of what they liked about it and what struck them as archaic. Such perceptions could also change in the course of time.

In addition to that, guidebooks alongside reports from veteran educational travelers also created expectations that did not necessarily meet with German reality once the students had reached Europe. One could argue, then, that Americans created a type of ideal, imaginary culture before their journeys, which they then tried to pin down while abroad by picking those aspects of foreign customs that were closest to their ideal. They thus came to Germany to shape their ideas of what American (university) culture should be like, whereby the different German ways helped clarify what exactly it was that they sought.

For many US students, one of the more fascinating elements of German student life was the fact that Germans would freely mix academic quests with jolly entertainment, such as when they organized club meetings during which they might discuss deeper philosophical questions in a beer hall. The example of such academic clubs probably had inspired US students at Leipzig in the early 1890s, as we have seen in chapter 6, to initiate an official American club. The one difference between the American Students Club and the various German academic clubs, though, was that Germans talked lofty philosophy, whereas Americas talked business as to how to improve US academia.

In the following, let me trace the different stages of guidebook, linguistic attainments, observation of German student life, and a reflecting of German culture in the activities of the American colony. It will become obvious that Americans did not necessarily come to Germany determined to merge cultures, but that they were often motivated by pragmatic, everyday needs—in combination with a healthy skepticism such as expressed in their keeping a distance from German culture. They nonetheless ended up doing what I described in this introduction: taking on aspects of the foreign customs to create a better America.

The Guidebook

US students prepared for their German venture by reading guidebooks such as James Morgan Hart's *German Universities* (1874) addressed to the US student in Germany and, of course, Baedeker.[1] Indeed, John W. Burgess, an Amherst graduate who traveled to Europe in the summer of 1871, remembered that his "friend and companion, [Elihu] Root, had been reading his guidebooks all the way over."[2] (This is *not* the Elihu Root who served under President Theodore Roosevelt.) Likewise, on his way to Leipzig in 1853,

Mason C. Weld "went to see and did pretty much all that Murrays hand-book says may be seen from the cars between O. and Cologne."[3] George H. Parker arrived in Leipzig having studied his Baedeker well, which served him also in his communication with his family back home. In October 1891, describing his journey from the Harz Mountains to Saxony, he wrote, "Next in the series comes Leipzig ... (see map Baedeker p. 342)."[4] In 1877/78, Calvin Thomas followed advice about culinary Leipzig: "Dined at Müller's Restaurant, recommended in Hart's German Universities, but too far off for my present purposes."[5]

Guidebooks were not just read for practical purposes relating to every-day life, and Leipzig Americans also viewed advice from such books with a critical eye. After all, Americans abroad were not a homogenous mass but a group with vastly differing opinions in spite of a type of American consensus that united them especially while abroad. By the end of his Leipzig stay, Thomas noted, "I have just been reading again the opening pages of Hart's book on the German Universities in which he says that he consumed the first six months in writing exercises and studying grammar. He defends the plan zealously, but for me that would certainly have been nearly a waste of time."[6] Of course, Thomas was a prospective linguist, which would explain why language came to him more easily. James McKeen Cattell informed his parents on 29 January 1886 that Hart made "great fuss over the examination—says he worked on it ten hours a day for I don't know how long, broke down in health &c. I am taking the matter very easily."[7] Writing to his parents, the criticism certainly also emphasized the fact that he was doing well at the German university, likely even better than his compatriots.

Language Considerations

Besides reading up on German culture, a thorough knowledge of the lan-guage was essential. US students' struggles with the German tongue illus-trate how seriously they were at work while abroad.[8] Whereas their first and foremost objective was to follow lectures, they soon learned that col-loquial German was equally necessary and actually harder to acquire. They consequently devised strategies to reach the high fluency that would allow them to spend their time efficiently, such as by planning on a few prepa-ratory weeks of language cramming in regions where a supposedly pure German dialect was spoken. Once they were enrolled at their university of choice, they tried to pick lectures by professors with a particularly clear pro-nunciation. Moreover, as mentioned before, the most ambitious frequented German churches to check on their linguistic progress and boarded with German families. Once they had reached high language proficiency, they relished peppering their English with interspersed German phrases. The poet William Carlos Williams, a medical student at Leipzig in 1909, summed up the development, "I am banging along at the usual gait trying to get some of the German-dictionary into my subconscious self's mind. It is one Hell of a ... language I can tell you and is pretty hard to manage. It is coming however and I expect to have plenty of fun later."[9]

While in 1827/28, Theodore Dwight Woolsey was still confronted with Latin lectures,[10] his fellow countrymen of later generations had to put their textbook knowledge of German to the test. The future physiologist Warren Plimpton Lombard, a Harvard graduate who later taught at the University of Michigan, in an autobiographical sketch remembered the "ridiculous course in German which I took in College" that had "left me with no real knowledge of the language."[11] In spite of a summer of cramming, in the fall of 1882 he "soon found that the Leipzig Professors used a vocabulary much greater than I had acquired." Likewise, Andrew C. McLaughlin shortly after his arrival in 1893 noted that he had "[h]eard the funniest lecture.... I could not understand much—Will try him again perhaps."[12] He did not. By the last day of December that year he confided to his diary: "My work in the Uni. has diminished to two sets of lectures—one by [Felician] Gess on the Fr. Rev. which I understand excellently and the other by [Karl] Lamprecht from whom now I can understand 2/3 by careful listening."[13]

Some professors were appreciated on account of their clear pronunciation. In the fall of 1895/96, Edith Hamilton delighted in Karl Brugmann's lectures, "And I don't know why it is," she mused, "but his German presents no difficulties to me. It is no exaggeration to say I understand him quite as well as if he spoke English. It seems as if his thought was so lucid that it lit up his language."[14] Similarly, Thomas Day Seymour was pleased to find that "Prof Dr [Georg] Curtius' lectures on Greek Grammar are the lectures which I am most anxious to hear and most fortunately for me his enunciation is very distinct, so already I can understand much."[15] Henry Pickering Bowditch went to Paris in 1868, moved on to Bonn the following year, and in the fall of 1869 settled in Leipzig. At Bonn, Bowditch was "following Max Schultze's lectures on histology," which were "really very admirable" for "I can understand a great deal of them & am every day improving."[16] A decade later, Calvin Thomas reported a similar success: "Today I had my first experience in the lecture room. Thanks to my previous study and the work I have done since reaching Leipsic I was able to understand from the outset. The lecture was Curtius[,] Subject: Griechische Literatur vorzüglich der Poesie [Greek Literature with Special Focus on Poetry]. I lost scarcely a word and although my notes were none of the best, it was not because I couldn't understand but because I tried to use the German schrift [Gothic script]. I shall take notes in Latin [letters] which is every way better."[17] Two months later, Thomas qualified the "German Schrift," as "an invention of the devil" to which he "won't give … countenance."[18]

A language needs work even—or especially after—one has acquired a high level of fluency. Not all US students at Leipzig might have been as serious in this respect as Thomas, who pledged early in his first Leipzig semester in the fall of 1877 "not to neglect German; to devote a portion of each day to its study, and to practice in composition. There is danger that one will relinquish all effort as soon as he can understand well and can make known his ordinary wants."[19] But the future professor of German did not quite achieve his goal. Towards the close of his year in Leipzig he came to control his ambitions and be content with his achievements. While translating Lithuanian in class, which he managed well, the professor "was not long in detecting that I was a foreigner. I am not so sensitive on this point as I once was, and shall be tolerably satisfied to speak German decently well and fluently even if I can't deceive people into the notion that I am a German."[20]

Bowditch, by contrast, had more difficulty in advancing his German, which might partly be explained by the fact that he was a physiologist rather than a linguist. While at Bonn, he struggled with German almost to desperation: "I devote a great deal of my time to the German language & shall have to do so for a long time before I acquire any proficiency in speaking it. This learning foreign languages is no joke, German least of all. There is no use in trying to make believe that it is not a terribly hard language. How much time students lose in learning foreign languages!"[21] This little outburst immediately gave him an idea:

> If we only had a common language such as Latin used to be in the last century we should save a great deal of time. Why should not an international congress construct from the already existing elements of speech an easily learnt, flexible, scientific language which should be taught in all the schools of the world & in which all books intended for a world wide circulation should be written. Such a language would probably in the course of time replace all the present languages & all mankind would be united by a common speech. About that time look out for the millennium.

In fact, already the 1850s had witnessed efforts in France to create a universal language. In 1887, Ludwig Lazarus Zamenhof from Russian Poland published his thoughts on an artificial language, Esperanto, which still has its followers today.[22] One of the most famous Leipzig professors of the late nineteenth century, the physical chemist Wilhelm Ostwald, was a fervent supporter of the idea and, after his retirement in 1905, devoted time and effort to the cause.[23] By contrast, the Leipzig philologists August Leskien and Karl Brugmann were more reserved about the issue.[24] Their professional interest in linguistics must have dimmed their enthusiasm regarding an artificial world language—after all, languages are always subject to change and thus a dynamic rather than a static phenomenon. An artificial language would necessarily develop and thus differentiate into new dialects and eventually new languages—especially if it were widely distributed and used by sizable portions of the world population.

By December 1869, Bowditch, now in Leipzig, after more than half a year of residence in Germany, sighed that the "language is still an obstacle. Even under the most favourable [*sic*] circumstances when I understand all the words perfectly I cant [*sic*] read German more than 1/2 as fast as English. It is an awfully hard language + I am afraid I shall never be able to use it with any facility."[25] Little surprising, then, that he rejoiced when a young Scotchman arrived at the laboratory in Leipzig a few weeks later. Bowditch now had a "little more occasion to use my own tongue."[26] Before leaving Germany in the summer of 1871, Bowditch, of course, married a young German, Selma Knauth, who was fluent in English.[27]

One cannot live on scholarship alone—a US student in Germany did not face the real linguistic challenge in the lecture hall, though not everyone was aware of that upon arrival. Thomas wrote to a Miss Davis shortly after he had reached Leipzig in September 1877:

> Now while I'm at it I want to explode one doctrine which has led me to the wasting of considerable time. Some lunatic or other whose book I read, says that the hardest thing in German is the vocabulary of abstract and philosophical terms—'Tis false! The hardest thing is the concretest. Zum Beispiel [for instance], to make a tailor understand how you want a suit of clothes cut, a waiter whether you'll have your steak rare or well-done +c: or to buy an article when you don't know what the name of it is.[28]

Thomas sighed in conclusion that "I never knew how many things there are in the world before and these things have names and in German the names have genders and these genders may be accompanied by Umlauts and no end of contrivances of ingenious villainy. But give us time—Was lange dauert, wird endlich gut [what takes long in the making will turn out well]."

Colloquial vocabulary could, however, hardly be learned in the lecture hall. But learning it from the locals proved slightly problematic. As Thomas noted in September 1877, "the Saxon pronunciation is notoriously bad."[29] He was by far not the only one to show concern with the local dialect. Upon his arrival in December 1827, Woolsey tried to be optimistic about his linguistic progress: "This language as spoken I cannot understand more than I could French on landing in France last spring but I have no doubt that it will come to me more easily than the French has done; so much does it resemble the English. A person hearing the salutation 'gut morgen (good morning)[']' with which we were repeatedly saluted along the road would have thought himself almost in some shire of England where they speak a corrupt English."[30] But few of his compatriots shared his optimism as to that.

Early in the century, a most persistent argument in favor of Göttingen as an ideal university for US students insisted that in the Hanover area the spoken German was much closer to the written word than elsewhere, particularly in the south. In the 1820s, it seemed unlikely to Henry Dwight that the German states could ever be united partly on account of the variety in dialects. For, as some neighboring Native American tribes supposedly had once complained about the Tuscaroras, Dwight observed, the southern Germans had a "harsh" and "barbarous" pronunciation that sounded like "white man's wagon going down stony hill."[31] He conceded, though, that both the Hanoverian *and* the Saxon dialects were more pleasing to the foreign ear, although:

> The Saxons are accused by the Hanoverians of having a harsh accent; though the Rhine states would be perfectly satisfied to speak as well as the former, whose pronunciation they place next to that of the German subjects of king George [i.e., the Hanoverians]. There is one sound which distinguishes a Hanoverian from every other German. All words beginning with the letter *s*, when followed by a consonant, they pronounce soft; for example, the words *sprechen, stein* [to speak, stone] they utter as they are written. The Saxons and others always give the *s* the sound of *sh;* as *shprechen, shtein.* This the Hanoverians condemn, as it makes their language very rough, which is of itself harsh enough to any foreign ear; and they also observe that the orthography ought to be followed. Their reasons appear conclusive to every foreigner; but they are not thus regarded by the other Germans.

How, then, could a stay at a Saxon university be justified from a purely linguistic point of view?

When, after 1870, Leipzig became one of the educational centers in Germany, the local dialect proved a crucial hurdle to be taken—although US students would now occasionally realize the absurdity of such language considerations. Some continued to voice the opinion that Hanoverian purity of dialect was uncontested, quickly adding that German was generally an ideal language for academic purposes.[32] The future Harvard philosopher William James, Bowditch's college friend, who roamed Europe in the late 1860s, however, made fun of the language purists in a letter to the latter dated 5 May 1868, that is, before Bowditch himself had crossed the Atlantic. James wrote from Heidelberg, situated in the south of Germany:

> [Heidelberg]'s a delicious place to live in, people say, altho' the Swabian German is laughed at by those of the North. So if you are intending to come to Germany this summer and to devote yourself to the language, which is the common plan,

you would hardly choose it for a residence. For my part, I think this universal fastidiousness on the part of Americans about hearing good German the first three months is the most ludicrous phenomenon of the 19th century. The common people you won't understand, no matter where you are, and your own dialect is so certain to be worse than the very worst you can possible hear from educated people, that to be particular is as absurd as for a chimney sweep to refuse to sit down because there's dust on the bench. The important gain in the first three months is leisure to read a lot of German, to get to think in it and to be forced to utter sentences in it.[33]

James concluded, "There is nothing which I would sooner sacrifice, in choosing a place to camp in and start my German, than a good accent in the people." Unhappy with the German lady he had hired as a teacher, Thomas also came to realize that the assistance of a native speaker was not necessarily the best road to acquiring a language: "I thought so once and now I know it."[34]

A German university was hardly ever chosen for a local dialect but for the academic opportunities to be found there as well as for the scholarly reputation of individual professors and lecturers. Local dialects could lend additional credit to an institution at best, or, alternatively, add difficulty to the German experience. Besides, the language problem could be approached, as James suggested, by devoting the first few weeks or months in Germany concentrating exclusively on the language. In 1882, Lombard decided on Weimar as an ideal place to cram "German for all I was worth during one Summer. I was quite proud of myself when I went to Leipzig in the Autumn."[35] That his preparation nonetheless proved unsatisfactory was mentioned already. No documents are available that would explain why Lombard had chosen Weimar in Thuringia. Possibly the fact that the great German poets Goethe and Friedrich Schiller had lived and lay buried there as well as the proximity to Leipzig might have influenced his decision. It is also possible that someone had recommended the town or even a particular pension to him.

James Rowland Angell first went to Braunschweig because his father had studied German there several decades before.[36] James Burrill Angell, president of the University of Michigan at Ann Arbor in the late nineteenth century, during the late 1850s had gone to Europe convinced that "the best German was that spoken in the free state of Brunswick."[37] In 1893, J. R. Angell's sister Lois and her husband Andrew C. McLaughlin also opted for a more provincial setting in order to work on their German. They chose Grimma, "a little town about half way between Leipsic and Dresden. Those weeks were devoted to a study of German of which I knew scarcely a word when I went there,"[38] wrote Andrew. Upon their departure for Leipzig, the couple reinforced their linguistic efforts:

We insisted on Katy's speaking Deutsch mit [with] the baby + with us + entered once more upon the effort to speak continually with each other. Six weeks in Germany finds us able to ramble along in bad German with each other whenever the conversation comes [to] very ordinary matters, + to understand a good deal of what is said directly to us—but not to follow a conversation between two natives—though Lois understands better than I. The ordinary words, such as verstehen [understand], or glauben [believe] are now in + part of our thinking material.[39]

Katy was the maid, the baby their toddler son Jamie.

Not all US students went to a remote area by free choice in order to exclusively study the language. In 1902, Irma C. Wieand had already spent two weeks in Leipzig when she decided to go to Bad Grüna for the summer:

This step was made from necessity, not from choice, as I had expected to travel during the summer instead of resting at a German Bad [spa]. However, my object to learn to speak German was perhaps furthered rather than defeated by this change in my plans, as I was obliged to use that language constantly, and the physical strength I gained was, no doubt, worth more to me, in view of the fact that I wish to study this winter, than sightseeing would have been.[40]

Wieand implied her worry about a contemporary concern: Would a female actually support without harm to her reproductive organs the exhaustive effects of intense study that was inevitable by a stint at an institution of higher learning? As late as in 1900, a Leipzig physician went so far as to "prove scientifically" that women were intellectually inferior.[41] Until 1922, twelve editions of his oeuvre were published.[42] There were similar arguments in the United States, the most famous being *Sex in Education* by Harvard's Dr. Clarke, which was published in 1873.[43] Wieand reassured herself as well as the readers of her class letter by pointing out that she kept an eye on the state of her health.

Impressions of German Student Life

According to the available sources that, unfortunately, allow us only a limited glimpse, US students for the most part appear to have remained observers of German culture while abroad. McLaughlin interwove a description of Germans into his account of matriculation procedures, turning his wait into an almost sociological study of a foreign Other. Interestingly, this foreign Other was above all else described as *not* being intellectually superior, which insinuates a conviction on McLaughlin's part that the United States could build up similar academic appeal. He observed that "The hall is very interesting + was to me especially so—filled as it was with a couple of hundred German students. They were of all sorts of appearance—... but I am sure appearing no brighter."[44]

German student life struck US visitors as different, diverse, and not necessarily in tune with their expectations—a sign that student culture was evolving. Indeed, US students in the German countries noticed that German student life must have changed in the course of the nineteenth century. In November 1871, Thomas Day Seymour told his classmates at Western Reserve that he was disappointed, because at Leipzig "there is none of that German Studentlife and German Studentsongs of which one hears so much"; it could be found only at smaller universities "and even there these are checked."[45] At Heidelberg, so he continued, "some Americans were sentenced to pay a fine of a hundred dollars or go to jail for six weeks, for singing on the streets as American students so love to do."

Some characteristics of German student life observed by earlier US students were evidently disappearing; but Americans' foci also shifted to embracing other aspects of German student culture as the century wore on. Drinking events and dueling would be examples. US students delighted in German academic clubs, which, as Boston's Eva Channing mockingly wrote in 1879, embraced "the free social life of the university, as embodied in its various 'Kneips' [ritualized drinking events] and literary 'Vereins' [clubs], where, indeed, the 'feast of reason and the flow of soul' are generously combined with the less ethereal delights of beer and tobacco."[46] At Leipzig, the Modern Philologists (Neuphilologen Verein) were especially popular with up to four official US members per semester in the 1890s. Among them were Thomas Marc Parrott and J. Duncan Spaeth, who later remembered Parrott's "ability to combine concentrated and strenuous study with hearty enjoyment of life."[47] Parrott had previously studied at Princeton, Spaeth at the University of Pennsylvania. They became colleagues in the Princeton English department.

US students were intrigued by ritualized beer-drinking during German academic club meetings. A *Kneipe* or *Kommers* allowed for fraternization between students and faculty. The future muckraker Lincoln Steffens's description of a *Kneipe* in 1890 was a succinct, chronological account suggestive of a sociologist's notes. The letter was addressed to Steffens's father rather than to a peer, which is probably why Steffens stressed the fact that he had not overstepped his limits, proof of his self-control abroad. Steffens was detached in noting differences to drinking in North America. He thus mirrored the guest lecturer who had discussed European drinking habits.[48] In 1905, Arthur Lamb described in a like manner a "King's *Kommers,*" a drinking event in honor of the Saxon king, Rector Magnificus of the University: "The affair was held in a large hall in the Zoological Garden. Between

2- and 3000 students and professors were there—seated at long tables—each with his stein of helles—or dunkles [light or dark beer] before him. The King entered—great applause—speech of welcome by the acting rector and by a representation of the students. Answering speech from the King—more applause. Then prosits to the King—and a steady consumption of beer—punctuated by splendid singing of student songs from printed slips—quite drowning out what seemed a crushing big orchestra."[49]

Scholarly zeal underneath the surface of mere drinking appealed to US visitors. In her autobiographical novel, the Chicagoan Elfrieda Hochbaum has Scott Leigh—the fictional counterpart of Paul Pope, a future Cornell professor whom she met in Leipzig around 1900—marvel at the intellectual undercurrents in both the *Kneipe* and the duel: "German students ... indulge not only in the physical duel, but in the intellectual one. While they are improving their fencing, they are not neglecting to sharpen their minds. While they are half-intoxicated, they extemporize poems in Latin. While they sit at their beer-tables, they discuss the foundations of society, the origins of religion, the influence of science on philosophy, and the political significance of the development of the navy. Most of them are under twenty-one."[50]

After their return, some US students adopted the beer and fraternization of students and professors at American institutions of higher learning. For instance, Parrott taught his younger colleagues and graduate students at Princeton "German songs, and drank pitchers of beer with them even in the days when there was supposed to be no beer in America."[51] Alice Hamilton observed that before World War I, German clubs were common at US universities. They allowed faculty members to meet and "to drink beer and sing German songs and reminisce tenderly about the golden days in Heidelberg, Bonn, Jena."[52]

US visitors were curious about dueling but did not participate to the same degree as they did in academic clubs. Eighteen-year-old Wymberly De Renne of Georgia enrolled at Leipzig in October 1871 to study *cameralia* (business). He heard lectures on philosophy, logic, and international law. But the—for him—most captivating aspect of the German university was the "subculture of duelists." De Renne joined the Saxonia Corps. When he "left Leipzig in the fall of 1873 he had both a certificate of studies completed and a large duelling scar that crisscrossed his left temple."[53] To date this is the only example of a Leipzig American who fought duels; that he was a Southerner does not mean, however, that all Southerners were less inclined to excel academically. Vanderbilt's James Hampton Kirkland would be an example to the contrary.[54] For the academically ambitious US students, dueling was a remnant of the past and generally a waste of time.[55] In late 1891, describing a walk through Leipzig, George Parker actually referred to German students organized into fraternities (*Burschenschaften*) as "sights."[56] German *Burschenschaften* kept dueling practices alive.

As it was then prohibited by law in the German state of Saxony, a late-nineteenth-century *Mensur* (duel) turned into a secretive affair. Leipzig students would cross the border into a neighboring state for that purpose. Parker described "the great oak under which the students used to duel but which the Saxon laws now forbid so that they all go to Halle, on Tuesdays I believe, and do their cutting on Prussian Soil." If a US student wished to attend it, he had to ask a German acquaintance to introduce him to the inner circle of a *schlagende Verbindung,* or dueling fraternity. In a letter to Rodney Howard True, the zoologist Joseph Stafford wrote, "I was told that I was probably the only American who ever saw such an occasion."[57] Conveying a stirring sense of secrecy, he nonetheless remained a sober observer fascinated with the human body's robustness: "It[']s surprising what it takes to kill a man." It brings to mind the attitude of another Leipzig American, the historian Andrew C. McLaughlin, who in 1893 noted with regard to German acting: "It's all too passionate for a cold blooded American."[58]

Reflecting German Student Culture in Activities of the American Students Club

In its activities, the American Students Club at Leipzig appeared to be an organization that had adjusted to German customs but applied them to serve US means, such as in the way in which the club members mixed scholarship and leisure without especially in later years losing track of advancing American higher education. They also always got entertained in the process. For example, when in February 1890 Arthur Amos Noyes wrote to his friend Harry M. Goodwin about the American Students Club, he started off with its academic aspects: "It brings the fellows in all the different branches of study together, and gets them acquainted. I have enjoyed the meetings exceedingly. Every night some member is selected who talks for half an hour or so on some subject he is interested in, and then a general discussion follows."[59] But the discussions were, just like those at German academic club meetings, meant not only to inform and educate but to entertain: "Time before last," Noyes continued, "one of the zoologists described a summer stay in the Bahama Islands, where he went to study sea animals. He told a number of anecdotes about the life of the people there, especially the Negroes, and related a number of their stories in the dialect. Then another night a fellow gave us an account of a trip to Greece."

The club's purpose was, however, not simply to share experiences but to help evaluate and thus to elevate US higher education, an aspect that seemed to become more pronounced after 1900. Lightner Witmer of the University of Pennsylvania did not join the club, though he attended a meeting in 1891: "It is quite a large club. That evening they had an address on an 'Ideal College Course in Political Science.' ... I got up and said that I should like to make a few remarks concerning the instruction given at the U. of P. [University of Pennsylvania], if it were permitted to a mere guest to address the meeting. Then I sailed in and unfolded to them the Wharton School in all its magnificence, and I think the little seed took root in all their hearts and will grow."[60] Not subject matter itself such as political science was discussed but the *ideal college course* in political science, that is, the way in which the subject could best be treated.

The topical choice of an ideal course reveals that not German but US education was the primary focus. US students in Leipzig took advantage of the multitude of backgrounds of their fellow countrymen in town (as well as their acquaintances elsewhere) to compare different college courses in the United States from first-hand experiences. The Witmer episode was no isolated incident. Morris Tilley informed Lane Cooper in 1901, "At the Club meeting ... we had a talk from Prof. Dunneway of Leland Stanford on Amer. and Ger. Univ[ersity] methods followed by a general discussion of the subject."[61] A Clyde Augustus Duniway was indeed on the Stanford history faculty as an instructor. He was on sabbatical leave during the 1901/02 academic year: "The greater portion of his vacation will be consumed in study at the Universities of Leipsic, Berlin, and Paris, with a side trip into Switzerland."[62] His name appears neither in the club's official membership list, nor in the Leipzig register. He had earned a PhD degree from Harvard in 1894 and ultimately became a university president.[63] Arthur Lamb provided another example in 1904: "Last evening ... Prof. Crowell of Brown Univ[ersity] gave us a talk on 'Germanics at Brown University.'"[64] Asa Clinton Crowell had earned a PhD degree at Brown in 1894 and subsequently became an assistant professor of Germanic languages there. He would promote the study of German into the 1920s.[65] Until early 1904, Morton Collins Stewart had been a member and an officer of the American Students Club. He had studied at Brown but appears to have left Leipzig before the 1904 fall term. He might have established the contact with Crowell.

The American Students Club at Leipzig was above all educational, not political. The club's 1899/1900 constitution explicitly stated, "Discussion of questions touching the German government or pertaining to partisan politics, American or British, will not be allowed,"[66] which was in accord with official university regulations[67] and might have been a reason why Witmer did not join. On 31 October 1891, he informed a friend about a socialist meeting, where he had met some of the most important German socialists including Wilhelm Liebknecht and August Bebel.[68] Witmer found political debate outside the university, although he was rather cynical about it. Interestingly, according to a letter written at Leipzig in September 1888, Witmer's US mentor, Leipzig-trained J. M. Cattell, had met Liebknecht during his European venture. Cattell also voiced sympathies with the socialists.[69]

In spite of its seriously academic ambitions, the American Students Club also provided a platform for social gatherings and a meeting place for pranksters, which might also be interpreted as a reviving American college traditions while in Germany. Lamb asked an unidentified friend in 1904: "Was the American Club in existence in your day? Did they ... then play the Cow Trick on callow neophytes?"[70] Americans also enjoyed alcoholic beverages during their club meetings, though it is not clear whether they performed the German drinking rituals; if they did, they did not deem it worthwhile to be recorded. On 2 March 1902, Morris Tilley wrote to Lane Cooper: "Last night at the American Club we had our Schluss Kneipe [final drinking entertainment] and then afterward free choice spirits [and] had an ex Kneipe until—well pretty early this morning. I wish you could have been along with us."[71] The academic discussions also drifted off into less serious waters. As Noyes related:

> Gill one night described a visit of his to a masked ball in Leipsic; they are not very respectable affairs, and yet he pretended to have seen most of the members of the club there. He usually asked them what they were doing there, and every one had some excuse. One of the "theologes" said he came there to study "total depravity." Our art student was there to study modern art as exemplified in female attire, so he told him. He had the audacity to say he met me there, and on expressing his surprise at seeing me in such a place, I replied that I came only to study the application of new aniline dyes to the human countenance, and he said that to change the subject I went off into a tedious discussion about tetramethyl-diamids tri-phenylcarbinol derivatives.[72]

Augustus Herman Gill was an MIT graduate who had studied chemistry at Leipzig since 1888. He had known Noyes already back in America, which might have prompted him to playfully accuse Noyes of being a killjoy. Noyes lived alone for most of his life. He arrived at his laboratory at 4 AM and left at 8 PM. He took his students on excursions into nature, both to get to know them and to develop a sense of their potential as scientists and researchers. He loved poetry.[73]

US students enjoyed entertainments such as balls, though their opinions of them varied over the years—earlier accounts told of important social gatherings that allowed students to meet and mix with Leipzig society, whereas later accounts mention disreputable affairs. George H. Parker went to one of the ill-famed masked balls in the 1891/92 fall term and fretted: "There is a Masked Ball almost every night. I have been to one—staid up and went between 12 and 1:30 A.M. It was frightful. An experience is quite enough."[74] By contrast, earlier US students, such as William H. Welch, had experienced balls as opportunities to meet Leipzig society. Welch told his father in December 1876: "Through the kindness of Prof. [Karl Hugo] Kronecker, the assistant professor of physiology, I have made the acquaintance of some of the professors here and have been able to see something of German social life. I attended as his guest one of the professor's balls which are held monthly and bring together in a very pleasant way the professors and their families."[75]

Welch then veered off into musing about differences in academic social life on both sides of the Atlantic: "After supper and toasts dancing began and was indulged in by nearly all of the professors. I was struck by the liveliness and mirth of the occasion without any sacrifice of good manners. I fancy that a gathering of professors and their families with us would be about as stiff and formal as can be imagined." Welch was quick to reassure his father, "My knowledge however of Leipsic society does not extend much deeper than this," a neglect that he explained with dress considerations: "I can not accept any invitations to social gatherings as I have no dress suit, and it would be absolutely unallowable to attend a dinner here without full dress."

Six years earlier, Bowditch had given a sober account of a professor's ball in January 1870: "I went to a professor's ball last Sunday in Leipzig on the invitation of Prof. Ludwig. There was nothing magnificent about the affair[.] The dresses were simple + in very good taste. There were many good pleasant faces amongst the young ladies but no striking beauties. There was the usual set-down supper towards midnight. Prof. Ludwig's daughter is quite pretty + yet bears a striking resemblance to her father who is anything but a beauty."[76] Unlike Welch, the son of a country doctor, Bowditch had, of course, sprung from New England aristocracy, which might explain differences in both men's impressions of Leipzig balls at roughly the same time.

Little America in Leipzig

Leipzig's American colony organized its own festivities as well as sports games. Alongside group visits to the concert hall and opera, such events united US students and residents and created a little America in Leipzig. As Hochbaum pointed out in her autobiographical novel, "Entering the ball-room, she was back in America. Here were the students of music, the transient tourists, the wives and chaperoning mothers; Americans who were living in Europe for the better living and the cheaper living, professors and those who hoped to be professors."[77] For some, social events of the American colony were great opportunities to overcome the blues.

US holidays provided welcome occasions for social gatherings, although non-American native English speakers also joined, and not all US students wanted to spend time with their fellow Americans. Lamb noted in 1905, "We celebrated Washington[']s Birthday by a Dance given by the Anglo-American Club—at which three English to one American showed up."[78] Of course, by then American student numbers were declining, and the British probably simply enjoyed the fun aspects of the occasion. As a matter of fact, though, not all US students wanted to celebrate US holidays in Leipzig. It did not mean that they were less patriotic, but that they preferred to advance their European studies instead, thus making the best possible use of their time abroad. On 8 July 1878, Thomas observed: "The national holiday passed without special demonstration on the part of the Americans resident in Leipzig, and I felt no pang of remorse."[79] Neither did the centennial of the Declaration of Independence stir all Leipzig Americans. Lanman mentioned the event in passing before referring to a pleasant evening at the house of a Leipzig professor: "The '4th' I spent at Leipsic. A number of my countrymen made an excursion. But the eve I spent very pleasantly at Prof. Curtius'."[80]

By 1900, the July 4th celebration attracted a large crowd, which might be explained at least partly by the boost in national self-confidence after the victorious 1898 war. Moreover, as I suggested earlier, among the students studying at Leipzig then might have been more Americans who had embarked on the educational journey not so much for the intellectual benefits to be derived from the experience but because everyone else seemed to be doing it. They were following well-trodden paths and eager to have some fun, such as the celebration of the national holiday. As Cooper wrote to his father from Berlin in July 1900, he experienced "a patriotic service in anticipation of the Fourth," with US ambassador Andrew D. White and his wife.[81] There were numerous serious students in attendance. The prospective chemist Frederick Gardner Cottrell reported in his diary a year later, "July 4-Thursday. Spent morning ... at lab then went to Waldshencke [*sic*, a restaurant] in Connewitz for Celebration (200 people there). See photos + programme. Knocked around with Prof. Lloyd of Columbia Teach College."[82] Yet another year later, Cottrell was busy polishing his thesis. The national holiday passed altogether unnoticed: "July 4 overhauled thesis + cut it down to dimension that might still squeeze through. Took stroll around cemetery to collect my thoughts + then had talk over the matter with [Robert] Luther who advised giving it to Ostwald direct."[83]

Most students arrived in Leipzig for the fall term. Their first major US holiday was Thanksgiving. In November 1904, Lamb looked forward to it with mixed feelings. He was homesick. "Tomorrow is Thanksgiving," he wrote, "and it seems hard to realize that I shan't sit down as usual to a real New England Dinner at Home!" He did not expect his German landlady or the American Students Club to make up for it: "Our landlady is going to have a real turkey, however, for dinner and during the evening the American Club is to give a dance. I fear the turkey will be a poor substitute for the genuine article and I don't expect that the dance will compare with real ones at home."[84] Apparently, his apprehensions were partly justified:

> The Thanksgiving Dinner was indeed a poor substitute, but our landlady did her best. The dance on the other hand was a very pleasant affair—There were more than 70 [90?] people present—almost equally divided between the two sexes. It was a delight to see so many Americans together especially so many American girls. The music was furnished by a German orchestra and wasn't especially good—for they play with quite a different accent; one which no doubt suits the German style of dancing admirably, but is quite difficult for Americans to dance by.

Thanksgiving was celebrated long before the American Students Club came into existence; it was certainly celebrated nonetheless. "There is going to be a big Thanksgiving dinner here next Thursday at one of the hotels," Bowditch told his mother on 14 November, probably in 1869, "where all the Americans in Leipzig will eat together."[85] Two years later, Seymour recorded in his diary: "Had a Thanksgiving dinner at the Hotel de Pruße. Very good. Ten courses. Wine etc. Ten of us there.... Eat for two hours, sang for two hours and then went to Gewandhaus [concert hall]. Lovely Day. Black clothes in evening without overcoat."[86]

While Seymour simply enjoyed the US festivity, by Christmas time Lamb was still homesick. He moaned on 13 December 1904: "*I'd like to spend next week at home!*"[87] Even lonelier was William James. On sabbatical leave from Harvard, he spent a few dreary days in Leipzig meeting Wilhelm Wundt in late 1882. On 11 November, he wrote a poetic letter to his wife Alice inspired by the Leipzig fall. Like others before and after him, he interspersed his letter with German expressions as if to emphasize the depth of his feelings:

> 8 P.M.
>
> Dearest! Theuerste!
>
> Altho I sent you a Briefchen [little letter] this morning I cannot refrain from turning once more in the lone evening hour to "one in whose tender bosom I" +c. Leipzig has been to day very gelid, with a filthy atmosphere, and altogether with the poetic "mellowness" I spoke of rather swamped by the genius of No-

vember. For the first time ~~since~~ yesterday, I have had to have fire, and the feeling of the immobile heat of the cast iron stove makes me feel like getting on to a land of open grates such as Paris is to be.... My journey runs down hill now to Paris—Berlin was the apex—and I grow impatient as I near the goal. Harry will be there.... I'm going now to bed early where I shall drop + sleep with thoughts of thee and thy babes.... I hope the photographs will soon be here. Good night! Good night![88]

Harry was, of course, James's younger brother, the novelist Henry James. The doctor-poet William C. Williams also never quite overcame his homesickness during the long Leipzig fall and winter. He wrote to his brother: "I've felt rotten since I've been here, not in health but from lon[e]liness,"[89] and again a few months later, "I must not stay here too long."[90]

By late December, spirits tended to rise again. For, the Christmas holidays also provided an opportunity to experience more German culture or to travel about. George H. Parker eased any traces of homesickness with a sense of humor, immediately delving into a description of the German ways: "As you know I was overtaken in my preparation for the feast by the feast itself. The first thing I knew the squares in Leipzig began filling up with Christmas trees and booths of toys etc and I ... early in the morning of my birthday [took] the first train out from Leipzig for St. Andreasberg."[91] Parker was born on 23 December 1864. He spent Christmas 1891 among friends in the Harz Mountains. To leave town at that time of the year was not uncommon. In December 1895, Edith Hamilton wrote to her cousin and friend Jesse Hamilton that together with her sister Alice she would leave for Dresden. In anticipation of the trip, Edith wrote: "I think I shall really feel that I am in Europe then. Leipzig has become so familiar and homelike. We have lost the sense of it being really foreign parts."[92]

The Saxon capital with its famous picture gallery was generally a favorite destination for short trips.[93] In 1875, Lanman had also planned to spend his Christmas break in Dresden, "as it is only a very short ride from here."[94] But it worked out differently. On 26 December, he sent a lengthy description of his German Christmas to his aunt, exclaiming, "It seems as though I had been the recipient of *too* much happiness and blessing at this blessed Christmas tide. I shall never forget my German Christmas."[95] The account is a mixture of academic excitements and Christmas celebrations. He first went to hear Christmas songs at the St. Thomas Church and then found that a German journal had blessed him with the publication of one of his writings. He subsequently exchanged gifts with his landlady and was invited to a Christmas dinner at Curtius's. He concluded with the exclamation "Oh! the Germans make a great deal of Christmas, and are n't they kind to strangers? I have had so much blessing beyond all hope or deserts."

With the days growing longer again starting in January, and with students typically arriving in Leipzig in the fall rather than in the spring, there are fewer incidents of homesickness on record after the Christmas days. Fun and different sports events instead became interesting diversions. For example, in 1904/05, Lamb related that US Consul Southard P. Warner had "challenged the Leipzig Hockey team to a game with a team of picked up Americans and English. There are 3 or 4 good players among us, but to make the necessary 7, 2 or 3 fellows like myself—who have never played the game will be pressed.... The game was scheduled for yesterday but as I said, the weather was bad—and the ice melted—so it has been postponed till Wednesday."[96] No records are available that reveal whether the game eventually took place.

There are other examples of American sports activities. On 8 October 1877 Thomas noted in his journal: "On Saturday I was so indiscreet as to play a game of base-ball and the result is a lameness still felt. While on the field made the acquaintance of several new Americans."[97] Although Thomas had vowed to record but his scholarly progress in his journal, when he composed his memoirs in old age, he described American baseball games at Leipzig in great detail (resorting to a personalized spelling):

> In the spring of 1878 we wer numerous enuf so that we could usually get out two nines for a game of base-ball on Saturday afternoons. On one occasion that I vividly remember a foul ball that I had pitcht struck a small boy on the nose and drew a little blood. The district police—our improvised diamond was out in what was then suburbs—at once interfered to stop so dangerous a sport. We argued that the accident was after all not so very serious and that probably nothing of the sort would ever happen again. But the local guardian of the law was obdurate; the utmost concession he would make was that we might submit our case to the central office.
>
> So we formed in line by twos and marcht solemly about a mile to the Central Polizeiamt [police office], where, by means of bat, ball, word and gesture, aided by an imaginary diagram on the floor, we explained to the Chief of Police the American game of baseball. After a while a gleam of almost human intelligence came into his eyes. Then his face darkend again and he demanded to know what the game was for anyway: *Aber, meine Herren, was ist der Zweck dieses Spiels ueberhaupt?* [But gentlemen, what's the point of this game?]
>
> And strange to tel, we wer able to answer the query to his satisfaction. He evidently thought it ridiculous that a lot of alien lunatics should *wish* to go through a cycle of such laborious movements for nothing, but at the same time concluded that the foolishness did not normally and necessarily call for blood from the spectators. Yes, we might go on. So we all marcht solemly back, showd our permission to the local potentate and resumed our game.[98]

Whether the incident took indeed place in this manner must remain unanswered. But it is quite certain that the American colony did organize American baseball games in Leipzig.

Less exclusively American sports were also attractive. In the winters of 1869 and 1870, Bowditch enjoyed skating.[99] He also experimented rather unsuccessfully with riding a bike: "I made another effort yesterday to ride on a velocipede. My success was not startling. I am afraid it would require rather too much time to learn. I was to have gone riding on horseback this morning with my Russian friend if the weather had been favorable, but good weather in the Winter months must be rather a rarity in the latitude according to all accounts."[100] In the warmer seasons, quite a few students—Americans as well as Germans—were fond of tennis.[101] Boating was a welcome spare time activity on Leipzig's rivers as well.[102]

Besides sports, US students enthusiastically took advantage of Leipzig's cultural offerings, such as concerts and operas. According to Parker, among Leipzig Americans opinions about the Leipzig music offerings came in two marked classes: "One class roundly condemns the performances and says the orchestra is a thing of past reputation only—this is too strong, for an orchestra that could play the Anakreon overture with the precision and delicacy with which this one did last Wednesday is not to be dismissed so. The other class lauds it to the skies."[103] Most US students whose letters and journals I examined did give a favorable impression of the music, particularly in comparison with the offerings at home.[104]

Trips to Leipzig's concert hall *Gewandhaus* or to the opera were not only affordable for students but once again provided an opportunity to meet fellow countrymen. Parker described a visit to the Leipzig opera in late 1891, adding, "Between the acts (the length of them is always noted on the program ...), you go out and walk up and down the large hall way around the 1st balcony. Here you meet your friends."[105] He listed a handful of acquaintances from his US student days at Harvard whom he had met in the Leipzig concert hall. Parker also explained in detail how a student benefited in going to the opera at Leipzig:

> The university is also involved in the city government so that students have certain priv[i]leges.... An ordinary Univ[ersity] student can buy tickets for the theater at half price. The way it is done is this. Sunday morning at 8.30 those who want good places, go to the Castellan's [janitor's] room in the Augusteum ... and sign in a book for each night that they want a ticket for the theater. For instance this morning I went over and signed for Wednesday (Faust) and Friday (Tannhäuser) and then on Wednesday our tickets will be waiting for us till 10 o'clock. If they are not called for by that time they are sold to others. All the tickets are for the Parterre right side and the best places are given to the first-

comers Sunday morning so you see the Univ[ersity] sets a premium on early Sunday rising. The floor of the theater is divided.... The fellows all sit together row behind row in Parterre rechts [right side]. The Conservatory girls and boys are in Parterre links [left side]. The seats are very good provided you are not too far back and cost the fabulous sum of 80 pfennigs (20 cents). Price reckoned as follows.

Reg. Price 1.50.Mark/ 1/2 price for student .75 Mk. to which is added 5 pfennigs for Castellan and his trouble in buying ticket. = in all 80pfgs.

Parker did not have qualms about going to the theater on Sunday, though it is evident from his letter that his family might have been estranged by this: "In this way tickets can be bought for the week but not for the Sunday night performance—I forgot to say that the theater is open on Sundays as on other days. The best opera of the week is usually on Sunday night ... and for Sunday night the students have to buy with the public."

One may wonder if German student days did not help change some customs at home in the long run. Hartmut Keil observed with regard to German immigrant neighborhoods in Chicago that "German gemütlichkeit was quite alien to puritanical values, especially when immigrants presumed to drink wine and beer in public places, much less to sing and go to the theater on Sundays and holidays."[106] In July 1853, Mason C. Weld was surprised to find that the Leipzigers went to concerts on Sundays. He observed (pointing out that he had inquired about these concerts rather than having attended one!): "We find on enquiring that these Sunday morning concerts are very well attended, a fine band of music plays at the Coffeehouse and multitudes go out and take their breakfast and listen to the music. The Germans one and all regard the day as one of enjoyment, and make little or no distinction between the religious enjoyment and that of worldly pleasures."[107] Later generations of Leipzig Americans were less puritanical. As Andrew McLaughlin noted in 1893, "We have of course enjoyed the music immensely + I see now how hard it[']s going to be when one goes back not to have any opportunity to let off ... occasionally. I am a great Phillistine, but I must confess I enjoy music better in a good bier halle [sic, restaurant where beer is served] than I do in too stiff a concert. One wants to wriggle around + tickle his gustatory nerve at the same time that his auditory is being fiddled on."[108]

Summary

American students abroad carefully observed the foreign customs they encountered and infused their activities with elements from that host culture. In spite of their keen observations, though, it would not quite be adequate to argue that they fully grasped what they saw—nor did they want to. Thanks to, for instance, guidebooks that prepared them for the transatlantic venture, they had clear ideas of what to expect, and, as their expectations did not necessarily meet reality, it may be suspected that, first of all, German culture too kept evolving as successive generations of US students crossed the Atlantic back and forth, and, second, American expectations reflected a certain ideal of what US university culture should be like. This latter point is crucial. It is the driving force behind the reform movements of the late nineteenth and early twentieth centuries that was fueled both by a willingness to push American culture ahead and by an openness to benefit from those nations that already appeared to be leading.

More specifically, US students adopted German forms of leisure associating with the purpose of nonetheless advancing the production of knowledge. Yet they used the format of club meetings also to benefit from the expertise of Americans in Leipzig who came from across the United States, thus allowing the East Coast scholar to learn more about science and certainly the organization of science on the West Coast or in the South of the United States. Interestingly, the earlier incarnation of the American Students Club seemed to be closer to the example of German academic university clubs. That is, even though academic networking was a central objective, the meetings in the early 1890s apparently served also to exchange experiences within one's research contexts that easily could veer off into entertainments. By contrast, the available examples from club meetings after 1900 reflect a greater focus on exchanging information related to US academe in its organization and offerings.

In spite of a curiosity about and interest in German culture, Americans were at times overcome by homesickness, a feeling over which they triumphed by participating in American festivities in Leipzig or by meeting up in order to play genuinely American games such as baseball. In reporting about American activities in Leipzig, US students often showed their pride in the nation. Those students did not want to copy the German ways. They wanted to look and learn at best and subsequently do it better the American way. They did not uniformly agree on what they saw abroad and what best to make of it. Different opinions may be heard ranging from enthusiastically embracing many aspects of German culture via actively participating in American activities in Leipzig to keeping a critical distance even to their compatriots.

Cultural transformation as a phenomenon is difficult to grasp but appears to become more tangible when examining a people against a foreign Other. That in addition to more or less elusive benefits from the German venture US students also brought material assets back home is yet another aspect to be examined in my eighth and final chapter.

Notes

1. Karl Baedeker, *Northern Germany. Handbook for Travellers,* 9th rev. ed. (Leipsic: Karl Baedeker, 1886); *Karl Baedeker 1827–1927* (Leipzig: Breikopf & Härtel, 1927).
2. John W. Burgess, *Reminiscences of an American Scholar* (New York: Columbia University Press, 1934), 88.
3. M. C. Weld, 22 June 1853 [Mason's III Eur fragment]. L. Weld Family Papers, Group 559, Box 1, Folder 2, YUL.
4. G. H. Parker to Family, 17 October 1891, also 22 January 1892. Parker Papers, HUG 4674.12, Box 2, HUL Pusey.
5. Journal, C. Thomas, 16 September 1877. C. Thomas Papers, 86180 Aa 2 Ac, Box 3, UM Bentley.
6. Journal, C. Thomas, 16 June 1878, ibid.
7. J. M. Cattell to Parents, 29 January 1886, reprinted in Michael M. Sokal, ed., *An Education in Psychology: James McKeen Cattell's Journal and Letters from Germany and England, 1880–1888* (Cambridge, MA: MIT Press, 1981), 202.
8. See also Anja Becker, "US-American Students in Leipzig and Their Struggle with the German Tongue, 1827 to 1909," in *Transatlantic Cultural Contexts. Essays in Honor of Eberhard Brüning,* ed. Hartmut Keil (Tübingen: Stauffenburg, 2005), 165–86.
9. W. C. Williams to Edgar Williams, 20 September 1909. MS Coll 395, Box 2, Folder 50, UP Van Pelt.
10. T. D. Woolsey to Laura Johnson (Sister), 3–5 January 1828. Woolsey Family Papers, Group 562 Series, I Box 3, Folder 39, YUL.
11. W. P. Lombard, typed CV with handwritten corrections. Warren Plimpton Lombard Correspondence 1877–1899, 85811 Aa2, Box I, Folder 3, UM Bentley. The corrected version is given here. Following quote ibid.
12. Journal, A. C. McLaughlin, 29 October 1893. McLaughlin Papers, 85536Aa2, Box 1, UM Bentley.
13. Journal, A. C. McLaughlin, 31 December 1893, ibid.
14. E. Hamilton to Jessie Hamilton (Cousin), 24 November 1895. Hamilton Family Papers, MC 278, microfilm 27, Folders 595/96, HUL Schlesinger. An unreliable resource about E. Hamilton is Doris Fielding Reid, *Edith Hamilton: An Intimate Portrait* (New York: W.W. Norton, 1967); see Anja Becker, "For the Sake of Old Leipzig Days ... Academic Networks of American Students at a German University, 1781–1914" (PhD dissertation, University of Leipzig, 2006), chapter 6 for an example of Reid's inaccuracy.
15. T. D. Seymour to Philo, 30 October 1870. Seymour Family Papers, Group 440, Box 25, Folder 200, Series VII, YUL.
16. H. P. Bowditch (Bonn) to Henry Ingersoll Bowditch (Uncle), 30 May 1869 [typed copy]. H. P. Bowditch Papers, H MS c 5.1, HUL Countway.
17. Journal, C. Thomas, 23 October 1877. C. Thomas Papers, 86180 Aa 2 Ac, Box 3, UM Bentley.
18. Journal, C. Thomas, 5 December 1877, ibid.
19. Journal, C. Thomas, 28 October 1877, ibid.
20. Journal, C. Thomas, 15 July 1878, ibid.
21. H. P. Bowditch (Bonn) to H. I. Bowditch (Uncle), 30 May 1869 [typed copy]. H. P. Bowditch Papers, H MS c 5.1, HUL Countway. Following quote ibid.
22. See for example Andrew Large, *The Artificial Language Movement* (Oxford: Blackwell, 1985).
23. Ostwald devoted the entire fifth chapter of the third volume of his memoirs to the subject

of a world language. See Wilhelm Ostwald, *Lebenslinien. Eine Selbstbiographie,* vol. 3 (Berlin: Klasing & Co., 1926–27), 141–81.

24. E. Eichler, "August Leskiens Wirken für die Slawistik," *ZfSl* 26, no. 2 (1981): 179.

25. H. P. Bowditch to Mother, 9 December 1869. Bowditch Papers, H MS c 5.1, HUL Countway. He made a similar observation in a letter to his Uncle H. I. Bowditch, 5 December 1869, ibid.

26. H. P. Bowditch (Dresden) to Lucy Bowditch (Mother), 23 January 1870 [?], ibid.

27. Walter B. Cannon, "Henry Pickering Bowditch," in *Biographical Memoirs of the National Academy of Sciences,* vol. 17 (1922), 183–86, reprinted in *The Life and Writings of Henry Pickering Bowditch,* vol. 1 (New York: Arno Press, 1980), 186. As to his wife's knowledge of English, see H. P. Bowditch to Mother, 3 October 1869. Bowditch Papers, HMSC 5.1, Folder 1869, HUL Countway.

28. C. Thomas to Miss Davis, 20 September 1877. Thomas Papers, 86180 Aa 2 A, Box 1, UM Bentley. Following quote ibid.

29. Ibid.

30. T. D. Woolsey to Mother, 17 December 1827. Woolsey Papers, Group 562 Series I Box 3 Folder 39, YUL.

31. Henry E. Dwight, *Travels in the North of Germany, in the Years 1825 and 1826* (New York: G. & C. & H. Carvill, 1829), 323–24, 238. Following quote ibid., 323–24.

32. James Morgan Hart, *German Universities: A Narrative of Personal Experience* (New York: G. P. Putnam's Sons, 1874 [reprinted London: Routledge/Thoemmes Press, 1994]), 51–52, also 6.

33. W. James (Teplitz, Bohemia) to H. P. Bowditch, 5 May 1868 [typed copy]. Bowditch Papers H MS c.5.2, Folder 1, Countway. Following quote ibid.

34. Journal, C. Thomas, 19 September 1877. Thomas Papers, 86180 Aa 2 Ac, Box 3, UM Bentley.

35. W. P. Lombard, typed CV with handwritten corrections. Lombard Correspondence 1877–1899, 85811 Aa2, Box I, Folder 3, UM Bentley. The corrected version is given here.

36. J. R. Angell, unpublished autobiographical sketch, 9–10. Angell Papers, Group 2, Series II Box 2 Folder 7a, YUL.

37. Shirley W. Smith, *James Burrill Angell: An American Influence* (Ann Arbor: University of Michigan Press, 1954), 45.

38. A. C. McLaughlin, autobiographical sketch, ca. 1938/39, 32–33. McLaughlin Papers, 855 36 Aa2, Box 1, UM Bentley.

39. Journal, A. C. McLaughlin, 27 September 1893, ibid.

40. Irma C. Wieand, "To my Classmates," in *Class Letter of the Class of 1901 of Mount Holyoke College,* 1902 edition, 95–97, MHA.

41. Paul Julius Möbius, *Ueber den physiologischen Schwachsinn des Weibes* (Halle: Verlag von Carl Marhold, 1900).

42. Lothar Mertens, *Vernachlässigte Töchter der Alma Mater,* Sozialwissenschaftliche Schriften, Heft 20 (Berlin: Duncker & Humblot, 1991), 25.

43. Edward H. Clarke, *Sex in Education; or a Fair Chance for Girls* (New York, 1873). See also Julia Ward Howe, *Sex and Education. A Reply to Dr. E. H. Clarke's "Sex in Education"* (Boston: Roberts Brothers, 1874).

44. Journal, A. C. McLaughlin, 25 October 1893. McLaughlin Papers, 85536Aa2 Box 1, UM Bentley.

45. T. D. Seymour to Classmates, November 5, 1871. Seymour Family Papers, Group 440, Series VII, Box 21, Folder 153, YUL. Following quote ibid.

46. Eva Channing, "The Contributors' Club," *The Atlantic Monthly. A Magazine of Literature, Science, Art, and Politics* 44 (December 1879): 789.

47. J. Duncan Spaeth, "Thomas Marc Parrot," 1, 4, Thomas Marc Parrott '88, Faculty File, PUL Mudd.

48. J. L. Steffens to Father, 23 November 1890, reprinted in Ella Winter and Granville Hicks, eds., *The Letters of Lincoln Steffens*, vol. 1 (New York: Harcourt, Brace and Company, 1938), 54–55.

49. A. B. Lamb to Family, n.d. [ca. late February 1905]. Lamb Papers HUG 4508.50, Box 2, HUL Pusey.

50. Elfrieda Hochbaum, *Burning Arrows* (Boston: Bruce Humphries Publishers, 1963), 263–64.

51. Obituary, typescript, p. 2. Thomas Marc Parrott '88, Faculty File, PUL Mudd.

52. Alice Hamilton, *Exploring the Dangerous Trades* (Boston: Little, Brown and Company, 1943), 163.

53. William Harris Bragg, *De Renne: Three Generations of a Georgia Family* (Athens: University of Georgia Press, 1999), 190–91.

54. Anja Becker, "Southern Academic Ambitions Meet German Scholarship: The Leipzig Networks of Vanderbilt University's James H. Kirkland in the Late Nineteenth Century," *Journal of Southern History* 74, no. 4 (November 2008): 855–86.

55. Journal, C. Thomas, 15 October 1877. Thomas Papers 86180 Aa 2 Ac, Box 3, UM Bentley. C. Thomas to "Meine liebe Freundin," 27 November 1877, ibid., Box 1.

56. G. H. Parker to Family, 13 December 1891. Parker Papers HUG 4674.12, Box 2, HUL Pusey. Following quote ibid.

57. J. Stafford to R. H. True, 14 July 1895. R. H. True Papers BT763, Series II, Box 8, APS. Following quote ibid.

58. A. C. McLaughlin, Journal, 1 November 1893. McLaughlin Papers 85536Aa2, Box 1, UM Bentley.

59. A. A. Noyes to H. M. Goodwin, 20 February 1890. H. M. Goodwin Papers MC121, Box 1, MIT Archives.

60. Lightner Witmer to John Stewart, 16 May, 1891. John Stewart Collection, Box 2, UP Van Pelt.

61. M. Tilley to L. Cooper, 23 December 1901. Cooper Papers 14/12/680, Box 16, Cornell Kroch.

62. *The Stanford Alumnus*, July 1901. Pat White, e-mail message to author, 21 May 2007.

63. *Quinquennial Catalogue of Harvard University 1636–1930* (Cambridge, MA: Harvard University Press), 70, 653. http://pds.lib.harvard.edu/pds/view/6796688.

64. A. B. Lamb to Family, started 23 November, continued 27 November 1904. Lamb Papers HUG 4508.50, Box 2, HUL Pusey.

65. Martha Mitchell, *Encyclopedia Brunoniana* (Providence, RI, 1993). http://www.brown.edu/Administration/News_Bureau/Databases/Encyclopedia/search.php?serial=C0760 and http://www.brown.edu/Administration/News_Bureau/Databases/Encyclopedia/search.php?serial=M0410.

66. Verzeichnis der Verbindungen, WS 1891/92, Rep. II/XVI/II, Nr. 17. 488/94, 0205, LUA.

67. Gesetz, die Studien auf der Universität Leipzig betreffend § 3, and Disziplinar-Ordnung § 36. See *Immatrikulations und Disziplinar-Ordnung für die Studierenden der Universität Leipzig vom 8. März 1903* (Leipzig: Alexander Edelmann, 1903), 3 and 20.

68. L. Witmer to J. Stewart, 31 October 1891. Stewart Collection, Box 2, UP Van Pelt.

69. J. M. Cattell to Parents, 10 September 1887, reprinted in Sokal, *Education in Psychology*, 277–78, also 146n3.

70. A. B. Lamb to Sam, 12 January 1904 [1905!]. Lamb Papers, HUG 4508.10, HUL Pusey.

71. M. Tilley to L. Cooper, 2 March 1902. Cooper Papers, 14/12/680, Box 16, Cornell Kroch.

72. A. A. Noyes to H. M. Goodwin, 20 February 1890. Goodwin Papers, MC121, Box 1, MIT Archives.

73. David L. Adams, "Arthur Amos Noyes—First in Chemical Education, First in Chemical Research, and First in the Northeastern Section," ms [published in *The Nucleus* (1997)], 9–10, MIT Museum. Linus Pauling, "Arthur Amos Noyes," in *Proceedings of the Robert A. Welch Foundation. Conferences on Chemical Research*, ed. W. O. Milligan (Houston, TX: 1977), 88–102.

74. G. H. Parker to Family, 22 January 1892. Parker Papers, HUG 4674.12, Box 2. HUL Pusey.

75. W. H. Welch to William Wickham Welch (Father), 19 December 1876. Welch Papers Box 68, Folder 5, JHU med. Following quote ibid.

76. H. P. Bowditch (Dresden) to Mother, 23 January 1870 [?]. Bowditch Papers, H MS c 5.1., HUL Countway.

77. Hochbaum, *Burning Arrows*, 262–63.

78. A. B. Lamb to Family, n.d. [week of Washington's birthday]. Lamb Papers, HUG 4508.50, Box 2, HUL Pusey.

79. Journal, C. Thomas, 8 July 1878. Thomas Papers, 86180 Aa 2 Ac, Box 3, UM Bentley.

80. C. R. Lanman to Aunt, 9 July 1876. Lanman Papers, HUG 4510.67, Letters from Europe, vol. 3, HUL Pusey. Emphasis in original.

81. L. Cooper (Berlin) to Father, 3 July 1900. L. Cooper Papers, 14/12/680, Box 18, Cornell Kroch.

82. Diary, F. G. Cottrell, 4 July 1901. Frederick Gardner Cottrell Papers, MMC 3121, Container #1, LC. As to Cottrell, see Frank Cameron, *Cottrell: Samaritan of Science* (Garden City, NY: Doubleday & Company, 1952).

83. Diary, F. G. Cottrell, 4 July 1902. Frederick Gardner Cottrell Papers, MMC 3121, Container #1, LC.

84. A. B. Lamb to Family, 23 November 1904. Lamb Papers, HUG 4508.50, Box 2, HUL Pusey. Following quote ibid.

85. H. P. Bowditch to Mother, 14 November [1869]. Bowditch Papers, HMS c5.1 HUL Countway.

86. Diary, T. D. Seymour, 24 November 1870. Seymour Family Papers, Box 25, Folder 200, YUL.

87. A. B. Lamb to Family, 13 December 1904. Lamb Papers, HUG 4508.50, Box 2, HUL Pusey. Emphasis in original.

88. W. James to Alice Howe (Gibbens) James, 11 November 1882. James Family, bMS Am 1092.9 items 1301–1306, Folder 31, HUL Houghton.

89. W. C. Williams to E. I. Williams, 17 August 1909. W. C. Williams, Ms. Coll. 395, Box 2, Folder 50, UP Van Pelt.

90. W. C. Williams to E. I. Williams, 7 November 1909, ibid., Folder 54.

91. G. H. Parker to Family, 29 December 1891. G. H. Parker Papers, HUG 4674.12, Box 2, HUL Pusey.

92. E. Hamilton to J. Hamilton (Cousin), 23 December 1895. Hamilton Family Papers, MC 278, microfilm 27, Folders 595/96, HUL Schlesinger.

93. H. P. Bowditch (Dresden) to Mother, 23 January 1870 [?]. Bowditch Papers, H MS c 5.1. HUL Countway.

94. C. R. Lanman to Aunt, 28 November 1875. Lanman Papers, HUG 4510.67, vol. 3, HUL Pusey.

95. C. R. Lanman to Aunt, 26 December 1875, ibid. Following quotes regarding Lanman's Christmas in 1875 from that source. Emphasis in original.

96. A. B. Lamb to Mother, n.d. [winter 1904/05]. Lamb Papers, HUG 4508.50, Box 2, HUL Pusey.

97. Journal, C. Thomas, 8 October 1877. C. Thomas Papers, 86180 Aa 2 Ac, Box 3, UM Bentley.

98. C. Thomas, unfinished, typed autobiography, 19–20, ibid., Box 1. Emphasis in original.

99. H. P. Bowditch to Mother, 22 January 1871. Bowditch Papers, H MS c 5.1., HUL Countway.

100. H. P. Bowditch to Mother, 31 October 1869, ibid.

101. A. B. Lamb to Family, Leipzig, n.d. [2nd week after arrival in Leipzig]. Lamb Papers, HUG 4508.50, Box 2, HUL Pusey. Cooper explained on 16 March 1901, that it was "a favorite game with the Germans too at present." L. Cooper (London) to Mother, 16 March 1901. Cooper Papers, #14/12/680, Box 18, Cornell Kroch. Also, J. M. Cattell to Parents, 25 February 1885, reprinted in Sokal, *Education in Psychology*, 162.

102. Postcard, H. P. Bowditch (Dresden) to Selma Knauth Bowditch (Wife), 19 August 1895. Bowditch Papers, H MS c 5.1, HUL Countway; Journal, A. C. McLaughlin, 24 March 1894. McLaughlin Papers, 85536Aa2, Box 1, UM Bentley; J. M. Cattell to Parents, 24 June 1887, reprinted in Sokal, *Education in Psychology*, 267.

103. G. H. Parker to Family, 13 December 1891. Parker Papers, HUG 4674.12, Box 2, HUL Pusey.

104. For example, Lanman exulted in an opera that had been sung "most beautifully" and soon thereafter mentioned another performance which he "liked ... very much." C. R. Lanman to Aunt, 28 November 1875 and 12 December 1875. Lanman Papers, HUG 4510.67, Letters from Europe, vol. 3, HUL Pusey. See also Carl Ludwig to Herrmann von Helmholtz, 25 December 1865. Reprinted in Herbert Hörz, *Physiologie und Kultur in der zweiten Hälfte des 19. Jahrhunderts. Briefe an Herman von Helmholtz* (Marburg/Lahn: Basilisken-Presse, 1994), 323–24.

105. G. H. Parker to Family, 13 December 1891. Parker Papers HUG 4674.12, Box 2, HUL Pusey. Following quotes ibid.

106. Hartmut Keil, "Immigrant Neighborhoods and American Society: German Immigrants on Chicago's Northwestern Side in the Late 19th Century," in *German Workers' Culture in the United States 1850–1920*, ed. Hartmut Keil (Washington, DC: Smithsonian Institution Press, 1988), 48.

107. M. C. Weld to Beloved-Ones, 24 July 1853. L. Weld Family Papers, G559, B1, F2, YUL. Emphasis in original.

108. A. C. McLaughlin to J.R. Angell, 13 February 1893 [1894!]. J. R. Angell Papers, G2, S II, B8, F55, YUL.

Chapter 8

RETURNING HOME

The German Venture and
the Transformation of US Higher Education

IN THE COURSE of the nineteenth century, reform movements in education were evident on both sides of the Atlantic, though German universities had begun to transform their organizational structures from older scholastic forms into modern research universities already in the eighteenth century. In the United States, reform activity became particularly pronounced after the US Civil War, a time that was also marked by a considerable student migration especially to German universities. Americans' striving for a "New Education" is consequently part of a transatlantic phenomenon. "New Education" refers to the reformist wave of the late nineteenth and early twentieth centuries. It is a "generic term to denote a complex, multiform movement for educational reform, which can be said to be an attribute of all efforts towards systematic education ... , but which took on a more tangible form after initial consolidation of national education systems in Europe and the USA in the last third of the 19th century."[1]

Following my examination of the phenomenon of US student migration to German universities between the late 1800s and 1914, the question remains to be discussed what exactly these students brought home and which effect their educational transatlantic journeys had on US higher education. I will trace manifestations of the German venture in US higher education by first of all exploring the state of mind of the transatlantic travelers, by which I mean their determination to affect changes in American education after having experienced German higher education. Closely linked to this topic is

---

the subject of US university leaders trying to recruit young Americans sometimes directly from German lecture halls. I will subsequently explore career
paths after a German venture by focusing specifically on women's colleges.
The example illustrates how closely male and female higher education were
linked and to what extent men and women could benefit from the system.
Moreover, a PhD degree became increasingly essential for an academic career, which is why I will also explore the influence of above all Leipzig- and
Halle-trained American PhDs and their influence on US higher education.
Finally, material aid was necessary to build up the American research university, which is why US students brought books, even entire libraries, and
apparatuses back home. They founded scientific and scholarly journals that
were inspired by German publications to establish national and international forums of communication for individual research disciplines.

Shifting the Scientific-Scholarly Focus to North America

William Welch's biographers observed that in 1878, "he returned across the
Atlantic with his eyes fixed on a vision: America too must become the home
of medical science."[2] Welch set up a course in pathology at Bellevue Hospital in New York, which soon "had begun to bridge the gap that separated
New York from European scientific developments."[3] Welch thus set out to
make US medicine as great as many of his countrymen already thought it
to be. That is, during Welch's student days in Germany, his stepmother had
lectured him on a lack of patriotism when he praised German education,
and his father had urged him to call on an *American* physician should he
fall ill while abroad.[4] But then, his father was a traditionally trained doctor to whom his son's scientific excitement and rigor might have appeared
somewhat bewildering.

Not only traditionally minded Americans deluded themselves about the
state of education. In his memoirs written in the 1920s, Wilhelm Ostwald
related a conversation with one of his former US students, Arthur Noyes,
at Harvard in 1905. As was the case with Welch, Noyes is portrayed as
strongly determined not simply to excel personally but to be speaking for
the entire nation in expressing his desire of turning the United States into
the world's educational and scientific center. The two chemists discussed the
question of how science could be advanced in America. Ostwald was dubious that willpower, resources, and ability were enough. He recalled with
hindsight:

> I pointed out that it needed an astonishing amount of time and a scientific tradi-
> tion to produce a worthwhile and lasting result. I referred to Clark University as

an example. That institution had been founded some ten years before, was very well funded, and had the objective to organize a scientific production with the best researchers but regardless of costs. The experiment had failed.

Noyes was not discouraged. He said one could learn from this how to do it better next time. New funds would be available when needed, and his people were determined to achieve greatness in this field as well. "It will take a long time until you even come close to the point where Germany is now," I said. Struggling with a slight embarrassment, Noyes fervently replied with shiny eyes: "*We hope in time to move the intellectual center of mankind across the Atlantic Ocean to America.*" As Noyes had always been a quiet and reserved person, I was surprised to find him speak with such ardor. It makes me pensive. Because of the destructive war in Europe, the United States is now a leading economic power. But at this point it cannot be said with certainty whether America will also experience an intellectual heyday.[5]

In fact, speaking with even more hindsight in the early twenty-first century, it may be doubted that in order to achieve academic greatness, a long-standing tradition of high culture is needed. It may be considered a European prejudice. Already Ostwald's account of his conversation with Noyes was overshadowed by gloomy apprehensions, though the German professor failed to see that tremendous changes had occurred in US education in the course of the previous decades. Moreover, as regarded the Clark experiment, the question is not so much that it failed, but why. To point out just one shortcoming—did Clark have administrators able to create the kind of appealing research atmosphere necessary to attract the brightest students for prolonged periods of time? Many interrelated factors usually contribute to failure or success of a university project.

Other German professors were aware of the fact that in some respects, America provided ideal conditions for achieving educational excellence. As early as in 1887, Wilhelm Wundt had envied US activism that provided for the creation of new departments: "During Christmas break Mr. Cattell visited us. He is in England this winter.... He already has an agreement with the University of Pennsylvania to establish psychology there. As you can see, it is easier in America to 'set up' a new discipline. But maybe one day we will get there, too."[6] Wundt nonetheless never traveled to the United States. When he was invited to attend the twentieth anniversary of Clark University, which G. Stanley Hall intended to turn into a psychological gathering attended by Sigmund Freud, Carl Gustav Jung, and William James, Wundt declined on account of old age, but also because the jubilee coincided with the five hundredth anniversary of the University of Leipzig.[7]

For those German professors who were willing to take advantage of the opportunity, American academic networks that were rooted in a German university experience could actually provide new academic experiences. As the above quote from Ostwald's memoirs insinuates, however, even if a German professor agreed to take advantage of that, it did not necessarily mean that he realized the significance of such activities in propelling US science and education to the top. Still, the fact that some Leipzig professors did actually travel to the United States after 1900 marks an undeniable tendency in that direction. For instance, in connection with the world fair held at St. Louis in 1904 on the occasion of the centennial celebration of the Louisiana Purchase, an international congress of the arts and sciences took place.[8] The motivation was "to highlight the entire spectrum of human knowledge as a well-organized entity and to present to the civilized world maybe two leading representatives of each individual discipline as speakers."[9] One of the participants was Ostwald, who pointed out that it was the first time that such a scientific conference had been undertaken. It was telling that it was staged in the New World, but Ostwald did not comment on that. He was younger than Wundt and showed a certain eagerness to attend scientific gatherings in the United States. Another delegate was Karl Lamprecht, whose best-known US student William Dodd had been instrumental in bringing him over.[10] A future professor at the University of Chicago, Dodd was then affiliated with Randolph-Macon College, which since 1903 had been under the presidency of Leipzig alumnus Robert Emory Blackwell. The example implies that by 1900, Leipzig Americans were well established in US academe.

Scouting Young Academic Talent in Europe

Academic leaders in the United States had closely observed educational developments in Europe since at least the late 1860s, looking especially for promising young talent in the universities. They did so from afar through correspondence but also by traveling to Europe themselves or by sending their representatives. As James McKeen Cattell suggested in an 1884 letter to his parents,[11] US university representatives would recruit promising US academicians directly from Leipzig lecture halls, whereby—as William James told James R. Angell in the early 1890s—it mattered above all that they had been associated in one way or another with a leading European or rather German authority in their fields of expertise.[12] Henry Pickering Bowditch,[13] William Welch, and Calvin Thomas all made connections in Leipzig or were recruited from Leipzig directly to a first promising teaching position at a notable US university in transformation.

If, however, US administrators were unable to recruit a promising German-trained American, they were quite willing to opt for a foreigner as long as they could hire the best possible candidate. Germans, by contrast, were much more reluctant to do so, although a few examples may be found.

The difference lay in the fact that in being determined to reach the top, US administrators could afford to take risks as they had nothing to lose. The Germans, in turn, already had the educational and scientific prestige that Americans craved, which is why they proceeded with more caution if not conservatism. International academic prestige and prospective candidates' skills were thus driving forces in building up US academia; networking was a vital tool to attain that goal. But one needed to have broad-minded recruiters who knew the European academic scene first hand. This broad mindedness also referred to being open towards a younger and yet unknown generation of scholars and scientists.

During his German student days, William Welch, a future luminary at the Johns Hopkins medical school, had realized that he was but one more representative in a succession of students from the New World at Carl Ludwig's laboratory. He regretted that the excellent training that US doctors received in Europe could hardly be of use in the United States later on as American universities lacked adequate facilities. But even though he had been aware of Bowditch before his Leipzig venture in 1875, he heard about and met a number of prospective US physiologists not in America but in Europe. In late 1876, he wrote to his stepmother Emily *Sedgwick* Welch: "Quite a number of Americans have done good work here. In the report of last year I notice a paper by Charles *Sedgwick* Minot of Boston, by whose name I was attracted. I was told that he is not here this winter."[14] Minot was actually one of Bowditch's disciples.[15]

While abroad, Welch wasn't shy about voicing his criticism of US academic potential versus actual opportunities there, interspersing a cautious optimism while assuring his parents of being on the road to success: "I am sure that American students over here prove themselves quite as diligent and capable as the native students, and I think often more so, but they rarely reap the fruit of their labors for when they return they find in America no market for their wares, so to speak, that i[s,] there are no opportunities open for purely scientific work…. This is inevitable in a new country, but there promises now to be a change for the better." This change for the better referred to the creation of Johns Hopkins medical school. John Shaw Billings, "Surgeon-general and librarian in Washington" had been "appointed to organize the hospital and medical department of the Johns Hopkins University."[16] He visited Leipzig in early November 1876 not simply to look at facilities but to scout young talent. Welch seized the opportunity that would ultimately get him involved in the Johns Hopkins medical school for the remainder of his career. He reported home: "I met him quite by accident. Prof. [Ernst Leberecht] Wagner was showing him around his pathological laboratory, when he brought him in where we were working and introduced him to two of his countrymen, [Walter] Stallo and myself. We accompanied him around the different medical buildings."[17] What followed was a lengthy description of Welch's impressions, which he was eager to pass on to his parents in most favorable terms:

> What he related concerning his plans regarding the Johns Hopkins pleased me very much. It seems to be the right sort of man for the important executive position which he holds. He says that the medical department will not be organized in less than four years, when it is hoped that the hospital will be completed. There are to be laboratories like the German, and the examinations for admission are to be so severe as to exclude all except those who can appreciate and profit by the instruction given. The classes will therefore necessarily always be small, and it is hoped to attract especially graduates of other colleges, who now go to foreign countries.

Soon a job opportunity presented itself: "He said that many of the professorships would have to be filled by young men, who if necessary would be sent to Germany, as there were, for instance, no men in New York whom he would consider for the chair of physiology. Of course such young men would at first be taken on trial and not made full professors." Welch did not hesitate: "He took my name and address and said that he should have to look to such men as we, who were pursuing our studies over here. He inquired minutely how I was spending my time and thought I was directing my studies wisely, and said that if I am to teach as he hoped I would I ought to spend not less than two years in German laboratories."

The letter now fulfilled the twofold purpose of assuring Welch's parents that the money in junior's overseas venture was well invested and that Welch was making wise decisions that had the potential of procuring a splendid position (which is how things turned out[18]). Welch concluded: "My aspirations for obtaining a position in the Johns Hopkins were rather strengthened, still there is nothing solid to build upon. If in the next four years I could only do something to prove that I should be competent to hold a position in that university, I think I might have some chance of securing the place, if they are to choose young men." Having stated his case, Welch was so cautious as to remind his parents of the uncertainty of his plans in spite of all, "But at present I have done nothing and when I return to America I must try to earn my living and can not afford to devote my time to a subject which has no immediate relation to that important end. However all these hopes seem very airy and egotistical when I think of the numbers of young men who have been and are over here, some having acquired already some reputation, and who are hoping for the same or similar prospects." One might, of course, interpret this caution as Welch's strategy to ensure that his parents would continue to support his education abroad until he himself thought that he was well prepared—after all, he had already proven to the visiting US authority that he was capable of prudent choices.

Almost a decade later, Welch returned to Leipzig to visit Ludwig. By that time, he himself was involved in building up the Johns Hopkins medical school. Once again, the stay at Leipzig provided him with contacts that would ultimately benefit Johns Hopkins. Dr. Henry L. Swain of New Haven, a medical student at Leipzig from the 1884/85 through the 1885/86 fall terms, remembered that in 1885, "[Franklin P.] Mall was one day much excited over a young American doctor who had visited Ludwig; he had listened to the two men talking and had been greatly attracted by the guest, Dr. William Welch."[19] According to the student directories, in the fall of 1885/86, Swain roomed in the same pension as Mall. Mall had enrolled at Leipzig on 25 October 1885 and just like Bowditch in 1869 originally intended to stay for one year only. He reconsidered on advice of the Leipzig anatomist Wilhelm His, whom he had befriended. Rather than leaving for Berlin, he stayed for two years, eventually receiving a place in Ludwig's still crowded laboratory.[20] Welch and Mall at once established cordial relations that would last for a lifetime. Indeed, Welch's biographers, Simon Flexner and James Thomas Flexner, never even mention when and how the two men met. Having described Welch's visit to Leipzig without mentioning Mall, the Flexners cite a personal 1890 letter from Welch to Mall suggesting a mutual understanding that apparently did not need any further explanation.[21]

When Calvin Thomas traveled to Leipzig in the summer of 1877, he was thinking of a German doctorate, yet not as a primary goal.[22] He never obtained that degree. In the winter of 1878, he encountered in Leipzig an Ann Arbor assistant professor of Greek on leave of absence, Albert H. Pattengill. A few months later, Thomas was appointed instructor in Greek, a position established instead of Pattengill's assistant professorship. The two men consulted, and Thomas accepted the offer. He left Leipzig in August 1878. Three weeks into the new semester, however, Pattengill was restored to his former position, which posed the problem of what to do with Thomas, who had cut short his German venture for the Ann Arbor position. Eventually, he was made instructor in German.[23]

The academic job offer from Ann Arbor successfully undermined Thomas's scheme to obtain a Leipzig PhD degree. It also undermined his plan to become a classicist—for the remainder of his career he would be devoted to Germanic languages. When viewing his fate from the perspective of Leipzig-American philologists, this change was well in tune with general trends. To the extent to which I was able to examine Leipzig-American philologists' subject interests and future career paths, it appears that philologists of the 1870s were keener on the classics, whereas later generations tended to focus on modern languages.[24]

The case of T. W. Richards illustrates that after the turn of the twentieth century, the United States was catching up with scientific Europe. In 1914, Richards would be the first American to be awarded the Nobel Prize in chemistry. Back in 1901, he had received a different honor—he became the first American to be called to a German university, Göttingen, a move that caused a stir in US academic circles. At Harvard, President Charles W. Eliot and Charles Loring Jackson, professor of chemistry,[25] both were highly concerned about the possibility of losing Richards. Eliot wrote to Richards on 15 July, "Professor Jackson has told me of the Göttingen proposal, which strikes me as unique and desirable—especially to decline. I should like to talk it over with you. C.W.E."[26] Two days before, Jackson had urged Richards to remain in Cambridge: "Your letter fills me with alarm. Do not go! I can see how tempting the offer is, and feel we have comparatively little to offer on our side, but here you are the biggest toad in the puddle, and I think after this will be treated as well as we can. I have written again to Eliot with this, and hope he will see you and talk over the affair.... I am mighty glad for the compliment to you, but if you go, you knock us all to pieces, to say nothing of the wrench to my heart in losing you."[27] Three days later, Jackson again pointed out that "in Göttingen there will be some embarrassment in your doing work in physical chemistry in competition with [Walther Hermann] Nernst whereas here you will have a perfectly free hand."[28]

Richards indeed declined the offer, strengthening his position at Harvard.[29] He told another colleague:

> The joyful news that I have to tell you may perhaps have been "discounted" already. The Göttingen letter, full of words of appreciation, but very positive in its declining, has been despatched. Pres. Eliot, thanks to the very kind representations of you and my two other good friends, has met me "more than half way" as Jackson said he would.... I must stop, for lack of time, because the mail goes in a few minutes. There is only time to say that a new laboratory is popping its masthead above the horizon—according to the President. It may sail the other way, but there is hope.[30]

Once it was certain that Richards would stay, the Ostwald students Arthur Noyes and Henry Paul Talbot, both then affiliated with MIT, congratulated Richards. Noyes wrote in the fall of that year: "Accept most hearty congratulations upon the unusual but well deserved honor which the University of Göttingen conferred on you this summer. I was delighted to hear, however, that you are to remain at Cambridge under conditions more favorable for your scientific work."[31] Talbot struck a similar chord in October 1901.[32]

Americans previously had taught at German universities. As, however, Richard's friend and colleague Jackson pointed out, "other Americans have grown up at the Universities where they are professors, and the men called from positions here have been foreigners."[33] Gregory would be an example. Richards was, of course, related to Gregory by marriage. When he refuted the claim that he was a first to be called to a German university, he referred to Gregory. But Eliot emphatically replied that the Göttingen call was a much different affair.[34]

As the Richards case showed, German universities were not entirely opposed to calling foreigners, although they proceeded with much more caution, for they were the ones with a reputation to lose—US universities, by contrast, were eagerly building up theirs, thus being rather daring and even aggressive in their recruitment attempts. After 1900, Leipzig cautiously opened up towards US scholarship. Two US students taught English there (see chapter 4). It illustrates a tendency that the Harvard zoologist George Howard Parker had already observed ten years earlier: by 1900, Germans were hard-up as regarded promising academic offspring.[35]

The reason for the decline in the number of promising young Germans at German universities might have been the fact that young Germans were lured to the United States. For example, academic circles in the United States became so enthused about linguistics that they repeatedly attempted to recruit German linguists. In a few instances they succeeded. The cases of Ewald Flügel and Hermann Collitz are particularly impressive. Collitz had studied at Halle and Göttingen. In 1886, he accepted the chair of comparative linguistics and German philology at Bryn Mawr College. He moved on to a professorship in German philology at Johns Hopkins in 1907.[36] In both positions he was of interest to Leipzig-American networks, particularly as the president of Bryn Mawr back then, M. Carey Thomas, had been one of the first women to study at Leipzig in the late 1870s.

Ewald Flügel, who had studied philology under Richard Wülker at Leipzig, accepted a full professorship of English at Stanford University in the spring of 1892. He explicitly desired, though, to remain on record as an adjunct of Leipzig's philosophical faculty,[37] which points to the academic unease he felt about moving to the New World. Flügel was the grandson of Johann Gottfried Flügel, who had spent the years from 1810 to 1819 in America, eventually becoming a US citizen. In 1824, he was made *lector publicus* in English at the University of Leipzig and thus pioneered in introducing the study of English to the Leipzig curriculum. He published a dictionary that also contained American expressions, an undertaking that his son Felix Flügel continued. When J. G. Flügel was appointed US consul in Leipzig in 1839, his teaching career ended. His grandson E. Flügel was awarded a Leipzig PhD degree in 1887 and from 1888 until 1892 was an adjunct in English. When Wülker published a new edition of his *History of English Literature* in 1906, for the first time it included a substantial entry on North American literature authored by Stanford's E. Flügel.[38]

Women's Colleges as a Career Boost

Whereas for a woman a professorship at a women's college in the United States typically meant the apex of her career, for a man it was but a step up the career ladder that might lead to one of the leading US universities, some of which (especially on the East Coast) tended to be for men above all. For the female students, it nonetheless meant to benefit from an upcoming academic elite. Of course, some Leipzig-trained men such as Herbert Maule Richards of Barnard or John Martyn Warbeke of Mount Holyoke would remain at a women's college for the better part of their careers. Others such as George Shannon Forbes of Harvard would be affiliated with a male institution while simultaneously committing themselves to female education—Forbes also taught at Radcliffe. Still others, however, would indeed move from female to male education. But even women increasingly could break into the male world of teaching if they were highly qualified.

It is not always possible to detect the men's attitudes toward teaching women. In the case of Paul Shorey, teaching at a women's college clearly was apparently but a stepping stone up the career ladder. After having obtained an AB degree from Harvard, Shorey registered at Leipzig in the fall of 1881 in order to study the classics. Three years later he obtained a PhD degree at Munich. He became an associate professor of Greek and Latin at the newly founded Bryn Mawr College for women in the following year, remaining there until 1892, when he was called to a chair in Greek at the new University of Chicago.

While Shorey's attitude towards teaching women is not known, another Leipzig American, George Augustus Hulett, thought his female students to be "interesting," a term that does not convey a whole lot of meaning. A member of the Princeton class of 1892 and subsequently a graduate student there, he enrolled at Leipzig on 17 October 1896 to pursue chemistry, earning a PhD degree in 1898. From 1899 to 1905, he was instructor and afterwards assistant professor of physical chemistry at the University of Michigan, a coeducational institution. He reminisced about his experiences there in a Princeton yearbook, "After studying in Germany, I had the good fortune to be connected with the University of Michigan, and found there much of interest.... Teaching the mixed classes was an interesting experience—the young ladies do most excellent work, and seem very much in earnest; but with all the pleasant work at Michigan, you can readily understand that I was quite ready to come back to Princeton."[39] One may wonder whether Hulett was so eager to return to Princeton because the institution happened to be his alma mater or whether—stress being on the '92 *men* whom he addressed—he might have looked forward to getting away from a place where his research and teaching was distracted by the presence of learned women.

An attitude is more clearly detectable in Edward Washburn Hopkins, who was more openly apprehensive about teaching female students. He had received a PhD degree from Leipzig in 1881 and would correspond with his professor of Sanskrit, Ernst Windisch, even years after he had left. For the better part of his career, Hopkins was affiliated with Yale as a professor of Sanskrit and comparative philology. But before he was called there, he had spent some ten years at Bryn Mawr College in the 1880s and early 1890s. Hopkins had known Eva Channing at Leipzig[40] and had probably also met M. Carey Thomas there, who had been involved in Bryn Mawr affairs since its beginnings.

Having accepted a call to Bryn Mawr in 1886, Hopkins looked at the idea of teaching at a women's college as a change away from "interesting men" to "lecturing to women." His choice of wording implied that the female student would be more passive and thus intellectually less stimulating than the male students. Still,

> the work to be done was such as it interests me much more than that in my former position at Columbia College. Sanskrit and comparative philology tempted me away from N.Y. and so I came, not without some apprehension of the ultimate result. But a year has now passed and our new college for women seems to have ... public confidence and to be on the way to success. You will perhaps wonder at the number of women who are anxious to obtain a classical education, but there seem to be many who have such aspirations and who seek to satisfy this thirst for knowledge by entering upon a collegiate course ... so that I feel confident that in a few years I may number several disciples among my students.[41]

In 1895, a call to Yale ended the uncertainty of teaching women. The previous Sanskrit professor, William Dwight Whitney,[42] having passed away, Hopkins rejoiced that the years at the women's college had been quite pleasant after all. Again he referred to the better conditions of the new job as the main reason for change: "I am very glad to leave Bryn Mawr; not that it is not a very pleasant [?] place, but my Sanskrit work was much hindered by the necessity of lecturing in a Greek Department at the same time. I shall now for the first time in my life be able to devote myself [to ?] Sanskrit without the necessity of working ten hours a week in classics."[43] In yet another, most enthusiastic letter written in October 1898, the thrill about the new job and interesting students culminated in the announcement that "[y]ou may be interested to know that I have added to my family since I saw you, three boys and a girl altogether."[44] In spite of the apprehensive teaching experience at the women's college, the years at Bryn Mawr were steps up the career ladder that in Hopkins's case led to Yale, which was then still mainly a men's school.

An ambitious US college or university would not shy away from hiring a woman if she happened to be the most highly qualified candidate. In the spring of 1907, a letter from the German Department at Western Reserve University in Cleveland, Ohio, addressed to Hermann Collitz at Johns Hopkins inquired whether Gertrude Charlotte Schmidt might be suited for an instructorship in German at their College for Women. If not, and if "you have no good woman in mind, can you suggest a good man? We want the best person we can get, man or woman."[45] In the United States, the gender of a teacher did not matter so much as long as the person was a first-rate choice. In those days, "best trained" meant having had some connection with German higher education. Schmidt was a promising Bryn Mawr student who traveled to Leipzig as a European Fellow recommended by M. Carey Thomas.[46]

The case of Alice Hamilton is even more impressive. Remembering her call to Harvard in 1919 as the first woman ever, she wrote not without a sense of humor:

> Harvard was then—and [in 1943] still is—the stronghold of masculinity against the inroads of women, who elsewhere were encroaching so alarmingly.... Harvard had not changed her attitude toward women students in any way, yet there she was putting a woman on the faculty. It seemed incredible at the time, but later on I came to understand it. The medical school faculty, which was more liberal in this respect than the Corporation, planned to develop the teaching of preventive medicine and public health more extensively than ever before. Industrial medicine had become a much more important branch during the war years, but it still had not attracted men, and I was really about the only candidate available. I was told that the Corporation was far from enthusiastic over this breaking away from tradition, and that one member had sworn roundly over it. "But then," said my informant, "you know, he always swears." Another member had asked anxiously if I would insist on my right to use the Harvard Club, which at that time had no ladies' entrance, and did not admit even members' wives. One of my backers had promised them I never would nor would I demand my quota of football tickets, and of course I assured him that I should never think of doing either. Nor did I embarrass the faculty by marching in the Commencement procession and sitting on the platform, though each year I received a printed invitation to do so. At the bottom of the page would be the warning that "under no circumstances may a woman sit on the platform," which seemed a bit tactless, but I was sure it was not intentional.[47]

She added, though, that a number of her colleagues, including Dean David Edsall of the Medical School, were rather cordial to her.[48] Long before women were admitted to Harvard as students, a woman was added to the faculty, as she was "really the only person available" for the new job, a fact that emphasizes how very determined US academe was on the whole to reach the educational top of the world.

The PhD Degree

US administrators of the late nineteenth century would hire students away from German lecture halls regardless of whether or not they had yet attained a PhD degree, though in the era of radically transforming higher education, it was but a matter of time until the PhD degree would become one of the highly prized goals to be obtained in Germany as a starting point for an academic career in the United States. Lester F. Goodchild and Margaret Miller established several stages in the development of the American doctorate and dissertation. Of particular interest to this monograph are the early stages they observed: the period 1787 to 1874, when American graduate education slowly emerged, and the period 1875 to 1899, at the beginning of which stood the founding of Johns Hopkins University and thus the creation of an institution with a specific emphasis on graduate studies (in contrast to undergraduate education).[49] The two phases describe, first of all, the initiation of US graduate education after the American Revolution with the introduction of the PhD degree by midcentury presenting an important stepping stone to the emergence of graduate programs. Second, on the eve of the twentieth century, graduate schools were implemented and firmly anchored at key institutions in America.

The idea of the PhD degree had been adopted from Germany,[50] and, thanks to Daniel Coit Gilman's activities at Yale after his return from a German study tour in the second half of the 1850s, the PhD had been molded into an American degree. During the 1870s and even the 1880s, we find US students speak with fascination of the degree that could be obtained with a certain academic prestige attached to it at German universities. For instance, Calvin Thomas reminisced towards the close of his life that during his student days at Ann Arbor in the early 1870s, instructors had recently returned from Germany "with an impressive PhD after their names."[51] Likewise, after Milton Wylie Humphreys of West Virginia had earned a PhD degree from Leipzig in 1874, he was treated as a celebrity upon his return to Virginia:

> Many [Washington and Lee] students, even students whom I did not know procured my photograph and brought it to me for my signature, and were uniformly disappointed because I would not add "Ph.D." to my name. So rare was the degree in those days in America. Puffs, more or less true, of the "brilliancy" of my achievement appeared in many papers, among them the New York Tribune.... One of the "Courants," I think it was the "Yale Courant," at the close of the session, collected a list of the doctorates ... and the one *genuine* doctorate was—mine.[52]

Humphreys was 28½ years old when he enrolled at Leipzig on 18 April 1873 to study philology. Since 1869, he had been assistant professor of ancient languages at his alma mater. He would later teach at Vanderbilt University, the University of Texas in Austin, and the University of Virginia.[53]

If, then, James McKeen Cattell claimed in an 1884 letter to his parents, "The Ph.D. has always appeared to me a minor matter—but its most fitting place is at the conclusion of my studies,"[54] it revealed that it was a new and yet somewhat unusual concept that nonetheless (or maybe even because of that) had fired his ambitions. Cattell's remark was likely at least to some extent intended to convince his parents that a longer stay at a German university would be more advantageous than returning prematurely to take over faculty duties in America.

When analyzing information about the PhD degrees that were conferred upon US students at the University of Leipzig, the most interesting finding is that among American students, the degree was obviously quickly winning in popularity. Of at least 150 Leipzig dissertations that are preserved at the Leipzig University Library, nine were printed during the 1870s, about seventeen during the 1880s, almost seventy during the 1890s, and the rest after the turn of the century. In the last three or four years before World War I, the number of US dissertations dropped to almost zero. Few Leipzig-American dissertations were consequently written in the 1870s but considerably more in the 1890s. After the turn of the century, the number diminished, which might also be a reflection of the fact that the American PhD programs had now matured to a degree that made a venture to Germany for that purpose unnecessary. The observation is furthermore in accordance with the fact that after 1900, US student numbers at Leipzig began generally to decline. The numbers of US dissertations submitted at Leipzig are thus somewhat representative of trends in US student numbers abroad (see Appendix 3).

The number of US dissertations that are preserved at the Leipzig University Library do not reflect the actual number of PhD degrees conferred upon US students during the same time period. US students earned at least 190 PhD and MD degrees at Leipzig between 1870 and 1914. In comparison, more than 60 of the 1,200 Americans on Shumway's list received a PhD degree from Göttingen.[55] Humphreys was one of the first US students to earn a Leipzig PhD degree. The earliest to do so was apparently Frederick De Forest Allen in 1870. He had registered at Leipzig in November 1868 to study philology under Georg Curtius. Then again, two Leipzig Americans from the pre-1914 period received their degrees as late as in 1915 and 1920. They were Marvin Beeson and Heinrich A. Koch.

Simultaneously, the first years of the twentieth century witnessed an increase in German doctors, which was viewed critically by some as a tendency of the German PhD degree to be losing in quality. Charles W. Super voiced his concern regarding the increasing quantity and decreasing quality of German learning in an article in *The Nation* in early 1914. His observations implied the old truth that too much of something good will turn bad. It also touched upon the question of higher learning for the masses, a problem for which the nineteenth-century university at least in Germany was not prepared. Super had found that "more than 5,500 dissertations were issued in 1910 from the German empire alone."[56] He fretted, "It is within bounds to say that of this enormous output not one thesis in ten is worth printing, and not one in a hundred has any permanent value.... Many German professors have expressed the opinion that at least 40 per cent. of their students ought not to be in a university at all." Super then voiced a warning lest the same trends might occur in the United States, "Too many young people are looking towards gaining a livelihood with their wits who should be using their hands for this purpose."

On the whole, only a small percentage of US students actually obtained a Leipzig doctorate, although it should be taken into account that some of them submitted dissertations at other universities in Europe and the United States—for instance, John Robert Sittlington Sterrett registered at Leipzig in the fall of 1872 but earned a PhD degree from Munich eight years later. The low total number of dissertations might be explained to some extent by monetary considerations. Writing about a fellow student of psychology at Leipzig, Harlow Gale, Lincoln Steffens observed that to obtain a PhD degree at Leipzig, $1,800 had to be paid. But Gale was unwilling to commit to such a sum: "He studied for Ph.D. and passed his ex's but never paid the necessary $1,800 for the degree, caring nothing for it."[57]

A few US women were awarded PhD degrees in the 1870s and 1880s. But while they could not accomplish that at Leipzig, some of them may be linked to the Saxon university more or less directly. Helen Magill was the first woman to earn a PhD degree on North American soil. She did so in 1877 at Boston University, where she had studied together with Eva Channing. Her subsequent academic career was not as satisfactory as she had expected. On 10 September 1890, she abandoned it altogether to become the second wife of the diplomat, historian, and former president of Cornell University, Andrew D. White, who was twenty-one years her senior. When in 1897 Andrew was appointed US ambassador to Germany, Helen accompanied him to Berlin, where they occasionally received Lane Cooper as a visitor, who in 1900/01 was working towards a PhD degree in philology at Leipzig. M. Carey Thomas obtained her PhD degree summa cum laude from Zurich in 1882, mainly because she was not accepted as a PhD candidate at Leipzig. She asked her family beforehand not to spread news of what she was attempting to do in order to avoid ridicule in case of failure. Then again, Laura Emilie Mau unsuccessfully tried to obtain a Leipzig PhD right before World War I.[58]

The preparation of a dissertation allowed for networking, for instance as regarded publication. William M. Baskervill taught and soon befriended James H. Kirkland at Wofford College, South Carolina, before they both obtained Leipzig PhD degrees and became colleagues at Vanderbilt University. The dissertations, which they submitted in 1881 and 1885, respectively, are similar in layout. They were printed by the same printer in Halle, Ehrhardt Karras. Baskervill worked with Wülker, as did Kirkland.[59] At least nine theological and philological US students at Leipzig had their theses printed by Karras. It may be suspected that Wülker advised them to do so, or, alternatively, that they advised one another. Similarly, Wilhelm Ostwald had a predilection for the printer Wilhelm Engelmann.[60] Many of the dissertations of Ostwald's US students were published by that printer.

Material Improvements I: Libraries and Books

Once US students had completed their German higher education ideally with a PhD attached to their names, and once they had possibly even secured already a first academic position in the United States, they set about to prepare themselves in more material ways for their new challenges. Already for the duration of a stay abroad, US students had described the state of libraries and laboratories both in private correspondence and in published journal articles, using the opportunity to think of ways of how to improve US academia. As they were getting ready to move on, they did not confine themselves to penning elaborate descriptions. They now also invested much time and efforts as well as considerable resources into acquiring books and apparatuses. In the course of the nineteenth century, their changing opinions about libraries and laboratories depicted Leipzig in a more favorable light at times when it was highly popular among US students. But even when Leipzig had little appeal as a university town, visitors from the New World would take advantage of its resources as the European center of the book trade.

At Leipzig in 1816, the greatest disappointment for young George Ticknor was its libraries. He mentioned it twice—once in the beginning, once in the middle of a lengthy journal entry written on 18 September. The university library was "in very bad order particularly the [Manuscripts Section, which] it is almost impossible & sometimes quite impossible to find."[61] Ticknor attempted to be fair, pointing out that the library did hold a few treasures among its manuscripts "that have considerable value." But the collection was open for public use "only four hours in the week" and was "certainly inadequate." Ticknor also visited other libraries such as the Rath's Bibliothek in the *Gewandhaus,* "a building erected in 1740 and unquestionably the finest in Leipzig." He was full of praise for that library, but not satisfied, as it was "a city library kept for show and almost inaccessible compared with Göttingen." To make matters worse, it housed "also a Cabinet of Minerals of 6000 pieces, not very rare, ... which we did not see, as this can be effected only by a special permission from the Burgsmeister [*sic,* mayor?]!" In short, the libraries left much to be desired. Spoilt by what he had seen at Göttingen, Ticknor concluded as to Leipzig's libraries in 1816: "This part of the University is almost contemptible."

From the point of view of US students, the library situation in Leipzig improved in the course of the nineteenth century, although every now and then criticisms would be heard, illustrating US educational travelers' search for an ideal. In the 1820s, Henry Dwight observed that in the German countries, libraries could be found even in the smallest towns. He concluded that German governments regarded "intellectual cultivation" a most important aspect of life.[62] By 1853, Mason C. Weld qualified the Leipzig University Library as "large and fine."[63] Lane Cooper did find it wanting in 1901, though "accessibility of various departmental libraries compensates to a certain extent for the superior facilities—or rather richness of the Royal Library in Berlin."[64] In 1877, William Welch had also pointed out that Leipzig's departmental libraries were a great asset.[65] In December 1875, Charles R. Lanman rejoiced in English and American papers at a Leipzig reading room as well as the "magnificent" selection of scientific journals.[66] Finally, Cooper observed in 1900 that the library was "well lighted, heated, and ventilated—more than can be said of many similar structures elsewhere."[67]

Comments about the libraries highlighted national perspectives and differences. When George H. Parker was unhappy about the cataloguing system, he remarked, "The library is the finest of the university buildings but like most German libraries it is not very convenient. The catalogue is not accessible—to get a book you make out a slip [and] leave it one day and call the next day—if the book is to be found you get it, if not you try another."[68] In addition to the complicated cataloguing system, German libraries were undemocratic in their accessibility by a broader public. As Andrew McLaughlin noted in February 1894, "It has just occurred to me that Germany has no great Public libraries—at least I know of none—like the Boston library.... The library here like so many other things is for the favored few—for the few I might say who will + can understand the intricacy of the catalogue [?] + the regulations."[69]

The greatest neglect on the part of European academia was—so US Students complained—that it did not make use of the opportunity of a considerable US student presence to find out more (on a larger scale) about scholarly-scientific advances on the other side of the Atlantic. As late as in the early 1890s, US academe was represented through the lens of German scholarly and scientific media; in a way, it was lacking independence. There were few American publications in European libraries, thus the Europeans' ignorance of US contributions to the state of Western science and scholarship even as regarded publications by Leipzig alumni such as G. Stanley Hall.[70] Already in 1869, Bowditch had complained to his uncle, writing from Paris, France: "I don't see why Americans are not as capable of doing good work in a scientific way as any other people. The great trouble is that American work is not known here."[71]

US students did not simply observe and analyze; they also acted to improve the situation back home. One way to achieve this was to send books and entire libraries to America, and, by doing so, to ensure that these materials would now be made available on much more democratic terms. In 1820/21, Edward Everett and Joseph Green Cogswell obtained from Johann Wolfgang von Goethe himself a twenty-volume edition of his works for the Harvard University Library.[72] Eighty years later, a Harvard University Annual Report actually pointed out with satisfaction the merits of such transactions:

> In regard to the value and character of the library, I cannot do better than quote from Professor [Georg] Witkowski, of the University of Leipzig, who, in a series of articles in the Allgemeine Zeitung ["general newspaper"], bewails the loss to German scholarship of the many private libraries which in recent years have found their way from Germany to America. The loss, he maintains, is irreparable, and cannot be counterbalanced by any corresponding advantage to American scholars … , impressing deeply the warning that Germans must not permit further inroads to be made on irreplaceable national possessions.[73]

The report concluded, "Such expressions bring home to us very pointedly the duty which the ownership of such treasures implies—the duty of making them as widely useful as possible, and of maintaining the collection in serviceable condition."

A center of the book trade, Leipzig was particularly suited for buying books. Already the earliest visitors appreciated this aspect of commercial Leipzig.[74] During Ticknor's second visit in the mid-1830s, he spent the little time he stayed in Leipzig getting in touch with book publishers and dealers rather than meeting scholars. He gave a not quite so flattering portrait of one of the two Brockhaus sons as "a ready, & sagacious person, entirely imbued with the spirit of trade"[75] (Ticknor was not sure whether he had encountered Heinrich or Friedrich; the father Friedrich Arnold was deceased by then). Ticknor returned another two decades later, as he told Edward Everett on 30 July 1856, to procure books for the new Boston Public Library. He stopped three times in Leipzig and "was busy for the Library."[76] Likewise, while George Lincoln Burr studied there in the 1884/85 fall term, he discussed new acquisitions for the White library with the founding president of Cornell, A. D. White.[77] Henry P. Bowditch wrote to William James in June 1871: "I have had a long list of books made out comprising the most important works on physiological subjects published within the last 15 or 20 years + I hope to induce the city library to purchase a part or all of them."[78] Later that year, Thomas Day Seymour informed his former classmates at Western Reserve that he had "had the pleasure of making out an order for the complete 'Bibliotheca Scriptorum Graecorum Teubneriana' for the College Library.—about a hundred volumes + comprising nearly all of the Greek authors who are at all prominent."[79] A few years later, Lanman, one of the most avid Leipzig-American book buyers, rejoiced that he had gotten hold of the same edition.[80]

Seymour's case suggests that it was a pleasure to build up a library while simultaneously supplying a college with important works. Indeed, to pile up books in one's room was to get to the bottom of the German experience—that is, for the time being to devote one's life to pure scholarship. Seymour wrote that he had "been settled in my room only three or four days but I have my books there and feel quite at home."[81] Similarly, Calvin Thomas reported: "Secured a room, unpacked my trunk and arranged my books ... am now ready for work."[82] When Thomas met the pastor of the American Church, Samuel Ives Curtiss, he envied his library.[83] Two years before, Lanman had delighted in Curtiss's "magnificent lot of books, elegantly bound,"[84] adding, "I am very well and happy and enjoying Leipsic immensely.... I have been making some important purchases of books."[85] Lane Cooper rejoiced in 1900 that "Living is cheap in Leipzig, consequently I can afford more for the gradual collection of necessary or even desirable books, many of which it is not easy to get in America."[86] Seymour noted in November 1871: "My father's library is so well supplied with the standard works that I have only to supplement it, but have already two large chests full of books and a long list of books to buy."[87] Shortly before leaving Leipzig in August 1878 to become instructor at the University of Michigan at Ann Arbor, Thomas prepared himself for the new challenge: "Last week I spent in buying books and getting them to the binder's. 'Tis pleasant work and not to be dispatched in a hurry."[88]

US students approached their book buying with scientific rigor, it seems, taking advantage of every opportunity with a critical eye. They read catalogues and engaged the services of book dealers, also advising one another in these regards. Bowditch, for example, asked his friend William James, "Shall I order it from *my* bookseller? Perhaps he will treat you better."[89] Seymour carefully examined catalogues for important upcoming sales.[90] As early as 1828, Theodore D. Woolsey had observed the practice of publishing catalogues in preparation of an upcoming book fair.[91]

Late-nineteenth-century US students also voiced criticisms of the German approach to the book trade, ironically missing what Ticknor had found in too great an abundance at Leipzig earlier in the century: a sense of business spirit as evident in America. Thomas fussed, "The book trade here disappoints me. There is absolutely no display. I look in at the shop windows and seldom see anything which excites my covetousness. I enter the shop and the chances are great of not getting what I want."[92] He found establishments in Detroit and even Grand Rapids more impressive than those in Leipzig and London, concluding, "People in Europe don't seem to have the notion of spreading out a $100000 stock of books for the public to handle and look at."

Material Improvements II: Laboratories, Apparatuses, and Journals

With the nineteenth-century scientific spirit holding everyone from classicist to chemist in a tight grip, US students not only curiously observed libraries but also showed an interest in laboratories and apparatuses and took note of German scientific journals as models for similar publications to be initiated back home. Shortly after his arrival in Leipzig in December 1869, Bowditch suggested to his uncle Henry Ingersoll Bowditch to publish a description of Carl Ludwig's new laboratory in a medical journal in the United States "in order that the medical profession may understand how science is valued here in Europe + if you think it worth while I will write a description."[93] The letter itself, in fact, formed the nucleus of the proposed article. H. I. Bowditch's reply was favorable.[94] H. P. Bowditch's 1870 letter to the editor of the *Boston Medical and Surgical Journal* started off with the observation that "Leipzig is a city very little visited by American medical men, for whom the larger cities, such as Berlin and Vienna, offer in general greater attractions in their superior opportunities for clinical observation. The student of physiology and chemistry, however, finds here facilities for prosecuting his studies which are not surpassed in any city in Germany."[95]

Bowditch's article was a deliberate attempt to inform interested circles at home about new opportunities abroad and thus possibly to attract others to the Saxon university. He was not the only one to do so—both in private letters and in publications several of his fellow Americans who were enrolled in European universities did the same. The descriptions overall tended to show an interest in physical detail such as buildings and their organization combined with background information and implied ponderings on how exactly the scientific creation of knowledge was achieved in Germany. By August 1887, James McKeen Cattell was contemplating a paper about Wundt's Leipzig laboratory, which he would indeed present in late 1887. It was published in *Mind* in 1888.[96] In 1905, Raymond Pearl described the Leipzig zoological laboratory in detail. The letter was addressed to his mother, which might account for the gossip items contained therein. He started out with a physical description: "Now I will tell you all about the lab. It is a big stone structure made in two wings and in three stories high besides the basement. The first floor contains the main laboratory and rooms for investigators; the second floor the zoological museum and the third floor the residence of the head professor [Carl] Chun and some other Prof. that I don't know. The German professors get this house rent thrown in by living in the laboratory. My room is a big room on the ground floor." This was immediately followed by working conditions blended with a description of the people:

> The people in the lab. are very nice and try to do every thing they can for me. The head man, [Carl] Chun, is a pleasant fatherly old chap, who comes in every day to see how I am getting along. He can speak English, but mostly won't. [Otto] Zur Strassen is the next man under him, and was married a little less than a year ago to Chun's daughter, who was reputed to be the most beautiful girl in Leipzig. We haven't seen her yet but hope to. Zur Strassen must be about 35 years old, but looks younger a great deal. Like most of the University men here, he has money. He gets practically no money from the University. Only the head profs. do, and so while they are working up they must depend on their own resources for a living.[97]

Pearl was far from happy about the laboratory, specifically in comparison with what he had seen back home. He thought the equipment "very poor, as judged by our standards." He fretted about having to procure some equipment himself, though he conceded that "being a guest of the place they tried their best to get everything I needed for me, but I finally had to turn to and buy some things, because they did not have them." Pearl had come to Leipzig on a scholarship of the Carnegie Institution. He continuously worried about money matters. Of all the US students whom I examined, he was the only one to complain about expensive Leipzig, a fact that should be taken into account when evaluating his grievances about Chun's laboratory.

Be that as it may, by 1905, the Leipzig zoological laboratory apparently still had less impressive resources at its disposal than the physiological laboratory of Bowditch's day and also some even earlier ones. Already in 1853, the prospective chemist Evan Pugh had sent letters to a US editor that also contained a description of Otto Linné Erdmann's Leipzig laboratory, thus introducing him to US scientific circles, starting by positioning the man as a scientist of the first rank, which was necessary especially at a time when Leipzig was not yet a first choice for US students: "Prof. Erdmann, though not generally known in America, stands high as a chemist in Europe. He is author of several books on chemistry, besides being an assistant editor of a chemical paper (a thing America has not yet supported) which is of strictly scientific character. We found him in his library."[98] This was followed by a description of the facilities in which Pugh did not restrict himself to describing both the professor and his laboratory but also gave attention to the generally pleasant atmosphere. Research facilities should not be crowded in ugly neighborhoods for mere money concerns, which could only hinder the build-up of prestige:

> His little laboratory is well supplied with the best apparatus, much of which, that has been adopted by chemists generally, he contrived himself. Passing through this room we entered the students' laboratory. This was large enough to accommodate sixteen or twenty students, giving each an experimenting table and a set of reagents. It is very comfortably arranged, and so situated as to give a fine view into an open square, and receiving the rays of the morning sun; contrasting in this respect finely with many of our American laboratories, which for want of their patronage, are crowded off into unpleasant parts of the towns, where rents are not so high.
>
> In another room were the materials for making poisonous and unpleasant gases, some of which are required at almost every step in chemical analysis. Adjoining this was the lecture room, which is capable of seating fifty students, and by an ingenious contrivance doors can be thrown open, so as to allow the lecturer to use the furnace and heating apparatus in one room, to make illustrations before the students in the lecture room.

Erdmann initiated a tradition of technical or physical chemistry at Leipzig that would experience a heyday after Ostwald's arrival in 1887.

One of Ostwald's early US students, Arthur A. Noyes of MIT, did not fail to depict Ostwald's laboratory in a letter to his friend Harry M. Goodwin, who would soon embark for Leipzig himself. Among student friends, the description focused on less serious aspects, for example, "One of the notices posted in the laboratory is to the effect that students who knock their cigar ashes on the floor are to be fined twenty pfennigs; and one important use of Bunsen burners is for lighting cigars."[99] Noyes very much regretted that "[e]verything is fined. If you drop a match on the floor, fine, twenty pfennigs, if you dont [sic] pick it up again right off. If you cause any 'übelriechende' [smelly] or 'schädlich' [dangerous] vapors to escape, –50 pfennigs; if you leave a reagent bottle off the shelf twenty pfennigs etc. I expect to have quite a bill for fines at the end of the year. I discover most every day that I have been doing something wrong."

From the point of view of Ostwald's US students, the establishment of laboratories staffed with US Ostwald students made less urgent a visit to physico-chemical Leipzig. In 1952, a German American, George Jaffé, published his recollections about "three great laboratories," listing Ostwald's research facilities first. Jaffé remembered a growing distance between the "master and his pupils,"[100] which increased after Ostwald had moved into a new laboratory on 3 January 1898. For Ostwald's former US students it was difficult to be present at the opening. They sent their regrets in a mixture of flattery and congratulations.[101] Harry Clary Jones saw to it that the opening of Ostwald's new laboratory was announced in *Science*.[102]

In addition to monitoring the appeal of Leipzig laboratories, US students also procured apparatuses. Bowditch, a member of a well-known and well-situated family, could afford to make substantial purchases financed entirely from his own pocket. In January 1870, he broached the issue with his father: "Do you know whether there is any money in the [Harvard] College funds which could be used for the purchase of apparatus for physiological experiments? Such a fund is a prime necessity for a physiological laboratory. New [missing words] needed + old ones need to be altered + repaired.... Thanks for your remittance of 300£."[103] Half a year before Bowditch returned home, his father informed him, "I have remitted (200£) two hundred pounds—I wish you to get every thing you may need & do not desire you to restrict yourselves to the (1000$) one thousand dollars, but purchase what in your judgment may be necessary...."[104] Bowditch replied, "If you see [Harvard president] Mr Eliot you can tell him that I hope he will give me a good laboratory for I am going to bring home quite a quantity of apparatus."[105] He also joyfully informed his friend William James of the developments, expressing hope for a future cooperation, "I shall bring home lots of apparatus with me + if the faculty will only give me a little money to buy animals we can set up a laboratory at once. I say *we* for I expect you to join me in working at experimental physiology."[106] Cattell was similarly fortunate as Bowditch. As a student in Leipzig, he had enough money to buy apparatuses and pay his friend Gustav Oscar Berger.[107] When it was decided that Cattell would be affiliated with the University of Pennsylvania, while still in England in late 1888 he was informed that $1,000 was at his disposal to buy apparatuses.[108]

Finally, upon their return to the United States, Leipzig Americans resorted to academic networks to furnish the market with new scientific publications made in America. They consulted with Leipzig professors (revealing internal rivalries in the process). For example, in 1893, Cattell informed Wundt about G. Stanley Hall's lack of commitment to an all-American journal of psychology. The program outlined for the journal was ambitious. Cattell cautiously suggested turning it into an international platform to make America more attractive for international scholarship.[109] In January 1897, Harry C. Jones told Ostwald that he did not think much of a new, Cornell-based US journal of physical chemistry.[110] John W. Servos discussed its fate in connection with Wilder Dwight Bancroft's career, which he summarized as a "qualified failure."[111] Such journals established in the United States—even if prepared by loyal and promising US disciples—were still likely to rival the Germans' own publications in time.

Summary

A student venture in Germany was geared toward finding oneself a professional future in the US—preferably in academia. Many US students worked throughout their German venture toward this goal and, having experienced a foreign model for up to several years, returned home determined to turn the United States into an academic Mecca. They had established numerous important contacts, which in some cases, had paved their ways into an American college or even research university while still abroad, especially as the administrators of such institutions after 1870 were particularly eager to recruit excellently trained young scholars and scientists directly out of the German lecture halls, seminars, and research laboratories. Ambitious to reach the top, administrators attempted to hire the best person they could get, regardless of gender or nationality (though race was likely a different issue to be explored more thoroughly elsewhere).

After the 1860s, the PhD degree became an important feature of the nascent US graduate schools. The PhD degree had been brought over from Germany and then adjusted to US higher education. It quickly took hold as a means to honor graduate students at the end of their successful studies and completion of a dissertation or independent research project. Until about 1900, though, the German PhD degree was still considered to be quite prestigious. But especially thereafter American higher education seemed to be catching up even if Germans were not necessarily aware of the development or did not quite understand its full significance.

With connections and the degree at hand, US students returned home with clear ideas also of the physical aspects and necessities of an ideal research university. They had checked out and described libraries and laboratories, and they had purchased books and apparatuses both for their private use and to be added to American college and university collections or public libraries. They had also closely observed and even participated in academic culture, such as by undergoing rigorous PhD examinations and by submitting their works to specialized scholarly and scientific journals in Germany. Such material and conceptual values were a part of the German influence upon US higher education especially in the period 1866 to 1914.

Notes

1. Rita Hofstetter and Bernard Schneuwly, eds., *Passion, Fusion, Tension: New Education and Educational Sciences: End 19th—Middle 20th Century = éducation nouvelle et sciences de l'éducation: fin du 19e—milieu du 20e siècle* (Bern: Peter Lang, 2006), 2n2.
2. Simon Flexner and James T. Flexner, *William Henry Welch and the Heroic Age of American Medicine* (Baltimore/London: Johns Hopkins University Press, 1993 [1941]), 5.
3. Ibid., 116.
4. Ibid., 102.
5. Wilhelm Ostwald, *Lebenslinien. Eine Selbstbiographie*, vol. 3 (Berlin: Klasing & Co., 1926–27), 56–57. My emphasis and translation, original: "ich wies auf den erstaunlich großen Einfluß der Zeit und die Notwendigkeit einer wissenschaftlichen Tradition zur Hervorbringung reichlicher und dauernder Hochleistungen hin. Als Beispiel konnte ich die Clark-Universität anführen, die vor etwa zehn Jahren mit sehr großen Mitteln und der ausgesprochenen Absicht gegründet worden war, eine Vereinigung der besten Forscher ohne Rücksicht auf die Kosten herzustellen, um eine große wissenschaftliche Produktion zu organisieren. Der Versuch war fehlgeschlagen. Noyes ließ sich dadurch nicht entmutigen und meinte, daß man hierbei lernen könnte, es demnächst besser zu machen, denn die Mittel ließen sich immer wieder beschaffen[,] und sein Volk habe den festen Willen, auch auf diesem Gebiet das Höchste zu erreichen. ,Es wird noch lange dauern, bis Sie dem Standpunkt nahe kommen,' sagte ich, ,den Deutschland schon jetzt erreicht hat.' Unter Überwindung einer leichten Verlegenheit, aber mit roten Backen und glänzenden Augen antwortete Noyes: ,Wir hoffen, zu gegebener Zeit den geistigen Schwerpunkt der gesamten Menschheit über den Atlantischen Ozean hierher zu verlegen.' Da Noyes stets ein überaus ruhiges, zurückhaltendes Wesen gezeigt hatte, überraschte mich diese innere Glut sehr und macht mich höchst nachdenklich. Ob der wirtschaftlich führenden Stelle, welche die Vereinigten Staaten inzwischen dank der wahnwitzigen Selbstzerfleischung Europas erreicht haben, auch eine geistige folgen wird, kann jetzt noch nicht mit Wahrscheinlichkeit vorausgesehen werden."
6. W. Wundt to Emil Kraeplin, 9 January 1887, NA Wundt, 327, LUA. My translation, original: "In den Weihnachtsferien besuchte uns Herr Cattell aus England, wo er diesen Winter ist.... Er besitzt bereits ein Anstellungspatent für Psychologie an der Pennsylvanian-Universität. Sie sehen, in Amerika werden leichter neue Fächer ,gegründet' als bei uns. Aber vielleicht kommt es doch noch einmal dazu."
7. Norma J. Bringmann and Wolfgang G. Bringmann, "Wilhelm Wundt and his first American Student," in *Wundt Studies,* ed. Wolfgang G. Bringmann and Ryan D. Tweney (Toronto: C. J. Hochgrefe, Inc., 1980), 185; Saul Rosenzweig, *Freud, Jung, and Hall the King-Maker: The Historic Expedition to America with G. Stanley Hall as Host and William James as Guest* (Seattle/Toronto/Bern/Göttingen: Rana House Press St. Louis, 1992), 47–49.
8. See also James Gilbert, *Whose Fair? Experience, Memory, and the History of the Great St. Louis Exposition* (Chicago: University of Chicago Press, 2009).
9. Ostwald, *Lebenslinien*, vol. 3, 390. My translation, original: "das ganze Gebiet menschlicher Geistesarbeit als wohlgeordnetes Ganzes zur Geltung zu bringen und für jedes Einzelfeld dieses gesamten Gebietes womöglich zwei führende Vertreter aus der Gelehrtenschaft der ganzen Kulturwelt als Redner zu gewinnen."
10. Lowry Price Ware, "The Academic Career of William E. Dodd," (PhD dissertation, University of South Carolina, 1956), 32.

11. J. M. Cattell to Parents, 30 August 1884, reprinted in Michael M. Sokal, ed., *An Education in Psychology: James McKeen Cattell's Journal and Letters from Germany and England, 1880–1888* (Cambridge, MA: MIT Press, 1981), 118.

12. J. R. Angell (Cambridge), 27 April 1892. Angell Papers, 85605 Aa 1, UM Bentley.

13. Bowditch's case may be traced in his correspondence with his father: H. P. Bowditch to Father, 2 and 9 January 1870, 21 April [1871]. Bowditch Papers, HMS c5.1, Folder 5, HUL Countway.

14. W. H. Welch to Stepmother, 8 November 1876. Welch Papers, Box 68, Folder 16, JHU med. My emphasis.

15. Frederick T. Lewis, "Charles Sedgwick Minot. December 23, 1852–November 19, 1914," (Harvard Medical School, booklet, 30 November 1914), HUG 1573 14, HUL Pusey; Charles Sedgwick Minot Papers, H MS c 21.2, HUL Countway; *Quinquennial Catalogue of Harvard University 1636–1930* (Cambridge, MA: Harvard University Press), 114, 642; Heinz Schröer, *Carl Ludwig. Begründer der messenden Experimentalphysiologie* (Stuttgart: Wissenschaftliche Verlagsgesellschaft M.B.H., 1967), 291; Frederic T. Lewis, "Charles Sedgwick Minot," in *Anatomical Record* 10, no. 3 (20 January 1916): 133–64; Frederic T. Lewis, "Obituary. Charles Sedgwick Minot. December 23, 1852–November 19, 1914," in *Boston Medical and Surgical Journal* 171, no. 24 (10 December 1914): 911–14. W. T. Porter, "Charles Sedgwick Minot, M.D.," in *Boston Medical and Surgical Journal* 172, no. 13 (1 April 1915): 467–70.

16. W. H. Welch to Stepmother, 8 November 1876. Welch Papers, Box 68, Folder 16, JHU med. Flexner and Flexner, *William Henry Welch*.

17. W. H. Welch to Stepmother, 8 November 1876, ibid. Following quotes ibid.

18. Flexner and Flexner, *William Henry Welch*.

19. Florence Rena Sabin, *Franklin Paine Mall: The Story of a Mind* (Baltimore: Johns Hopkins Press, 1934), 37–38.

20. Ibid., 55–56.

21. Flexner and Flexner, *William Henry Welch*, 146.

22. Ibid., 21.

23. As to the Pattengill affair, see journal, C. Thomas, 6 August 1878, Thomas Papers, 86180 Aa 2 Ac, Box 3, UM Bentley. Also, C. Thomas, unfinished, typed Autobiography, 20–21, 24, ibid., Box 1.

24. See Anja Becker, "For the Sake of Old Leipzig Days ... Academic Networks of American Students at a German University, 1781–1914" (PhD dissertation, University of Leipzig, 2006).

25. *Quinquennial Catalogue*, 96.

26. C. W. Eliot to T. W. Richards, 15 July 1901. Richards Papers, HUG 1743.1.5, Box 2, Folder EF, HUL Pusey.

27. C. L. Jackson to T. W. Richards, 13 July 1901, ibid., Folder Misc.

28. C. L. Jackson to T. W. Richards, 16 July 1901, ibid.

29. C. W. Eliot to T. W. Richards, 29 July and 29 August 1901, ibid., Folder EF.

30. T. W. Richards to Charles Robert Sanger, 25/26 July 1901, ibid., Folder Misc. Sanger was professor of chemistry at Harvard. *Quinquennial Catalogue*, 134.

31. A. A. Noyes to T. W. Richards, 11 October 1901. Richards Papers, HUG 1743.1.5, Box 2, Folder Misc., HUL Pusey.

32. H. P. Talbot (Boston) to T. W. Richards, 7 October 1901, ibid.

33. C. L. Jackson to T. W. Richards, 13 July 1901, ibid., Folder Misc.

34. C. W. Eliot to T. W. Richards, 26 August 1901, ibid., Folder EF.

35. G. H. Parker, *The World Expands: Recollections of a Zoologist* (Cambridge, MA: Harvard University Press, 1946), 88–89.

36. Eveline Einhauser, ed., *Lieber Freund... Die Briefe Hermann Osthoffs an Karl Brugmann, 1875–1904* (Trier: WVT, 1992), 264–65. Eduard Prokosch, "Hermann Collitz," *Journal of English and Germanic Philology* 35 (1936): 454–57, reprinted in Thomas A. Sebeok, *Portraits of Linguists. A Biographical Source for the History of Western Linguistics, 1746–1963. Vol. 2. From Eduard Sievers to Benjamin Lee Whorf* (Bristol: Thoemmes Press, 2002 [1966]), 74–77. G. Schlimpert and R. Eckert, "Briefe Leskiens an Karl Brugmann," *ZfSl* 26, no. 2 (1981): 229 n52.

37. Personalakte Ewald Flügl, PA 462, LUA.

38. Anja Becker, "Amerikanistik [American Studies]," in *Geschichte der Universität Leipzig. Band IV: Fakultäten, Institute, Zentrale Einrichtungen (1. Halbband)* [History of the University of Leipzig. Volume IV: Departments, Institutes, Centers (Part 1)], ed. Ulrich von Hehl, Uwe John, and Manfred Rudersdorf (Leipzig: Universitätsverlag, 2009); Also Eberhard Brüning, *Das Konsulat der Vereinigten Staaten von Amerika zu Leipzig* (Berlin, Akademie Verlag, 1994), and Eberhard Brüning, *Humanistische Tradition und Progressives Erbe der Leipziger Anglistik/Amerikanistik. 100 Jahre Lehrstuhl für englische Sprache und Literatur and der Karl-Marx-Universität* (Berlin: Akademie Verlag, 1977). Ewald Flügel, "Carlyles religiöse und sittliche Entwicklung und Weltanschauung. Zweiter Teil," (PhD dissertation, University of Leipzig, 1887), printed by Verlag [publisher] Fr. Wilh. Brunow; see Ewald Flügel, "III. Die nordamerikanische Literatur," in *Geschichte der englischen Literatur von den ältesten Zeiten bis zur Gegenwart*, by Richard Wülker, vol. 2, 2nd rev. and exp. ed. (Leipzig/Wien: Verlag des Bibliographischen Instituts, 1907), 413–541.

39. 15th Year Book Class of 1892, Faculty File George Augustus Hulett '92, PUL Mudd.

40. E. Channing (Jamaica Plain) to E. Windisch, 25 November 1888. NA Windisch, 2.85.1, LUA.

41. E. W. Hopkins (Bryn Mawr) to E. Windisch, 5 October 1886. Ibid., 2.247.2, LUA.

42. For a biographical note on Whitney, see Ward W. Briggs, Jr., ed., *The Letters of Basil Lanneau Gildersleeve* (Baltimore/London: Johns Hopkins University Press, 1987), 386.

43. E. W. Hopkins (New York) to E. Windisch, 8 September 1895. NA Windisch, 2.247.5, LUA.

44. E. W. Hopkins (New Haven) to E. Windisch, 23 October 1898. Ibid., 2.247.7.

45. R. W. Deering (Western Reserve University) to H. Collitz, 6 May 1907. Collitz Papers, MS 14, B. 8, JHU MEL. Deering was a Leipzig-trained Vanderbilt graduate. Anja Becker, "Southern Academic Ambitions Meet German Scholarship: The Leipzig Networks of Vanderbilt University's James H. Kirkland in the Late Nineteenth Century," *Journal of Southern History* 74, no. 4 (November 2008): 855–86.

46. G. C. Schmidt (Leipzig) to Immatrikulations-Kommission, 10 October 1905. Enclosed is a letter of recommendation from M. Carey Thomas to University of Geneva, 21 June 1905. Acta, Zulassung weiblicher Personen zum Besuche von Vorlesungen an der Universität Leipzig betr. (1905), Rep. II no. 60 vol. 5, microfilm 429, p. 0529 [45], LUA.

47. Alice Hamilton, *Exploring the Dangerous Trades* (Boston: Little, Brown and Company, 1943), 252–53. See also Barbara Sichermann, *Alice Hamilton: A Life in Letters* (Cambridge, MA: Harvard University Press, 1984); Joseph J. Elia, Jr., "Alice Hamilton—1869–1970," *New England Journal of Medicine* 283. no. 18 (29 October 1970): 993–94; and Alice Hamilton, "Edith and Alice Hamilton. Students in Germany," *Atlantic Monthly* 215, no. 3 (March 1965): 129–32.

48. Hamilton, *Exploring the Dangerous Trades*, 266.

49. Lester F. Goodchild and Margaret M. Miller, "The American Doctorate and Dissertation: Six Development Stages" in *Rethinking the Dissertation Process: Tackling Personal and Institutional Obstacles*, ed. Lester F. Goodchild, Kathy E. Green, Elinor Katz, and Raymond C. Kluever (San Francisco: Jossey-Bass Publishers, 1997), 17–32.

50. William Clark devotes an entire chapter to the history of the PhD degree in his *Academic Charisma and the Origins of the Research University* (Chicago: University of Chicago Press, 2006), 183–238.

51. C. Thomas, unfinished, typed Autobiography, c.1919, 9. C. Thomas Papers, 86180 Aa 2 Ac, Box 1, UM Bentley.

52. Unpublished memoirs, M. W. Humphrey. Quoted in Ollinger Crenshaw and William Pusey III, "An American Classical Scholar in Germany, 1874," *American-German Review* 22, no. 6 (August/September 1956): 33. Emphasis in original.

53. John R. Durbin, "In Memoriam Milton Wylie Humphreys." 2 Apr 2002. http://www .utexas.edu/faculty/council/2000–2001/memorials/AMR/Humphreys/humphreys.html. [28 August 2005]. Also, Briggs, *The Letters of Basil Lanneau Gildersleeve*.

54. J. M. Cattell to Parents, 30 August 1884, reprinted in Sokal, *Education in Psychology*, 118. Following quote ibid.

55. Sokal, *Education in Psychology*, 2. Without giving a specific page, he cites Daniel Bussey Shumway, "The American Students of the University of Göttingen," *Americana Germanica* 8, nos. 5 and 6 (September–December 1910) and Paul G. Buchloh, ed., *American Colony of Göttingen. Historical Data Collected Between the Years 1855 and 1888* (Göttingen: Vandenhoek & Ruprecht, 1976).

56. Charles W. Super, "German Degrees," in *The Nation* 98, no. 2531 (1 January 1914): 9. Following quotes ibid.

57. L. Steffens to Frederick M. Willis, 29 January 1891, reprinted in Ella Winter and Granville Hicks, eds., *The Letters of Lincoln Steffens*, vol. 1 (New York: Harcourt, Brace and Company, 1938), 59.

58. As regards Magill, Glenn C. Altschuler, *Better Than Second Best: Love and Work in the Life of Helen Magill* (Urbana/Chicago: University of Illinois Press, 1990), 38–40, 108, 127–28. See also Glenn C. Altschuler, *Andrew D. White—Educator, Historian, Diplomat* (Ithaca, NY: Cornell University Press, 1979) and L. Cooper (Berlin) to Father, 3 July 1900, Cooper Papers, 14/12/680, Box 18, Cornell Kroch. As regards Thomas, see M. C. Thomas (Zurich) to Mother, 25 June 1882, reprinted in Marjorie Housepian Dobkin, ed., *The Making of a Feminist: Early Journals of M. Carey Thomas* (Kent, OH: Kent State University Press, 1979), 257. As to her desire not to spread the news before the examination, see the same to Uncle Allen, 1 June 1882, ibid., 255. As regards Mau, see Sandra L. Singer, *Adventures Abroad: North American Women at German-Speaking Universities, 1868–1915*, Contributions in Women's Studies 201 (Westport, CT: Praeger, 2003), 149–50.

59. Edwin Mims, *Chancellor Kirkland of Vanderbilt* (Nashville: Vanderbilt University Press 1940), 46–47.

60. Konrad Krause, *Alma Mater Lipsiensis. Geschichte der Universität Leipzig von 1409 bis zur Gegenwart* (Leipzig: Universitätsverlag, 2003), 481.

61. Journal, G. Ticknor, 18 September 1816. Ticknor Journals, microfilm W 3275, reel II, vol. II, HUL Lamont. Following quotes ibid.

62. Henry E. Dwight, *Travels in the North of Germany, in the Years 1825 and 1826* (New York: G. & C. & H. Carvill, 1829), 74. The same had been observed by Madame de Staël in the chapter on Saxony in Madame de Staël, *De l'Allemagne*, vol. 1 (Paris: GF Flammarion, 1968 [1810]), 119–20. Dwight proceeded to list the names of towns and the number of volumes stored in local libraries. At Leipzig he found two libraries containing one hundred thousand volumes. Dwight, *Travels in the North of Germany*, 75.

63. M. C. Weld to Family, 22 June 1853 (Mason's III Eur fragment). L. Weld Family Papers, Group 559, Box 1, Folder 2, YUL.

64. L. Cooper to Mother, 4 [?] November 1900. Cooper Papers, 14/12/680, Box 18, Cornell Kroch.

65. W. H. Welch to Stepmother, 29 January 1877. Welch Papers, Box 68, Folder 17, JHU med.
66. C. R. Lanman to Aunt, 5 December 1875. Lanman Papers, HUG 4510.67, Letters from Europe, vol. 3, HUL Pusey.
67. L. Cooper to Mother, 4 [?] November 1900. Cooper Papers, 14/12/680, Box 18, Cornell Kroch.
68. G. H. Parker to Family, 13 December 1891. Parker Papers, HUG 4674.12, Box 2, HUL Pusey.
69. Journal, A. C. McLaughlin, 27 February 1894. McLaughlin Papers, 85536 Aa 2, Box 1, UM Bentley.
70. L. Witmer to J. Stewart, n.d. John Stewart Collection, Box 2, Folder Witmer, UP Van Pelt.
71. H. P. Bowditch to H. I. Bowditch, 26 January 1869. H. P. Bowditch Papers, HMS c5.1, Folder 2. HUL Countway. He proceeded to give an example about how he had enlightened the French on the work of Jeffries Wyman, professor of anatomy at Harvard until 1874. On Bowditch and Wyman, see W. Bruce Fye, *The Development of American Physiology: Scientific Medicine in the Nineteenth Century* (Baltimore: Johns Hopkins University Press, 1987), 93–98; *Quinquennial Catalogue*, 161.
72. Orie William Long, *Literary Pioneers: Early American Explorers of European Culture* (New York: Gordon Press, 1975 [1935]), 87–90.
73. *Reports of the President and the Treasurer of Harvard College, 1903–1904.* Harvard Library, 214–15. http://pds.lib.harvard.edu/pds/view/2574586?n=216&s=4. Following quote ibid. As to Prof. Witkowski, see Walter Dietze, *Georg Witkowski (1863–1939)* (Leipzig: Karl-Marx-Universität, 1973).
74. Philip Schaff, *Germany; Its Universities, Theology, and Religion* (Philadelphia: Lindsay and Blakiston/New York: Sheldon, Blakeman & Co., 1857), 80. T. Parker (Auerbach's Keller) to Dr. Francis, 12 June 1844, reprinted in John Weiss, *Life and Correspondence of Theodore Parker*, vol. 1 (New York: D. Appleton & Company, 1864), 240. Dwight, *Travels in the North of Germany*, 335; Anonymous, *The Tourist in Europe: or A Concise Summary of the Various Routes, Objects of Interests, &c.* (New York: Wiley & Putnam, 1838), 247; G. Stanley Hall, *Aspects of German Culture* (Boston: James R. Osgood and Company, 1881), 74.
75. Journal, G. Ticknor, 14 May 1836. Ticknor Journals, microfilm W3275, reel 2, vol. IV, HUL Lamont.
76. George Ticknor, *Life, Letters, and Journals of George Ticknor*, vol. 2 (London: Sampson Low, Marston, Searle, & Rivington, 1876), 312, 330.
77. E.g., A. D. White (Cornell) to G. L. Burr (Leipzig), 8 December 1884. White Papers, 1/2/2 Box 46, Cornell Kroch.
78. H. P. Bowditch to W. James, 11 June 1871. James Papers, bMS Am 1092.9 (77–84), Folder 2, HUL Houghton.
79. T. D. Seymour to Classmates, 3 November 1871. Seymour Family Papers, G440, B25, F200, SVII, YUL.
80. C. R. Lanman to Aunt, 7 November 1875, also the same, 21 November 1875. Lanman Papers, HUG 4510.67, Letters from Europe, vol. 3, HUL Pusey. Emphasis in original.
81. T. D. Seymour to Classmates, 3 November 1871. Seymour Family Papers, G440, B25, F200, SVII, YUL.
82. Journal, C. Thomas, 6 September 1877. Thomas Papers, 86180 Aa 2 Ac, Box 3, UM Bentley. Emphasis in original.
83. Journal, C. Thomas, 2 October 1877, ibid.
84. C. R. Lanman to Aunt, 14 November 1875. Lanman Papers, HUG 4510.67, Letters from Europe, vol. 3, HUL Pusey.

85. C. R. Lanman to Aunt, 7 November 1875, ibid.
86. L. Cooper to Mother, 4 [?] November 1900. Cooper Papers, 14/12/680, Box 18, Cornell Kroch.
87. T. D. Seymour to Classmates, 3 November 1871. Seymour Family Papers, G440, B25, F200, SVII, YUL.
88. Journal, C. Thomas, 6 and 16 August 1878. Thomas Papers, 86180 Aa 2 Ac, Box 3, UM Bentley.
89. H. P. Bowditch to W. James, 11 June 1871. James Papers, bMS Am 1092.9 (77–84), Folder 2, HUL Houghton. Emphasis in the original. Benjamin Ide Wheeler, the Leipzig-trained classicist and president of the University of California at Berkeley, also resorted to the services of Leipzig book dealers long after he had left. B. I. Wheeler to Buchhandlung Gustav Fock (Leipzig), 31 October 1900. Benjamin Ide Wheeler Correspondence and Papers, ca. 1870–1923, C-B 1044, Box 1, Folder: Wheeler, Benjamin Ide: Outgoing Letters, September–December 1900, Berkeley Bancroft.
90. Diary, T. D. Seymour, 12 November 1870. Seymour Family Papers, Group 440, Box 25, Folder 200, Series VII, YUL.
91. T. D. Woolsey to Sarah D. Woolsey (Sister), 21 April 1828. Woolsey Family Papers, Group 562, Series I, Box 3, Folder 42, YUL. He also noted the names of English-speaking authors who seemed to be more popular with the German reading public than German authors: Walter Scott, James Fennimore Cooper, and Washington Irving.
92. Journal, C. Thomas, 18 September 1877. C. Thomas Papers, 86180 Aa 2 Ac, Box 3, UM Bentley. Following quite ibid.
93. H. P. Bowditch to H. I. Bowditch, 5 December 1869. H. P. Bowditch Papers, HMS c5.1 Folder 2, HUL Countway.
94. H. P. Bowditch to Mother, 15 March 1870, ibid.
95. Henry Pickering Bowditch, "Letter from Leipzig," *Boston Medical and Surgical Journal* 82 (1870): 305–7. See also Benjamin Joy Jeffries, "Letter to the Editor [on Professor Ludwig]," ibid., 421.
96. J. M. Cattell to Parents, 6 August 1887, reprinted in Sokal, *Education on Psychology*, 274. See *Mind* 13 (1888): 37–51. See also Joseph Jastrow, "Experimental Psychology in Leipzig," *Science* 8, no. 198 (19 November 1886): 459–62.
97. R. Pearl to Mother, 30 July 1905. Pearl Papers, B:P312, Series II, APS. Following quote ibid.
98. E. Pugh to Editor, 31 October 1853, in C. A. Browne, "European Laboratory Experiences of an Early American Agricultural Chemist—Dr. Evan Pugh (1828–1864)," *Journal of Chemical Education* 7, no. 3 (March 1930): 500–502. Following quote ibid.
99. A. A. Noyes to H. M. Goodwin, 1 November 1888. Goodwin Papers, MC 121, Box 1, MIT Archives. Following quote ibid.
100. George Jaffé, "Recollections of Three Great Laboratories," in *Journal of Chemical Engineering* 29 (1952): 230–31, 235. See also "Some Scientific Centres. I.—The Leipzig Chemical Laboratory." *Nature* 64 (June 6, 1901): 127–29. Ed. by Sir Norman Lockyer.
101. A. A. Noyes to W. Ostwald, 18 May 1893, 17 November 1896, and 11 January 1897. NL Ostwald, BBAW, 153/5, 153/10, 153/11; H. C. Jones to W. Ostwald, 6 August 1895 and 13 July 1897, ibid., 146/6, 146/13, and 146/14; T. W. Richards to W. Ostwald, 19 December 1897, ibid., 106/10; L. Kahlenberg to W. Ostwald, 9 October 1897 and 31 January 1898, ibid., 2098/2, 2098/3; L. Morgan to W. Ostwald, 16 December 1897, 150/4.
102. H. C. Jones to W. Ostwald, 15 June 1898. NL Ostwald, 146/15, BBAW. *Science* was founded by Thomas Edison in 1880, but was owned and edited by James McKeen Cat-

tell and his family from 1894 until the year after his death in 1944. Sokal, *Education in Psychology*, 339–41.

103. H. P. Bowditch to Father, 2 January 1870. Bowditch Papers, HMS c5.1, Folder 5. HUL Countway.

104. Jonathan Ingersoll Bowditch (Father) to H. P. Bowditch, 22 March 1871. Reprinted in Bruce Fye, "Why a Physiologist?—The Case of Henry P. Bowditch," *Bulletin of the History of Medicine* 56 (1982): 27n44. See also Frederick W. Ellis, "Henry Pickering Bowditch and the Development of the Harvard Laboratory of Physiology," *New England Journal of Medicine* 219, no. 21 (24 November 1938): 819–28.

105. H. P. Bowditch to Father, 21 April [1871]. Bowditch Papers, HMS c5.1, Folder 5. HUL Countway.

106. H. P. Bowditch to W. James, 11 June 1871. James Papers, bMS Am 1092.9 (77–84), Folder 1, Harvard Houghton. Emphasis in the original.

107. Sokal, *Education in Psychology*, letters 4.15, 5.14, 5.18, 5.58, 5.120, 5.14, 6.45, 6.51, 6.105.

108. J. M. Cattell (Cambridge, GB) to Parents, 20 November 1888, reprinted in Sokal, *Education in Psychology*, 310–11. See also ibid., n.2 and 3.

109. J. M. Cattell (New York) to W. Wundt, 31 July 1893. NA Wundt, 1089/1, LUA. Emphasis in original.

110. H. C. Jones to W. Ostwald, 10 January 1897. NL Ostwald, 146/12, BBAW.

111. John W. Servos, "A Disciplinary Program That Failed: Wilder D. Bancroft and the Journal of Physical Chemistry, 1896–1933," *ISIS* 74 (1982): 207. Preserved in Fac. Biog. File Wilder D. Bancroft, Cornell Kroch.

CONCLUSION

IN HIS 1925 NOVEL *Arrowsmith*, the Nobel laureate Sinclair Lewis intro-
duces his readers to "John A. Robertshaw, John Aldington Robertshaw, professor of physiology in the medical school"[1] of the fictitious University of
Winnemac in the fictitious state of Winnemac, which, like "Michigan, Ohio,
Illinois, and Indiana," is "half Eastern and half Midwestern."[2] Robertshaw
is a living caricature of the US professor at the turn of the twentieth century. He "was rather deaf, and he was the only teacher in the University of
Winnemac who still wore mutton-chop whiskers.... On all occasions he
remarked, '*When I was studying with Ludwig in Germany*—'."[3] Carl Ludwig, of course, was not a fiction but from 1865 until his death in 1895 the
spearhead of physiology at the University of Leipzig, where he attracted
numerous illustrious US disciples. One of them, Warren P. Lombard, Warren
Plimpton Lombard, Harvard-educated and affiliated with the University of
Michigan, was the real-life counterpart of Lewis's Robertshaw.[4]

The example suggests that the nineteenth-century German venture
did not simply influence US academic culture but—in more or less subtle
was—left its imprint on US culture at large. Lombard's German experience
became such a defining characteristic of his personality that it was later on
remembered by his students and even immortalized in literature. Lombard
was not the only physiologist so rewarded. Another Ludwig student from
the United States, Franklin Paine Mall, was honored in a similar way by
Gertrude Stein, who was his student in the first decade of the twentieth century at Johns Hopkins University. In her *Autobiography of Alice B. Toklas,*
Stein confessed that she "delighted in Doctor Mall, professor of anatomy,
who directed her work."[5] Mall was a central figure in US physiology networks at that time.

Apparently, US student migration touched upon different aspects of life,
such as everyday transactions, wars, educational reforms as well as travel

Notes for this section begin on page 267.

and the encounter with foreign cultures. Until recently, however, student migration abroad was studied as a seemingly straight movement at the end of which educational and organizational concepts as well as materials were brought home to be instilled into ongoing reform processes there. My research shows instead that student migration is a multilayered cultural phenomenon that involves a movement through space and time, in the course of which subject matter evolves and transformations may occur in the cultural realm. The more interest Americans showed in foreign travel, the more exposure to foreign culture they gained. As a result, they on the whole opened up to supporting new ideas that might be considered foreign but that could as well have lurked beneath mainstream cultural conformism at home in the form of extant but less widely acknowledged and accepted norms.

Student migrations abroad were also intertwined with other, simultaneous travel movements, such as the movement of visitors and advanced scholars and scientists, but also travelers and families on the grand tour as well as diplomats. Especially at times of intense student migrations, American colonies emerged in cultural centers in Europe that also communicated with one another thanks to movements on the part of Americans while in Europe. In the case of students, I refer to these movements as routes of study, for they were to a considerable degree determined by their desire to visit several scholarly and scientific centers of interest to them. Study trajectories in Europe therefore reflect paths of knowledge in specific or closely related disciplines. Trips for leisure and sightseeing need to be added, which took place during semester breaks or at the beginning or end of a student venture.

These basic considerations led me to reconstruct student migrations from two different but interrelated angles. First, I traced developments in numbers and thus established sound statistical foundations. Second, I unearthed the human beings behind the numbers and explored their interactions, to which I refer as my biographical approach. As already the statistical data revealed a considerable amount of available sources and thus multiple possibilities for biographical approach, I decided to zoom in on Leipzig's American colony and explore it from the perspective of academic networking activities. The two approaches allowed me to draw a number of conclusions with considerable implications for American higher education.

I structured my statistical examination into four different aspects. First, I examined overall developments of US student numbers abroad; second, I traced individual developments of US student numbers at a chosen few German universities; third, I undertook comparisons with developments of general student numbers at German institutions of higher learning; fourth I prepared statistical analyses of the US student body at one German university, which provided answers to the question of where students came from, where they had been educated previously, and how old they were on average upon their first arrival. All of these statistical observations provided me with insights that did not necessarily apply to only one side of the Atlantic.

My statistics illustrate first and foremost that developments in US student numbers differed from German university to German university, though larger tendencies were similar and might not necessarily match trends in total enrollments (especially after the onset of the twentieth century). In other words, US students benefited from German education in the eighteen hundreds, but by the twentieth century the tides had turned. One explanation for that might be the fact that nineteenth-century US student migration was motivated by an increasing desire to improve US education, for which German universities—so it was generally acknowledged—could serve as suitable examples. By the twentieth century, however, American opinions of German education were becoming more critical, while simultaneously US higher education was in the process of transforming. It now provide much better opportunities and boasted improved resources, which made a trip abroad for educational purposes no longer a vital necessity.

Moreover, my analysis proves that US students at German universities as a group transformed in the course of the nineteenth century. They became more diverse with regard to gender, ethnicity, and socioeconomic backgrounds. They also became older upon their first enrollment abroad, which might be explained by the fact that, as graduate programs were initiated at US universities, they began to study longer before embarking for Europe. Increasingly, though, and especially after the turn of the twentieth century, the age range of US students who registered at Halle and Leipzig widened, now including very young students fresh out of high school besides senior citizens near retirement age. While this could be interpreted as an ever-broadening appeal of the German university, I consider it instead to be an example of the fact that studying at a German university by 1900 had become so popular that it was something of a fad, and everyone wanted to have a part of it—rather than those bright minds exclusively who would push American scholarship and sciences into new directions in the future. The fact that already during the 1890s US student numbers had experienced an all-time high also speaks to this development.

By 1900, pioneering US students of the—for student migration—so intensive previous three decades were well established in US academia, operating at Johns Hopkins and the University of Chicago, among others, as well as at less prosperous and smaller institutions that were nonetheless equally ambitious at least in some respects, such as Vanderbilt. These German-trained Americans could thus act within research structures that had not existed a few years before. While a foreign venture was thus still deemed an appropriate step to further one's education by benefitting from the prestige of German education, it became less vital for young, ambitious graduates in order to actually obtain the necessary knowledge and methods to embark on their own research ventures.

My biographical in connection with my statistical approach revealed that the academic associations one could establish and strengthen in the course of a German venture were vital factors to further the academic careers of US students; they were thus vital also for American higher education. I call this phenomenon *academic networking*. Academic networking happened on various levels and to varying degrees of intensity. It happened between US students and German professors, among American students, between American students and other US visitors in Europe, as well as between US students and their fellow students either from Germany or from third countries. It could be entirely formal and pragmatic such as when US students abroad interacted with German professors in preparation of a PhD degree or, alternatively, when Americans met within established organizational frameworks abroad to discuss the future of American higher education. But it could also border the realm of the personal when intense friendships formed in the process or family members got involved to further one's prospects.

I observed a pattern that reflected more formal academic networking and that was rooted in enrollment practices. Apparently, a pioneering US student first found out about new developments at a German university such as the arrival of a new luminary. Sometimes they found out by chance. Others, in turn, asked their peers in Germany for advice and thus stayed on top of things. In general, pioneers were likely to become influential in the future by introducing new disciplines and approaches to the United States, as did Henry Pickering Bowditch and William James. Once they were established in US academia, they would send their own students to German universities. Of those, while the earlier students might be likely to still contribute to introducing the innovations that their American mentors had initiated, the later ones could become innovators in new directions. For example, Calvin Thomas had expected to became a classicist when arriving in Germany but eventually devoted his career to Germanics.

Besides mentor-disciple relationships that required networking such as in the form of letters of recommendation, Americans abroad also created different organizational structures to further professional quests in the academic sphere and also to smooth over homesickness at times. The most comprehensive structure was the idea of an American colony in a European center of culture and learning. The American colony embraced different Americans in town, be they students, businessmen, artists, resident families, or travelers on the grand tour.

My focus was, however, on the organizational structures that served academic means and involved students above all. At Leipzig, I discovered an American Students Club that was part of the American colony but explicitly devoted its activities to helping make contacts in academic circles and also assisting new arrivals in town. It thus reflected my idea of academic networking quite closely. In addition to that, there was an American Church—which also catered to the American colony and, in later years, to English-speaking Leipzig residents more generally. For the periods during which I could find proof of the existence of the American Church, it may be said that American students organized it who at the same time were also available for informal and academic networking activities in their homes. Other resident Americans also opened their homes to US students. All of this shows that it was difficult to separate leisure from academe.

Whereas some forms of association while at Leipzig related back to America—such as when old acquaintances met again or students of former Leipzig Americans arrived—US students in Leipzig also closely observed German (university) culture and got involved in those aspects that interested them. Local academic university clubs were comparatively popular among US students and might have inspired the idea of eventually creating an American Students Club. Other aspects of German student life such as matriculation rituals were observed with curiosity, and yet others were viewed in a critical light. Duels would be an example of the latter especially in the late nineteenth century. The more ambitious Americans carefully prepared for the German venture by reading guidebooks and studying the language. I focused on such students, though their letters, journals, and memoirs also attest to the fact that the American student colony was diverse—some were simply after the fun; others managed to mix hard work with leisure-time excursions.

Women were part of transatlantic academic networks. By contrast, too little information is available about representatives of other US student groups such as African Americans to draw general conclusions about their activities within such networks. Then again, disabled Americans, who were also quite few in number, maybe for that reason did not appear to have a group identity as such. But no matter if they were women or men, white or black, physically challenged or able bodied, US students were ambitious to advance America in various ways—only their priorities differed. African Americans certainly felt first and foremost a desire to improve race relations, whereas women pushed for gender equality. Disabled Americans simply fit in for as long as they accepted the standards of the able-bodied mainstream.

Women made up the most substantial group of an Other in the US student body abroad. Enough sources are available to illustrate that they were part of mentor-disciple relationships and could even pioneer in introducing a German luminary in US academia—as was the case with Ellen Churchill

Semple and Friedrich Ratzel. While especially in the early years women represented a microcosm within the university's male student body, they nonetheless made the best of it. Many of the female Leipzig Americans embarked on notable academic careers typically at women's colleges in the United States—though Leipzig-trained Alice Hamilton eventually became the first female professor at Harvard in 1919.

The case of women also contributed in another way to academic networking. Indeed, it appears that some Leipzig Americans—not just women—actually found first teaching and research opportunities at women's colleges. From there, a few of them would move on to the elite Northeastern universities that at least in their undergraduate programs continued to be all male. Others would get involved in women's education at coeducational or coordinate colleges, where they would be able to teach both men and women.

When they returned home, US students on the whole brought along visions, concepts, organizational ideas, and material goods to turn America into nothing less but the scientific and scholarly center of the (Western) world. Their personal ambitions reflected the ambitions of a young nation to become a major power player besides the old European nations. Education was viewed as an important asset to gain international prestige; the fact that initially US students had to turn to Old Europe for innovation seemed hardly in step with such ambitions, which is why student migration—as it took on momentum—became a catalyst for reform movements at home.

To achieve the transformation of American higher education, US students closely observed and described in letters and published journals what they saw abroad. They picked out the aspects of German university life that seemed most promising to advance their own search for an American university ideal. These aspects included concepts such as the idea of research rather than speculation and of seminary and laboratory methods rather than lecturing (which could be considered a way of active do-science-yourself rather than being passively told what there was to know). US students were inspired abroad, which led for example to the creation of US graduate schools in addition to undergraduate colleges—in this way, the American system could be remodeled without adopting the German university with its traditional four faculties that by the late nineteenth century were beginning to break up, anyway. As a part of the new US graduate schools, the PhD degree was introduced to highlight the differences in achievement as compared with undergraduate education. The launching of scholarly and scientific journals as observed in Germany may furthermore be added. Such journals were founded for specific academic disciplines to provide platforms for academic exchanges. Finally, the remodeling of American higher education required also material support, which is why Americans shipped loads of books, entire libraries, and apparatuses back home.

What made US higher education leading in the world in the twentieth century was that an increasing number of nineteenth-century students had been willing and even eager to look and think outside the American box. In spite of many individual points of view, an educational consensus existed by the late 1800s to the effect that things would have to change, and that the Germans came much closer to the ideal but that they did not quite represent it thoroughly and exclusively.

Based on my research, I would argue that Americans developed their motivation to reform America and specifically its education against a foreign matrix without simply accepting, consuming, and adopting the foreign culture. Instead, on the whole (there were exceptions, of course), US students also located weaknesses in the German system—such as the German/European faculty's neglect to follow scholarly and scientific advancements in the United States. German-trained Americans, in turn, were, of course, in an advantageous position, as they had a thorough knowledge of both German *and* American academia. Ironically, their knowledge of American academia was strengthened also thanks to their interaction with their compatriots, for example during meetings of the American Students Club at Leipzig.

I consider networking the most decisive achievement of nineteenth-century US students in Europe—even if often their connecting with, for instance, Leipzig professors and fellow students abroad had been initiated prior to their departure from the United States. American students' eagerness to explore the possibilities offered by foreign professors and their openness to benefitting from them in order to advance their own careers ultimately instilled in them the desire, if not determination, to have similar opportunities at home and thus indeed to transfer the academic center of the Western world from Europe to North America. The result of this persisting determination may be witnessed in the numerous internationally appealing US universities today.

Academic networking was the essence of the nineteenth-century German experience. In other words, the "German ideal" or "German model" can be grasped by tracing and understanding the processes that happened with and among American students during their extended stays at German centers of higher learning while remaining in close touch with American education, such as in the form of American microcosms (that is, American colonies) abroad. One could argue, then, that the modern American university was born in direct contact with a foreign culture. It was not so much a trans*ferr*ing of German concepts *somehow* to America after the event of a German student venture, but a trans*form*ing of US academic culture in contact with a foreign setting that seemed closer to ideal education. The various academic networking activities promoted these transformations.

Time and again, though, my analysis reached points where the serious and ambitiously focused academic networking on the part of US students crisscrossed with more personal interests and leisure—Americans actually were aware of that as something desirable when observing German academic club meetings. An intriguing aspect about student migration to German universities was consequently the fact that besides the hard work, there was time simply to enjoy associating with both Americans and Europeans. These associations once again were of differing intensity and warmth, ranging from finding a spouse or a lifelong friend and colleague to mere pragmatic interaction simply to make the best of the stay abroad.

No matter if friend, relative, or colleague, successful networking necessitated a certain chemistry. As Charles Newton Zueblin appealed to Winthrop Moore Daniels for the sake of old Leipzig days to write an article about Woodrow Wilson, it must have triggered a number of pleasant memories of jolly German student days and agreeable associations, which made it hard to turn down the request. The idea of such an emotional undercurrent is expressed in a greeting with which Joseph Stafford, still at Leipzig, finished a July 1895 letter to his Leipzig friend Howard Rodney True, who had left already: "Holding the kindest remembrances of our Leipzig acquaintance I remain ever yours very truly...."[6]

Notes

1. Sinclair Lewis, *Arrowsmith* (New York: Signet Classic, 1998 [1925]), 19.
2. Ibid., 6.
3. Ibid., 19. My emphasis.
4. Horace Willard Davenport, "A University of Michigan Faculty Life, Warren Plimpton Lombard in Ann Arbor, 1892–1939," 1992, DB 2 L841 D247, UM Bentley.
5. Gertrude Stein, *The Autobiography of Alice B. Toklas* (New York: Vintage Books, 1990 [1933]), 81. Mall had studied under Henry Sewall at Ann Arbor and received a MD degree there in 1883. From the fall term 1884 until 1886, he worked with Ludwig. Afterwards he was affiliated with Johns Hopkins and Clark University. In 1893, he came to head the anatomical department of the new medical school at the Johns Hopkins, also thanks to William Henry Welch, whom he had first met at Leipzig. Anonymous, "Memorial Services in Honor of Franklin Paine Mall, Professor of Anatomy, Johns Hopkins University, 1893 to 1917," *Bulletin of the Johns Hopkins Hospital* 29, no. 327 (May 1918): 109–23; Florence Rena Sabin, "Dr. Franklin P. Mall: An Appreciation," in *Science* 47, no. 1211 (15 March 1918): 249–61; Florence Rena Sabin, *Franklin Paine Mall: The Story of a Mind* (Baltimore: Johns Hopkins Press, 1934); Gerald B. Webb and Desmond Powell, *Henry Sewall. Physiologist and Physician* (Baltimore: Johns Hopkins University Press, 1946).
6. J. Stafford to R. H. True, 14 July 1895. True Papers, BT763, Series II, Box 8, APS.

Appendix 1

FIGURES

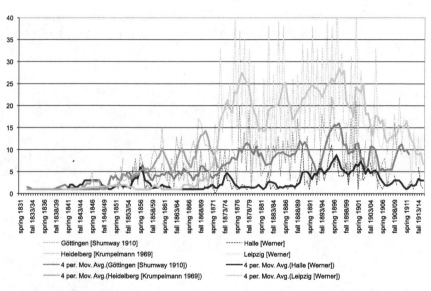

Figure 1. US Students at Göttingen, Halle, Heidelberg, Leipzig, 1831–1914

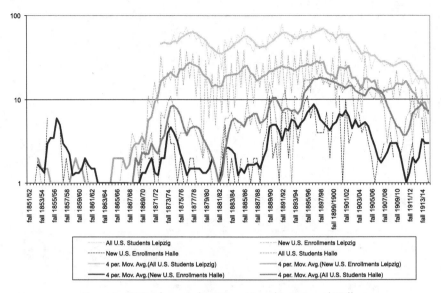

Figure 2. US Students at the Universities of Leipzig and Halle

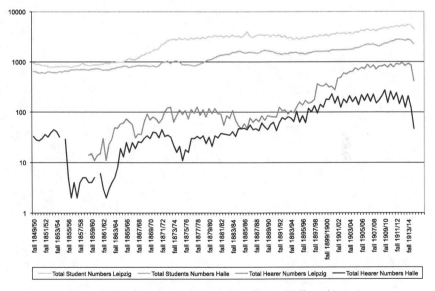

Figure 3. Total Student and Hearer Numbers at Halle and Leipzig

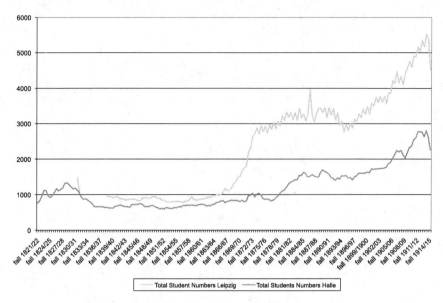

Figure 4. Total Student Numbers at Halle and Leipzig

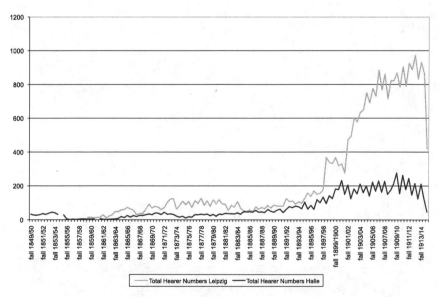

Figure 5. Total Hearer Numbers at Halle and Leipzig

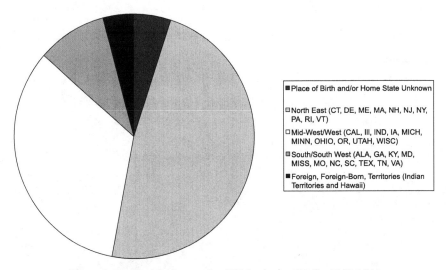

Figure 6. Regional Backgrounds of US Students at Halle, 1769–1914

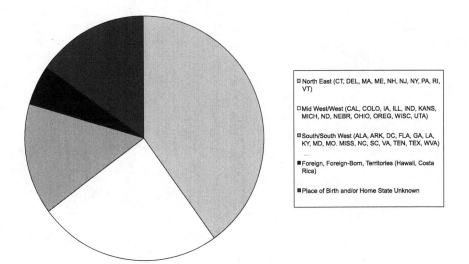

Figure 7. Regional Backgrounds of US Students at Leipzig, 1781–1914

Figure 8a. Shifts in Regional Backgrounds
at Halle over Time

1769-1861

> □ North East □ Mid West ▣ South ■ Foreign ■ Unknown

1866-1879

> □ North East □ Mid West ▣ South/South West ■ Foreign ■ Unknown

1880-1889

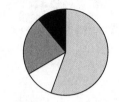

> □ North East □ Mid West ▣ South/South West ■ Foreign ■ Unknown

Figure 9a. Shifts in Regional Backgrounds
at Leipzig over Time

1781-1865

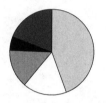

> □ North East □ Mid West/West ▣ South ■ Foreign ■ Unknown

1866-1879

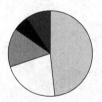

> □ North East □ Mid West/West ▣ South ■ Foreign ■ Unknown

1880-1889

> □ North East □ Mid West/West ▣ South ■ Foreign ■ Unknown

Figure 8b. Shifts in Regional Backgrounds
at Halle over Time

Figure 9b. Shifts in Regional Backgrounds
at Leipzig over Time

1890-1899

☐North East ☐Mid West/West ▨South/South West ■Foreign ■Unknown

1890-1899

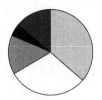

☐North East ☐Mid West/West ▨South ■Foreign ■Unknown

1900-1914

☐North East ☐Mid West/West ▨South/South West
■Foreign/Territories ■Unknown

1900-1914

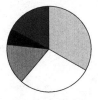

☐North East ☐Mid West/West ▨South ■Foreign/Territory ■Unknown

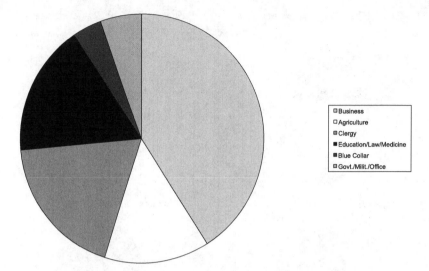

Figure 10. Socioeconomic Backgrounds, Halle

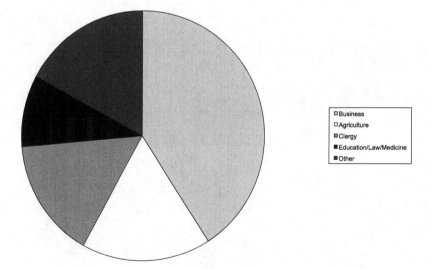

Figure 11. Socioeconomic Backgrounds, Leipzig

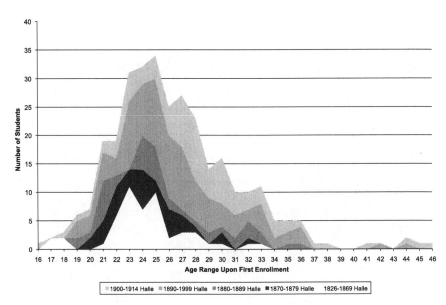

Figure 12. Age Range, Halle

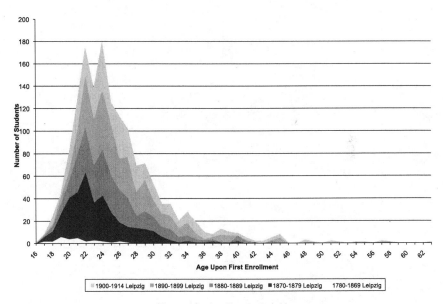

Figure 13. Age Range, Leipzig

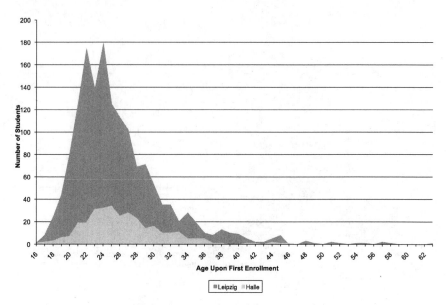

Figure 14. Age Ranges, Halle and Leipzig

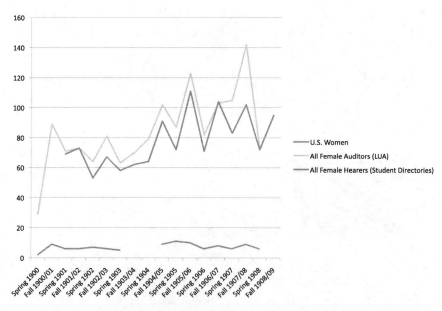

Figure 15. Female Auditors at Leipzig, 1900–1908

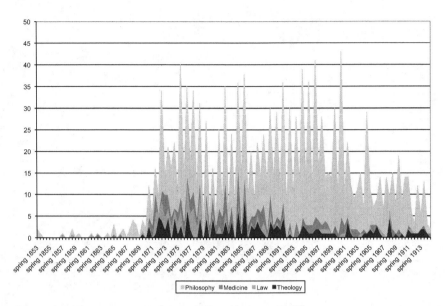

Figure 16. Subject Choices at Halle

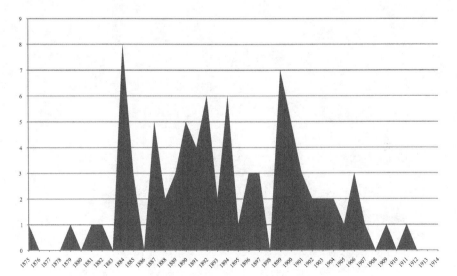

Figure 17. Subject Choices at Leipzig

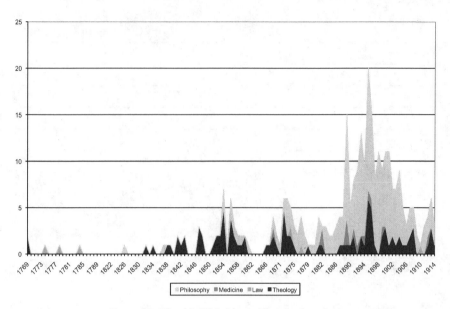

Figure 18. Wundt's US Students (First Registration)

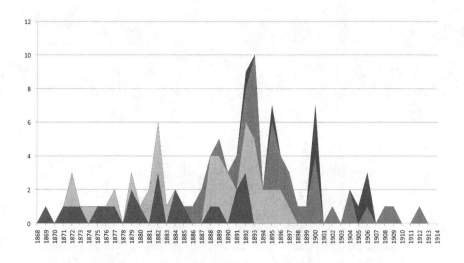

Figure 19. Appeal of Leipzig Physiologists and Biologists

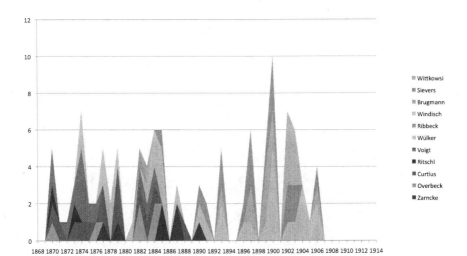

Figure 20. Appeal of a Succession of Leipzig Linguists

Appendix 2

List of Leipzig Professors
of Interest to US Students

Note: The individual entries below list "professor's name (subject; life span, affiliation with Leipzig, miscellanea)." If only one year is given as "Leipzig affiliation," it means that the professor in question remained at the University of Leipzig for the remainder of his career. Earliest known faculty association with Leipzig noted.

Before 1820s

Gottfried Hermann (Greek; 1772–1848, Leipzig since 1797)

1820s

Ernst Heinrich Weber (psychology, physiology, pharmacology; 1795–1878, since 1821)

Moritz Wilhelm Drobisch (philosophy, mathematics, psychology; 1802–1896, since 1825)

Otto Linné Erdmann (technical chemistry; 1804–1869, since 1827)

1830s

Gustav Theodor Fechner (psychology, physiology, pharmacology; 1801–1887, Leipzig 1834–1840 but remained for the rest of his life)

Konstantin von Tischendorf (theology; 1815–1874, since 1834, first as a student)

1840s

Wilhelm Roscher (economy; 1817–1894, since 1848)

1850s

Wilhelm Scheibner (mathematics; 1826–1908, since 1853)
Friedrich Zarncke (German; 1825–1891, since 1854)
Johannes Overbeck (archaeology; 1826–1895, since 1858)

1860s

Rudolf Georg Karl Seydel (philosophy; 1835–1892, since 1860)
Georg Curtius (Greek; 1820–1885, since 1861)
Carl Ludwig (physiology; 1816–1895, since 1865)
Adolph Mayer (mathematics; 1839–1908, since 1865)
Friedrich Wilhelm Ritschl (Classics; 1806–1876, since 1865)
Georg Voigt (history; 1827–1891, since 1866)
Franz Delitzsch (theology; 1813–1890, since 1867)
Rudolf Leuckart (zoology; 1822–1898, since 1868)
Carl Neumann (mathematics; 1832–1925, since 1868)
Johann Nepomuk Czermark (physiology; 1828–1873, since 1869)
Ernst Leberecht Wagner (pathology; 1829–1888, since 1869)

1870s

August Leskien (Slavonic languages; 1840–1916, since 1870)
Gustav Heinrich Wiedemann (physical chemistry; 1826–1899, succeeded
    Erdmann in 1871)
Wilhelm His (anatomy; 1831–1904, since 1872)
Max Heinze (history of philosophy; 1835–1909, since 1875)
Richard Wülker (first chair in English; 1845–1910, since 1875; originally
    spelled Wülcker)
Wilhelm Wundt (philosophy, psychology, anthropology; 1832–1920, since
    1875)
Carl von Noorden (history; 1833–1883, Leipzig since 1876)
Otto Ribbeck (Classics; 1827–1898, succeeded Ritschl in 1876)
Ernst Windisch (Sanskrit and Celtic languages; 1844–1918, since 1877)

1880s

Felix Klein (mathematics; 1849–1925, Leipzig 1880–1885)
Karl von Bahder (Germanics; 1852–1932, Leipzig 1881–1918)
Caspar René Gregory (theology; 1846–1917, since 1883 but as student
    since 1873)

Rudolf Boehm (pharmacology; 1844–1926, since 1884 on initiative of
    Ludwig, His, and Wagner)
Wilhelm Maurenbrecher (history; 1838–1892, since 1884)
Johannes Wislicenus (organic chemistry; 1835–1902, since 1885)
Eduard Study (mathematics; 1862–1930, Leipzig 1885–1888)
Karl Brugmann (Greek and Italic; 1849–1919, succeeded Curtius in 1886)
Sophus Lie (mathematics; 1842–1899, Leipzig 1886–1898)
Friedrich Engel (mathematics; 1861–1941, since 1886)
Friedrich Ratzel (anthropogeography; 1844–1904, since 1886)
Kurt Wachsmuth (history; 1837–1905, since 1886)
Wilhelm Ostwald (physical chemistry; 1853–1932, since 1887)
Wilhelm Pfeffer (botany; 1845–1920, since 1887)
Ewald Flügel (English; 1863–1914, Leipzig 1888–1892)
Felician Gess (history; 1861–1938; Leipzig 1888–1894)
Georg Witkowski (German language and literature; 1863–1939, Leipzig
    since 1889)

1890s

Adolf Birch-Hirschfeld (Romance languages; 1849–1917, since 1891)
Karl Lamprecht (history; 1856–1915 succeeded Georg Voigt in 1891)
Karl Bücher (economy; 1847–1930, since 1892)
Eduard Sievers (Germanics; 1850–1932, since 1892)
Erich Marcks (history; 1861–1938, succeeded Maurenbrecher, Leipzig
    1894–1901)
Robert Luther (physical chemistry; 1867/68–1945, Leipzig 1896–1908)
Otto zur Strassen (zoology; 1869–1961; Leipzig 1896–1909)
Carl Chun (zoology; 1852–1914; succeeded Leuckart in 1898)
Albert Köster (Germanics; 1862–1924, since 1899)
Franz Eulenburg (political economy; 1867–1943, Leipzig 1899–1917)

After 1900

Arthur Hantzsch (organic chemistry; 1857–1935, succeeded Wislicenus in
    1903)

Appendix 3

LIST OF LEIPZIG-AMERICAN DISSERTATIONS

Note: This list is based on the holdings of the Leipzig University Library Albertina. It is therefore incomplete. Added are a few dissertations by Leipzig Americans who graduated elsewhere in Europe and North America as well as a few Leipzig dissertations by non-Americans who later embarked on careers in the United States, such as Hugo Münsterberg.

Allen, Frederick. "De Dialecto Locorensium." Diss., Leipzig: Melzer, 1870.

Andrews, Frank Marion. "Ueber die Wirkung der Centrifugalkraft auf Pflanzen." Diss., Leipzig: Gebrüder Borntraeger, 1902.

Arnold, J. Loring. "King Alfred in English Poetry." Diss., Meiningen: K. Keyssner, 1898.

Arps, G. F. "Über den Anstieg der Druckempfindlichkeit." Diss., Leipzig: Wilhelm Engelmann, 1908.

Ayer, Joseph Cullen, Jr. "Versuch einer Darstellung der Ethik Joseph Butlers." Diss., Leipzig: G. Kreysing, 1893.

Baer, Samuel H. "Ueber die Synthese eines inactiven Menthens." Diss., Leipzig: Metzger & Wittig, 1898.

Baker, Theodor. "Über die Musik der nordamerikanischen Wilden." Diss., Leipzig: Breitkopf & Härtel, 1882.

Ball, Oscar Melville. "Der Einfluss von Zug auf die Ausbildung von Festigungsgewebe." Diss., Leipzig: Gebrüder Borntraeger, 1903.

Bancroft, Wilder D. "Über Oxydationsketten." Diss., Leipzig: Wilhelm Engelmann, 1892.

Baskerville, William Malone. "The Anglo-Saxon Version of the Epistola Alexandriaa Aristotelem." Diss., Halle: E. Karras, Printer, 1881.

Beeson, Marvin F. "Die Organisation der Negererziehung in den Vereinigten Staaten von Amerika seit 1860." Diss., Halle: Heinrich John, 1915.

Bell, Robert Mowry. "Der Artikel bei Otfrid." Diss., Leipzig: 1907/08.

Bennett, Charles Gibson "Das allgemeine Stimmrecht in den Vereinigten Staaten von Nord-Amerika mit Hinblick auf Frankreich und die Schweiz." Diss., Berlin: Ernst Siegfried Mittler und Sohn, 1877.

Bigelow, Samuel Lawrence. "Katalytische Wirkung auf die Geschwindigkeit der Oxydation des Natriumsulfits durch den Sauerstoff der Luft." Diss., Leipzig: Wilhelm Engelmann, 1898.

Bissell, Allen Page. "The Law of Asylum in Israel Historically and Critically Examined." Diss., Leipzig: Theodor Stauffer, 1884.

Blackburn, Francis Adelbert. "The English Future. Its Origin and Development." Diss., Leipzig: Oswald Schmidt, 1892.

Blanchard, Arthur A. "Über die Zersetzung des Ammoniumnitrits." Diss., Leipzig: Wilhelm Engelmann, 1902.

Bloomfield, Leonard. "A Semasiologic Differentiation in Germanic Secondary Ablaut." Diss. University of Chicago, 1909. Also published in *Modern Philology* (October 1909): 245–382.

Bouton, Charles L. "Invariants of the General Linear Differential Equation and their Relation to the Theory of Continuous Groups." Diss., Baltimore: Lord Baltimore Press, ca. 1898.

Breck, Edward. "Fragment of Ælfric's Translation of Æthelwold's De Consuetudine Monachorum and Its Relation to Other Mss. Critically Edited from the Ms. Cotton. Tib. A. III. In the British Museum." Diss., Leipzig: W. Drugulin's Printing Office, 1887.

Buckingham, Edgar. "Über einige Fluoreszenzerscheinungen." Diss., Leipzig: Wilhelm Engelmann, 1894.

Burns, P. S. "Chemisches Verhalten einiger dimolekularen Nitrile." Diss., Leipzig: Johann Ambrosius Barth, 1893.

Campbell, Thomas Moody. "Longfellows Wechselbeziehungen zu der Deutschen Literatur." Diss., Leipzig: Dr. Seele & Co., 1907.

Carr, Joseph. "Über das Verhältnis der Wiclifitischen und der Purvey'schen Bibelübersetzung zur Vulgata und zu Einander." Diss., Leipzig: Philos. Diss. 1901/02.

Cattell, James McKeen. "Psychometrische Untersuchungen." Diss., Leipzig: Wilhelm Engelmann, 1886.

Chapin, Paul. "Einfluss der Kohlensäure auf das Wachsthum." Diss., München: Val. Höfling, 1902.

Cheney, James Loring. "The Sources of Tindale's New Testament." Diss., Halle: E. Karras, 1883.

Child, Charles Manning. "Ein bisher wenig beachtetes Antennales Sinnesorgan der Insekten." Diss., Leipzig: Wilhelm Engelmann, 1894.

Coggeshall, George Whiteley. "Über die Konstanz der Kalomel-Elektrode." Diss., Leipzig: Wilhelm Engelmann, 1895.

Collins, George Stuart. "Dryden's Dramatic Theory and Praxis." Diss., Leipzig: Oswald Schmidt, 1892.

Cooper, Lane. "The Prose Poetry of Thomas de Qunicey." Diss., Leipzig: Dr. Seele & Co., 1902.

Copeland, Edw. Bingham. "Über den Einfluss von Licht und Temperatur auf den Turgor." Diss., Halle: Wischan & Wettengel, 1896.

Cottrell, Frederick Gardner. "Der Reststrom bei galvanischer Polarisation betrachtet als ein Diffusionsproblem." Diss., Leipzig: Wilhelm Engelmann, 1903.

Culley, David E. "Konrad von Gelnhausen. Sein Leben, seine Werke und seine Quellen." Diss., Halle: Heinrich John, 1913.

Curtis, Mattoon Monroe. "An Outline of Locke's Ethical Philosophy." Diss., Leipzig: Gustav Fock, 1890.

Davies, James. "'A Myrroure for Magistrates' Considered with Special Reference to the Sources of Sackville's Contributions." Diss. Leipzig: Dr. Seele & Co., 1906.

Dawson, Edgar. "Byron und Moore." Diss. Leipzig: Verlag von Dr. Seele & Co., 1902.

Dieckhoff, Tobias. "Der zusammengesetzte Satz im Reinke de Dos." Diss., Leipzig: August Hoffmann, 1899.

Dodd, William Edward. "Thomas Jeffersons Rückkehr zur Politik 1796." Diss., Leipzig: Grübel & Sommerlatte, ca. 1899.

Dohmen, Franz Joseph. "Darstellung der Berührungstransformationen in Konnexkoordinaten." Diss., Leipzig: B. G. Teubner, 1905.

Dye, Vincent. "Die Beziehung von Elisabeth Barrett Brownings Leben zu ihrer Dichtkunst." Diss., Leipzig: Bruno Zechel, 1905.

Earp, Edwin L. "Die relative Vollständigkeit und Hinlänglichkeit der Entwicklungs-Ethik und der Christlichen Ethik." Diss., Leipzig: Emil Glausch, 1901.

Eastman, Clarence Willis. "Die Syntax des Dativs bei Notker." Diss., Leipzig: Max Hoffmann, 1898.

Emerton, Ephraim. "Sir William Temple und die Tripleallianz vom Jahre 1668." Diss., Berlin: Carl Jahncke'S Buchdruckerei, 1877.

Evans, Hubert "F.H. Bradley's Metaphysiik." Diss., Leipzig: Buchdruckerei d. Leipz. Tagebl. E. Polz, 1902.

Evjen, John O. "Die Staatsumwälzung in Dänemark im Jahre 1660." Diss., Leipzig: Emil Glausch, 1903.

Fife, Robert Herndon. Jr., "Der Wortschatz des Englischen Maundevillen ach der Version der Cotton Handschrift (Brit. Museum, London) Titus C. XVI." Diss., Leipzig: Dr. Seele & Co., 1902.

Findlay, Alexander. "Theorie der fraktionierten Fällung von Neutralsalzen und ihre Anwendung in der analytischen Chemie." Diss., Leipzig: Wilhelm Engelmann, 1900.

Fink, Colin G. "Die Kinetik der Kontaktschwefelsäure." Diss., Leipzig: Wilhelm Engelmann, 1907.

Friedel, Charles. "Ueber die Absorption der strahlenden Wärme durch Flüssigkeiten." Diss., Leipzig: Johann Ambrosius Barth [Arthur Meiner], 1895.

Fruit, John Phelps. "Determinism from Hobbes to Hume." Diss., Leipzig, G. Kreysing, 1895.

Gage, Frank Wellington. "The Negro Problem in the United States." Diss., Leipzig: Oswald Schmidt, 1892.

Gay, Edwin Francis. "Zur geschichte der einhegungen in England." Diss., Berlin, Altenburg: Stephan Geibel, 1902.

Geer, Curtis Manning. "English Colonization Ideas in the Reign of Elizabeth." Diss., Danvers, MA: Danvers Mirror Press, 1895.

Geselbracht, Franklin. "Das Verfahren bei den deutschen Bischofswahlen in der zweiten Hälfte des 12. Jahrhunderts." Diss., Weida i. Th.: Thomas & Hubert, 1905.

Gibson, Howard B. "On the Liberation of Nitrogen during the Process of Putrefaction." Diss., Baltimore: Press of the Friedenwald Company, 1893.

Goodnight, Scott Holland. "German Literature in American Magazines Prior to 1846." Diss. University of Wisconsin–Madison, 1907.

Goodwin, Elliot H. "The Equity of the King's Court Before the Reign of Edward the First." Diss., Leipzig: Grübel & Sommerlatte, 1899/ 1900.

Goodwin, Harry Manley. "Studien zur Voltaschen Kette." Diss., Leipzig: Wilhelm Engelmann, 1894.

Gordy, John P. "Hume as Sceptic." Diss., Berlin: Berliner Buchdruckerei-Actien-Gesellschaft, 1885.

Griggs, John Cornelius. "Studien über die Musik in Amerika." Diss., Leipzig: Breitkopf & Härtel, 1894.

Hall, Arthur Graham. "Bestimmung der Definitionsgleichungen aller endlichen continuirlichen Gruppen von Punkttransformationen in der Ebene." Diss., Leipzig: Breitkopf & Härtel, 1902.

Hall, Elliot Snell. "A Study of Some New Semipermeable Membranes and Experiments on the Preparation of Porous Cups Suitable for the Measurement of Osmotic Pressure." Diss., Lancaster, PA: The New Printing Company, 1904.

Heald, Fred De Forest. "Gametophytic Regeneration as Exhibited by Mosses, and Conditions for the Germination of Cryptogam Spores." Diss., Leipzig: Oswald Schmidt, 1897.

Henderson, Charles Richmond. "Die ökonomische Lage u. die Mittel der Collegien im Staate Illinois U.St.A.." Diss., Leipzig: 1901/02.

Herman, John Edward. "Locke as Pedagogue." Diss., Leipzig: Oswald Schmidt, 1890.

Hildner, Jonathan. "Untersuchungen über die Syntax der Konditionalsätze bei Burchard Waldis. Ein Beitrag zur Grammatik des Frühnhd." Diss., Leipzig: August Hoffmann, 1899.

Holzwarth, Charles H. "Zu Otfrids Reim, eine rhythmisch-melodische Studie." Diss., Borna/Leipzig: Robert Noske, 1909.

Hopkins, Edward W. "The Mutual Relations of the Four Castes According to the Mānavadharamaçā." Diss., Leipzig: Breitkopf and Härtel, 1881.

Hudnall, Richard H. "A Presentation of the Grammatical Inflexions in Andrew of Wyntoun's 'Orygynale Cronykil of Scotland.'" Diss., Leipzig: Oswald Schmidt, 1898.

Hulett, George Augustus. "Der stetige Übergang fest-flüssig." Diss., Leipzig, Wilhelm Engelmann, 1899.

Humphreys, Milton Wylie. "Quaestiones Metricae de Accentus Momento in Versu Heroico." Diss., Leipzig: Andrae, 1874.

Jarmulowsky, Harry. "Zur Statistik der Sectio caesarea mit besonderer Berücksichtigung der Indication der conservativen Methode und der Porro-Operation." Diss. Christian-Albrechts-Universität zu Kiel, Kiel: H. Fiencke, 1906.

Jastrow, Morris, Jr. "Abu Zakarijjâ Jahja ben Dawûd Hajjûg und seine zwei grammatischen Schriften: über die Verben mit schwachen Buchstaben und die Verben mit Doppelbuchstaben." Diss., Universität Leipzig, 1884; Giessen: W. Keller, 1885.

Johnson, John W. "Researches on Heat of Obscure Rays." Diss., Leipzig: 1892.

Judd, Charles Hubbard. "Ueber Raumwahrnehmungen im Gebiet des Tastsinnes." Diss., Leipzig: Wilhelm Engelmann, 1896.

Kahlenberg, Louis. "Über komplexe Tartrate und gewisse alkalische Lösungen des Kupfers und des Bleies." Diss., Leipzig: Wilhelm Engelmann, 1895.

Kirkland, James Hampton. "A Study of the Anglo-Saxon Poem, The Harrowing of Hell (Grein's Höllenfahrt Christi)." Diss., Halle: Ehrhardt Karras, Printer, 1885.

Knowlton, Pitt G. "Origin and Nature of Conscience." Diss., Oberlin, O.: News Press, 1896/97.

Koch, Heinrich A. "Quellenuntersuchungen zu Nemesios von Emesa." Diss., Leipzig: Bernhard Tauchnitz, 1920.

Kubler, Conrad. "Beitrag zur Chemie der Condurangorinde." Diss., Weida i. Th.: Thomas & Hubert, 1908.

LeRossignol, James Edward. "The Ethical Philosophy of Samuel Clarke." Diss., Leipzig: G. Kreysing, 1892.

Lind, S. C. "Über die Bildung des Bromwasserstoffgases aus den Elementen." Diss., Leipzig: Emil Glausch, 1906.

Little, Arthur M. "Mendelssohn's Music to the Antigone of Sophocles." Diss., Washington, D.C.: Gibson Brothers, 1893.

Lovett, Edgar Odell. "The Theory of Perturbations and Lie's Theory of Contact Transformations." Diss., 1898/99, Leipzig: 1897.

Mac Dougall, Frank H. "Über die Reaktion zwischen Chlorsäure und Salzsäure." Diss., Leipzig: Wilhelm Engelmann, 1908.

Mac Lean, George Edwin. "Alfric's Anglo-Saxon Version of Alcuini Interrogationes Sigeuulfi Presbyteri in Genesin." Diss., Halle: Karras, 1883.

MacHarg, John Brainerd. "Visual Representations of the Trinity: An Historical Survey." Diss. Columbia University, Cooperstown, NY: Arthur H. Crist Publishing Co., 1917.

Manly, George W. "Contradictions in Locke's Theory of Knowledge." Diss., Leipzig: C. G. Röder, ca. 1892.

Manthey-Zorn, Otto. "Johann Georg Jacobis Iris." Diss., Zwickau: Johannes Herrmann, 1905.

Masius, Morton. "Über die Adsorption in Gemischen." Diss., Borna-Leipzig: Robert Noske, 1908.

McClumpha, Charles Flint. "The Alliteration of Chaucer." Diss., Leipzig: Grimme & Trömel, 1888.

McKenney, Randolph E. B. "Observations on the Conditions of Light Production in Luminous Bacteria." Diss. Basel. In *Proceedings of the Biological Society of Washington* 15, (29 November 1902): 213–34.

McKim, W. Duncan. "Über den Nephridialen Trichterapparat von Hirudo." Diss., Leipzig: Wilhelm Engelmann, 1895.

Mead, William Edward. "The Versification of Pope in Its Relations to the Seventeenth Century." Diss., Leipzig: Frankenstein and Wagner, 1889.

Mellby, Carl August. "Vonrad Vorstius. Ein Vorkämpfer religiöser Duldung am Anfang des 17. Jahrhundert." Diss., Leipzig: Oswald Schmidt, 1901.

Meyer, Ernst C. "Wahlamt und Vorwahl in den Vereinigten Staaten von Nord-Amerika." Diss., Leipzig: R. Voigtlander, 1908.

Meyerholz, Charles. "Die Federal-Konvention vom Jahre 1787. Ein Beitrag zur Verfassungsgeschichte der Vereinigten Staaten." Diss., Leipzig: R. Voigtlander, 1907.

Morgan, Bayard Quincy. "Zur Lehre von der Alliteration in der Westgermanischen Dichtung." Diss., Halle: Ehrhardt Karra, 1907.

Morgan, J. Livingston Rutgers. "Die Bestimmung von Cianionen auf elektrometrischem Wege." Diss., Leipzig: Wilhelm Engelmann, 1895.

Morgenthau, Julius C. "Ueber den Zusammenhang der Bilder auf Griechischen Vasen." Diss., Leipzig: Bär & Hermann, 1886.

Morse, Harry. "Über die Dissociation der Merkurihaloide." Diss., Leipzig: Wilhelm Engelmann, 1902.

Mottier, David M. "Ueber das Verhalten der Kerne bei der Entwicklung des Embryosacks und die Vorgänge der Befruchtung." Diss., Berlin: Gebrüder Borntraeger, 1897.

Münsterberg, Hugo. "Die Lehre von der Natürlichen Anpassung in ihrer Entwicklung, Anwendung und Bedeutung." Diss., Leipzig: Metzger & Wittig, 1885.

Murbach, Lewis. "Beiträge zur Kenntnis der Anatomie und Entwicklung der Nesselorgane der Hydroiden." Diss., Berlin: Nicolaische Verlags-Buchhandlung R. Stricker, 1894.

Myhrman, David W. "Die Labartu-Texte." Diss., Strassburg: Karl J. Trübner, 1902.

Pace, Edward. "Das Relativitätsprincip in Herbert Spencer's psychologischer Entwicklungslehre." Diss., Leipzig: Wilhelm Engelmann, 1891.

Page, Thomas Walker. "Die Umwandlung der Frohndienste in Geldrenten in den Oestlichen, Mittleren und Südlichen Grafschaften Englands." Diss., Baltimore: Guggenheimer, Weil & Co, 1896/97.

Parrott, Thomas M. "An Examination of the Non-Dramatic Poems in Robert Browning's First and Second Periods, to Which is Added a Bibliography." Diss., Leipzig: Oswald Schmidt, 1893.

Patten, William. "The Development of Phryganides, with a Preliminary Note on the Development of Blatta Germanica." Diss., London: J. E. Adlard, Bartholomew Close, 1884. Reprinted from *Quarterly Journal of Microscopical Science* (1884).

Peirce, Benjamin Osgood, Jun. "Über die electromagnetischen Kräfte von Gaselementen." Diss. Leipzig: Metzger & Wittig, 1879.

Peirce, George J. "A Contribution to the Physiology of the Genus Cuscuta." Diss., Oxford: Horace Hart, 1894.

Phelan, James. "On Philip Massinger." Diss., Halle: E. Karras, 1878.

Pope, Paul R. "Die Anwendung der Epitheta im Tristan Gottfrieds von Strassburg." Diss., Halle: Ehrhardt Karras, 1903.

Price, M. B. "Teutonic Antiquities in the Generally Acknowledged Cynewulfian Poetry." Diss., Leipzig: Ernst Hedrich, 1896.

Price, Orlo Josiah. "Martineau's Religionsphilosophie. Darstellung und Kritik." Diss., Newark, OH: Express Printing Co., 1902/03.

Remley, Frederick A. "The Relation of State and Church in Zurich—1519 to the First Disputation." Diss., Leipzig: Ernst Hedrich, 1895.

Retzer, Robert. "Über die Musculöse Verbindung zwischen Vorhof und Ventrikel des Säugethierherzens." Diss. Leipzig: Veit & Comp., 1904.

Richardson, Burt P. "Elektroanalytische Studien." Diss., Leipzig/Hamburg: Leopold Voss, 1913.

Riemer, Guido C.L. "Die Adjektiva bei Wolfram von Eschenbach stillistisch betrachtet. Der Wort- und Begriffsschatz." Diss., Halle: Ehrhardt Karras, 1906.

Robinson, George Livingston. "The Prophecies of Zechariah. With Special Reference to the Origin and Date of Chapters 9–14." Diss., Chicago: University of Chicago Press, 1896.

Roe, John C. "Some Obscure Points in Byronic Biography." Diss., Leipzig: Oswald Schmidt, 1893.

Russell, James Earl. "The Extension of University Teaching in England and America." Diss., Leipzig: 1895. See also *Extension Bulletin* 10 (October 1895): 147–253. University of the State of New York.

Sammet, Viktor. "Die Gleichgewichte [...], chemisch und elektromotorisch bestimmt." Diss., Leipzig: Wilhelm Engelmann, 1905.

Scripture, E. W. "Ueber den asociativen Verlauf der Vorstellungen." Diss., Leipzig: Wilhelm Engelmann, 1891.

Sheib, Edward E. "The Public Schools in the United States of America." Diss., Baltimore: C. W. Schneidereith, 1877.

Sill, Herbert F. "Über das Gleichgewicht zwischen einer Stickstoffbase und organischen Säuren in verschiedenen Lösungsmitteln." Diss., Leipzig: Wilhelm Engelmann, 1905.

Smith, Frank Clifton. "Die Sprache der Handboc Byrhtferths und des Brieffragments eines unbekannten Verfassers. Ein Beitrag zur Lautlehre des Spätangelsächsischen." Diss., Leipzig: Pöschel & Trepte, 1905.

Smith, W. A. "Über die stufenweise Dissociation zweibasischer organischer Säuren." Diss., Leipzig: Wilhelm Engelmann, 1898.

Spaeth, J. D. "Die Syntax des Verbums in dem Angelsächsischen Gedicht Daniel." Diss., Leipzig: Emil Freter, 1893.

Spalding, Volney M. "The Traumatropic Curvature of Roots." Diss., 1894.

Spaulding, Frank E. "Richard Cumberland als Begründer der Englischen Ethik." Diss., Leipzig: Gustav Fock, 1894.

Squires, William Harder. "Jonathan Edwards und seine Willenslehre." Diss., [Leipzig?]: Berger & Behrendt, 1901.

Stafford, Joseph. "Anatomical Structure of Aspidogaster conchicola." Diss., Jena: Gustav Fischer, 1896.

Stanclift, Henry Clay. "Queen Elizabeth and the French Protestants in the Years 1559 and 1560." Diss., Leipzig: Oswald Schmidt, 1892.

Sterenberg, James. "The Use of Conditional Sentences in the Alexandrian Version of the Pentateuch." Diss., University of Munich, Munich: F. Straub, 1908.

Stewart, Andrew. "Ueber einige neue Synthesen von Diketochinazolinen und Monothiodiketochinazolinen." Diss., Leipzig: Metzger & Wittig, 1895.

Story, William E. "On the Algebraic Relations Existing Between The Polars of a Binary Quantic." Diss., Leipzig: Metzger & Wittig, 1875.

Stratton, George Malcolm. "Ueber die Wahrnehmung von Druckveränderungen bei verschiedenen Geschwindigkeiten." Diss., Leipzig: Wilhelm Engelmann, 1896.

Sullivan, Eugene C. "Studien über einige Jodverbindungen." Diss., Leipzig: Wilhelm Engelmann, 1899.

Sussmann, Martin. "Ueber einen Fall von multipler Neuritis mit perverser Temperaturempfindung." Diss., Friedrich-Wilhelms-University zu Berlin, Berlin: Gustav Schade [Otto Francke], 1891.

Tawney, Guy A. "Die Wahrnehmung zweier Punkte mittels des Tastsinns, mit Rücksicht auf die Frage der Uebung und die Entstehung der Vexirfehler." Diss., Leipzig: Wilhelm Engelmann, 1897.

Thatcher, C. J. "Die elektrolytische Oxydation von Natriumthiosulfat und ihr Mechanismus." Diss., Leipzig: Wilhelm Engelmann, 1904.

Tilley, Morris Palmer. "Zur Syntax Wærferths." Diss., Leipzig: Gustav Fock, 1903.

Titchener, E. Bradford. "Ueber binoculare Wirkung monocularer Reize." Diss., Leipzig: Wilhelm Engelmann, 1892.

Tower, Olin Freeman. "Studien über Superoxyd-Elektroden." Diss., Leipzig: Wilhelm Engelmann, 1895.

Townsend, Charles Orrin. "Der Einfluss des Zellkerns auf die Zellhaut." Diss., Berlin: Gebrüder Borntraeger, 1897.

Tressler, Victor G. A. "Die politische Entwicklung Sir Robert Cecils bis zum Tode Lord Burleighs." Diss., Leipzig: Emil Glausch, 1901.

Trevor, J. E. "Über die Messung kleiner Dissociationsgrade." Diss., Leipzig: Wilhelm Engelmann, 1892.

True, Rodney H. "On the Influence of Sudden Changes of Turgor and of Temperature on Growth." Diss., Leipzig: 1895.

Tschirner, Frederick. "Über die Oxydation aromatischer Basen insbesondere über die Oxydation von Anilin." Diss., University of Munich, Zürich: J. Leemann vormals J. Schabeliz, 1900.

Turk, Milton Haight. "The Legal Code of Aelfred the Great." Diss., Halle: Ehrhardt Karras, 1890.

Voss, Ernst. "Der Genitiv bei Thomas Murner." Diss., Leipzig: Gustav Fock, 1895.

Wakeman, Alfred J. "Über die Beeinflussung der Molekular-Leitfähigkeit der Essigsäure durch kleine Mengen anderer elektrolytischer Substanzen. Anwendung der Theorie der isohydrischen Lösungen." Diss., Leipzig: Wilhelm Engelmann, 1894.

Warbeke, John Martyn. "Das Homogenitätsprinzip in der Spencerschen Psychologie und die Beziehungen desselben zu der Erkenntnislehre der 'First Principles.'" Diss., Leipzig: Dr. Seele & Co., 1907.

Warner, Jr., Brainard H. "Die Organisation und Bedeutung der freien Öffentlichen Arbeitsnachweisämter in den vereinigten Staaaten von Nordamerika." Diss., Leipzig: Jäh & Schunke, 1903.

Westhaver, J. B. "Über das Verhalten von Anoden aus Iridium, Platin und Rhodium bei der Elektrolyse verdünnter Schwefelsäure." Diss., Leipzig: Wilhelm Engelmann, 1905.

Westfall, John van Etten. "On a Category of Transformation Groups in Three and Four Dimensions." Diss., Ithaca, NY: Andrus & Church, 1899.

Weyer, Eduard Moffat. "Die Zeitschwellen gleichartiger und disparater Sinneseindrücke." Diss., Leipzig: Wilhelm Engelmann, 1898.

Whitney, Willis Rodney. "Untersuchungen über Chromsulfat-Verbindungen." Diss., Leipzig: Wilhelm Engelmann, 1896.

Wilkinson, John J. "James Martineaus Ethik. Darstellung, Kritik und pädagogische Konsequenzen." Diss., Leipzig: Sellmann & Henne, 1898.

Witmer, Lightner. "Zur experimentellen Aesthetik einfacher räumlicher Formverhältnisse." Diss., Leipzig: Wilhelm Engelmann, 1893.

Woelfel, Albert. "Ueber die Symptomatologie und Pathologie der Strangulation." Diss., Leipzig: Bruno Georgi, 1902.

Wolfe, Harry Kirke. "Untersuchungen über das Tongedächtnis." Diss., Leipzig: Wilhelm Engelmann, 1886.

Wood, Frank Hoyt. "Ursprung und Entwicklung der Sklaverei in den Ursprünglich von Frankreich und Spanien besessenen Teilen der Vereinigten Staaten und Canadas." Diss., Leipzig: Bruno Zechel, 1900.

Wood, Henry. "Chaucer's Influence Upon King James I. of Scotland as Poet." Diss., Halle: E. Karras, 1879.

Worcester, Elwood Ernest. "The Religious Opinions of John Locke." Diss., Geneva, NY: W. F. Humphrey, 1889.

Ylvisaker, Sigurd C. "Zur Babylonischen und Assyrischen Grammatik. Eine Untersuchung auf Grund der Briefe aus der Sargonidenzeit." Diss., Leipzig: August Pries, 1911.

Zalinski, Edward Robins. "Untersuchungen über Thuringit und Chamosit aus Thüringen und Umgebung," Diss., Stuttgart: E. Schweizbart'sche Verlagshandlung E. Nägele, 1904.

BIBLIOGRAPHY

Abbreviations

APS	American Philosophical Society, Philadelphia
BBAW	Berlin Brandenburgische Akademie der Wissenschaften
Berkeley Bancroft	University of California at Berkeley—Bancroft Library
Cornell Kroch	Cornell University, Ithaca, NY—Kroch Library Manuscripts and Rare Books
HUL Countway	Harvard University—Countway Library
HUL Houghton	Harvard University—Houghton Library
HUL Lamont	Harvard University—Lamont Library
HUL Pusey	Harvard University—Pusey Library
HUL Schlesinger	Harvard University—Schlesinger Library
JHU med	Johns Hopkins University—Alan Macon Chesney Medical Archives
LC	Library of Congress
LUL Albertina	Leipzig University Library Albertina (Sondersammlung)
LUA	Leipzig University Archives
MHCA	Mount Holyoke College Archives
MIT Archives	Massachussetts Institute of Technology—Archives
MIT Museum	Massachussetts Institute of Technology—Museum
NARA	National Archives and Records Administration
PUL Firestone	Princeton University—Firestone Library
PUL Mudd	Princeton University—Seeley G. Mudd Manuscript Library
Rice Fondren	Rice University—Fondren Library
SUA	Stanford University Archives
UAH	University Archives Halle
UM Bentley	University of Michigan, Ann Arbor—Bentley Historical Library
UP Van Pelt	University of Pennsylvania—Van Pelt Rare Book and Manuscript Library
VU SCUA	Vanderbilt University—Special Collections and University Archives
Vevey	Vevey Community Archives, Vevey, Switzerland
YUL	Yale University Library—Manuscripts and Archives

Archival Materials

APS: Benjamin Franklin Papers, BF85.

APS: Raymond Pearl Papers, B:P312.

APS: Rodney Howard True Papers, BT763.

BBAW: Nachlass (NL) Wilhelm Ostwald.

Berkeley Bancroft: Benjamin Ide Wheeler Correspondence and Papers, ca. 1870–1923, C-B 1044, Box 1, Folder: Wheeler, Benjamin Ide: Outgoing Letters, September–December 1900.

Cornell Kroch: Faculty Biographical File Wilder D. Bancroft.

Cornell Kroch: Faculty Biographical File Paul Russell Pope.

Cornell Kroch: George Lincoln Burr Papers, 14/17/22.

Cornell Kroch: Graduate Student Folder Mrs. Paul Russell Pope.

Cornell Kroch: Lane Cooper Papers, 14/12/680.

Cornell Kroch: Andrew Dickson White Papers, 1/2/2.

HUL Countway: Charles Sedgwick Minot Papers, H MS c 21.2.

HUL Countway: Henry Pickering Bowditch Papers, H MS c 5.1.

HUL Houghton: James Family Papers, bMS Am 1092.9.

HUL Lamont: George and Anna Ticknor, Travel Journals, microfilm W 3275.

HUL Pusey: Arthur Becket Lamb Papers, HUG 4508.50, Corresp. with Parents, 1903–1905.

HUL Pusey: Biographical Folder, HUG 300 Arthur Becket Lamb A.M. '03.

HUL Pusey: Biographical Folder, HUG 300 Charles Carlton Ayer '89.

HUL Pusey: Biographical Folder, HUG 300 George Draper Osgood '12.

HUL Pusey: Biographical Folder, HUG 300 Ralph Thacher.

HUL Pusey: Charles W. Eliot, "Address at Southwestern Association of Northern Colleges, San Antonio," San Antonio Express, 27 February 1909, clipping, Eliot Papers, Box 273.

HUL Pusey Charles Rockwell Lanman Papers, HUG 4510.67, Letters from Europe, vol. 3, and Diaries, HUG 4510.5.

HUL Pusey, Frederick T. Lewis, "Charles Sedgwick Minot. 23 December 1852–19 November 1914," (Harvard Medical School, booklet, 30 November 1914), HUG 1573.14.

HUL Pusey: George Howard Parker Papers, Personal Correspondence, HUG 4674.12.

HUL Pusey: Harvard College Class of 1912. Twenty-Fifth Anniversary Report, Sixth Report, June 1937.

HUL Pusey: Josiah Royce MSS, HUG 1755.5.

HUL Pusey: Theodore William Richards Papers, HUG 1743.6.5 and HUG 1743.1.5.

HUL Schlesinger: Hamilton Family Papers, MC 278, microfilm 27.

JHU med: William Henry Welch Papers, I Correspondence with Individuals.

LC: Frederick Gardner Cottrell Papers, MMC 3121.

LUL Albertina: Gregory Papers, Box MS 0994, MS 0995, MS 0996 (letters to Gregory).

LUA: Acten des akademischen Senates der Universität LEIPZIG die Zulassung Hörer weibli-chen Geschlechts zu den academischen Vorlesungen betr., 6 December 1873, Rep. II/IV, Nr. 35.

LUA: Acta, die Immatrikulation weiblicher Studierender betr. (1906–?), Rep. II/IV, Nr. 67, microfilm 434.

LUA: Akten der Universität Leipzig betreffend: "Hörerinnen" (1907–18), Rep. II/IV, Nr. 60 Bd. 6., microfilm 430.

LUA: Acta, [Un]sittlichen Verkehr Studi[ren]der mit Frauenpersonen betr. (1893–1914), Rep II/IV, Nr. 55a.

LUA: Acta, Zulassung weiblicher Personen zum Besuche von Vorlesungen an der Universität Leipzig betr. (1900), Rep. II/IV, Nr. 60 Bde. 2–5, microfilms 428 + 429.

LUA: American Students Club = Klub der *amerikanischen* und *englischen* Stud. (Verein *amerikanischer* Studenten/Amerikaner-Verein), Rep. II/XVI/III, Nr. 16 and 17, microfilm 488/94.

LUA: Leipzig hearer lists = Verzeichnisse der nicht immatrikulierten Zuhörer an der Universität Leipzig (1873/74–1902/03), GAXM1 to GAXM4, microfilm 502/94.

LUA: Leipzig Matrikel 1781–1914, Rektor M, M11, microfilm 583; M12–M29, microfilms 600/95–604/95; M30, 584; M31–M51, microfilms 631–635; M44–M44a, microfilms 1337; M52–M67, microfilms 679–683.

LUA: Nachlass (NA) Windisch.

LUA: Nachlass (NA) Wundt.

LUA: Personalakte Ewald Flügl, PA 462.

LUA: Student. Körperschaften, Rep. II/XVI/II, WS 1899/1900 Nr. 6 Bd. 5, microfilm 476/94; SS 1905 Bd. 16, 478/94; SS 1909 Bd. 24, 479/94; SS 1911 Bd. 28, 480/94; and WS 1914/15 Bd. 35, 481/94.

LUA: Verzeichnis der Verbindungen pro S.S. 1890, Rep. II/XVI/II, Nr. 3 Bd. 10, microfilm 474/94.

LUA: Verzeichnis der Verbindungen, WS 1891/92, Rep. II/XVI/II, Nr. 17, microfilm 488/94.

MHCA: 1903 *Class Letter* no. 2 (1906), LD 7096.5 1903 E.

MHCA: *Class Letter of the Class of 1901 of Mount Holyoke College*, 1902 ed., 95–9, LD 7096.5 1903 E.

MIT Archives: Harry Manly Goodwin Papers, MC121.

MIT Museum: David L. Adams, "Arthur Amos Noyes—First in Chemical Education, First in Chemical Research, and First in the Northeastern Section," ms [published in *The Nucleus* (1997)], 9–10.

NARA: Appointment Papers and Letters of Recommendation, Record Group 59, General Records of the Department of State. [Arthur Payson's father].

NARA: Card Record Of Appointments Made From 1776 To 1968 (RG 59 Entry A1–798).

NARA: D[i]spatches from U.S. Consuls in Leipzig, 1828–1906, microfilm T-215, roll 11, 10 July 1890–16 October 1903.

PUL Firestone: Winthrop Moore Daniels Papers, CO734.

PUL Mudd: Alumni File of James Mark Baldwin 1884, Biographical Information.

PUL Mudd: Allen Welsh Dulles Papers, Todd Family Correspondence.

PUL Mudd: Faculty File George Augustus Hulett '92.

PUL Mudd: Faculty File Thomas Marc Parrott '88.

Rice Fondren: President's Papers E.O. Lovett.

SUA: *The Stanford Alumnus* (July 1901). Pat White, email message to author, 21 May 2007.

UAH: Matrikel Halle.

UM Bentley: James Rowland Angell Papers, 85605 Aa 1.

UM Bentley: Horace Willard Davenport, *A University of Michigan Faculty Life, Warren Plimpton Lombard in Ann Arbor, 1892–1939* (1992). DB 2 L841 D247.

UM Bentley: Warren Plimpton Lombard, Correspondence 1877–1899, 85811 Aa 2.

UM Bentley: Andrew Cunningham McLaughlin Papers, 85536 Aa 2.

UM Bentley: Necrology File George Allen Briggs.

UM Bentley: Necrology File Theodore Hitchcock Johnston.

UM Bentley: Necrology File Percy Ripley Wilson.

UM Bentley: Volney Morgan Spalding Papers.

UM Bentley: Calvin Thomas Papers, 86180 Aa 2 Ac.

UP Van Pelt: John Stewart Collection, letters from Lightner Witmer.

UP Van Pelt: William Carlos Williams, letters to his brother, MS Coll 395.

VU SCUA: James Hampton Kirkland Papers.

Vevey: A. Scheiterberg, *Bellerive. Institution Sillig 1836–1892. Souvenir du Jubilé du 15 Juillet 1886* 2nd ed. (Vevey: Imprimerie Alph. Recordon, 1892).

Vevey: Student lists.

YUL: James Rowland Angell Papers, Manuscript Group 2.

YUL: Yale Class Reports of Lewis Weld '18 and Mason Cogswell Weld '52 (Sheffield Scientific School).

YUL: *A History of the Yale Class of 1851, for forty years. Mainly by themselves* (Boston: Alfred Mudge & Son, no. 24 Franklin Street, 1893). Ybb Class Histories.

YUL: Obituary Record of Graduates of Yale University Deceased during the Academic Year Ending in June 1888, no. 8, Series 3.

YUL: Obituary Record of Graduates of Yale University Deceased During the Academic Year Ending in June 1895.

YUL: Seymour Family Papers, Thomas Day Seymour Correspondence, Manuscript Group 440.

YUL: Lewis Weld Family Papers, Mason Cogswell Weld's Letters from Germany, Manuscript Group 559.

YUL: Woolsey Family Papers, Manuscript Group 562.

Miscellaneous Resources

Dr. William Roba of the Eastern Iowa Community College, Bettendorf, Iowa provided me with materials on St. Sebald:
- George J. Zeilinger, *1854–1929, A Missionary Synod With a Mission* (1929).
- Guy Reed Ramsey, *Postmarked Iowa: A List of Discontinued and Renamed Post Offices* (Crete, NE: J-B Publishing Company, 1976).
- "History of Clayton County," in *Cass Township Close Knit German Village* (1984).

Gästebuch der Samuel-Heinicke-Schule 1803–1852, A IV 64,2, Spezialbibliothek für Hör- und Sprachschädigung, Samuel-Heinicke-Schule Leipzig.

The University Archives Halle has information regarding the Mühlenbergs. Also: Franckeschen Stiftungen <archiv@francke-halle.de>.

The University Archives Heidelberg have documents regarding Gideon Emmet Moore, including his Latin CV, H-IV-102/72.

Biographical Dictionaries and Student Directories

Allgemeine Deutsche Biographie (ADB). 1875–1912. http://www.deutsche-biographie.de/~ndb/index.html.

Biographical Memoirs of the National Academy of Sciences. http://www.nasonline.org/site/PageServer?pagename=MEMOIRS_B.

Garraty, John A., and Mark C. Carnes, general eds. *American National Biography*. 24 vols. New York/Oxford: Oxford University Press, 1999.

Gillispie, Charles Coulston, ed. in chief. *Dictionary of Scientific Biography*. 9 vols. New York: Charles Scribner's Sons, 1970–1974.

James, Edward T. et al., eds. *Notable American Women, 1607–1950. A Biographical Dictionary*. 3 vols. Prepared under the auspices of Radcliffe College. Cambridge, MA: Belknap Press of Harvard University Press, 1971.

Meyers Konversationslexikon. 4th ed., vol. 4. Leipzig/Wien: Verlag des Bibliographischen Instituts, 1885–1892.

National Cyclopedia of American Biography. Vol. 23. Clifton, NJ: White, 1967.

Neue Deutsche Biographie (NDB). Berlin: Duncker & Humblot, 1953. http://www.deutsche-biographie.de/~ndb/index.html.

The Quinquennial Catalogue of Harvard University 1636–1930. Cambridge, MA: Harvard University Press. http://pds.lib.harvard.edu/pds/view/6796688.

Online Search Engines, University/College Websites, and University/College Histories

Amherst College Biographical Record. 1921. [Online search engine of Amherst Coll. Alumni]. http://www.amherst.edu/~rjyanco/genealogy/acbiorecord/menu.html.

Harvard Annual Reports, http://hul.harvard.edu/huarc/refshelf/AnnualReportsCites.htm#ta rHarvardPresidents.

Reports of the President and the Treasurer of Harvard College, 1903–1904. Harvard Library, 214–15. http://pds.lib.harvard.edu/pds/view/2574586?n=216&s=4.

Personal-Verzeichniß der Universität Leipzig WS 1849/1850 (Nr. XXVI) to SS 1853 (Nr. XLIII) printed by Wilh. Staritz, Universitäts-Buchdrucker, Leipzig. http://ubimg.ub.uni-leipzig .de/.

Personal-Verzeichniß der Universität Leipzig WS 1853/54 (Nr. XLIV) to SS 1860 (Nr. LVII) printed by Alexander Edelmann, Universitätsbuchdrucker, Leipzig. http://ubimg.ub.uni-leipzig.de/.

Personal-Verzeichniß der Universität Leipzig WS 1860/1861 (Nr. LVIII) to WS 1914/15 (Nr. CLXVI), Commissions-Verlag Alexander Edelmann, Universitäts-Buchhändler, Leipzig. http://ubimg.ub.uni-leipzig.de/.

Published Sources, Secondary Sources, Biographical and Autobiographical Sources

Adams, Herbert B. *Thomas Jefferson and the University of Virginia.* Washington, DC: Government Printing Office, 1888.

Adams, J.F.A. "Is Botany a Suitable Study for Young Men?" *Science* 9 (1887): 117–18.

Adler, Margot. "Some Students Look for Hidden-Gem Colleges." NPR, *Morning Edition,* 22 February 2007. http://www.npr.org/templates/story/story.php?storyId=7384194.

Albisetti, James C. "German Influence on the Higher Education of American Women, 1865–1914." In *German Influences on Education in the United States to 1917,* eds. Geitz, Heideking, and Herbst, 227–44.

———. *Schooling German Girls and Women: Secondary Education in the Nineteenth Century.* Princeton, NJ: Princeton University Press, 1988.

Altschuler, Glenn C. *Andrew D. White—Educator, Historian, Diplomat.* Ithaca, NY: Cornell University Press, 1979.

———. *Better Than Second Best: Love and Work in the Life of Helen Magill.* Urbana/Chicago: University of Illinois Press, 1990.

Anderson, Benedict. *Imagined Communities. Reflections on the Origin and Spread of Nationalism.* London: Verso, 1989 [1983].

Anderson, Robert David. *Education and Opportunity in Victorian Scotland: Schools and Universities.* Edinburgh: Edinburgh University Press, 1983/1989.

Anonymous. "Higher Education for Women in Germany.—I." *The Nation. A Weekly Journal Devoted to Politics, Literature, Science & Arts* 44, no. 1274 (November 28, 1890): 426–27.

Anonymous. "Memorial Services in Honor of Franklin Paine Mall, Professor of Anatomy, Johns Hopkins University, 1893 to 1917." *Bulletin of the Johns Hopkins Hospital* 29, no. 327 (May 1918): 109–23.

Anonymous. *The Tourist in Europe: or A Concise Summary of the Various Routes, Objects of Interests, &c.* New York: Wiley & Putnam, 1838.

Aptheker, Herbert, ed. *The Correspondence of W.E.B. DuBois. Selections 1877–1934.* Vol. 1. Amherst: University of Massachusetts Press, 1973–1978.

Baedeker, Karl. *Northern Germany. Handbook for Travellers.* 9th rev. ed. Leipsic: Karl Baedeker, 1886.

Bailey, Fred Arthur. *William Edward Dodd: The South's Yeoman Scholar.* Charlottesville: University Press of Virginia, 1997.

Baldwin, Bird T., ed. "In Memory of Wilhelm Wundt." *Psychological Review* 28 (May 1921): 153–88. Reprinted in *Wundt Studies,* ed. Bringmann and Tweney, 280–308.

Baldwin, James Mark. *Between Two Wars: 1861–1921.* 2 vols. Boston: Stratford Company, 1926.

———. "Autobiography." In *A History of Psychology in Autobiography,* ed. Carl Murchison, vol. 1, 1–30. Worcester, MA: Clark University Press, 1930.

Barasch, Moshe. *Blindness: The History of a Mental Image in Western Thought.* New York: Routledge, 2001.

Barkin, Kenneth. "W.E.B. Du Bois' Love Affair with Imperial Germany." *German Studies Review* 28 (May 2005): 284–302.

Barnard, Harry. *The Forging of an American Jew: The Life and Times of Judge Julian W. Mack.* New York: Herzl Press, 1974.

Barton, Len. *Overcoming Disabling Barriers: 18 Years of Disability and Society.* London: Routledge, 2006.

Bauman, H-Dirksen L. *Open Your Eyes: Deaf Studies Talking.* Minneapolis: University of Minnesota Press, 2008.

Baumgarten, Marita. *Professoren und Universitäten im 19. Jahrhundert.* Göttingen: Vandenhoek & Ruprecht, 1997.

Becker, Anja. "Amerikanistik [American Studies]." In *Geschichte der Universität Leipzig.* Band IV: Fakultäten, Institute, Zentrale Einrichtungen (1. Halbband), ed. Ulrich von Hehl, Uwe John, and Manfred Rudersdorf, 12–31. Leipzig: Universitätsverlag, 2009. English version: http://americanstudies.uni-leipzig.de/the_leipzig_model/institute_for_american_studies/.

———. "Crossing Disciplinary Boundaries." *Our Hemisphere—Nuetro hemisferio. A Newsletter of the Center for the Americas at Vanderbilt* (Fall 2007).

———. "For the Sake of Old Leipzig Days… Academic Networks of American Students at a German University, 1781–1914." PhD dissertation, University of Leipzig, 2006.

———. "How Daring She Was! The Female American Colony at Leipzig University, 1877–1914." In *Taking Up Space. New Approaches to American History,* mosaic 21, ed. Anke Ortlepp and Christoph Ribbat, 31–46. Trier: Wissenschaftlicher Verlag Trier, 2004.

———. "Southern Academic Ambitions Meet German Scholarship: The Leipzig Networks of Vanderbilt University's James H. Kirkland in the Late Nineteenth Century." *Journal of Southern History* 74, no. 4 (November 2008): 855–86.

———. "US-American Students in Leipzig and Their Struggle with the German Tongue, 1827 to 1909." In *Transatlantic Cultural Contexts. Essays in Honor of Eberhard Brüning,* ed. Hartmut Keil, 165–86. Tübingen: Stauffenburg, 2005.

———, and Tobias Brinkmann, "Transatlantische Bildungsmigration: Amerikanisch-jüdische Stundenten an der Universität Leipzig 1872 bis 1914." In *Bausteine einer jüdischen Geschichte der Universität Leipzig im Auftrag des Simon-Dubnow-Instituts für Jüdische Geschichte und Kultur an der Universität Leipzig,* ed. Stephan Wendehorst, 61–98. Leipziger Beiträge zur Jüdischen Geschichte und Kultur, ed. Dan Diner, vol. IV. Leipzig: Universitätsverlag, 2006.

Beckert, Herbert, and Horst Schumann, eds. *100 Jahre Mathematisches Seminar der Karl-Marx-Universität Leipzig.* Berlin: VEB Deutscher Verlag der Wissenschaften, 1981.

Bederman, Gail. *Manliness & Civilization: A Cultural History of Gender and Race in the United States, 1880–1917.* Chicago: University of Chicago Press, 1995.

Bell, Whitfield J., Jr. "Philadelphia Medical Students in Europe, 1750–1800." *Pennsylvania Magazine of History and Biography* 47, no. 1 (January 1943): 1–29.

Best, John Hardin. "Education in the Forming of the American South," in *Essays in Twentieth-Century Southern Education. Exceptionalism and Its Limits*, ed. Wayne J. Urban, 14–15. New York/London: Garland Publishing, 1999. An earlier edition was published in *History of Education Quarterly* 36, no. 1 (Spring 1996): 39–51.

Betts, Edwin M., and James A. Bear, Jr., eds. *The Family Letters of Thomas Jefferson.* Columbia: University of Missouri Press, 1966.

Bickel, Marcel H. *Die Entwicklung zur experimentellen Pharmakologie 1790–1850. Wegbereiter von Rudolf Buchheim.* Basel: Schwabe & Co. AG Verlag, 2000.

Black History Month. *The Role of Afro-American Churches in Economic, Political and Social Development at Home and Abroad.* Columbia: University of Missouri-Columbia, 1989.

Blackbourn, David. *The Long Nineteenth Century: A History of Germany, 1780–1918.* New York: Oxford University Press, 1998.

Blaschke, Karlheinz. "Die Universität Leipzig im Wandel vom Ancien Régime zum bürgerlichen Staat." In *Wissenschafts- und Universitätsgeschichte*, ed. Karl Czok, 133–53.

Bodenstedt, Friedrich. *Vom Atlantischen zum Stillen Ozean.* Leipzig: Brockhaus, 1882.

Böhmer, Julius. "Das Geheimnis um die Geburt von Franz Delitzsch." *Saat auf Hoffnung* 71, no. 2/3 (1934): 63–75, 110–20.

Bog, Ingomar. "Ist die Kameralistik eine untergegangene Wissenschaft?" In *Berichte zur Wissenschafttsgeschichte*, ed. Fritz Krafft, vol. 4, 61–72. Wiesbaden: Akademische Verlagsgesellschaft Athenaion, 1981.

Boles, John B. *University Builder: Edgar Odell Lovett and the Founding of the Rice Institute.* Baton Rouge: Louisiana State University Press, 2007.

———. *A University So Conceived: A Brief History of Rice.* 3rd rev. and exp. ed. Houston: Rice University, 2006 [1992].

Bonner, Thomas Neville. *American Doctors in German Universities: A Chapter in International Intellectual Relations.* Lincoln: University of Nebraska Press, 1963.

———. *To the Ends of the Earth: Women's Search for Education in Medicine.* Cambridge, MA: Harvard University Press, 1992.

Boring, Edward G. "Edward Bradford Titchener, 1867–1927." *American Journal of Psychology* 38, no. 4 (October 1927): 489–506.

Bowditch, Henry Pickering. "Letter from Leipzig." *Boston Medical and Surgical Journal* 82 (1870): 305–7.

Bowditch, Manfred. "Henry Pickering Bowditch. An Intimate Memoir." *Physiologist* 1, no. 5 (November 1958): 7–11.

Bowditch, Vincent Y. *Life and Correspondence of Henry Ingersoll Bowditch.* 2 vols. Freeport, NY: Books for Libraries Press, 1902.

Bragg, William Harris. *De Renne: Three Generations of a Georgia Family.* Athens: University of Georgia Press, 1999.

Brandenburg, Erich. "Die Universität Leipzig im ersten halben Jahrtausend ihres Bestehens." In *Die Universität Leipzig 1409–1909. Gedenkblätter zum 30. Juli 1909.* Leipzig: Günther, Kirstein & Wendler, 1909.

Brentjes, Sonja, and Karl-Heinz Schlote. "Zum Frauenstudium an der Universität Leipzig in der Zeit von 1870 bis 1910." In *Jahrbuch für Regionalgeschichte und Landeskunde 19*, 57–75. Weimar: Verlag Herrmann Böhlaus Nachfolger, 1993/94.

Briggs, Ward W. Jr., ed. *The Letters of Basil Lanneau Gildersleeve.* Baltimore: Johns Hopkins University Press, 1987.

Bringmann, Norma J., and Wolfgang G. Bringmann. "Wilhelm Wundt and His First American Student." In *Wundt Studies*, ed. Bringmann and Tweney, 176–92.

Bringmann, Wolfgang G., Norma J. Bringmann, and Gustav A. Ungerer. "The Establishment of Wundt's Laboratory: An Archival and Documentary Study." In *Wundt Studies*, ed. Bringmann and Tweney, 123–57.

Bringmann, Wolfgang G., and Ryan D. Tweney, eds. *Wundt Studies*. Toronto: C. J. Hochgrefe, 1980.

Broadie, Alexander. *The Scottish Enlightenment: The Historical Age of the Historical Nation*. Edinburgh: Birlinn, 2001/2007.

Brocke, Bernhard von. *Wissenschaftsgeschichte und Wissenschaftspolitik im Industriezeitalter: das "System Althoff" in historischer Perspektive*. Hildesheim: Lax, 1991.

Bronk, Isabelle. "Women at the University of Leipzig." *The Nation* 51, no. 1329 (18 December 1890): 480–81.

Brown, William Wells. *The American Fugitive in Europe Sketches of Places and People Abroad*. Boston: John P. Jewett and Co, 1855. Chapel Hill, NC: Academic Affairs Library, University of North Carolina at Chapel Hill, 2000. http://docsouth.unc.edu/neh/brown55/brown55.sgml.

Browne, C. A. "European Laboratory Experiences of an Early American Agricultural Chemist—Dr. Evan Pugh (1828–1864)." *Journal of Chemical Education* 7, no. 3 (March 1930): 499–517.

Brückner, Isabell, and Karl Hansel, eds. "Zum Ausscheiden Wilhelm Ostwalds aus der Universitätslaufbahn." *Mitteilungen der Wilhelm-Ostwald-Gesellschaft zu Großbothen e.V.* 6, no. 1 (2001): 45–69.

Brugmann, Karl. "Hermann Osthoff." *Indogermanische Forschungen* 24 (1909): 218–23. Reprinted in Sebeok, *Portraits of Linguists*, vol. 1, 555–62.

Brüning, Eberhard. *Humanistische Tradition und Progressives Erbe der Leipziger Anglistik/ Amerikanistik. 100 Jahre Lehrstuhl für englische Sprache und Literatur and der Karl-Marx-Universität*. Abhandlungen der sächsischen Akademie der Wissenschaften zu Leipzig 67.1. Berlin: Akademie Verlag, 1977.

———. *Das Konsulat der Vereinigten Staaten von Amerika zu Leipzig*. Berlin, Akademie Verlag, 1994.

———. "Die Universität Leipzig im 19. Jahrhundert aus amerikanischer Sicht." *Jahrbuch für Regionalgeschichte und Landeskunde 20, 1995–96*, 101–11. Stuttgart: Verlag der Sächsischen Akademie der Wissenschaften zu Leipzig in Kommission bei Franz Steiner Verlag, 1996.

Buchan, James. *Crowded with Genius: The Scottish Enlightenment: Edinburgh's Moment of the Mind*. New York: HarperCollins Publishers, 2003/2004.

Buchheim, Liselotte. "Als die ersten Medizinerinnen in Leipzig promoviert wurden." *Wissenschaftliche Zeitschrift der Karl-Marx-Universität Leipzig* 6 (1956/57): 365–81.

Buchloh, Paul G. ed. *American Colony of Göttingen. Historical Data Collected Between the Years 1855 and 1888*. Göttingen: Vandenhoek & Ruprecht, 1976.

Bünning, Erwin. *Wilhelm Pfeffer. Apotheker, Chemiker, Botaniker, Physiologe 1845–1920*. Reihe Große Naturforscher Band 37. Stuttgart: Wissenschaftliche Verlagsgesellschaft mbH, 1975.

Burgess, John W. *Reminiscences of an American Scholar*. New York: Columbia University Press, 1934.

Bursian, Conrad. *Geschichte der classischen Philologie in Deutschland von den Anfängen bis zur Gegenwart*. München and Leipzig: Oldenbourg, 1883.

Bushong, Allen D. "Semple, Ellen Churchill." *American National Biography Online* (February 2000). http://www.anb.org/articles/14/14–00552.html.

Buttmann, Günther. *Friedrich Ratzel. Das Leben und Werk eines deutschen Geographen*. Große Naturforscher Band 40. Stuttgart: Wissenschaftl. Verlagsgesellschaft MBH, 1977.

Calkins, Mary Whiton. "Autobiographical Sketch." In *A History of Psychology in Autobiography*, vol. 1, ed. Carl Murchison, 31–62. Worcester, MA: Clark University Press, 1930.

Calvin, Melvin. "Gilbert Newton Lewis." In *Proceedings*, ed. W. O. Milligan, 116–45.

Cameron, Frank. *Cottrell: Samaritan of Science*. Garden City, NY: Doubleday & Company, 1952.

Cannon, Walter B. "Henry Pickering Bowditch." *Biographical Memoirs of the National Academy of Sciences* 17 (1922): 183–86. Reprinted in *The Life and Writings of Henry Pickering Bowditch*. vol. 1. New York: Arno Press, 1980.

———. "Henry Pickering Bowditch, Physiologist." *Science* 87, no. 2265 (27 May 1938): 471–78.

Cappon, Lester J., ed. *The Adams-Jefferson Letters: The Complete Correspondence between Thomas Jefferson and John Adams*. Chapel Hill: University of North Carolina Press, 1959.

Cattell, James McKeen. "The Psychological Laboratory at Leipsic," *Mind* 13 (1888): 37–51.

Chambers II, John Whiteclay. *The Tyranny of Change: America in the Progressive Era, 1890–1920*. 2nd ed. New Brunswick, NJ: Rutgers University Press, 2001 [1992].

Channing, Eva. "The Contributors' Club." *The Atlantic Monthly. A Magazine of Literature, Science, Art, and Politics* 44 (December 1879): 788–91.

Chickering, Roger. *Karl Lamprecht. A German Academic Life (1856–1915)*. Atlantic Highlands, NJ: Humanities Press, 1993.

———. "Das Leipziger 'Positivisten-Kränzchen' um die Jahrhundertwende." In *Kultur und Kulturwissenschaften um 1900 II Idealismus und Positivismus*, ed. Gangolf Hübinger, Rüdiger vom Bruch, and Friedrich Wilhelm Graf, 227–45. Stuttgart: Franz Steiner Verlag, 1997.

Clark, Walter Eugene. "Charles Rockwell Lanman, 1850–1941*." *Journal of the Oriental Society* 61, no. 3 (September 1941): 191–92.

Clark, William. *Academic Charisma and the Origins of the Research University*. Chicago: University of Chicago Press, 2006.

Clarke, Edward H. *Sex in Education; or a Fair Chance for Girls*. New York, 1873.

Clausewitz, Carl von. *On War*, translated from the German. London: Penguin Books, 2007 [1832].

Clendenning, John, ed. *The Letters of Josiah Royce*. Chicago: University of Chicago Press, 1970.

———. *The Life and Thought of Josiah Royce*. Rev. and exp. ed. Nashville: Vanderbilt University Press, 1999.

Cobb, James C. *Away Down South. A History of Southern Identity*. Oxford: Oxford University Press, 2005.

Collini, Stefan. "Introduction," in C. P. Snow, *The Two Cultures*. Cambridge: Cambridge University Press, 1998.

Cohen, Arthur M. *The Shaping of American Higher Education: Emergence and Growth of the Contemporary System*. San Francisco: Jossey-Bass, John Wiley & Sons, 1998.

Cohen, Arthur M., and Carrie B. Kisker. *The Shaping of American Higher Education: Emergence and Growth of the Contemporary System*. 2nd ed. San Francisco: Jossey-Bass, John Wiley & Sons, 2009.

Come, Donald Robert. "The Influence of Princeton on Higher Education in the South before 1825." *William and Mary Quarterly* 3rd Ser. 2, no. 4 (October 1945): 359–96.

Conrad, Johannes. *The German Universities for the Last Fifty Years,* translated by John Hutchinson, with a preface by later Ambassador James Bryce. Glasgow: David Bryce and Son, 1885.

————. *Das Universitätsstudium in Deutschland während der letzten fünfzig Jahre* (Jena: 1884).

Cordasco, Francesco. *The Shaping of American Graduate Education; Daniel Coit Gilman and the Protean PhD*. Totowa, NJ: Rowman and Littlefield, 1960/1973.

Costas, Ilse. "Der Zugang von Frauen zu akademischen Karrieren. Ein internationaler Überblick." In *Bedrohlich gescheit. Ein Jahrhundert Frauen und Wissenschaft in Bayern*, ed. Hiltrud Häntzschel and Hadumod Bußmann. München: Verlag C. H. Beck, 1997, 20–21.

Coulter, E. Merton. *College Life in the Old South. As Seen at the University of Georgia*. Athens: Brown Thrasher Books, University of Georgia Press, 1983 [1928].

Cowley, W.H. "European Influences upon American Higher Education." *Educational Record* 20 (April 1939): 165–90.

Craig, John E. *Scholarship and Nation Building: The Universities of Strasbourg and Alsatian Society, 1870–1939*. Chicago: University of Chicago Press, 1984.

Crandall, David L. "From Roxbury to Richmond: The Military Career of Henry P. Bowditch." *The Physiologist* 32, no. 4 (1989): 88–95.

Crenshaw, Ollinger, and William Pusey III. "An American Classical Scholar in Germany, 1874." *American-German Review* 22, no. 6 (August/September 1956): 30–33.

Cunningham, Raymond J. "The German Historical World of Herbert Baxter Adams: 1874–1876." *Journal of American History* 68, no. 2 (September 1981): 261–75.

Curtiss, Samuel Ives. *Franz Delitzsch: A Memorial Tribute*. Edinburgh: T. & T. Clark, 1891.

Czok, Karl, ed. *Geschichte Sachsens*. Weimar: Hermann Böhlaus Nachfolger, 1989.

————. *Wissenschafts- und Universitätsgeschichte in Sachsen im 18. und 19. Jahrhundert*. Berlin: Akademie-Verlag, 1987.

Dabney, Charles William. *Universal Education in the South*. Vol. 1. Chapel Hill: University of North Carolina Press, 1936.

Dallek, Robert. *Democrat and Diplomat: The Life of William E. Dodd*. New York: Oxford University Press, 1968.

Dédéyan, Charles in *L'Année balzacienne*, ed. Michel Lichtle, Nouvelle serie. Paris: PUF, 1997.

Diehl, Carl. *American and German Scholarship, 1770–1870*. New Haven, CT: Yale University Press, 1978.

————. "Innocents Abroad: American Students in German Universities, 1810–1870." *History of Education Quarterly* 16, no. 3 (Fall 1976): 321–41.

Diehl, Karl. "Johannes Konrad." *Jahrbücher für Nationalökonomie und Statistik* CIV, 3rd Series, vol. 49 (June 1915): 753.

Dietze, Walter. *Georg Witkowski (1863–1939)*. Leipzig: Karl-Marx-Universität, 1973.

Dobkin, Marjorie Housepian, ed. *The Making of a Feminist: Early Journals of M. Carey Thomas*. Kent, OH: Kent State University Press, 1979.

Dodd, William E. "Karl Lamprecht and Kulturgeschichte." *Popular Science Monthly* 63 (September 1903): 419–20.

Downer, Harry E. *History of Davenport and Scott County*. Vol. 2. Chicago: S. J. Clarke Publishing, 1910. http://www.celticcousins.net/scott/1910vol2bios25.htm.

Driver, S. R. "Professor Franz Delitzsch." In *The Expository Times*, vol. 1, ed. J. Hastings, 197–201. Edinburgh: T. & T. Clark, October 1889–September 1890.

Drucker, Renate. "Zur Vorgeschichte des Frauenstudiums an der Universität Leipzig. Aktenbericht." In *Vom Mittelalter zur Neuzeit*, ed. Hellmut Kretzschmar, 278–91. Berlin: Rütten & Loening, 1956.

DuBois, W.E.B. *The Autobiography of W.E.B. DuBois; a Soliloquy on Viewing My Life from the Last Decade of Its First Century*. New York: International Publishers, 1968.

Dulles, Eleanor Lansing. *Chances of a Lifetime: A Memoir.* Englewood Cliffs, NJ: Prentice-Hall, 1980.

Dunn, Ernest. *Survey of the Black Experience in America and Abroad.* Dubuque, IA: Kendall/Hunt, 1996.

Durbin, John R. "In Memoriam Milton Wylie Humphreys." http://www.utexas.edu/faculty/council/2000–2001/memorials/AMR/Humphreys/humphreys.html.

Dwight, Henry E. *Travels in the North of Germany, in the Years 1825 and 1826.* New York: G. & C. & H. Carvill, 1829.

Dykhuizen, George. *The Life and Mind of John Dewey.* Carbondale: Southern Illinois University Press, 1973.

Edgerton, Franklin. "Charles Rockwell Lanman." In *The American Philosophical Society Year-book 1941,* 1 January–31 December 1941 (Philadelphia: 1942): 348–86.

Eichler, E. "August Leskiens Wirken für die Slawistik." *Zeitschrift für Slawistik [ZfSl]* 26, no. 2 (1981): 168–91.

Einhauser, Eveline. *Die Junggrammatiker. Ein Problem für die Sprachwissenschaftsgeschichtsschreibung.* Trier: WTV, 1989.

———, ed. *Lieber Freund ... Die Briefe Hermann Osthoffs an Karl Brugmann, 1875–1904.* Trier: WVT, 1992.

Eisenberg, W., et al. *Ernst Heinrich Weber.* Heft 6 der Reiher Synergie Syntropie Nichtlineare Systeme. Leipzig: Verlag im Wissenschaftszentrum, 2000.

Elia, Joseph J., Jr. "Alice Hamilton—1869–1970." *New England Journal of Medicine* 283, no. 18 (29 October 1970): 993–94.

Ellis, Frederick W. "Henry Pickering Bowditch and the Development of the Harvard Laboratory of Physiology." *New England Journal of Medicine* 219, no. 21 (24 November 1938): 819–28.

Ette, Ottmar. *ÜberLebenswissen. Die Aufgabe der Philologie.* Berlin: Kadmos, 2004.

Eulenburg, Franz. *Die Frequenz der deutschen Universitäten von ihrer Gründung bis zur Gegenwart.* Leipzig: Teubner 1904. Reprint Berlin: Akademie Verlag, 1994.

Evans, Stephanie Y. *Black Women in the Ivory Tower, 1850–1954: An Intellectual History.* Gainesville: University Press of Florida, 2007.

Fay, Amy. *Music-Study in Germany.* 2nd ed., rev. and enl. Chicago: Jansen, McClurg & Co., 1881.

Fernberger, Samuel W. "Howard Crosby Warren 1867–1934." *Psychological Bulletin* 31, no. 1 (January 1934): 1–4.

———. "The American Psychological Association. A Historical Summary, 1892–1930." *Psychological Bulletin* 29, no. 1 (January 1932): 1–89.

Ferris, William Henry. *The Black Man in America and Beyond the Seas: Advertising Prospectus for a Book of This Title, with Extracts from It on P. 16–36.* New Haven, CT: s.n, 1912.

Finch, Edith. *Carey Thomas of Bryn Mawr.* New York/London: Harper & Brothers Publishers, 1947.

Fläschendräger, Werner. "Die Universität vom Ausgang des 18. Jahrhunderts bis zur Universitätsreform von 1830." In *Alma Mater Lipsiensis,* ed. Lothar Rathmann, 126–40.

Flexner, Abraham. *The American College; a Criticism.* New York: Century Co., 1908.

———. "The German Side of Medical Education." *Atlantic Monthly* 112 (1913): 654–55.

———. *Medical Education in Europe; a Report to the Carnegie Foundation for the Advancement of Teaching.* New York: 1912.

———. *Medical Education in the United States and Canada; a Report to the Carnegie Foundation for the Advancement of Teaching.* New York: 1910.

———. *Universities. American. English. German.* With a new introduction by Clark Kerr. London: Oxford University Press, 1968 [1930].

Flexner, Helen Thomas. *A Quaker Childhood.* New Haven, CT: Yale University Press, 1940.

Flexner, James Thomas. *An American Saga. The Story of Helen Thomas & Simon Flexner.* New York: Fordham University Press, 1993 [1984].

Flexner, Simon, and James Thomas Flexner. *William Henry Welch and the Heroic Age of American Medicine.* Baltimore: Johns Hopkins University Press, 1993 [1941].

Flügel, Ewald. "III. Die nordamerikanische Literatur." In *Geschichte der englischen Literatur von den ältesten Zeiten bis zur Gegenwart,* Richard Wülker, vol. 2, 2nd rev. and exp. ed., 413–541. Leipzig/Wien: Verlag des Bibliographischen Instituts, 1907.

Franklin, Fabian. *The Life of Daniel Coit Gilman.* New York: Dodd, Mead and Company, 1910.

Freeberg, Ernest. "'More Important Than a Rabble of Common Kings': Dr. Howe's Education of Laura Bridgman." *History of Education Quarterly* 34, no. 3 (Fall 1994): 305–27.

Frevert, Ute. "Die Zukunft der Geschlechterordnung. Diagnosen und Erwartungen an der Jahrhundertwende." In *Das Neue Jahrhundert. Europäische Zeitdiagnosen und Zukunftsentwürfe um 1990,* ed. Ute Frevert. Göttingen: Vandenhoek & Ruprecht, 2000, 146–84.

Friedrich, Karl Josef. *Professor Gregory. Amerikaner, Christ, Volksfreund, deutscher Held.* Gotha: Friedrich Andreas Perthes, 1917.

Frings, Theodor. "Eduard Sievers." *Berichte über die Verhandlungen der Sächsischen Akademie der Wissenschaften zu Leipzig. Philologisch-historische Klasse* 85, no. 1 (1933): 1–36. Reprinted in Sebeok, *Portraits of Linguists,* vol. 2, 1–52.

Frost, Dan R. *Thinking Confederates: Academia and the Idea of Progress in the New South.* Knoxville: University of Tennessee Press, 2000.

Fye, W. Bruce. "Carl Ludwig and the Leipzig Physiological Institute: 'A Factory of New Knowledge.'" *Circulation* 74, no. 5 (November 1986): 920–28.

———. *The Development of American Physiology: Scientific Medicine in the Nineteenth Century.* Baltimore: Johns Hopkins University Press, 1987.

———. "Why a Physiologist?—The Case of Henry P. Bowditch." *Bulletin of the History of Medicine* 56 (1982): 19–29.

Gannon, Jack R. *Deaf Heritage: A Narrative History of Deaf America.* Silver Spring, MD: National Association of the Deaf, 1981.

Geier, Wolfgang, and Harald Homann, eds., *Karl Lamprecht im Kontext. Ein Kolloquium.* Leipzig: Schriften des Instituts für Kulturwissenschaften i.Gr. der Universität Leipzig, 1993.

Geiger, Roger I., ed. *The American College in the Nineteenth Century.* Nashville: Vanderbilt University Press, 2000.

———. "Introduction," and "The Rise and Fall of Useful Knowledge. Higher Education for Science, Agriculture, and the Mechanic Arts, 1850–1875." In *The American College in the 19th Century,* ed. Geiger, 1–36, 153–68.

———. "Southern Higher Education in the 20th Century. Introduction to Volume 19. A Special Issue of the *History of Higher Education.* Editor's Introduction." *History of Higher Education Annual* (1999): 7–24.

Geitz, Henry; Jürgen Heideking, and Jurgen Herbst, eds. *German Influences on Education in the United States to 1917.* Washington, DC: German Historical Institute, and Cambridge: Cambridge University Press, 1995.

Genthe, Martha Krug, and Ellen Churchill Semple. "Tributes to Friedrich Ratzel." *Bulletin (formerly Journal) of the American Geographical Society of New York* 36 (1904): 550–53.

Giauque, W. F. "Gilbert Newton Lewis (1875–1946)." In *The American Philosophical Society. Year Book 1946,* 317–322. Philadelphia: 1947.

Gilbert, James. *Whose Fair? Experience, Memory, and the History of the Great St. Louis Exposition.* Chicago: University of Chicago Press, 2009.

Gilman, Daniel Coit. *The Launching of a University.* New York: Dodd, Mead & Company, 1906.

Glatthaar, Joseph T. *Forged in Battle. The Civil War Alliance of Black Soldiers and White Officers.* Baton Rouge: Louisiana State University Press, 2000.

Goldschmidt, Dietrich. "Historical Interaction Between Higher Education in Germany and in the United States." In *German and American Universities,* ed. Ulrich Teichler and Henry Wasser, 11–33. Werkstadtberichte, vol. 36. Kassel: Wissenschaftliches Zentrum für Berufs- und Hochschulforschung, Gesamthochschule Kassel, 1992.

Goodchild, Lester F., and Margaret M. Miller. "The American Doctorate and Dissertation: Six Development Stages." In *Rethinking the Dissertation Process: Tackling Personal and Institutional Obstacles,* ed. Lester F. Goodchild, Kathy E. Green, Elinor Katz, and Raymond C. Kluever, 17–32. San Francisco: Jossey-Bass Publishers, 1997.

Gürüz, Kemal. *Higher Education and International Student Mobility in the Global Knowledge Economy.* Albany: State University of New York Press, 2008.

Häntzschel, Hiltrud, and Hadumod Bußmann, eds. *Bedrohlich gescheit. Ein Jahrhundert Frauen und Wissenschaft in Bayern.* München: Verlag C. H. Beck, 1997.

Haley, Alex. *The Autobiography of Malcolm X as Told to Alex Haley.* New York: Ballantine Books, 1992 [1964].

Hall, G. Stanley. *Aspects of German Culture.* Boston: James R. Osgood and Company, 1881.

———. *Die Begründer der Modernen Psychologie (Lotze, Fechner, Helmholtz, Wundt),* translated by Raymund Schmidt. Leipzig: Felix Meiner Verlag, 1914.

———. *Life and Confessions of a Psychologist.* New York/London: D. Appleton and Company, 1924.

———. "Philosophy in the United States," *Popular Science Monthly* 1 (1879); no page number given, quoted in Veysey, *The Emergence,* 129.

Hall, Peter Dobkin. "Noah Porter Writ Large? Reflections on the Modernization of American Education and Its Crisis." In *The American College in the Nineteenth Century,* ed. Geiger, 196–220.

Hamilton, Alice. "Edith and Alice Hamilton. Students in Germany." *Atlantic Monthly* 215, no. 3 (March 1965): 129–32.

———. *Exploring the Dangerous Trades.* Boston: Little Brown and Company, 1943.

Hamilton, J. G. de Roulhac. "Southern Members of the Inns of Court." *North Carolina Historical Review* 10, no. 4 (October 1933): 273–86.

Handlin, Lilian. *George Bancroft. The Intellectual as Democrat* (New York: Harper & Row, 1984).

Hammer, Carl, Jr. "John T. Krumpelmann." In *Studies in German Literature,* ed. Carl Hammer, Jr. Baton Rouge: Louisiana State University Press, 1963.

Hansel, Karl, and Christa Pludra, eds. "Die Vorbereitung des Harvard-Aufenthaltes Wilhelm Ostwalds." *Mitteilungen der Wilhelm-Ostwald-Gesellschaft zu Großbothen e.V.* 6, no. 1 (2001): 27–43.

Hart, James Morgan. *German Universities. A Narrative of Personal Experience.* New York: G. P. Putnam's Sons, 1874. Reprinted London: Routledge/Thoemmes Press, 1994.

Heinze, Andrew R. *Jews and the American Soul: Human Nature in the Twentieth Century.* Princeton, NJ: Princeton University Press, 2004.

Hellenbrand, Harold. *The Unfinished Revolution. Education and Politics in the Thought of Thomas Jefferson.* Newark: University of Delaware Press and London/Toronto: Associated University Press, 1990.

Hendrick, Burton J. *The Training of an American: The Earlier Life and Letters of Walter H. Page 1855–1913.* Boston and New York: Houghton Mifflin Company, 1928.

Herbst, Jurgen. "Francis Greenwood Peabody: Harvard's Theologian of the Social Gospel." *Harvard Theological Review* 5 (1961): 45–69.

———. *The German Historical School in American Scholarship*. Ithaca, NY: Cornell University Press, 1965.

Herget, Winfried. "Overcoming the 'Mortifying Distance': American Impressions of German Universities in the Nineteenth and Early Twentieth Centuries." In *Transatlantische Partnerschaft. Kulturelle Aspekte der deutsch-amerikanischen Beziehungen*, ed. Dieter Gutzen, Winfried Herget, and Hans-Adolf Jacobsen, 195–208. Bonn: Bouvier, 1992.

Hinsdale, Burke A. "Chapter XIII. Notes on the History of Foreign Influence upon Education in the United States." In *United States Bureau of Education. Report of the Commissioner of Education for the Year 1897–98*, vol. 1, 591–629. Washington: Government Printing Office, 1899.

Hirschberg, Walter, ed. *Neues Wörterbuch der Völkerkunde*. Berlin: Dietrich Reimer Verlag, 1988.

His, Wilhelm, Jr. *Wilhelm His der Anatom. Ein Lebensbild von Wilhelm His*. Berlin/Wien: Urban und Schwarzenberg, 1931.

Hobsbawm, Eric. *The Age of Empire*. New York: Vintage Books, 1987.

Hochbaum, Elfrieda. *Burning Arrows*. Boston: Bruce Humphries Publishers, 1963.

Hörz, Herbert. *Physiologie und Kultur in der zweiten Hälfte des 19. Jahrhunderts. Briefe an Herman von Helmholtz*. Marburg/Lahn: Basilisken-Presse, 1994.

Hofstetter, Rita, and Bernard Schneuwly, eds. *Passion, Fusion, Tension: New Education and Educational Sciences: End 19th–Middle 20th Century = éducation nouvelle et sciences de l'éducation: fin du 19e–milieu du 20e siècle*. Bern: Peter Lang, 2006.

Holmes, Oliver Wendell. *One Hundred Days in Europe*. Works vol. 10. Boston: Houghton, Mifflin, 1891.

Horowitz, Helen Lefkowitz. *The Power and Passion of M. Carey Thomas*. New York: Alfred A. Knopf, 1994.

Howe, Julia Ward. *Sex and Education: A Reply to Dr. E. H. Clarke's "Sex in Education."* Boston: Roberts Brothers, 1874.

Hoyer, Siegfried. "Studenten aus dem zaristischen Russland an der Uniersität Leipzig 1870/ 1914." In *Recht—Idee—Geschichte. Beiträge zur Rechts- und Ideengeschichte*, ed. Heiner Lück and Bernd Schildt, 431–49. Köln/Weimar/Wien: Böhlau Verlag, 2000.

Hugo, Markus M. "'Uncle Sam I Cannot Stand, for Spain I Have No Sympathy': An Analysis of Discourse About the Spanish-American War in Imperial Germany, 1898–1899," in *European Perceptions of the Spanish-American War of 1898*, ed. Sylvia L. Hilton and Steve J. S. Ickringill. Bern: Peter Lang, 1999, 71–91.

Immatrikulations und Disziplinar-Ordnung für die Studierenden der Universität Leipzig vom 8. März 1903. Leipzig: Alexander Edelmann, 1903.

Jacobs, Wilbur R. *The Historical World of Frederick Jackson Turner. With Selections from His Correspondence*. New Haven, CT: Yale University Press, 1968.

Jaffé, George. "Recollections of Three Great Laboratories." *Journal of Chemical Engineering* 29 (1952): 230–38.

James, Henry [William James' eldest son]. *Charles W. Elliot*. Boston/New York: Houghton Mifflin Company, 1930.

Jarausch, Konrad. "American Students in Germany, 1815–1914: The Structure of German and U.S. Matriculations at Göttingen University." In *German Influences*, ed. Geitz et al., 195–211.

———. *Students, Society, and Politics in Imperial Germany. The Rise of Academic Illiberalism*. Princeton, NJ: Princeton University Press, 1982.

———. *Deutsche Studenten, 1800–1970*. Frankfurt a./M.: Suhrkamp, 1984.

Jaritz, Peter. *Sprachwissenschaft und Psychologie. Begründungsprobleme der Sprachwissenschaft im ausgehenden 19. und beginnenden 20. Jahrhundert.* Serie OBST, no. 10. Habilitationsschrift 1988; Osnabrück: Universität, 1990.

Jastrow, Joseph. "Experimental Psychology in Leipzig." *Science* 8, no. 198 (19 November 1886): 459–62.

Jeffries, Benjamin Joy. "Letter to the Editor [on Professor Ludwig]." *Boston Medical and Surgical Journal* 82 (1870): 421.

Jeismann, Karl-Heinz. "American Observations Concerning the Prussian Educational System in the Nineteenth Centrury." In *German Influences*, ed. Geitz et al., 21–41.

Jensen, William B. "Harry Jones Meets the Famous." *Bulletin for the History of Chemistry* 7 (Fall 1990): 26–33.

Joas, Hans. *G. H. Mead. A Contemporary Re-Examination of His Thought.* Translated by Raymond Meyer. Cambridge, MA: MIT Press, 1997.

Johnson, R. J., Derek Gregory, and David M. Smith, eds. *The Dictionary of Human Geography.* 3rd ed. Cambridge, MA: Blackwell, 1994.

Kallen, Horace M. "Julian William Mack, 1866–1943." *American Jewish Year Book* 46 (18 September 1944 to 7 September 1945): 35–46.

Kaplan, Justin. *Lincoln Steffens. A Biography.* New York: Simon and Schuster, 1974.

Karl Baedeker 1827–1927 (Leipzig: Breikopf & Härtel, 1927).

Keil, Hartmut. "Immigrant Neighborhoods and American Society. German Immigrants on Chicago's Northwestern Side in the Late 19th Century." In *German Workers' Culture in the United States 1850–1920*, ed. Hartmut Keil, 25–58. Washington, DC: Smithsonian Institution Press, 1988.

Kelley, Brooks Mather. *Yale: A History.* New Haven, CT: Yale University Press, 1974.

Kersten, H. *Die Frau und das Universitätsstudium.* Stuttgart: 1892.

Keys, Frederick G. *Arthur Becket Lamb 1880–1952. A Biographical Memoir.* National Academy of Sciences by Columbia University Press. Reprinted from *Biographical Memoirs of the National Academy of Sciences* (1956): 201–34.

Koenen, Erik. "Verzeichnis der Hochschulschriften." In *Karl Bücher*, ed. Koenen and Meyen, 49–121.

———, and Michael Meyen, eds. *Karl Bücher. Leipziger Hochschulschriften 1892–1926.* Leipzig: Universitätsverlag, 2002.

Koestler, Frances A. *The Unseen Minority: A Social History of Blindness in the United States.* New York: AFB Press, 2005 [1976].

Koslowski, Peter, ed. *The Theory of Ethical Economy in the Historical School. Wilhelm Roscher, Lorenz von Stein, Gustav Schmoller, Wilhelm Dilthey and Contemporary Theory.* Berlin: Springer-Verlag, 1995.

Krakau, Knud. "Einführende Überlegungen zur Entstehung und Wirkung von Bildern, die sich Nationen von sich und anderen machen." *Deutschland und Amerika. Perzeption und historische Realität*, ed. Willi Paul Adams and Knud Krakau. Berlin: Colloquium Verlag, 1985.

Krause, Konrad. *Alma Mater Lipsiensis. Geschichte der Universität Leipzig von 1409 bis zur Gegenwart.* Leipzig: Universitätsverlag, 2003.

Krumpelmann, John T. "The American Students of Heidelberg University 1830–1870." In *Jahrbuch für Americastudien*, vol. 14, ed. Ernst Fraenkel, Hans Galinsky, Eberhard Kessel, Ursula Brumm, and H.-J. Lang, 167–84. Heidelberg: Carl Winter Universitätsverlag, 1969.

———. *Southern Scholars in Goethe's Germany.* Chapel Hill: University of North Carolina Press, 1965.

Lachman, Arthur. *Borderland of the Unknown: The Life Story of Gilbert Newton Lewis, One of the World's Great Scientists.* New York: Pageant Press, 1955.

Lamberti, Georg. *Wilhelm Maximilian Wundt (1832–1920)*. Bonn: Deutscher Psychologen Verlag, 1995.

Lane, Harlan. *When the Mind Hears. A History of the Deaf*. London: Penguin, 1988 [1984].

Langfeld, H. S. "Howard Crosby Warren: 1867–1934." *American Journal of Psychology* 46, no. 2 (1934): 340–42.

Large, Andrew. *The Artificial Language Movement*. Oxford: Blackwell, 1985.

Lea, Elisabeth, und Gerald Wiemers. "Eine Sächsische Gesellschaft der Wissenschaften 'zum Flor und Ruhme unserer Universität.'" In *Wissenschafts- und Universitätsgeschichte*, ed. Karl Czok, 185–206.

LeDuc, Thomas H. "German Influences at Amherst." *Amherst Graduate Quarterly* (May 1940): 205–10.

———. *Piety and Intellect at Amherst College. 1865–1912*. New York: Columbia University Press, 1946.

Lee, Frederic S. "Carl Ludwig." *Science* 1, no. 23 (Friday, 7 June 1895): 630–32.

Legaré, Hugh Swinton. *The Writings of Hugh Swinton Legaré [...] Prefaced by a Memoir of his Life [...] Edited by his Sister*. Vol. 1. Charleston, SC: Burges & James, 1846.

Lewis, Frederic T. "Charles Sedgwick Minot." *Anatomical Record* 10, no. 3 (20 January 1916): 133–64.

———. "Obituary. Charles Sedgwick Minot. December 23, 1852–November 19, 1914." *Boston Medical and Surgical Journal* 171, no. 24 (10 December 1914): 911–14.

Lewis, Sinclair. *Arrowsmith*. New York: Signet Classic, 1998 [1925].

Lindberg, David C. *The Beginnings of Western Science: The European Scientific Tradition in Philosophical, Religious, and Institutional Contexts, 600 B.C. to A.D. 1450*. Chicago: University of Chicago Press, 1992.

Lippmann, Walter. *Public Opinion*. New York: Simon & Schuster, 1965 [1922].

Lischke, Ralph-Jürgen. *Friedrich Althoff und sein Beitrag zur Entwicklung des Berliner Wissenschaftssystems an der Wende vom 19. zum 20. Jahrhundert*. Berlin: ERS Verlag, 1991.

Lombard, Warren P. "The Life and Work of Carl Ludwig." *Science* 44, no. 1133 (15 September 1916): 363–75.

Long, Orie William. *Literary Pioneers: Early American Explorers of European Culture*. New York: Gordon Press, 1975 [1935].

Lord, Louis E. *A History of the American School of Classical Studies at Athens. 1882–1942*. Cambridge, MA: Harvard University Press, 1947.

Lucas, Christopher J. *American Higher Education. A History*. 2nd ed. New York: Palgrave Macmillan, 2006 [1994].

Malone, Dumas. *Jefferson & His Time. Volume 6. The Sage of Monticello*. Charlottesville: University of Virginia Press, 1981.

Marquardt, Hertha. "Die ersten Amerikanischen Studenten an der Universität Göttingen." In *Göttinger Jahrbuch 1955/56*, 23–33. Göttingen: Heinz Reise Verlag, 1956.

Marsden, George M. *The Soul of the American University: From Protestant Establishment to Established Nonbelief*. New York: Oxford University Press, 1994.

Martin, Jay. *The Education of John Dewey: A Biography*. New York: Columbia University Press, 2002.

Mason, C. W. "Wilder Dwight Bancroft 1867–1953." *Journal of the American Chemical Society* 76, no. 10 (26 May 1954): 2601–2.

Matthiessen, F. O. *The James Family: A Group Biography, Together with Selections from the Writings of Henry James Senior, William, Henry and Alice James*. New York: Vintage Books, 1974 [1947].

Mazón, Patricia. "Die Auswahl der 'besseren Elemente.' Ausländische und jüdische Studentinnen und die Zulassung von Frauen an deutschen Universitäten 1890–1909." *Jahrbuch für*

Universitätsgeschichte, vol. 5, ed. Rüdiger vom Bruch, transl. Axel Fair-Schulz, 185–98. Stuttgart: Franz Steiner Verlag, 2002.

———. *Gender and the Modern Research University: The Admission of Women to German Higher Education, 1865–1914*. Stanford, CA: Stanford University Press, 2003.

MacDonald, Arthur. "A Short Auto-Biography." *Indian Medical Record 55* (January 1935): 23–32.

McClelland, Charles E. *State, Society, and University in Germany 1700–1914*. Cambridge: Cambridge University Press, 1980.

McCullough, David. *The Greater Journey: Americans in Paris*. New York: Simon & Schuster, 2011.

McReynolds, Paul. *Lightner Witmer: His Life and Times*. Washington, DC: American Psychological Association, 1997.

Mertens, Lothar. *Vernachlässigte Töchter der Alma Mater*. Sozialwissenschaftliche Schriften, Heft 20. Berlin: Duncker & Humblot, 1991.

Miller, Walter. "Necrology Overbeck." *American Journal of Archaeology* 11, no. 3 (July–September 1896): 361–70.

Milligan, W. O., ed. *Proceedings of the Robert A. Welch Foundation. Conferences on Chemical Research*. Houston, TX: 1977.

Mims, Edwin. *Chancellor Kirkland of Vanderbilt*. Nashville, TN: Vanderbilt University Press, 1940.

Minot, C. S. "Henry Pickering Bowditch," *Science* 33, no. 851 (21 April 1911): 598–601.

Mitchell, Martha. *Encyclopedia Brunoniana*. Providence, RI: 1993. http://www.brown.edu/Administration/News_Bureau/Databases/Encyclopedia/search.php?serial=C0760, http://www.brown.edu/Administration/News_Bureau/Databases/Encyclopedia/search.php?serial=M0410.

Mitteilungen der Wilhelm-Ostwald-Gesellschaft zu Großbothen e.V. 2, no. 1 (1997); 2, no. 3 (1997); 3, no. 4 (1998); 4, no. 2 (1999); 5, no. 4 (2000); 7. no. 2 (2002). [Ostwald student lists.]

Möbius, Paul Julius. *Ueber den physiologischen Schwachsinn des Weibes*. Halle: Verlag von Carl Marhold, 1900.

Monaghan, Leila Frances. "A World's Eye View: Deaf Cultures in Global Perspective." In *Many Ways to Be Deaf*, ed. Leila Frances Monaghan et al., 1–24. Washington, DC: Gallaudet University Press, 2003.

Monaghan, Leila Frances, et al., eds. *Many Ways to Be Deaf*. Washington, DC: Gallaudet University Press, 2003.

Morgenthau III, Henry. *Mostly Morgenthaus: A Family History*. New York: Ticknor & Fields, 1991.

Morrison, Toni. *Playing in the Dark. Whiteness and the Literary Imagination*. London: Picador, 1993 [1992].

Moss, Hilary J. *Schooling Citizens: The Struggle for African American Education in Antebellum America*. Chicago: University of Chicago Press, 2009.

Mühlpfordt, Günter. "Die 'Sächsischen Universitäten' Leipzig, Jena, Halle und Wittenberg als Vorhut der deutschen Aufklärung." In *Wissenschafts- und Universitätsgeschichte*, ed. Karl Czok, 25–50.

Nash, Paul. "Innocents Abroad: American Students at British Universities in the Early Nineteenth Century." *History of Education Quarterly* 1, no. 2 (June 1961): 32–44.

Neubert-Drobisch, Walther. *Moritz Wilhelm Drobisch. Ein Gelehrtenleben*. Leipzig: Dieterich'sche Verlagsbuchhandlung Theodor Weicher, 1902.

Novick, Peter. *That Noble Dream: The "Objectivity Question" and the American Historical Profession*. Cambridge: Cambridge University Press, 1988.

Nye, Russel B. *George Bancroft*. New York: Twayne Publishers, 1964.

Oleson, Alexandra, and John Voss, eds. *The Organization of Knowledge in Modern America, 1860–1920*. Baltimore: Johns Hopkins University Press, 1979.

Olin, Stephen. *Inaugural Address, 5 March 1834*. Quoted in Scanlon, *Randolph-Macon College*.

Oriol, Philippe. *L'affaire du capitaine Dreyfus, 1894–1897*. Paris: Stock, 2008.

Osborne, Elizabeth A., ed. *From the Letter-Files of S. W. Johnson*. New Haven, CT: Yale University Press, 1913.

Ostwald, Wilhelm. *Lebenslinien. Eine Selbstbiographie*. 3 vols. Berlin: Klasing & Co., 1926–1927.

Parker, George Howard. *The World Expands: Recollections of a Zoologist*. Cambridge, MA: Harvard University Press, 1946.

Parshall, Karen Hunger, and David E. Rowe. *The Emergence of the American Mathematical Research Community 1876–1900: J. J. Sylvester, Felix Klein, and E. H. Moore*. Providence, RI: American Mathematical Society/London Mathematical Society, 1994 [1991].

Patrick, George Thomas White. *An Autobiography*. Iowa City: University of Iowa Press, 1947.

Patrick, Mary Mills. *Under Five Sultans*. London: Williams and Norgate, 1930.

Pauling, Linus. "Arthur Amos Noyes." In *Proceedings*, ed. W. O. Milligan, 88–102.

Peabody, Francis Greenwood. *Reminiscences of Present-Day Saints*. Boston and New York: Houghton Mifflin Company, 1927.

Perry, Lewis. *Intellectual Life in America: A History*. Chicago: University of Chicago Press, 1984/1989.

Pickus, Keith H. *Constructing Modern Identities: Jewish University Students in Germany; 1815–1914*. Detroit: Wayne State University Press, 1999.

Pierson, Mary Bynum. *Graduate Work in the South, Published under the Sponsorship of the Conference of Deans of Southern Graduate Schools*. Chapel Hill: University of North Carolina Press, 1947.

Pochmann, Henry A. *German Culture in America: Philosophical and Literary Influences, 1600–1900*. Madison: University of Wisconsin Press, 1957.

Porter, W. T. "Charles Sedgwick Minot, M.D." *Boston Medical and Surgical Journal* 172. no. 13 (1 April 1915): 467–70.

Potter, David M. "The Enigma of the South." *Yale Review* 51 (October 1961): 142–51.

Potts, David B. "Curriculum and Enrollment. Assessing the Popularity of Antebellum Colleges." In *The American College in the Nineteenth Century*, ed. Geiger, 37–45.

———. *Liberal Education for a Land of Colleges: Yale's Reports of 1828* (New York: Palgrave Macmillan, 2010).

Prokosch, Eduard. "Hermann Collitz." *Journal of English and Germanic Philology* 35 (1936): 454–57. Reprinted in Sebeok, *Portraits of Linguists*, vol. 2, 74–77.

Radcliffe, Kendahl, Jennifer Scott, and Anja Werner, eds. *Black Intellectuals: The Atlantic World and Beyond*. Jackson: University of Mississippi Press, forthcoming.

Raphelson, Alfred C. "Lincoln Steffens at the Leipzig Psychological Institute, 1890–1891." *Journal of the History of the Behavioral Sciences* 3, no. 1 (January 1967): 38–42.

Rathmann, Lothar, ed. *Alma Mater Lipsiensis. Geschichte der Karl-Marx-Universität Leipzig*. Leipzig: Edition Leipzig, 1984.

Ratzel, Friedrich. *Die Vereinigten Staaten von Amerika*. München: Oldenbourg, 1878–1880. [A 2nd ed. was published in 1893 as *Politische Geographie der Vereinigten Staaten von Amerika*.]

———. *Völkerkunde*. 3 vols. Leipzig: Bibliograph. Institut, 1885, 1886, 1888.

Reid, Doris Fielding. *Edith Hamilton. An Intimate Portrait*. New York: W. W. Norton & Company, 1967.

Reid, Joseph J. "Minority Student Participation in International Study Abroad Programs: A Family Perspective." MS Thesis, East Carolina University, 1995.

Reinach, Joseph, and Pierre Vidal-Naquet. *Histoire de l'affaire Dreyfus*. Bouquins. Paris: Éditions Robert Laffont, 2006 [1900].

Rektor and Senate of Leipzig University, eds. *Festschrift zur Feier des 500 Jährigen Bestehens der Universität Leipzig*. Vol. 4, pts. 1 + 2. Leipzig: Verlag von S. Hirzel, 1909.

Reports on the Course of Instruction in Yale College. New Haven, CT: Hezekiah Hower, 1828. http://www.yale.edu/yale300/collectiblesandpublications/specialdocuments/Historical_Documents/1828_curriculum.pdf.

Reports on the Course of Instruction in Yale College, Part II: "Liberal Education and the Classical Curriculum." http://collegiateway.org/reading/yale-report-1828/curriculum.

Retallack, James N. *Saxony in German History: Culture, Society, and Politics, 1830–1933*. Ann Arbor: University of Michigan Press, 2000.

Ribbeck, Emma, ed. *Otto Ribbeck. Ein Bild seines Lebens aus seinen Briefen 1846–1898*. Stuttgart: Cotta'sche Buchhandlung Nachfolger, 1901.

Richards, Robert J. "The Linguistic Creation of Man: Charles Darwin, August Schleicher, Ernst Haeckel, and the Missing Link in Nineteenth-Century Evolutionary Theory." *Experimenting in Tongues: Studies in Science and Language*, ed. Matthias Doerres. Stanford, CA: Stanford University Press, 2002.

———. *The Romantic Conception of Life: Science and Philosophy in the Age of Goethe*. Chicago: University of Chicago Press, 2002/04.

Richardson, Henry Handel. *Maurice Guest*. London: Virago, 1981 [1908].

Richter, A. "100 Jahre deutsche Slawistik, Teil VII. Deutsche Slawisten sowie Vertreter anderer Philologien in ihren Beziehungen zu dem neuen Leipziger Lehrstuhl." *Wissenschaftliche Zeitschrift der TH Magdeburg* 15, no. 5 (1971): 531–50.

Ringer, Fritz K. *The Decline of the German Mandarins: The German Academic Community, 1890–1933*. Cambridge, MA: Harvard University Press, 1969.

———. "The German Universities and the Crisis of Learning, 1918–1932." PhD dissertation, Harvard University, 1960.

———. "The German Academic Community." In *The Organization of Knowledge in Modern America, 1860–1920*, ed. Alexandra Oleson and John Voss, 409–29. Baltimore: Johns Hopkins University Press, 1979.

Rodgers, Daniel T. *Atlantic Crossings: Social Politics in a Progressive Age*. Cambridge, MA: Belknap Press of Harvard University Press, 1998.

Roizen, Ron. "E.M. Jellinek and All That! A Brief Look Back at the Origins of Post-Repeal Alcohol Science in the United States." http://www.roizen.com/ron/jellinek-pres.htm.

———. "Ranes Report: Roizen's Alcohol News & Editorial Service. RR #11: Jellinek's Phantom Doctorate." http://www.roizen.com/ron/rr11.htm.

Roosevelt, Theodore. *Rough Riders*. 1899.

Rosen, George. "Carl Ludwig and his American Students." *Bulletin of the Institute of the History of Medicine* (Johns Hopkins University) 4, no. 8 (October 1936): 609–49.

Rosenberg, Matt T. "Ellen Churchill Semple. America's First Influential Female Geographer." http://geography.about.com/library/weekly/aa022301a.htm.

Rosenzweig, Saul. *Freud, Jung, and Hall the King-Maker. The Historic Expedition to America with G. Stanley Hall as Host and William James as Guest*. Seattle/Toronto/Bern/Göttingen: Rana House Press St. Louis, 1992.

Ross, Dorothy. *G. Stanley Hall: The Psychologist as Prophet*. Chicago: University of Chicago Press, 1972.

Rossiter, Margaret W. *Women Scientists in America: Struggles and Strategies to 1940*. Baltimore: Johns Hopkins University Press, 1982.

Rudolph, Emmanuel D. "How It Developed that Botany Was the Science Thought Most Suitable for Victorian Young Ladies." *Children's Literature* 2 (1973): 92–97.

Rudolph, Frederick. *The American College & University: A History*. 1962; Athens: University of Georgia Press, 1990.

Růžička, Rudolf. "Historie und Historizität der Junggrammatiker." In *Sitzungsberichte der Sächsischen Akademie der Wissenschaften zu Leipzig* 119, no. 3. Berlin: Akademie Verlag, 1977.

Sabin, Florence Rena. "Dr. Franklin P. Mall: An Appreciation." *Science* 47, no. 1211 (15 March 1918): 249–61.

———. *Franklin Paine Mall: The Story of a Mind*. Baltimore: Johns Hopkins Press, 1934.

Salmond, S.D.F. "Franz Delitzsch: The Tribute of a Friend and Pupil." In *The Expository Times*, vol. 1, ed. J. Hastings, 201–03. Edinburgh: T. & T. Clark, October 1889–September 1890.

Sandys, John Edwin. *A History of Classical Scholarship. The Eighteenth Century in Germany, and the Nineteenth Century in Europe and the United States of America*. Vol. 3. Cambridge: Cambridge University Press, 1908.

Scanlon, James Edward. *Randolph-Macon College. A Southern History. 1825–1967*. Charlottesville: University of Virginia Press, 1983.

Schaff, Philip. *Germany; Its Universities, Theology, and Religion*. Philadelphia: Lindsay and Blakiston/New York: Sheldon, Blakeman & Co., 1857.

Schlimpert, G. "August Leskien im Lichte seiner Briefe an Karl Brugmann." *Zeitschrift für Slawistik [ZfSl]* 26, no. 2 (1981): 216–21.

Schlimpert, G., and R. Eckert. "Briefe Leskiens an Karl Brugmann." *Zeitschrift für Slawistik [ZfSl]* 26, no. 2 (1981): 222–38.

Schorn-Schütte, Luise. *Karl Lamprecht. Kulturgeschichtsschreibung zwischen Wissenschaft und Politik*. Göttingen: Vandenhoek & Ruprecht, 1984.

———. "Kulturgeschichte als Aufklärungswissenschaft. Karl Lamprecht's Bemühungen zur Reform der historischen Bildung im Kontext der internationalen Reformbewegung an der Jahrhundertwende." In *Transformation des Historismus. Wissenschaftsorganisation und Bildungspolitik vor dem Ersten Weltkrieg*, ed. Horst Walter Blank, 64–84. Waltrop: Hartmut Spenner, 1994.

Schröer, Heinz. *Carl Ludwig. Begründer der messenden Experimentalphysiologie*. Stuttgart: Wissenschaftliche Verlagsgesellschaft M.B.H., 1967.

"Die Schüler Wilhelm Pfeffers und ihre in den botanischen Instituten zu Tübingen und Leipzig unter seiner Leitung ausgeführten oder auf seine Anregung begonnenen Arbeiten." *Jahrbücher für wissenschaftliche Botanik* 56 (1915): 805–32.

Sebeok, Thomas A. *Portraits of Linguists. A Biographical Source for the History of Western Linguistics, 1746–1963. Vol. 1. From Sir William Jones to Karl Brugmann*. Bristol: Thoemmes Press, 2002 [1966].

———. *Portraits of Linguists. A Biographical Source for the History of Western Linguistics, 1746–1963. Vol. 2. From Eduard Sievers to Benjamin Lee Whorf*. Bristol: Thoemmes Press, 2002 [1966].

Servos, John W. *Physical Chemistry from Ostwald to Pauling: The Making of a Science in America*. Princeton, NY: Princeton University Press, 1990.

———. "A Disciplinary Program That Failed: Wilder D. Bancroft and the Journal of Physical Chemistry, 1896–1933." *ISIS* 74 (1982): 207–32.

Shumway, Daniel Bussey. "The American Students of the University of Göttingen." *Americana Germanica* (University of Pennsylvania) 8, no. 5/6 (September–December 1910): 171–254.

Sichermann, Barbara. *Alice Hamilton: A Life in Letters*. Cambridge, MA: Harvard University Press, 1984.

Sievers, Eduard. "Zarncke." In *Allgemeine Deutsche Biographie*, vol. 44, 700–706. Leipzig: Verlag von Duncker & Humblot, 1898.

Singer, Sandra L. *Adventures Abroad: North American Women at German-Speaking Universities, 1868–1915*. Contributions in Women's Studies 201. Westport, CT: Praeger, 2003.

Sloan, Douglas. *The Scottish Enlightenment and the American College Ideal*. New York: Teachers College Press, Columbia University, 1971.

Smith, Shirley W. *James Burrill Angell: An American Influence*. Ann Arbor: University of Michigan Press, 1954.

Sokal, Michael M., ed. *An Education in Psychology: James McKeen Cattell's Journal and Letters from Germany and England, 1880–1888*. Cambridge, MA: MIT Press, 1981.

———. "Biographical Approach: The Psychological Career of Edward Wheeler Scripture." *Historiography of Modern Psychology. Aims. Resources. Approaches*, ed. Josef Brozek and Judwig J. Pongratz. Toronto: C. J. Hogrefe, 1980, 255–78.

"Some Scientific Centres. I.—The Leipzig Chemical Laboratory." *Nature* 64 (June 6, 1901): 127–29. Ed. Sir Norman Lockyer.

Staël, Madame de. *De l'Allemagne*. Vol. 1. Paris: GF Flammarion, 1968 [1810].

Stagl, Justin. "Ratzel." In *Neues Wörterbuch der Völkerkunde*, ed. Hirschberg, 329.

———. "Wundt." In *Neues Wörterbuch der Völkerkunde*, ed. Hirschberg, 527.

Steffens, Josephine Bontecou. *Letitia Berkeley, A.M.* New York: A. Stokes Company, 1899.

Steffens, Lincoln. *The Autobiography of Lincoln Steffens, Complete in One Volume*. New York: Harcourt, Brace and Company, 1931.

Stein, Gertrude. *The Autobiography of Alice B. Toklas*. New York: Vintage Books, 1990 [1933].

Strong, Michael. *Language Learning and Deafness*, 4th printing. Cambridge: Cambridge University Press: 1995 [1987].

Strøm, Elin. *Sophus Lie 1842–1899*. Oslo: University of Oslo, printed at Godfreds trykkeri, 1992.

Streck, Bernhard. "Wilhelm Maximilian Wundt." In *Hauptwerke der Ethnologie*, ed. Christian F. Feest and Karl-Heinz Kohl, 524–31. Stuttgardt: Alfred Kröner Verlag, 2001.

Stevenson, Louise L. *Scholarly Means to Evangelical Ends: The New Haven Scholars and the Transformation of Higher Learning in America, 1830–1890*. Baltimore: Johns Hopkins University Press, 1986.

Stubhaug, Arild. *The Mathematician Sophus Lie: It Was the Audacity of My Thinking*, translated from the Norwegian by Richard H. Daly. Berlin, New York: Springer, 2002 [2000].

Student. "Women at the German Universities." *The Nation* 58, no. 1498 (15 March 1894): 193–94.

Super, Charles W. "German Degrees." *The Nation* 98, no. 2531 (1 January 1914): 9.

Thelin, John R. *A History of American Higher Education*. Baltimore: Johns Hopkins University Press, 2004.

Thwing, Charles Franklin. *The American and the German University*. New York: Macmillan, 1928.

———. *The College of the Future: An Address Delivered at the Commencement of Miami University, June 7th, 1897*. Cleveland, OH: Williams Publishing and Electric Co., 1897.

Ticknor, Anna, George Ticknor, Thomas Adam, and Gisela Mettele, *Two Boston Brahmins in Goethe's Germany: The Travel Journals of Anna and George Ticknor*. Lanham, MD: Lexington Books, 2009.

Ticknor, George. *Life, Letters, and Journals of George Ticknor*. 2 vols. London: Sampson Low, Marston, Searle, & Rivington, 1876.

Tinker, Miles A. "Wundt's Doctorate Students and Their Theses 1875–1920." *Wundt Studies*, ed. Bringmann and Tweney, 269–79.

Tischner, Wolfgang. "Das Universitätsjubiläum 1909 zwischen universitärer Selbstvergewisserung und monarchischer Legitimitätsstiftung." In *Sachsens Landesuniversität in Monarchie, Republik und Diktatur. Beiträge zur Geschichte der Universität Leipzig vom Kaiserreich bis zur Auflösung des Landes Sachsen 1952*, ed. Ulrich Von Hehl, 95–114. Beiträge zur Leipziger Universitäts- und Wissenschaftsgeschichte (BLUWiG) A 3. Leipzig: Evangelische Verlagsanstalt, 2005.

Titze, Hartmut. *Der Akademikerzyklus: historische Untersuchungen über die Wiederkehr von Überfüllung und Mangel in akademischen Karrieren*. Göttingen: Vandenhoeck & Ruprecht, 1990.

Tobies, Renate. "Mathematikerinnen und ihre Doktorväter." In *Aller Männerkultur zum Trotz. Frauen in Mathematik und Naturwissenschaften*, ed. Renate Tobies, 131–58. Frankfurt: Campus Verlag: 1997.

Todte, Mario. *Georg Voigt (1827–1891). Pionier der historischen Humanismusforschung*. Leipzig: Universitätsverlag, 2004.

Tewksbury, Donald G. *The Founding of American Colleges and Universities Before the Civil War. With Particular Reference to the Religious Influences Bearing Upon the College Movement*. Hamden, CT: Archon Books, 1965 [1932].

Tourgée, Albion Winegar. *A Fool's Errand*. 1879.

Troup, G. Elmslie. "Franz Delitzsch." In *The Expository Times*, vol. 1, ed. J. Hastings, 174–77. Edinburgh: T. & T. Clark, October 1889–September 1890.

Trow, Martin. "American Higher Education–Past, Present and Future." *Studies in Higher Education* 14, no. 1 (1989): 5–22.

Tuchman, Arleen. *Science, Medicine, and the State in Germany: The Case of Baden, 1815–1871*. New York: Oxford University Press, 1993.

Turner, Frederick Jackson. "The Significance of the Frontier in American History." In *The Frontier in American History*. New York: Henry Holt, 1920 [1893].

Turner, James, and Paul Bernard. "The German Model and the Graduate School: The University of Michigan and the Origin Myth of the American University." In *The American College in the Nineteenth Century*, ed. Geiger, 221–41.

Üner, Elfriede. *Kultur- und Universalgeschichte an der Schwelle der Zeiten. Exemplarische Entwicklungslinien der Leipziger Schule in den deutschen Sozial- und Geschichtswissenschaften*. Leipzig: Karl-Lamprecht-Gesellschaft e.V., 1993.

Van Cleve, John Vickrey, and Barry A. Crouch. *A Place of Their Own: Creating the Deaf Community in America*. Washington, DC: Gallaudet University Press, 1990 [1989].

Veysey, Laurence R. *The Emergence of the American University*. Chicago: University of Chicago Press, 1965.

Wagner, Siegfried. *Franz Delitzsch*. München: Kaiser, 1978.

Wagner-Hasel, Beate. *Die Arbeit des Gelehrten: Der Nationalökonom Karl Bücher (1847–1930)*. Frankfurt am Main: Campus, 2011.

Wagoner, Jr. Jennings L. *Jefferson and Education*. Charlottesville, VA: Thomas Jefferson Foundation; Chapel Hill, NC: Distributed by University of North Carolina Press, 2004.

Walker, Corey D. B. "'Of the Coming of John [and Jane]': African American Intellectuals in Europe, 1888–1938." *American Studies Quarterly* 47, no. 1 (2002): 7–22.

Walter, H. "Schüler Leskiens aus dem Südslawischen Bereich." *Zeitschrift für Slawistik [ZfSl]* 26, no. 2 (1981): 192–98.

Wanklyn, Harriet Grace. *Friedrich Ratzel*. Cambridge: Cambridge University Press, 1961.

Ware, Lowry Price. "The Academic Career of William E. Dodd." PhD dissertation, University of South Carolina, 1956.

Warren, Howard Crosby. "Autobiography." *A History of Psychology in Autobiography*, vol. 2, ed. Carl Murchison, 443–69. Worcester, MA: Clark University Press, 1932.

Warren, Jonathan Mason, John Collins Warren, and Russell M. Jones. *The Parisian Education of an American Surgeon: Letters of Jonathan Mason Warren, 1832–1835.* Philadelphia: American Philosophical Society, 1978.

Wasserloos, Yvonne. *Das Leipziger Konservatorium der Musik im 19. Jahrhundert. Anziehungs- und Ausstrahlungskraft eines Musikpädagogischen Modells auf das internationale Musikleben.* Hildesheim et. al: Olms, 2004.

Watson, Robert L. "Lightner Witmer: 1867–1956." *American Journal of Psychology* 69 (1956): 680–82.

Webb, Gerald B., and Desmond Powell. *Henry Sewall: Physiologist and Physician.* Baltimore: Johns Hopkins University Press, 1946.

Weiss, John. *Life and Correspondence of Theodore Parker.* Vol. 1. New York: D. Appelton & Company, 1864.

Werner, Anja. "Striving for the Top: German-Trained Southern, Southwestern, and Western University Leaders in the Early 20th Century." In *Education and the USA,* ed. Laurenz Volkmann, 87–103. Heidelberg: WINTER Universitätsverlag, 2011.

Whimster, Sam. "The Significance of Karl Lamprecht and His Work for Contemporary Cultural Studies." In *Karl Lamprecht im Kontext,* ed. Geier and Homann, 70–9.

White, Andrew D. *Autobiography.* 2 vols. New York: The Century Co., 1906.

White, John Williams. "Thomas Day Seymour 1848–1907." Memorial Address Given at Yale University on 12 February 1908. Published by the classical Club of Yale University.

Whitehouse, Owen C. "Franz Delitzsch—Eregete and Theologian." In *The Expository Times,* vol. 1, ed. J. Hastings, 177–79. Edinburgh: T. & T. Clark, October 1889–September 1890.

Wiemers, Gerald. "Ernst Heinrich Weber und die Königlich Sächsische Gesellschaft der Wissenschaften zu Leipzig." In *Ernst Heinrich Weber,* ed. W. Eisenberg et al., 31–40.

Williams, Gertrude S., and Jo Ann Robinson. *Education as My Agenda: Gertrude Williams, Race, and the Baltimore Public Schools.* Palgrave Studies in Oral History. New York: Palgrave Macmillan, 2005.

Williams, William Carlos. *The Autobiography of William Carlos Williams.* 1948.

Wilkins, A. S. "Georg Curtius. Eine Charakteristik by E. Windisch." *Classical Review* 1, no. 9 (November 1887): 263. In Sebeok, *Portraits of Linguists,* vol. 1.

Wilson, E. Bright. "Theodore William Richards." In *Proceedings,* ed. W. O. Milligan, 106–13.

Windisch, Ernst. "Georg Curtius." *Biographisches Jahrbuch für Altertumskunde* 9 (1886). Reprinted in Sebeok, *Portraits of Linguists,* vol. 1, 311–73.

———. *Georg Curtius. Eine Charakteristik.* Berlin: Verlag von S. Calvary & Co., 1887.

Windsor, Philip. *Strategic Thinking: An Introduction and Farewell,* ed. Mats R. Berdal and Spyros Economides. Boulder, CO: Lynne Rienner, 2002.

Winkler, Heinrich August. *Deutsche Geschichte vom Ende des Alten Reiches bis zum Untergang der Weimarer Republik.* Bonn: Bundeszentrale für politische Bildung [Sonderausgabe], 2000.

Winter, Ella, and Granville Hicks, eds. *The Letters of Lincoln Steffens.* 2 vols. New York: Harcourt, Brace and Company, 1938.

Willis, N. Parker. *Rural Letters and Other Records of Thoughts at Leisure.* Auburn/Rochester: Breadsley & Co., 1854.

Wright, Richard R., Jr. *87 Years behind the Black Curtain: An Autobiography.* Philadelphia: Rare Book Company, 1965.

Wunderlich, K. *Rudolf Leuckart. Weg und Werk.* Jena: Gustav Fischer Verlag, 1978.

Wundt, Wilhelm. *Erlebtes und Erkanntes.* Stuttgart: Alfred Kröner Verlag, 1920.

Yancy, George. "In the Spirit of the A.M.E. Church: Gilbert Haven Jones as an Early Black Philosopher and Educator." *A.M.E. Church Review* 118, no. 388 (2002): 43–57. Reprinted in

The American Philosophical Association Newsletter on Philosophy and the Black Experience 2, no. 2 (Spring 2003): 42–48.

Zieren, Gregory R. "From Halle to Harvard: Johannes Conrad as Transatlantic Mediator of Economic Thought." In _Tangenten: Literatur und Geschichte_, ed. Martin Meyer, Gabrielle Spengemann, and Wolf Kindermann. Münster: Lit Verlag, 1996.

Zimmerman, Jonathan. _Innocents Abroad: American Teachers in the American Century_. Cambridge, MA: Harvard University Press, 2006.

Zlatevka, Minka. "Bulgarische Doktoranden von Karl Bücher." In _Karl Bücher_, ed. Koenen and Meyen, 201–28.

Zwahr, Hartmut. "Von der zweiten Universitätsreform bis zur Reichsgründung, 1830 bis 1870." _Alma Mater Lipsiensis_, ed. Lothar Rathmann, 141–90.

Zwahr, Hartmut, Thomas Topfstedt, and Günter Bentele, eds. _Leipzigs Messen 1497–1997: Gestaltwandel, Umbrüche, Neubeginn_. 2 vols. Köln: Böhlau, 1999.

INDEX